Catching Up with the Competition

SIE *Studies in International Economics* includes works dealing with the theory, empirical analysis, and evaluation of international policies and institutions, in the area of international macroeconomics and finance, international trade theory and policy, as well as international legal and political economy.

Keith E. Maskus, Peter M. Hooper, Edward E. Leamer, and
J. David Richardson, Editors
Quiet Pioneering: Robert M. Stern and His International Economic Legacy

Bjarne S. Jensen and Kar-yiu Wong, Editors
Dynamics, Economic Growth, and International Trade

Jagdish Bhagwati and Mathias Hirsch, Editors
The Uruguay Round and Beyond: Essays in Honor of Arthur Dunkel

Kala Marathe Krishna and Ling Hui Tan
Rags and Riches: Implementing Apparel Quotas under the Multi-Fibre Arrangement

Alan V. Deardorff and Robert M. Stern
Measurement of Nontariff Barriers

Thomas Cottier and Petros C. Mavroidis, Editors
The World Trade Forum, Volume I: State Trading in the Twenty-First Century

Rajesh Chadha, Sanjib Pohit, Alan V. Deardorff, and Robert M. Stern
The Impact of Trade and Domestic Policy Reforms in India: A CGE Modeling Approach

Alan V. Deardorff and Robert M. Stern, Editors
Constituent Interests and U.S. Trade Policies

Gary R. Saxonhouse and T. N. Srinivasan, Editors
Development, Duality, and the International Economic Regime: Essays in Honor of Gustav Ranis

Charles P. Kindleberger
Essays in History: Financial, Economic, Personal

Keith Acheson and Christopher Maule
Much Ado about Culture: North American Trade Disputes

Alan V. Deardorff and Robert M. Stern
Social Dimensions of U.S. Trade Policies

Thomas Cottier and Petros C. Mavroidis, Editors
Regulatory Barriers and the Principle of Non-Discrimination in World Trade Law

Bernard Hoekman and Jamel Zarrouk
Catching Up with the Competition: Trade Opportunities and Challenges for Arab Countries

Catching Up with the Competition

Trade Opportunities and Challenges for Arab Countries

Bernard Hoekman and Jamel Zarrouk, Editors

Ann Arbor

THE UNIVERSITY OF MICHIGAN PRESS

Published in the United States of America by
The University of Michigan Press
Manufactured in the United States of America
♾ Printed on acid-free paper

2003 2002 2001 2000 4 3 2 1

A CIP catalog record for this book is available from the British Library.

Library of Congress Cataloging-in-Publication Data applied for
ISBN 0-472-11154-X (cloth : alk. paper)

Contents

Preface vii

Tables, Figures, and Boxes ix

Abbreviations and Acronyms xii

Introduction 1

PART ONE Where Does the Region Stand?

1. Beyond the Year 2000: Implications of the Middle East's Recent Trade Performance
Alexander J. Yeats and Francis Ng 9

2. Agricultural Trade and Rural Development in the Middle East and North Africa
Dean A. DeRosa 45

3. Intra-Industry Trade of Arab Countries: An Indicator of Potential Competitiveness
Oleh Havrylyshyn and Peter Kunzel 81

PART TWO Quantifying the Gains from Liberalization

4. Assessing the Implications for Lebanon of Free Trade with the European Union
Will Martin 103

5. A Free Trade Agreement between the European Union and a Representative Arab Mediterranean Country: A Quantitative Assessment
Thomas F. Rutherford, Elisabet E. Rutström, and David Tarr 145

6. Rents, Red Tape, and Regionalism: Economic Effects of Deeper Integration
Bernard Hoekman and Denise Konan 171

PART THREE Policy Challenges

7. Enhancing Egypt's Exports
James H. Cassing, Samiha Fawzy, Denis Gallagher, and Hanaa Kheir-El-Din 207

8. Regulatory Regimes and Trade Costs
Jamel Zarrouk 227

9. Strengthening Intellectual Property Rights in Lebanon
Keith E. Maskus 251

PART FOUR Institutional Options

10. The Greater Arab Free Trade Area: Limits and Possibilities
Jamel Zarrouk 285

11. Benefiting from WTO Accession and Membership
Bernard Hoekman and Jayanta Roy 307

Contributors 325

References 327

Preface

The Middle East and North Africa region has been lagging behind much of the developing world in integrating into the world economy, as measured by the ratio of trade to GDP, growth of nontraditional exports, the share of intra-industry trade, and inward foreign direct investment flows. The papers collected in this book analyze the recent trade performance of Arab countries and the trade policy strategies that have been pursued by governments in the region. Preferential trade agreements, both among Arab countries and between Arab countries and the European Union, have become a major instrument of trade policy reforms in the region. Many of the contributions to this volume explore the implications of the regional integration strategies that are being implemented and discuss options that might be considered by governments to further the objective of greater integration into the world economy.

Acknowledgements

A number of the papers that are included were originally prepared for other purposes and required significant reworking. We are very grateful to the authors of the papers for agreeing to undertake revisions and to have their work published in this book. We are also indebted to two anonymous referees for constructive comments on the draft manuscript, to Susan Al-Baker for copyediting and putting together the camera-ready manuscript, to Maria Kasilag for helping finalize the manuscript, and to Ellen McCarthy of the University of Michigan Press for helping to bring this project to fruition.

Disclaimer

All opinions expressed by the authors are strictly personal and should not be attributed to any government, official agency, or institution with which they may be, or have been, affiliated.

Bernard Hoekman and Jamel Zarrouk

Tables, Figures, and Boxes

Tables

1.1	The Most Recent Year of Availability for Middle Eastern Countries' Trade Data	11
1.2	The 1997 Geographic Destination of Middle Eastern Countries' Exports	12
1.3	The Share of Middle Eastern Countries in OECD Total and Non-Oil Imports 1980, 1988, and 1997	14
1.4	The 1997 Product Composition of OECD Imports from the Middle East	16
1.5	Industrial Countries' Thirty Largest 3-Digit SITC Non-Energy Import Products from the Middle East	18
1.6	Dynamic Products in Industrial Countries' Imports from the Middle East	21
1.7	1985 and 1997 IIT Ratios for Middle Eastern Countries	22
1.8	The Relative Importance of Parts and Components in Individual Middle Eastern Countries' Trade	24
1.9	The Impact of Competition, Demand, and Diversification on Middle Eastern Non-Oil Exports	27
1.10	The Share of Individual Countries in Intraregional Exports in the mid-1980s and 1990s	29
1.11	Middle Eastern Countries' Thirty Largest 3-Digit SITC Intraregional Exports in the mid-1980s and mid-1990s	30
1.12	Dynamic Products in Middle Eastern Countries' Regional Exports	32
1.13	1997 "Trade Intensity" Indices for Middle Eastern Countries' Exports	33
1.14	Implications of Middle Eastern Countries' Export Diversification Indices	35
1.15	Middle Eastern Countries' Trade Complementarity Indices	36

1.16 Middle Eastern Countries' 1985 and 1997 Revealed Comparative Advantage in Broad Product Groups 38
2.1 Economic Growth and Other Indicators of Social Welfare 1993 48
2.2 Agricultural Production 1990-92 52
2.3 Exports and Imports of MENA Countries by World Regions 1992-94 54
2.4 Revealed Comparative Advantage of MENA Countries in International and Intraregional Trade 1992-94 60
2.5 Import Restrictions in MENA Countries by Product Category 1984-93 62
2.6 Economic Cooperation in MENA 68
3.1 IIT Indices in Manufactures: Total Trade 85
3.2 Direction of Trade: IIT Trade Indices in Manufactures 1992-94 87
3.3 IIT Regression Fit: Deviations from Predicted Levels 94
3.4 Intra-Industry Trade by Product Group 95
3.5 Arab Countries: Intra-Industry Trade Indices in Manufactures for Selected Commodities 96
4.1 The Commodity Composition of Lebanon's Imports by Source 112
4.2 Nominal Tariff Rates on Imports from the EU and the World 113
4.3 Tariffs Imposed by Lebanon on Imports from Supplying Countries 114
4.4 Differentials between Lebanese Prices and Those in Qatar and the Middle East 116
4.5 ERPs Provided to Selected Lebanese Industries by Tariffs 117
4.6 Post Uruguay Round Tariff Rates and Lebanese Exports to the EU 122
4.7 Protection Rates in Lebanon's Major Trading Partners 123
4.8 Key Consequences of Liberalization by Lebanon 124
4.9 Estimated Impacts of Changes in Domestic Prices of Importables for Prices of Non-Traded Goods 128
4.10 Key Consequences of Liberalization by Lebanon with High Import Substitutability 129
4.11 Key Consequences of Liberalization by Lebanon with Balanced Trade 130
4.12 Consequences of Liberalizing Both Tariff and Nontariff Barriers 131
4.13 Consequences of Halving Financial Inflows in Lebanon 134
5.1 Key Sectoral Data for the Typical Arab Mediterranean Country 148
5.2 Elasticities of Substitution between Labor and Capital Use 151
5.3 Aggregate Effects 153
5.4 Percentage Change in Exports and Imports (Short Run) 158
5.5 Percentage Change in Prices (Short Run) 160
5.6 Short-Run Percentage Changes in Labor Use and Production 160

5.7	Changes in Prices of Sector-Specific Capital and Labor (Short Run)	162
5.8	Long-Run Percentage Changes in Labor Use and Production	164
6.1	Benchmark Output and Trade Shares	178
6.2	Government Policy and Elasticity Parameters	187
6.3	Impacts of Egyptian-EU Trade Agreement with Service NTBs Fixed	188
6.4	Impacts of Egyptian-EU Trade Agreement with Service NTBs Liberalized	190
6.5	Sectoral Impacts of Egyptian-EU Trade Agreement and Frictional Import NTBs	193
6.6	Egyptian-EU Trade Agreement with Arab League FTA Service NTBs Fixed	194
6.7	Egyptian-EU Trade Agreement with Arab League FTA Service NTBs Liberalized	196
7.1	Nominal and Effective Protection Rates in 1997	209
7.2	Effective Rates of Protection to Exports in 1997	210
7.3	The Extent of Tariff Induced Bias against Exports 1994 and 1997	212
7.4	Results of Studies of the Egyptian Standardization System	214
7.5	Unit Labor Cost of Production in Manufacturing ($) 1992	216
7.6	Efficiency Indicators 1994/95	217
7.7	Performance Indicators of Selected Industries	221
8.1	MENA Traders' Ranking of Regulatory Constraints	237
8.2	Main Indicators on Telecommunications Services in MENA Countries, 1999 data	240
8.3	Dealing with Regulatory Regimes at the Multilateral, Regional, and National Levels	244
9.1	Static Effects of Stronger Patent and Trademark Protection on Pharmaceuticals	262
9.2	Simulated Effects of Stronger Copyrights on Software	270
9.3	Effects of Stronger Copyrights on Printing and Publishing	274
9.4	Stronger Copyrights on Music and Video, and Film Industries	276
10.1	Intraregional Trade	286
10.2	Basic Economic Indicators of GAFTA Member Countries 1997	289
10.3	Status of Tariffs, Surcharges, and Internal Taxes on International Trade in Selected GAFTA Member Countries 1997	291
10.4	Tariff Structure in Selected GAFTA Member Countries 1997	293
10.5	Comparative Shares of Intraregional Trade in Merchandise and Services for Selected GAFTA Member Countries 1997	298

Figures

1.1	Trade Integration 1970-97	3
3.1	Summary Regression Plots for Selected Arab and Sample Countries	93
4.1	The Market for Goods Imported from the EU	105
4.2	The Market for Goods Imported from Non-EU Suppliers	106
4.3	The Market for Exports from Lebanon to the Partner Country	107
4.4	Lebanon's Source of Imports 1996	108
4.5	Lebanon's Source of Imports 1974	109
4.6	The Direction of Lebanon's Merchandise Exports 1996	110
4.7	Export Destinations for Lebanon 1974	111
4.8	The Relationship between Labor Intensity and Effective Assistance in Lebanon 1996	119
4.9	Determination of the Real Exchange Rate with No Trade Deficit	132
4.10	Determination of the Real Exchange Rate with Financial Inflows	133
6.1	Structure of the Model	183
7.1	Overall Ranking of Institutional Constraints	218
7.2	Export Constraints: Industrial Sector	219
7.3	Export Constraints: Cross-Industries	220
11.1	Possible Structure of a Trade Policy Department	317

Boxes

3.1	Regression for Trade Orientation Derivation	90
3.2	IIT Regressions	92
5.1	Simulation Scenarios	152
8.1	SASO International Conformity Certification Program	233
8.2	International Convention on the Simplification and Harmonization of Customs Procedures in the MENA Region: The Revised Kyoto Convention	248
10.1	A Scenario for Deep Integration under GAFTA	304

Appendix Tables

2.1	The MENA Economies 1993	74
4.1	GTAP Commodities and Broader Commodity Aggregates	135

Abbreviations and Acronyms

ACM	Arab Common Market
ATFP	Arab Trade Financing Program
APEC	Asia-Pacific Economic Cooperation
ASEAN	Association of Southeast Asian Nations
CAEU	Council of Arab Economic Unity
CAP	Common Agricultural Policy (EU)
CARICOM	Caribbean Community
CES	constant elasticity of substitution
CET	constant elasticity of transformation
CGE	computable general equilibrium
CPI	consumer price index
DOT	Direction of Trade
DSB	Dispute Settlement Body (WTO)
EFTA	European Free Trade Association
EMA	Euro-Mediterranean Agreement
ERP	effective rate of protection
EU	European Union
FDI	foreign direct investment
FTA	free trade agreement
GAFTA	Greater Arab Free Trade Area
GATS	General Agreement on Trade in Services
GATT	General Agreement on Tariffs and Trade
GCC	Gulf Cooperation Council
GDP	gross domestic product
GNP	gross national product
GOE	Government of Egypt
GOEIC	General Organization for Exports and Imports Control (Egypt)
GSP	Generalized System of Preferences
GST	Goods and Service Tax
GTAP	Global Trade Analysis Project
ICCP	International Conformity Certification Program
ICP	International Comparisons Project
IIT	intra-industry trade
IMF	International Monetary Fund
IMWG	Interministerial Working Group

IO	input-output
ISO	International Organization for Standardization
IP	intellectual property
IPR	intellectual property rights
LAFTA	Latin American Free Trade Association
MENA	Middle East and North Africa
MFA	Multi-Fibre Arrangement
MFN	most favored nation
MNE	multi-national enterprise
MRA	mutual recognition agreement
NAFTA	North American Free Trade Agreement
NTB	nontariff barrier
OECD	Organization for Economic Co-operation and Development
PC	personal computer
PCI	per capita income
PTA	preferential trade agreement
QR	quantitative restriction
R&D	research and development
RCA	revealed comparative advantage
RIA	regional integration arrangement
ROW	rest of the world
RTA	regional trade arrangement
SAM	Social Accounting Matrix
SASO	Saudi Arabian Standards Organization
SITC	Standard International Trade Classification
SPS	sanitary and phytosanitary
TARS	Trade Analysis Reporting System
TBT	technical barriers to trade
TOT	terms of trade
TPD	Trade Policy Department
TRIM	Trade-Related Investment Measure
TRIPS	Trade-Related Intellectual Property Rights
UAE	United Arab Emirates
UL	Underwriters Laboratories
UN	United Nations
UNCTAD	United Nations Conference on Trade and Development
UNSO	United Nations Statistical Office
VAT	value added tax
WIPO	World Intellectual Property Organization
WTO	World Trade Organization

Note: Not all abbreviations used in this volume are listed above.

Introduction

Bernard Hoekman and Jamel Zarrouk

Many developing countries have taken up the challenge of using international trade as an engine of economic growth and development by launching an unparalleled wave of trade reforms. The prevalence of traditional nontariff barriers (NTBs) such as import prohibitions and quotas has been greatly reduced if not fully abolished in many countries, and the average level and dispersion of tariffs has fallen significantly. At the same time, technological developments are greatly facilitating international exchange and specialization. These global trends have had a number of consequences.

- The more open international trading system has led to more intense competition in world markets, both raising the bar confronting countries that have lagged behind the more dynamic developing countries and increasing the pressure to undertake the reforms needed to enhance the performance of the economy.

- Technological changes—the information and telecommunications revolutions—have led to a change in the nature of international economic transactions. Services have become more tradable as digitization has become more feasible, and communications and transportation costs have fallen. The service content of the production and sale of goods has increased substantially. "Ship and forget" type of trade is more and more a thing of the past; increasingly products are tailored to the needs of consumers, and maintenance and follow-up services are an integral component of the value-added bundle.

- Trade and foreign direct investment (FDI) have become complements rather than substitutes, giving rise to ever larger flows of FDI, much of which involves "cross-hauling," with firms in similar lines of business located in different countries investing in each others' home markets.

- Much trade today involves trade in components and "production sharing"—different parts of the production chain are out-sourced to those geographic locations where they can be undertaken most efficiently. Such trade and specialization is heavily dependent on efficient logistics.

- As tariffs and other border barriers are reduced, the attention of business and policymakers moves to focus on those aspects of prevailing domestic regulatory regimes that are perceived to impede access to markets or to give rise to "unfair" competition. Greater attention is centering on the justification for the pursuit of national regulation, and pressures are mounting for harmonization of regulatory regimes. Greater emphasis is also put on ensuring that the enforcement of regulatory regimes does not needlessly impede trade by creating major resource costs for firms.

These developments are well known and often discussed. But, the extent to which countries in different parts of the world have increased their integration into the world economy varies substantially. Some countries such as China or the former centrally planned economies of Europe have greatly increased their participation in the international economy in the last decade. Others have not. This is the case in particular for many Arab countries in the Middle East and North Africa (MENA). Virtually all Arab countries, extending from Morocco in the west to Oman in the east, have undertaken major steps to implement tariff and fiscal reforms and to dismantle quantitative import restrictions. Notwithstanding these efforts, the pace of integration into the world economy achieved by the region has been slow. The trade integration ratio for Arab economies as a group (i.e., trade in goods and non-factor services as a share of GDP) showed no change in the 1990-97 period (fig. I.1). It increased in all other regions of the world.

A corollary of this is that Arab countries have lost market share on major markets. For example, the share of Arab exports in total European Union (EU) imports fell from over 20 percent in 1980 to only 6 percent in 1997. To a large extent, this decline reflects the real reduction in oil prices that occurred over this period, but it is also a reflection of the massive rise in exports from newly industrializing economies in Asia and the transition economies in Central and Eastern Europe. Recently, some countries in the region have begun to experience an improvement in trade performance, although Arab countries lag behind Israel and Turkey (see chap. 1 by Alexander Yeats and Francis Ng). The emerging competition from countries with an abundance of unskilled labor (Bangladesh, China, India) that have been integrating rapidly into the world market puts substantial pressure on Arab countries (e.g., Egypt, Morocco, and Tunisia) that have specialized in low-skilled labor-intensive industries. Finally, as argued by Oleh Havrylyshyn and Peter Kunzel in chapter 3, the relatively low levels of intra-industry trade (IIT) registered by countries in the region is another telling indicator. Clearly a major challenge facing Arab economies is to confront and catch up with the competition.

Reasons for the under-performance of Arab countries are numerous and complex.[1] Identifying the economic costs and benefits of alternative reform options and international trade agreements is an important task for researchers. The chapters collected in this volume analyze trade policy-related factors that constrain the ability of Arab businesses to compete on world markets and employ a variety of analytical tools to assess both the status quo and policy options. In some cases, numerical analysis extends to issues that do not lend themselves readily to quantification. Noteworthy in this regard are the studies of trade policy in Lebanon included in this volume—chapter 4 by Will Martin assessing the effects of trade liberalization and chapter 9 by Keith Maskus on the implications of strengthening intellectual property right (IPR) protection.

As discussed by James Cassing et al. in chapter 7 and Jamel Zarrouk in chapter 8, although tariffs have fallen and quotas have largely been abolished, transactions costs associated with international trade are frequently very high. Inefficiencies in customs clearance procedures, port and ancillary services, and

FIGURE 1.1 Trade Integration 1970-97

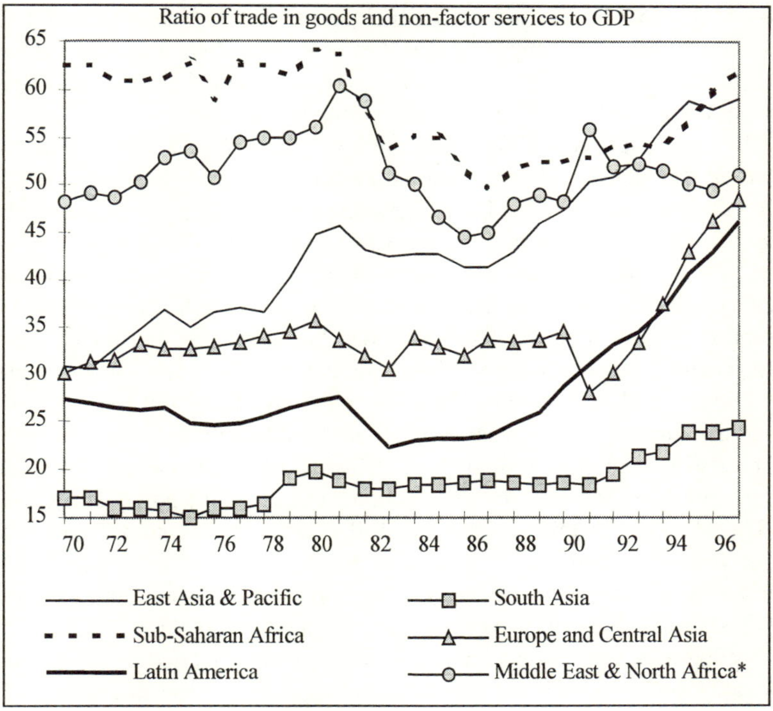

*Excludes Libya, Lebanon, and Qatar.

Source: Nabli and De Kleine (2000).

transportation and telecommunications services impose needless burdens on enterprises. Administrative red tape and redundant procedures are a major problem in some economies in the region. Relatively high import duties and inadequate duty drawback mechanisms add an additional burden by raising the costs of imported inputs and technology.

Many countries all over the world are complementing autonomous economic reform programs with international cooperative efforts that aim at liberalizing access to markets on a reciprocal basis. Such trade agreements may also extend to disciplines that pertain to various aspects of domestic regulatory regimes. Arab countries have been actively involved in regional integration efforts since the 1960s. These efforts have not been very successful, and in practice have been limited to a series of bilateral trade agreements with limited product coverage. Starting in the mid-1990s this began to change, with Mediterranean Arab countries concluding reciprocal free trade agreements (FTAs) with the EU covering all manufactures. A primary motivation for these FTAs was the conclusion of FTAs between the EU and Central and Eastern European countries (CEECs). The advent of EU-CEEC free trade raised concerns that the Mediterranean Arab countries might be "marginalized" in EU markets as the competitive advantage that they once enjoyed (due to geographic proximity and preferential access) would be eroded. So far, Jordan, Morocco, and Tunisia have concluded so-called Euro-Mediterranean Partnership Agreements, implying that they will open their domestic markets to EU producers over a ten-year period. Algeria, Egypt, Lebanon, and Syria are negotiating with the EU to conclude similar agreements.

The impact of such FTAs with the EU is the subject of a number of chapters in this volume. A large amount of analytical work has been done in recent years on the Euro-Mediterranean agreements (EMAs). A theme that emerges from this work is that the benefits of such FTAs will be greatly enhanced if they are used as instruments to pursue more general trade and regulatory reforms. Of particular importance is lowering tariffs against non-EU exporters as well as the EU (to reduce the scope for detrimental trade diversion) and incorporating mechanisms to reduce real resource costs created by inefficient and duplicative administrative procedures (customs control, product standards conformity assessment, etc.). Although rigorous quantification of the effects of current policies is difficult, existing modeling techniques are very useful is assessing the relative impact of alternative policy options.

The chapters in this volume by Will Martin, by Thomas Rutherford, Elisabet Rutström, and David Tarr, and by Bernard Hoekman and Denise Konan illustrate both the feasibility and the importance of undertaking ex-ante analysis of the likely economic effects of preferential trade liberalization.

Economic reform efforts in Arab countries have tended to be pursued with caution so as to limit social adjustment costs and social disruption. The consequence has been a slow reform process that is accompanied by substantial resistance from protected industries. This creates uncertainty on the part of the private sector and households and has reduced the credibility of reform programs. This in turn has limited the hoped-for investment and supply response. FDI flows to the region have been relatively small and concentrated in a limited number of sectors (Nabli and De Kleine 2000). The slow pace and limited scope of reforms undertaken in the region in comparison with more dynamic parts of the developing world implies that the ability of Arab firms to confront international competition, be it at home or on the world market, is adversely affected. There is an urgent need for accelerating and deepening trade reforms to enhance the ability of firms to produce goods and services efficiently.

Pressure for regulatory reform is also emanating from major trading partners such as the EU and the United States. This is reflected in the evolving and expanding agenda of the World Trade Organization (WTO), which now covers trade and investment in services, agriculture, and intellectual property, and may in the medium term come to include disciplines in areas such as investment and competition (antitrust) policy. The increasing focus on domestic regulatory issues in both regional forums such as the EMAs and the WTO confronts Arab governments with the need to clearly define what regulatory reforms they wish to pursue and how to go about doing so. Jamel Zarrouk discusses a number of key reform measures that Arab countries need to consider in their efforts to deal with regulatory challenges (chap. 8).

One issue that is of great concern to a number of countries in the region is the adoption of intellectual property right (IPR) protection that conforms to WTO standards. In chapter 9, Keith Maskus analyzes in some detail what the impact of strengthening IPRs might be for different industries in Lebanon. He emphasizes the importance of implementing complementary policies to maximize competition on markets and notes that competition policy (antitrust) disciplines have an important role to play in this regard. For example, sole agency and related exclusive distribution arrangements could significantly lower the net benefits of stronger IPRs.

International cooperation can help in mobilizing support for reforms by making best practices a focal point for discussions and lobbying and by mobilizing the technical and financial resources that are required to implement the needed reforms. In many areas what is required is institutional strengthening and training, not simply changes in legislation. This often takes a substantial amount of time. Technical and financial assistance may be more forthcoming if reform efforts are embedded in international agreements, especially if aid is part of the overall package; the reform path may become more credible to civil society as well.

A major policy issue confronting governments in the region is to ensure coherence between the pursuit of regional as opposed to multilateral integration. There are a number of major regional arrangements to which countries in the region belong: the Euro-Med FTAs, the Greater Arab Free Trade Area (GAFTA), and the Gulf Cooperation Council (GCC). At the same time many countries are WTO members, but most are not. Only nine of the twenty member states of the Arab League are WTO members (Bahrain, Djibouti, Egypt, Kuwait, Qatar, Mauritania, Morocco, Tunisia, and the United Arab Emirates [UAE]). Five are negotiating their accession (Algeria, Jordan, Oman, Saudi Arabia, and Sudan). Iraq, Lebanon, Libya, Syria, Yemen, and the Comoros Islands have yet to express an interest in initiating accession procedures. Membership in the WTO can do much to enhance transparency of trade regimes through adoption of "good practices." Potentially, regional integration agreements can do the same. But to do so, the agreements must address existing constraints and problems directly in a way that will be conducive to economic growth. As discussed by Jamel Zarrouk in chapter 10, that is not currently the case as regards the GAFTA.

All Arab countries have much to gain from becoming active WTO members and exploiting to the fullest extent the possibilities offered by this institution to spell out and commit to trade-related reforms and to defend their access to foreign markets. As argued by Hoekman and Jayanta Roy in chapter 11, currently Arab countries are not fully exploiting the potential of the WTO. Similarly, the potential benefits that could be obtained from regional integration efforts could be greatly enhanced by extending their reach to cover aspects of the enforcement of regulatory regimes that impose excessive costs on international trade (see chaps. 6 and 10). But equally important is to ensure that regional agreements cover all goods and services markets, including agriculture. As emphasized by Dean DeRosa (chap. 2), agricultural policies in the region remain highly distortive, and the fact that the EMAs do not imply full liberalization of EU agricultural markets is a major factor reducing their value to Mediterranean partner countries.

Collectively, the chapters in this volume provide an analysis of the trade performance of Arab countries, the trade policy choices that have been made in recent years, and the challenges that remain to be addressed. Much has been done in the last decade to liberalize trade but, as the contributions to this book reveal, much also remains to be done—both at the domestic level and in terms of maximizing the benefits of regional integration and membership in the WTO.

Notes

1. For discussions of some of the relevant factors, see the contributions in Shafik (1998).

PART ONE

Where Does the Region Stand?

CHAPTER 1

Beyond the Year 2000: Implications of the Middle East's Recent Trade Performance

Alexander J. Yeats and Francis Ng

Major changes that have occurred recently in external markets have important implications for Middle Eastern countries' export prospects.[1] The North American Free Trade Agreement (NAFTA) liberalized barriers to the intratrade of Canada, Mexico, and the United States, while further integration efforts continued in Europe. Regional integration arrangements (RIAs) strengthened and expanded in Latin America, with Mercosur and Andean Pact countries adopting average discriminatory tariffs against nonmembers in the range of 10 to 15 percent. The Uruguay Round agreement will also have a major impact on international trading conditions when fully implemented. Among the Round's achievements were an average 40 percent reduction in industrial countries' most-favored-nation (MFN) tariffs, an agreement on a phase-out of the Multifibre Accord (MFA), NTBs on agricultural products were converted to tariffs and then lowered, "voluntary" export restraints were abolished, and some progress was made in the liberalization of barriers to trade in services.

While many of these developments have positive implications for Middle Eastern countries, there are some potentially negative aspects. Regional integration initiatives like NAFTA, Mercosur, or the extended EU give member countries preferential (discriminatory) access to each other's markets, which may displace nonmembers' exports. This raises the question of whether a significant volume of Middle East exports may be displaced and, if so, which product sectors will be most affected? Similarly, the Uruguay Round's reduction of MFN tariffs may have negative implications since these cuts will lower (or eliminate) preferences some Middle East exporters receive under the Organisation for Economic Co-operation and Development (OECD) countries' Generalized

System of Preference (GSP) programs, or EU and United States (with Israel) free trade arrangements.[2] The phase-out of the MFA, tariffication of agricultural NTBs, and initiatives to liberalize services trade seemingly have positive implications for the Middle East if regional countries can compete with other producers. However, if they are not fully competitive in what promises to be a dramatically altered post-Uruguay Round external environment, the Middle East may experience significant negative trade effects.

Recognizing that improved trade opportunities can make a positive contribution to regional economic growth and also help reinforce the peace process, this chapter examines the implications of recent changes in Middle East global and intraregional exports. In recognition of the fact that there has been a strong continuing interest in regional trade arrangements (RTAs), the magnitude and composition of Middle East intratrade is analyzed and information relating to future prospects for this exchange is assessed. Measures such as the "revealed" comparative advantage (RCA) index, trade intensity ratios, IIT ratios (including statistics on trade in parts and components), changes in export diversification measures, and trade complementarity indices are employed to help assess Middle East export opportunities (and constraints) within and outside the region. However, before proceeding with these policy-related analyses, some discussion is required concerning the availability of and deficiencies in official Middle Eastern trade statistics.

Data Sources on Middle East Trade

Accurate information on the level and composition of trade is essential for the formulation of policy reforms or the negotiation of RTAs. Several statistical sources are available for analyzing Middle East countries' trade performance, but all have important limitations. The broadest database in terms of country coverage is compiled by the International Monetary Fund (IMF) and published in the *Direction of Trade (DOT) Statistics Yearbook.* This annual report provides information on the destination of exports and origins of imports for all sixteen Middle East countries. The DOT database's major limitation is that it only reports total import and export statistics and provides no information on the composition of trade—even at very aggregate levels.

The most detailed source of internationally comparable statistics on trade, tabulated both in terms of product composition and direction, is the COMTRADE database maintained by the United Nations Statistical Office (UNSO).[3] Since these records contain detailed trade statistics for each UN member, with imports and exports reported by country and by product, generally down to the 5-digit level of the Standard International Trade Classification (SITC) system, they should constitute a very useful source for analyzing Middle Eastern trade. However, a deficiency of the COMTRADE records is the tardy and uneven (and sometimes inaccurate) reporting practices of some Middle East countries (see table 1.1 for the latest year trade data were available as of June 1999). Furthermore, there are missing years in some countries historical COMTRADE records, which makes it difficult to accurately track longer-term trade trends.[4] Clearly, there is a pressing need for some Middle East countries to improve their reporting practices in order to facilitate empirical research on global and regional trade policy issues.

A second related problem is that the Middle Eastern countries that reported to the UNSO often have not done so for common years. For example, 1997 was the most recent year of data availability for Cyprus, Egypt, Israel, Kuwait, Oman, Syria, and Turkey, while Jordan and Qatar last reported statistics for 1995 and 1994 respectively. In order to construct a common database on Middle Eastern trade, it was necessary to "pool" annual information for several contiguous years. The rule followed was to aggregate data for the most recent year available in the 1990s to produce a "composite mid-1990s" trade database.[5] This required the merger of 1997 COMTRADE statistics for countries like Turkey, Israel, and UAE with other Middle East countries' latest available data. Given the interest in the magnitude and nature of recent changes, a similar procedure was used to compile a Middle East trade database for contiguous years in the early 1980s. This procedure produced a comprehensive database on the sixteen Middle Eastern countries' global and regional trade, both in total and down to the 4-digit level of the SITC (Revision 1) system. This was the primary data source used in this chapter, although in some cases, where information on the composition of trade was not needed, more recent IMF or United Nations Conference on Trade and Development (UNCTAD) statistics were employed.

Characteristics of Middle Eastern Global Exports

Recent international developments show that the geographic destinations of a country's exports can have important implications for its economic prospects. For example, countries whose exports were heavily directed toward Far

TABLE 1.1 The Most Recent Year of Availability for Middle Eastern Countries' Trade Data

Middle East Country and Year of Latest Available UN COMTRADE Statistics			
Bahrain (1996)	Israel (1997)	Libya (1991)	Syria (1997)
Cyprus (1997)	Jordan (1995)	Oman (1997)	Turkey (1997)
Egypt (1997)	Kuwait (1997)	Qatar (1994)	UAE (1993)
Iran (1983)	Lebanon (1983)	Saudi Arabia (1996)	Yemen (1995)

Source: Data availability from UN COMTRADE as of June 1999.

TABLE 1.2 The 1997 Geographic Destination of Middle East Countries' Exports

			Of which:						of which:			
Exporting Country	World ($ million)	Industrial Countries	Europe	North America	Asia	Other Countries	Africa	Asia	Europe	Middle East	Latin America	Not Specified
						(percent of total exports)						
Bahrain	3,174	25.0	8.8	3.7	12.6	75.0	1.7	46.1	5.3	20.3	0.3	1.4
Cyprus	1,248	29.4	28.0	1.2	0.2	70.6	2.1	2.9	36.5	23.2	0.5	5.4
Egypt	3,908	55.7	41.7	11.6	2.4	44.3	3.1	9.9	6.3	19.2	0.5	5.5
Iran	24,925	39.5	25.1	1.5	12.9	60.5	6.2	19.4	5.7	3.4	1.6	24.3
Israel	22,477	70.7	32.1	32.8	5.8	29.3	1.9	13.7	5.5	0.3	3.5	4.4
Jordan	1,451	18.8	12.4	1.7	4.9	81.2	7.8	19.9	4.5	40.2	0.7	8.1
Kuwait	14,091	48.1	10.7	12.9	24.5	51.9	3.8	46.1	1.2	0.6	0.3	0.0
Lebanon	711	33.6	25.3	6.8	1.5	66.4	6.0	1.7	9.3	45.5	0.9	3.1
Libya	9,716	84.2	84.2	0.0	0.1	15.8	5.4	1.4	7.1	1.4	0.5	0.0
Oman	6,515	33.4	3.0	3.65	26.7	66.6	3.4	60.9	0.0	2.3	0.0	0.0
Qatar	5,562	55.1	1.0	3.2	50.8	44.9	1.5	36.7	0.2	4.3	0.0	2.3
Saudi Arabia	61,603	53.5	18.5	16.0	19.0	46.5	2.5	34.3	1.6	6.2	1.9	0.2
Syria	4,017	56.7	55.1	0.7	0.8	43.3	2.5	1.5	17.3	18.8	0.1	3.0
Turkey	26,246	57.2	48.2	8.1	0.8	42.8	2.8	4.6	18.8	10.7	0.9	4.9
UAE	30,442	46.3	4.8	2.9	38.6	53.7	2.2	29.6	0.9	7.8	0.1	13.3
Yemen	2,479	17.8	12.2	0.3	5.3	82.2	2.5	71.2	0.0	2.9	5.5	0.0
ALL MIDDLE EAST	218,566	52.4	24.7	10.8	16.9	47.6	3.1	25.6	5.2	6.4	1.3	6.0
MEMO ITEM:												
All Non-Industrial Countries	1,908,775	53.7	21.7	21.7	10.3	46.3	2.7	26.4	6.6	2.8	5.0	2.8

Source: International Monetary Fund, *Direction of Trade Statistics Yearbook*, 1998.

Eastern markets have seen their growth prospects weakened due to this region's major recession. Similarly, exports to markets where RTAs are in the process of forming or strengthening (like NAFTA or the EU) might experience some displacement. Export prospects can also be affected by the product composition of trade. If exports are concentrated in goods with low income elasticities of demand, this could cause its marginalization in world trade. What does the available evidence concerning these points show for the Middle East?

Geographic Trade Patterns

Where are the primary outlets for Middle East exports and what factors in these markets might affect their level of import demand? Table 1.2 provides relevant information by showing the total value of Middle East global exports and the shares going to different destinations, i.e., all industrial countries (defined as all original members of the OECD with the exception of Turkey), industrial countries in Europe, North America, or Asia, and several other non-industrial regional groups. These figures indicate that more than half (52 percent) of all Middle Eastern exports go to industrial countries, yet three different trade patterns are evident in the individual country data. First, countries like Libya, Syria, and Turkey are primarily dependent on European markets and they may be negatively affected by integration efforts like the extension of the EU, adoption of a common currency, or new EU RTAs.[6] In contrast, Israel, Saudi Arabia, and UAE have a larger share of their exports destined for North America so these countries should be more concerned with the developments in this areas—such as the potential trade diverting effects of NAFTA. Third, five of the sixteen Middle East countries rely heavily on non-industrial country markets. Over 60 percent of Bahrain, Cyprus, Jordan, Lebanon, Oman, and Yemen's exports go to developing countries, most of which are in the Middle East or in Asia. These exporters are potentially vulnerable to adverse developments in the regional markets they service.

Table 1.2 also compares the direction of Middle Eastern exports with that of all non-industrial countries combined (see the memo item). Overall, very little difference is observed between the two groups' trade shares; 52 percent of Middle East exports go to industrial markets as opposed to 54 percent for all developing countries combined. The overall "geographic vulnerability" of the Middle East does not appear to be much different than most other developing countries. However, the Middle East does have a greater dependence on OECD Europe and Asia (41.6 percent versus 32 percent for all developing countries), while the share of exports going to OECD America is 11 points below average. For the region as a whole, these data accent the potential importance of changes in European market access conditions.

TABLE 1.3 The Share of Middle Eastern Countries in OECD Total and Non-Oil Imports 1980, 1988, and 1997

	Value of Industrial Countries Imports ($ million)			Share of Industrial Countries Imports (%)			Growth Rate	
Product Exporter	1980	1988	1997	1980	1988	1997	1980-1988	1988-1996
ALL GOODS								
Bahrain	799	671	867	0.5	1.0	0.7	-2.2	3.2
Cyprus	451	554	443	0.3	0.8	0.4	2.6	-2.8
Egypt	4,462	2,586	3,919	2.9	3.8	3.2	-6.8	5.2
Iran	10,010	5,369	9,551	6.4	8.0	7.7	-7.8	7.2
Israel	4,017	8,050	16,519	2.6	11.9	13.3	8.7	9.0
Jordan	70	185	300	0.1	0.3	0.2	12.2	6.0
Kuwait	9,785	4,587	7,458	6.3	6.8	6.0	-9.5	6.1
Lebanon	149	263	411	0.1	0.4	0.3	7.1	5.6
Libya	19,079	6,451	8,684	12.3	9.6	7.0	-13.6	3.7
Oman	2,811	2,147	2,372	1.8	3.2	1.9	-3.4	1.2
Qatar	4,546	1,268	3,372	2.9	1.9	2.7	-16.0	12.2
Saudi Arabia	77,751	19,958	35,604	50.0	29.6	28.8	-17.0	7.2
Syria	1,422	532	2,367	0.9	0.8	1.9	-12.3	18.7
Turkey	1,904	7,294	16,070	1.2	10.8	13.0	16.8	9.9
UAE	18,335	6,966	15,434	11.8	10.3	12.5	-12.1	9.9
Yemen	11	487	427	--	0.7	0.3	47.6	-1.6
ALL MIDDLE EAST	155,602	67,371	123,799	100.0	100.0	100.0	-10.5	7.6
NON-ENERGY GOODS								
Bahrain	111	408	538	1.1	1.9	1.2	16.2	3.5
Cyprus	439	554	442	4.4	2.6	1.0	2.9	-2.8
Egypt	747	978	2,148	7.6	4.5	4.7	3.4	9.8
Iran,	877	905	1,438	8.9	4.2	3.2	0.4	5.8
Israel	3,910	8,003	16,418	39.6	37.0	36.2	9.0	9.0
Jordan	70	175	300	0.7	0.8	0.7	11.4	6.8
Kuwait	108	207	251	1.1	1.0	0.6	8.1	2.4
Lebanon	149	263	405	1.5	1.2	0.9	7.1	5.4
Libya	132	302	314	1.3	1.4	0.7	10.4	0.5
Oman	73	309	410	0.7	1.4	0.9	18.0	3.5
Qatar	22	56	219	0.2	0.3	0.5	12.1	16.9
Saudi Arabia	696	2,367	3,497	7.0	10.9	7.7	15.3	4.9
Syria	111	94	434	1.1	0.4	1.0	-2.1	19.3
Turkey	1,887	6,295	15,918	19.1	29.1	35.1	15.1	11.6
UAE	542	682	2,591	5.5	3.1	5.7	2.9	16.7
Yemen	9	42	45	0.1	0.2	0.1	19.4	0.9
ALL MIDDLE EAST	9,882	21,640	45,366	100.0	100.0	100.0	9.8	9.3

Source: OECD countries import statistics as reported in the UN COMTRADE Database.

Industrial markets constitute the most important destinations for all Middle Eastern exports, but a related question is which Middle East countries originate this exchange? If one or two countries are excluded from the tabulation, would this influence perceptions concerning the direction of trade? Also, has their relative importance been stable, or do some regional countries now account for a significantly larger, or smaller, share of imports from the Middle East? For answers, the top half of table 1.3 shows the value, share, and growth rates for OECD imports from each regional country in 1980, 1988, and 1997, while the lower half shows similar statistics excluding fuels. These results change markedly depending on whether or not petroleum is included. If oil is included, Saudi Arabia accounts for almost 30 percent of all regional exports to the OECD. In contrast, Israel and Turkey are by far the two largest regional non-oil exporters, accounting for over $32 billion, or 71 percent of OECD imports from the Middle East.[7] However, while Israel's share of Middle Eastern exports to the EU declined slightly from its 1980 level of 39.6 percent, Turkey's share rose by a dramatic 16 points to 35 percent. The underlying trade statistics shows that textiles and clothing accounted for $7 billion, or 52 percent of the total increase that occurred in Turkey's exports.

However, as noted, when energy products are included in the statistics, the relative importance of individual countries changes significantly. Saudi Arabia alone accounts for about 30 percent of all OECD imports from the region while Iran and UAE combined add a further 26 percent. The underlying data for table 1.3 suggests the Middle Eastern trade shares are sensitive to the time periods used for comparison and changes in petroleum prices. For example, UNCTAD (1996, 48) estimates that 1988 crude oil prices were 60 percent below their corresponding levels in 1980, which resulted in the negative trade growth rates for those countries with highly specialized in energy exports.

The Composition of Middle East Exports

Economists often argue that developing countries that concentrate in the export of primary commodities may face detrimental long-term growth prospects. Unstable commodity prices and resulting unpredictable export earnings may make development planning difficult. As noted, the income elasticities of most primary commodities including fuels are low, so countries specializing in their production might expect to be increasingly marginalized in world trade. Third, export prospects for some primary commodities are diminished by synthetic substitutes (that is, plastics are increasingly being substituted for metals, synthetic fibers are being substituted for hard fibers, etc.). Is the composition of Middle Eastern countries' exports shifting toward manufactures or other goods with more promising prospects? In order to

TABLE 1.4 The 1997 Product Composition of OECD Imports from the Middle East

		Product Group as a Percentage of Total Exports							
		Major Product Groups					Select Commodity Groups		
Exporting Country	Total Exports ($ million)	All Foods	Agricultural Materials	Fuels	Ores & Metals	All Manufactures	Textiles & Clothing	Chemicals	Transport & Machinery
Bahrain	885.5	0.8	0.2	37.1	30.2	30.3	11.5	5.1	5.3
Cyprus	451.5	25.5	1.6	0.3	8.6	62.6	25.6	3.5	22.2
Egypt	4,318.0	4.2	3.0	48.5	4.7	37.2	25.9	2.1	2.2
Iran	10,197.6	5.1	1.7	85.1	0.5	7.5	4.9	0.5	0.4
Israel	16,753.0	5.2	2.3	0.6	1.3	88.6	6.2	12.7	24.1
Jordan	330.2	3.5	3.9	0.0	34.7	52.6	8.4	22.6	16.4
Kuwait	7,629.7	0.1	0.1	96.6	0.1	2.1	0.1	0.3	0.8
Lebanon	446.1	8.8	4.0	1.4	9.9	69.9	4.8	8.5	9.5
Libya	9,216.7	0.0	0.2	96.3	0.0	3.3	0.0	2.8	0.1
Oman	2,372.3	1.8	0.0	82.7	0.3	14.3	5.7	0.1	4.2
Qatar	3,385.9	0.0	0.1	93.3	0.0	5.7	3.0	1.6	0.8
Saudi Arabia	36,621.9	0.1	0.1	90.2	0.3	9.0	0.1	4.1	2.6
Syria	2,823.6	3.0	7.7	80.7	1.0	7.5	4.2	0.1	0.3
Turkey	16,068.8	17.0	1.7	0.9	3.0	76.6	47.6	2.2	12.1
UAE	15,459.2	0.6	0.1	83.1	2.0	10.9	3.9	1.0	3.5
Yemen	427.7	4.8	2.3	89.4	0.6	2.7	0.0	0.0	1.7
ALL MIDDLE EAST	127,387.8	3.7	1.0	66.8	1.5	28.8	9.1	3.8	6.3
MEMO ITEM:									
ALL Non-Industrial Countries	109,792.0	9.0	2.4	17.6	4.2	64.5	12.0	3.5	28.3

Source: United Nations Series D Trade Tapes. Import statistics as reported (c.i.f.) by the OECD countries. Product groups are defined as follows: All foods and feeds (SITC 0+1+22+4); agricultural materials (2-22-27-28); mineral fuels (3); ores minerals and nonferrous metals (27+28+68); all manufactures (5 to 8 less 68); yarns, textiles and clothing (26+65+84); chemicals (5); transport and machinery(7).

examine this question in markets with different demand prospects, we first analyze Middle Eastern trade with OECD countries (the major Middle Eastern markets) and later turn to developments in intraregional trade.

Table 1.4 provides summary statistics on the product composition of each Middle Eastern country's exports to the original OECD members by showing the share of trade occurring in broad product groups like foodstuffs, agricultural raw materials, ores and metals, or manufactures. As indicated, mineral fuels are by far the largest product group accounting for approximately 67 percent of all regional exports. This is almost four times higher than energy products' share in the exports of all non-industrial countries combined (see the memo item). The value of fuel exports ($85 billion) is about $48 billion higher than the second largest product group, manufactured goods (which account for 29 percent of regional exports).

Eight countries (Iran, Kuwait, Libya, Oman, Qatar, Saudi Arabia, UAE, and Yemen) have developed only a limited capacity for exports of manufactures and are almost totally reliant on mineral fuels, which account for more than 80 percent of their total exports. However, on the positive side, there clearly has been a longer-term decline in the relative importance of energy products in regional exports and an increase in the importance of manufactures. From 1975 to 1982, for example, the available COMTRADE data show petroleum products accounted for 90 percent or more of Middle East exports while the share of manufactures fluctuated between 3 and 4 percent. At this point, the share of fuels began a steady decline while manufactures share rose seven-fold to the value shown in table 1.4.

Table 1.4 shows that the exports of Israel, Lebanon, Turkey, and, to a lesser extent Cyprus and Jordan are more heavily concentrated in manufactures than other Middle Eastern countries (77 percent of Turkey's exports are manufactured goods, and their share in Israel's exports is 89 percent). Countries like these, which are not specializing in energy products, probably hold the key to increased regional trade opportunities since they have the capacity to export non-oil products competitively to third markets. Increased opportunities for intraregional trade may exist in foodstuffs, the third largest Middle East export group (12 percent of total exports).

What major non-energy products are regional countries now exporting to the OECD, and how has the composition of this trade changed? Table 1.5 lists the thirty largest non-oil exports and also shows the shares of these goods in 1980 and 1988. One 3-digit SITC product (non-fur clothing) now accounts for almost one-fifth of all Middle East exports and also has had one of the highest growth rates for the listed products. However, in spite of the Middle East's past success in exporting these goods, there is a degree of uncertainty concerning future trade prospects due to the Uruguay Round's scheduled elimination of quotas applied under the MFA. When the MFA quotas are phased out, textile and clothing trade should be subject to intense international competition, and the displacement of some established regional suppliers could occur. As such, Middle Eastern countries should assign a high priority to restructuring their industries, reducing costs, and improving quality to compete in the new competitive environment that is likely to occur.

Does table 1.5 suggest that a pattern or profile exists for the types of goods the Middle East may be able to export competitively? It may initially not be apparent, but most of the products listed have at least one of four common

TABLE 1.5 Industrial Countries' Thirty Largest 3-Digit SITC Non-Energy Import Products from the Middle East

	Value of Industrial Countries Imports ($ million)			Percent of Total Imports (%)		
Description (SITC)	1980	1988	1997	1980	1988	1997
Clothing not of fur (841)	413	2,847	8,067	4.2	13.1	17.8
Pearls and precious stones (667)	1,174	2,629	5,370	11.9	12.1	11.6
Organic chemicals (512)	198	1,220	2,048	2.0	5.6	4.4
Telecommunications equipment (724)	59	354	1,869	0.6	1.6	4.0
Fresh fruit and nuts (051)	905	988	1,500	9.2	4.6	3.2
Non-electric power machinery (711)	277	735	1,309	2.8	3.4	2.8
Gold and silverware (897)	124	408	1,258	1.3	1.9	2.7
Non-electric machinery, nes (719)	89	290	1,037	0.9	1.3	2.2
Scientific instruments (861)	58	273	992	0.6	1.3	2.1
Textile yarns (651)	345	627	811	3.5	2.9	1.7
Plastic materials (581)	47	503	789	0.5	2.3	1.7
Aluminum (684)	149	720	772	1.5	3.3	1.7
Floor covers (657)	677	599	751	6.9	2.8	1.6
Textile products, nes (656)	59	194	659	0.6	0.9	1.4
Woven non-cotton textiles	21	163	614	0.2	0.8	1.3
Electrical machinery, nes (729)	99	352	603	1.0	1.6	1.3
Preserved fruit (053)	178	470	544	1.8	2.2	1.2
Office machinery (714)	32	207	544	0.3	1.0	1.2
Fresh vegetables (054)	233	356	529	2.4	1.6	1.1
Electric power machinery (722)	40	114	473	0.4	0.5	1.0
Unmanufactured tobacco (121)	205	184	459	2.1	0.9	1.0
Dried fruit (052)	195	249	452	2.0	1.1	1.0
Woven cotton fabrics (652)	55	166	445	0.6	0.8	1.0
Medicinal products (541)	9	53	436	0.1	0.2	0.9
Road motor vehicles (732)	22	92	417	0.2	0.4	0.9
Articles of plastic, nes (893)	35	105	408	0.4	0.5	0.9
Manufactured fertilizers (561)	110	312	390	1.1	1.4	0.8
Cotton (263)	566	348	384	5.7	1.6	0.8
Crude vegetable materials (292)	209	232	358	2.1	1.1	0.8
Tools (695)	27	91	328	0.3	0.4	0.7
Total of Above Products	6,610	15,879	34,612	66.9	73.3	74.6
All Nonfuel Products	9,882	21,640	45,366	100.0	100.0	100.0

Source: United Nations Series D Trade Tapes. The above statistics exclude aircraft and special transactions (SITC 931).

characteristics. First, some goods, such as clothing, textile yarns, and floor covers are labor-intensive in production, and countries like Egypt and Jordan with relatively low wages should have a comparative advantage in these sectors.[8] Second, there are several products like organic chemicals, plastic materials, and aluminum that are energy-intensive, and the Middle East may be able to capitalize on its energy resources to further expand exports of such items. For example, energy-intensive products like glass and glassware or ferrous metals may be suitable for local manufacture. Third, several Middle Eastern countries are now intensively importing parts and components and using these materials for local assembly of items such as telecommunications equipment, nonelectrical machinery, and office machinery. Since the assembly operations are generally labor-intensive in nature, Middle Eastern countries may have the capacity to expand these types of "production sharing" operations. Finally, several agricultural products appear in table 1.5. Many Middle East countries are "off-season" producers (relative to Europe), and the Uruguay Round's lowering of agricultural trade barriers may enable them to better exploit opportunities in this sector.

Are There "Dynamic" Middle Eastern Exports?

Although they presently may not constitute a large share of Middle East exports, there are reasons why one should identify "dynamic" (i.e., fast growing) exports. If their current above-average growth continues for an extended period, these items may eventually become an important source of a country's export earnings. Second, if the dynamic products have specific production characteristics, this could convey important information. For example, if they are highly labor- or resource-intensive, both the reasons for their growth and whether similar export opportunities exist in other related goods should be determined. Third, there is an obvious interest in identifying dynamic products to focus future multilateral trade negotiations, like the previous Uruguay Round, on the removal of important foreign trade barriers they face.

Table 1.6 lists the thirty fastest-growing 3-digit exports from the region over 1993-97. It shows the value of trade involved, their growth rates, and whether or not the item is normally produced by labor- or capital-intensive manufacturing procedures. This latter classification is based on a recent analysis by the World Bank (1992) which attempted to measure factor intensities for the manufacture of different products. To guard against the results being biased by items with a very low initial trade base, products with exports of under $100,000 in 1993 were excluded from the comparisons.

Several interesting points are evident. First, these fast-growing products currently account for a relatively small share of all Middle East exports. In 1997, they totaled $2.4 billion or about 2 percent of all regional exports. Second, sixty percent of the Middle East dynamic products are manufactured goods—several of which often require locally available natural resource or agricultural production inputs, i.e., products like vegetable oils, paper and board, or leather. Could similar export opportunities be developed utilizing further processing of domestically available natural resources? Petroleum-based chemical and plastic industries may be one such suitable sector for further export development given the availability of crude petroleum in many Middle Eastern countries.

The fact that several of the dynamic products are foodstuffs, coupled with the Uruguay Round's tariffication and reduction of NTBs on agricultural trade, should focus attention on whether there are further agricultural export opportunities. Increased agricultural exports could assume special importance for Egypt, Turkey, Cyprus, and some other Middle Eastern countries, since these goods are highly labor intensive in production—a factor which could help alleviate the situation of the rural poor. Studies by the International Labor Office show that developing countries may use on average up to thirty times as much labor per unit of agricultural output as some developed countries, so expanded trade in these goods could have major job-creating effects.

One troubling aspect associated with table 1.6 is that Turkey, and to a lesser extent Israel, are the major suppliers for most of the Middle East's dynamic products. For only twelve of the thirty products do other countries register a significant presence. This suggests that the origins of the recent rapid growth of exports from the region have been concentrated and that most countries are not strongly involved in the rapid growth sectors. Egypt appears as a primary supplier for only three products (butter, stone and gravel, and iron wire) while Iran, Libya, and the smaller regional countries fail to appear on the list for any product. In addition, it is also surprising that 40 percent of the dynamic products are normally manufactured using relatively capital intensive procedures. Developing countries normally do not export these types of goods competitively unless they are highly subsidized (Lary 1968, Yeats 1990).

How Important is Intra-Industry Trade?

Some analyses of factors influencing the success or failure of efforts to promote industrialization and growth conclude that a growing level of IIT plays an important positive role. There are several reasons for this assumption. First, intra-industry exchange produces extra gains from international trade (over and above those from comparative advantage) because it allows countries to take advantage of larger markets. By engaging in IIT, a country can simultaneously reduce the number of similar goods it produces while the variety of goods available to domestic consumers is increased. By manufacturing fewer varieties, a country can produce each at a larger scale, with higher productivity and lower cost. At the same time, consumers benefit from an increased range of choices.

TABLE 1.6 Dynamic Products in Industrial Countries' Imports from the Middle East

Product (SITC) & Factor Intensity	Major 1997 Suppliers (share)	OECD Imports ($ million) 1993	1997	Growth Rate
Iron and steel plate (674)***	Turkey (94)	1.5	151.2	115.7
Zinc (686)***	Turkey (95)	0.4	7.5	75.8
Live animals (001)*	UAE (92)	4.1	75.5	72.9
Silver and platinum (681)***	UAE (74)	1.9	31.1	70.0
Fixed vegetable oils (421)*	Turkey (93)	8.0	87.5	59.8
Dyeing products (532)**	Israel (53)	1.1	7.6	47.9
Other manufactures (899)*	Israel (88)	30.5	182.8	44.8
Pulp & waste paper (251)***	Israel (80)	1.3	7.7	44.7
Iron ore (281)***	Cyprus (56)	1.4	7.1	39.9
Leather (611)*	Syria (34)	21.2	102.2	39.4
Butter (023)**	Egypt (76)	0.1	0.4	39.0
Primary iron forms (672)**	Turkey (54)	50.5	238.1	38.9
Stone & gravel (273)***	Egypt (42)	14.0	54.2	33.8
Synthetic rubber (231)***	S. Arabia (29)	2.2	8.2	33.1
Structures & parts (691)***	Turkey (38)	16.3	59.3	32.2
Non-gold coins (961)****	Jordan (53)	0.7	2.5	32.2
Pottery (666)*	Turkey (69)	7.0	25.5	32.2
Nonferrous metals (689)***	Israel (63)	9.3	32.9	31.6
Paints & pigments (533)**	S. Arabia (51)	14.0	47.0	30.3
Iron Shapes (673)***	Turkey (84)	84.0	274.6	29.6
Medicinal products (541)****	Israel (86)	133.3	435.7	29.6
Tobacco products (122)***	Cyprus (33)	1.0	3.2	28.3
Iron wire (677)**	Egypt (50)	4.5	12.9	26.3
Iron tubes (678)**	Turkey (78)	58.3	164.8	26.0
Wire products (693)**	Turkey (65)	22.7	60.8	24.6
Dressed fur skins (613)*	Turkey (75)	1.1	2.8	24.4
Sulphur (274)***	S. Arabia (73)	2.2	5.6	23.75
Wood manufactures (632)*	Israel (55)	7.6	19.5	23.68
Domestic electric equipment (725)**	Turkey (93)	84.7	216.6	23.48
Paper & board (641)***	Turkey (27)	17.4	43.3	22.78
ALL ABOVE PRODUCTS				
Value	Turkey (48)	602.2	2,368.0	34.2
Percent of all Imports		0.6	1.9	

* Generally manufactured by relatively labor-intensive techniques.

** Generally manufactured by techniques of average labor intensity.

*** Generally manufactured by relatively capital-intensive techniques.

**** Factor intensity information was not available from the World Bank (1992).

Source: United Nations Series D trade tapes. To be included in the above tabulations, OECD imports of the product had to total at least $100,000 in 1993.

Several summary indices provide useful insights as to the extent that IIT is taking place or is changing. One such measure is the IIT ratio. This index ranges between zero and one, with larger values indicating a greater level of trade between firms in the same industry. Higher IIT ratios suggest gains from specialization in differentiated products are being exploited and that the participating country is increasing its integration into the global economy.[9]

Table 1.7 presents Middle Eastern intra-industry ratios for all manufactures and several fabricated product sub-groups in 1985 and 1997. This relatively wide time span was chosen to help assess the magnitude of longer-term changes that may have occurred in this activity. For comparison, the table also shows similar ratios for five non-regional countries, all of which may be at a similar, or somewhat more advanced, stage of industrialization.

The key point evident from the table is that a relatively small IIT base exists in most of the Middle East as the IIT ratios are under 0.2 for 10 of the sixteen countries. This is far lower than the indices for Korea, Malaysia, and Taiwan, which range between 0.60 and 0.64. Israel is currently the only Middle Eastern country where a similar level of IIT is occurring. Perhaps an even more striking point is that the indices for several Middle Eastern

TABLE 1.7 1985 and 1997 IIT Ratios for Middle Eastern Countries

	Chemicals		Machinery & Transport		Other Manufactures		All Manufactures	
Country	1985	1997	1985	1997	1985	1997	1985	1997
Bahrain	0.31	0.16	0.25	0.24	0.16	0.44	0.21	0.31
Cyprus	0.29	0.28	0.30	0.24	0.29	0.35	0.30	0.29
Egypt	0.07	0.17	0.04	0.04	0.11	0.37	0.07	0.17
Iran	0.12	0.36	0.04	0.04	0.47	0.13	0.23	0.13
Israel	0.66	0.70	0.51	0.60	0.62	0.68	0.59	0.66
Jordan	0.21	0.20	0.15	0.13	0.09	0.16	0.14	0.16
Kuwait	0.17	0.08	0.09	0.06	0.15	0.11	0.12	0.08
Lebanon	0.25	0.12	0.13	0.06	0.29	0.30	0.24	0.18
Libya	0.59	0.36	0.10	0.02	0.15	0.22	0.20	0.16
Oman	0.14	0.27	0.14	0.22	0.09	0.27	0.12	0.24
Qatar	0.13	0.11	0.04	0.03	0.12	0.15	0.09	0.07
Saudi Arabia	0.39	0.25	0.07	0.13	0.04	0.30	0.09	0.19
Syria	0.05	0.06	0.03	0.02	0.11	0.11	0.07	0.07
Turkey	0.24	0.23	0.09	0.26	0.22	0.42	0.16	0.33
UAE	0.25	0.37	0.24	0.23	0.31	0.32	0.28	0.28
Yemen	0.14	0.18	0.08	0.05	0.14	0.25	0.12	0.14
MEMO ITEM:								
Brazil	0.71	0.57	0.70	0.58	0.21	0.47	0.51	0.54
Chile	0.38	0.43	0.14	0.10	0.21	0.37	0.22	0.24
Korea	0.49	0.63	0.56	0.67	0.29	0.56	0.41	0.61
Malaysia	0.38	0.70	0.67	0.67	0.38	0.52	0.57	0.64
Taiwan	0.52	0.57	0.58	0.68	0.18	0.45	0.36	0.60

Source: Computed from UN COMTRADE records.

countries have been essentially static at low levels (Cyprus, Jordan, and Syria), or have in fact have declined (Iran, Kuwait, Lebanon, Libya, and Qatar). Overall, the data fail to suggest that this type of exchange is currently developing within most of the Middle Eastern countries and, compared to other countries, its level is relatively low.

An activity closely related to IIT involves global production sharing and international trade in parts and components. Estimates suggest that this activity now accounts for at least 30 percent of world trade in manufactured goods and that global production sharing, in which several countries complete different stages of a manufacturing process, has grown considerably faster than overall trade in manufactures (Yeats 1998). Production sharing may have many positive attractions for the participating countries if it allows them to capitalize on their comparative advantage in different stages of a manufacturing process. One should, however, distinguish between two types of production sharing. Countries that are large net importers of components generally have sizeable pools of low-cost unskilled labor available, are normally at a relatively low level of industrialization, and lack the technical capacity to produce some sophisticated types of components (e.g., transistors, switch gear, automotive parts, etc.). On the other hand, net exporters of components are typically more industrialized countries with a relatively high skilled high cost labor force, which makes it advantageous for them to shift assembly operations abroad (Ng and Yeats 1999). Have the Middle Eastern countries been able to capitalize on this type of production sharing?

Revision 2 of the SITC system tabulates fairly detailed statistics on international trade in components that can be used to analyze the level of the Middle East's involvement in this exchange.[10] Table 1.8 draws upon these data and shows the value of components in global exports to and imports from the Middle Eastern countries in the most recent year for which UN COMTRADE data were available. To provide a "benchmark" for assessing the relative importance of this exchange, the table shows the share of components imports and exports in all manufactures trade. Finally, the table also provides similar statistics for several non-Middle Eastern countries for comparison.

The data reveal several interesting points. First, the region as a whole has a very large negative trade balance for parts and components with imports of these goods (about $20 billion) being approximately four times higher than exports. Several countries, like Oman and Saudi Arabia, appear to be making fairly extensive use of foreign-produced components in domestic assembly operations as "parts" account for twenty percent or more of all manufactured imports. On average, components account for 15 percent of the Middle East's imports of manufactured goods—a figure that is roughly comparable to that for the United States or Japan (see the memo item). An analysis of the composition of the Middle Eastern countries' imports of components shows that three items (parts of telecommunications equipment, automobile parts, and switch gear) account for about half of the total trade in these goods. This corresponds closely to the relative importance of these items on a global level.

On the export side, a different picture emerges. First, Israel dominates this exchange and accounts for 75 percent of all regional exports of components. The fact that parts account for about 18 percent of all Israeli manufactured exports indicates that it has achieved a level of involvement in this aspect of production sharing similar to most of the countries listed in the memo item. The underlying statistics show Israel's exports are concentrated in products that are of relatively high importance in global components trade, i.e., telecommunication parts account for 54 percent of all Israeli components exported, with switch gear and office machine parts accounting for a further 16 percent. Although components appear to represent a high share (21.8 percent)

TABLE 1.8 The Relative Importance of Parts and Components in Individual Middle Eastern Countries' Trade

		Value of Parts and Components Trade ($ million)		Share of Components in Total Manufactures Trade (%)	
Country	Year	Imports	Exports	Imports	Exports
Bahrain	1996	227.0	13.2	13.8	2.4
Cyprus	1997	168.5	6.3	8.0	2.6
Egypt	1997	980.6	31.8	11.9	2.1
Iran	*	1,244.1	29.8	15.8	2.6
Israel	1997	2,879.7	3,794.9	12.3	18.3
Jordan	1995	281.8	12.4	12.6	1.8
Kuwait	1997	986.4	33.4	15.0	5.6
Lebanon	*	529.0	12.1	13.3	2.4
Libya	1991	689.3	1.1	17.7	0.3
Oman	1997	832.5	275.3	22.7	21.8
Qatar	1994	219.5	0.1	14.3	0.0
Saudi Arabia	1997	4,672.6	13.6	23.1	0.3
Syria	1997	207.0	1.5	7.6	0.4
Turkey	1997	4,359.4	773.5	12.5	3.9
UAE	1993	1,203.4	6.3	10.5	1.3
Yemen	1995	82.3	0.0	10.7	0.2
ALL ABOVE COUNTRIES		19,563.2	5,005.3	14.5	9.2
MEMO ITEM:					
United States	1997	112,381.3	133,384.8	16.7	26.0
Germany	1997	52,302.1	74,144.7	16.7	16.6
Japan	1997	24,786.5	79,356.4	13.5	19.9
Singapore	1997	27,619.8	24,703.8	25.4	23.6
Malaysia	1997	20,304.2	13,333.8	31.2	22.1
Taiwan, China	1997	7,709.6	21,520.6	10.5	20.0

*Due to the failure of this country to report to UN COMTRADE, the statistics shown are based on partner country data.

Source: Computed from UN COMTRADE Statistics.

of Oman's total manufactured exports, the fact that motor vehicle and construction machinery parts account for three-quarters of these goods makes these statistics suspect. One possibility is that Oman may be incorrectly reporting some transshipments in its national export statistics.

Overall, what does the available information suggest concerning the prospects for increased Middle East involvement in production sharing? First, relative wage costs are acknowledged to be one major determinant of where component assembly operations are located, and the available statistics indicate some Middle Eastern countries should be attractive in this respect. According to the World Bank (1999), annual manufacturing wage costs in Egypt and Jordan range between $1,863 to $3,125, and are approximately 4 to 6 percent of those in Germany. On the negative side, the location of assembly operations is also strongly affected by the availability of adequate transport and communications infrastructure as well as government policies toward business. The available evidence suggest these are strong negative factors in some Middle Eastern countries which will have to be addressed before the Middle East more fully participates in this aspect of global production sharing.[11]

Competitive Factors and the Change in Middle Eastern Exports

The previous analysis (table 1.3) showed Middle Eastern non-oil exports expanded at a fairly rapid pace over 1988-96. Factors relating to both supply and demand influenced this recent trade change, and an important question concerns the extent to which changes in international competitiveness contribute to this favorable trade performance. This question can be addressed by decomposing a country's export growth into three factors, two of which relate to changes in global demand and competitive conditions.[12] The influence of demand for traditional goods (which are defined as products exported in a specified base period) is measured by the change in the total value of world trade in these items. In calculating the influence of this factor, one assumes that a country maintains its global trade share for a commodity. Specifically, if $D_{o,j}$ and $D_{t,j}$ represent world trade in product *j*, at time period *o* and *t* respectively, the change in exports attributed solely to demand $\Delta E_{d,i}$ is:

$$\Delta E_{d,i} = \sum (s_{o,j}) \cdot (D_{t,j} - D_{o,j}) \qquad (1)$$

where $s_{o,j}$ is the share of the country *i* in global exports of product *j* in the base period *o*, and the summation is over all goods exported. Therefore, equation (1) shows the change in country *i*'s exports that would have occurred if only changes in demand took place.

Second, the change in the competitive position of country i is measured by the difference between the exports that would have occurred in period t if the country's initial market share had not changed and those exports that were realized. This factor $(E_{c,i})$ is:

$$\Delta E_{c,i} = \sum(s_{t,j} - s_{o,j})(D_{t,j}) \qquad (2)$$

where $s_{t,j}$ is the share of the country in global exports of product j in period t, and the summation is over all goods exported. Equation (2) shows how much exports changed, above or below the level associated with pure demand changes, due to changes in a country's market shares. Any differences between changes in a country's total exports and the sum of these "demand" and "competitive" changes are due to product diversification.[13]

Table 1.9 summarizes the results when each of these equations was applied to statistics on all 3-digit SITC products exported by the Middle Eastern countries in 1988, 1992, and 1996. The table shows the total value of exports in each year along with changes due to the supply and demand factors. For example, Bahrain's 1988 non-oil exports totaled $710 million, and the 1988-94 market demand factor generated a potential increase in annual exports worth $104 million. However, Bahrain's improved ability to compete, as reflected in its higher market shares (particularly for aluminum products), resulted in a further export increase of $18 million. Bahrain's market shares experienced an even greater increase over 1992-96 which resulted in "competitive factor" export gains of about $267 million.

Several important positive points are evident from the statistics reported in table 1.9. First, while general improvements in the market shares of the Middle Eastern countries resulted in combined export gains of approximately $1.1 billion over the 1988-92 interval, this was largely due to the trade performance of four countries, namely Egypt, Iran, Turkey, and UAE. In fact, eight of the Middle Eastern countries experienced a general erosion of their market shares as well as losses for the export competitiveness factor. However, the data show that the Middle East experienced a significant improvement in trade perfor-mance over 1992-1996 as the competitiveness factor ($7.2 billion) was almost seven times higher than in the early period and, equally important, was positive in all but three (Libya, Oman, Qatar) of the sixteen countries. Israel's competitive gains ($2.5 billion) were the largest recorded, but six other countries recorded competitive gains of one-quarter billion dollars or more.

What caused these impressive Middle East market share trade gains? An examination of the underlying statistics indicates that the causes varied from country to country. The results for Saudi Arabia were largely a result of efforts to move into the manufacture and export of items, e.g., organic chemicals, plastic materials, and manufactured fertilizers that employ petroleum as a major input. Israel experienced a doubling of its market share for cut diamonds—exports rose by over $2 billion—while competitive share gains for clothing, fresh fruit and vegetables, textile yarns, and electrical machinery increased Turkey's exports of these products by one-half billion dollars or more. In Egypt and Jordan, the product base for the export expansion is somewhat broader, and there is some indication that they are connected to comprehensive structural adjustment programs, which started in the late 1980s. Altogether, the recent trade performance conveys a positive picture concerning the Middle East's general international competitiveness.

TABLE 1.9 The Impact of Competition, Demand, and Diversification Middle Eastern Non-Oil Exports

	Exports ($ million)			Factors Underlying the 1988-92 Export Change* ($ million)		Factors Underlying the 1992-96 Export Change* ($ million)	
Country	1988	1992	1996	Overall Demand	Competitive Factor	Overall Demand	Competitive Factor
Bahrain	710.4	832.4	1,430.4	103.7	18.3	331.0	267.0
Cyprus	658.5	701.6	1,107.7	260.4	-217.3	208.1	198.0
Egypt	1,207.2	1,939.7	2,419.8	297.7	520.1	504.9	75.2
Iran	1,006.6	1,726.5	2,359.6	239.8	480.1	256.8	376.3
Israel	903.3	11,647.0	18,727.2	2,813.1	-198.3	4,560.2	2,520.0
Jordan	678.6	703.4	894.4	127.4	-102.6	139.5	51.5
Kuwait**	514.1	253.3	571.0	169.2	-430.1	82.6	235.0
Lebanon	511.8	423.7	626.8	190.8	-278.1	124.9	78.3
Libya	457.9	409.9	516.0	108.6	-122.9	168.6	-62.5
Oman	308.0	462.2	577.2	90.9	2.9	126.8	-11.8
Qatar	417.3	480.2	629.0	84.1	19.8	173.7	-24.9
S. Arabia	4,364.9	4,278.2	7,000.3	1,228.9	-1,315.6	1,681.2	1,040.9
Syria	167.1	569.4	816.7	31.0	371.3	138.2	109.1
Turkey	8,133.6	12,631.8	18,105.8	3,313.3	1,184.9	3,389.9	2,084.1
UAE	1,692.4	3,392.3	4,764.6	538.7	1,161.2	1,132.8	239.4
Yemen	77.4	73.9	116.0	20.4	-23.9	26.1	16.1
ALL ABOVE	21,809.1	40,525.5	60,662.5	9,618.1	1,069.1	13,045.3	7,191.7

* The demand factor isolates the effects of the increase or decrease in global demand for Middle Eastern countries' exports. This factor shows the increase or decrease in exports that would have occurred had there been no change in a country's import market shares. The competitive factor shows the change in exports over or under that associated with the demand changes that is due solely to changes in a country's import market shares. Any differences between changes in a country's total exports and the sum of these "demand" and "competitive" changes are due to product diversification.

** Due to the Gulf War, 1988-90 and 1993-96 have been used for the analysis of Kuwait's export performance.

Prospects for Intraregional Trade

The historical record shows that countries have experienced varying degrees of success (and failure) in attempts to form RTAs. According to Viatsos (1978), the Latin American Free Trade Association (LAFTA) and the Andean Pact eventually collapsed due to reasons such as disagreements about how costs and benefits of the arrangements were being shared and a lack of complementarity in member countries' exports and imports. Others, like the Caribbean Community (CARICOM) or most of the regional arrangements in Sub-Saharan Africa, continue to officially function although members clearly have had major difficulties in implementing the original terms of the agreements (Yeats 1998). NAFTA was initiated too recently for determination of its full effects, but the real success of regional arrangements appears to have occurred in Europe. This uncertainty as to the eventual outcome of a RTA, and the time, effort, and costs that accompany its negotiation and implementation, generated an interest in the development of procedures for identifying countries that might form successful arrangements.[14]

Although their results must be analyzed with caution, comparisons of the "complementarity" of potential partners' imports and exports and measures of the diversity of products in a country's exports may convey some useful information. Examination of recent trade trends may be informative if it focuses on whether intratrade among potential partners is growing faster than average, or whether the structure of global exports is shifting toward products of major importance in the perspective partners' imports. Measures of national RCA may be useful if they show how well a country's international competitiveness corresponds to the potential partners' import needs.

Who Originates Intraregional Trade?

One question of major interest is which countries are now of primary importance as "originators" of intraregional trade and how has their relative importance changed over time? Table 1.10 employs the database developed in this chapter (see section 2) to determine the share of individual countries in this exchange in the mid-1980s and 1990s. As indicated, Turkey now accounts for almost one quarter of all regional exports (up from 17 percent in the mid-1980s) followed by Saudi Arabia and Egypt with 17 and 10 percent respectively.[15] However, the most striking change is the decline in the relative importance of Saudi Arabia whose intraregional export share fell from 34 percent in the mid-1980s to half that value a decade later.

Two additional surprising points evident in table 1.10 are that the overall level of regional trade in the 1990s (about $12.9 billion) is virtually the same as it was a decade earlier and that the intratrade growth rates for seven of the sixteen countries are negative. The current level of Libya's regional exports are about 12 percent below what they were in the mid-1980s, while exports from Saudi Arabia and UAE are 4 to 5 percent lower. However, the underlying statistics suggest these aggregate data may be biased by developments relating to one major product (petroleum) and do not accurately reflect what is in fact happening in other sectors of regional trade.

Implications of the Composition of Middle Eastern Intratrade

Table 1.11 provides relevant evidence concerning this point by identifying the thirty largest 3-digit SITC products in intraregional trade and showing their estimated value, share, and growth rates. As indicated, intraregional petroleum exports fell by over $4 billion during the last decade, and their current regional trade share (12 percent) is about one-quarter of its level in the mid-1980s. This in large part is a result of price changes as UNCTAD estimates that crude petroleum prices in the mid-1990s were almost 60 percent below their corresponding level in the 1980s. The magnitude of the price changes, coupled with the importance petroleum in intraregional trade, explains why this total exchange was essentially static from the mid-1980s to the 1990s.

TABLE 1.10 The Share of Individual Countries in Intraregional Exports in the mid-1980s and 1990s

	Intra-Regional Exports ($ million)		Share of Intra-Regional Exports (%)		Growth Rate
Exporter	Mid-1980s	Mid-1990s	Mid-1980s	Mid-1990s	Mid-1980s-1990s
Bahrain	114	486	0.9	3.8	11.1
Cyprus	232	129	1.9	1.0	-4.2
Egypt	541	839	4.5	6.5	3.4
Iran	1,278	1,237	10.5	9.6	-0.2
Israel	51	447	0.4	3.5	15.6
Jordan	171	392	1.4	3.0	6.9
Kuwait	1,152	409	9.5	3.2	-7.4
Lebanon	564	390	4.6	3.0	-2.8
Libya	743	295	6.1	2.3	-11.6
Oman	278	1,146	2.3	8.9	10.1
Qatar	234	311	1.9	2.4	5.7
Saudi Arabia	4,160	2,251	34.3	17.4	-4.4
Syria	228	1,184	1.9	9.2	11.8
Turkey	2,086	3,047	17.2	23.5	2.7
UAE	304	238	2.5	1.8	-4.9
Yemen	8	139	0.1	1.1	24.3
ALL MIDDLE EAST	12,144	12,940	100.0	100.0	0.5

Source: Estimates based on United Nations COMTRADE records.

When statistics for the other major products are examined, a far more dynamic impression of intraregional trade changes emerges. Excluding petroleum, exports of these "major" items approximately doubled over the decade to about $7.1 billion with an annual growth rate of close to 7 percent. Organic chemicals, plastic materials, electrical distribution machinery, and several other relatively sophisticated products recorded intraregional growth rates well

TABLE 1.11 Middle Eastern Countries' Thirty Largest 3-Digit SITC Intraregional Exports in the mid-1980s and mid-1990s

	Value of Exports ($ million)		Percent of All Exports (%)		Growth Rate
Commodity (SITC)	Mid-1980s	Mid-1990s	Mid-1980s	Mid-1990s	
Crude petroleum (331)	5,648.9	1,581.4	46.5	12.5	-9.8
Iron and steel shapes (673)	337.9	761.7	2.8	6.0	6.3
Plastic materials (581)	108.9	570.7	0.9	4.5	12.7
Road motor vehicles (732)	566.3	567.9	4.7	4.5	0.0
Petroleum products (332)	473.1	478.4	3.9	3.8	0.1
Fresh vegetables (054)	242.4	463.0	2.0	3.7	5.0
Clothing, non-fur (841)	172.2	384.5	1.4	3.0	6.2
Fresh fruit and nuts (051)	247.3	341.7	2.0	2.7	2.5
Aluminum (684)	102.5	318.9	0.8	2.5	8.7
Cement and building products (661)	124.5	295.4	1.0	2.3	6.6
Non-electric machinery, nes (719)	81.9	234.8	0.7	1.9	8.1
Live animals (991)	355.8	223.9	2.9	1.8	-3.6
Tobacco manufactures (122)	30.5	193.6	0.3	1.5	14.2
Elec. distribution machinery (723)	37.5	190.0	0.3	1.5	12.5
Articles of paper (642)	39.8	182.3	0.3	1.4	11.7
Textile yarn and thread (651)	163.7	181.6	1.3	1.4	0.8
Chemicals, nes (599)	29.7	170.3	0.2	1.3	13.4
Cleaning preparations (554)	41.3	145.8	0.3	1.2	9.7
Floor coverings (657)	68.7	133.2	0.6	1.1	5.1
Organic chemicals (512)	29.9	131.2	0.2	1.0	11.4
Woven non-cotton textiles (653)	119.8	124.7	1.0	1.0	0.3
Iron and steel tubes (678)	69.7	121.0	0.6	1.0	4.2
Machines for special industries (718)	68.3	115.6	0.6	0.9	4.0
Iron and steel primary forms (672)	26.4	114.9	0.2	0.9	11.3
Copper (682)	20.9	114.3	0.2	0.9	13.1
Articles of plastic, nes (893)	38.5	113.6	0.3	0.9	8.3
Medicinal products (541)	35.8	110.9	0.3	0.9	8.7
Inorganic elements and oxides (513)	38.1	109.2	0.3	0.9	8.1
Structures and parts (691)	83.0	104.9	0.7	0.8	1.8
Cotton (263)	8.4	103.8	0.1	0.8	19.3
ALL ABOVE PRODUCTS	9,411.5	8,683.3	77.5	68.5	-0.6
Excluding Petroleum	3,762.6	7,101.9	31.0	56.1	6.6
ALL EXPORTS	12,143.9	12,671.8	100.0	100.0	0.3

Source: United Nations Series D Trade Tapes.

above the corresponding growth in world trade (10 percent) over 1985-1995. Furthermore, the importance of manufactures in these products is evident as they account for almost three-quarters of the items listed in the table.

Dynamic Products in Intraregional Trade

The previous analysis of dynamic (fast growing) export products identified items that were growing at a far above average pace in the trade of Middle Eastern countries with OECD members. Two surprising points were evident in these results. First, there was a relatively high percentage (40 percent) of products in this list that were normally manufactured by capital-intensive production procedures. Second was the fact that Turkey was a principal supplier for many of these goods. Are the same general patterns reflected in statistics on intraregional trade?

Table 1.12 lists the thirty fastest-growing 3-digit SITC products in regional intratrade from the mid-1980s to 1990s. It shows the value of exports, their annualized growth rates, and also identifies the major supplier and its share in the exchange of each product. As indicated, these items now account for approximately $2.3 billion (up from about $322 million in the mid-1980s), or close to 20 percent of all intraregional trade. The compound growth rates for these products range from over 30 percent for pig iron and iron wire down to about 12 percent for electrical distributing machinery and paper pulp.

The major similarity with the dynamic products in OECD trade is that the same share (40 percent) of these goods are also normally manufactured by capital intensive production techniques. However, only three items appearing on the OECD list (iron wire, sulfur, and tobacco products) are among the fastest-growing products in intraregional trade. A second dissimilarity is that there is considerably less "country concentration" in the origin for these dynamic products than was the case in OECD trade. Turkey originates about 23 percent of all Middle East intraregional exports, but this is half its share in dynamic products going to industrial countries. In fact, Saudi Arabia and Turkey are both identified as the major supplier of the same number (seven) of the thirty dynamic products.

How "Intense" is Intraregional Trade?

Several statistical indices can provide useful insights concerning some aspects of international trade. One such measure—the so-called "trade intensity" index—has been used to determine whether the value of trade between two countries is greater or smaller than what would be expected based on their importance in world trade. For example, table 1.2 showed that approximately 12 percent of Egypt's exports go to North America. Is this above or below

TABLE 1.12 Dynamic Products in Middle Eastern Countries' Regional Exports

		Exports to the Region ($ million)		
Product (SITC) & Factor Intensity	Major 1990s Supplier (share)	Mid-1980s	Mid-1990s	Growth Rate
Pig iron (671)***	Bahrain (93)	0.7	99.3	38.6
Iron wire (677)**	Libya (48)	0.5	27.1	30.3
Aircraft (734)***	Turkey (87)	1.1	53.4	29.7
Fixed vegetable oils (422)*	Bahrain (39)	2.0	89.2	29.1
Leather (611)*	Egypt (31)	0.7	27.6	28.8
Zoo animals (941)****	Oman (78)	1.1	25.7	24.0
Milk and cream (022)**	S. Arabia (79)	5.3	96.2	22.3
Lead (685)***	S. Arabia (77)	0.6	9.3	21.0
Cotton (263)*	Syria (46)	8.4	103.8	19.3
Crude animal materials (291)*	Yemen (21)	0.8	7.4	19.1
Preserved meat (013)**	UAE (51)	2.1	23.7	18.5
Synthetic dyes (531)***	Turkey (40)	0.5	5.4	18.3
Pearls & precious stones (667)****	Israel (57)	0.9	9.4	18.1
Sulphur (274)***	Iran (69)	0.7	6.8	17.5
Iron and steel strip (675)**	Libya (100)	1.0	9.0	17.2
Undressed hides (211)*	Iran (46)	5.9	52.1	16.6
Chocolate and products (073)**	Turkey (65)	4.1	33.6	16.1
Margarine & shortening (091)**	Turkey (86)	7.7	61.1	16.0
Photographic supplies (862)***	Oman (70)	1.3	8.6	14.3
Tobacco products (122)***	Oman (56)	30.5	193.6	14.2
Essential oils (551)**	S. Arabia (50)	0.9	5.8	14.0
Animal & vegetable oils (431)*	Turkey (82)	9.7	59.7	14.0
Chemicals, nes (599)***	Israel (60)	29.7	170.3	13.4
Special textile products (655)*	Turkey (86)	12.7	70.5	13.2
Copper (682)***	Turkey (48)	20.9	114.3	13.1
Wheat meal or flour (046)**	Oman (44)	9.4	51.1	13.0
Plastic materials (581)***	S. Arabia (67)	108.9	570.7	12.7
Wire products (693)**	S. Arabia (79)	16.3	83.3	12.6
Elec. distributing machines (723)***	S. Arabia (55)	37.5	190.0	12.5
Paper pulp & waste (251)***	S. Arabia (51)	0.5	2.5	12.2
ALL ABOVE PRODUCTS	Turkey (23)	322.3	2,260.5	15.0
As % of All Regional Exports		2.7	17.8	
ALL REGIONAL EXPORTS		12,143.9	12,671.8	0.3

* Generally manufactured by relatively labor-intensive techniques.

** Generally manufactured by techniques of average labor intensity.

*** Generally manufactured by relatively capital-intensive techniques.

**** Factor intensity information was not available from the World Bank (1992).

Source: United Nations Series D trade tapes.

what would be expected on the basis of the two partner's relative size in global trade? Is Egypt's trade with other regional countries, about 19 percent of total exports, higher or lower than might be expected? Identification of bilateral combinations where trade is well below expected levels may help focus attempts to identify and remove constraints to trade and also assist in other aspects of trade policy formulation.

Table 1.13 shows 1997 "trade intensity" indices between individual Middle Eastern countries and regional and other selected trading partners. The index may range between zero and infinity, and has a relatively simple interpretation.[16] Values below unity indicate that trade between two countries is lower than expected, while values above one indicate it is relatively larger. A point to note is that, on average, Middle Eastern countries absorb about 3 to 4 percent of global exports. Therefore, any regional country that had a higher share of total exports going to the Middle East could be said to have an above average tendency to trade within the region.

Table 1.13 suggests that most intraregional trade flows are not consistently lower than what should be expected, although Israel and Libya's trade is lower and their trade with Europe is relatively higher. As an example of how to interpret these data, table 1.13 indicates that the share of Egypt's exports to region is about

TABLE 1.13 1997 "Trade Intensity" Indices for Middle Eastern Countries' Exports

	Partner Country				
Exporter	All OECD Countries	European Union	North America	Japan	Middle East Region
Bahrain	0.383	0.215	0.190	2.005	6.682
Cyprus	0.452	0.751	0.061	0.021	7.656
Egypt	0.855	1.202	0.602	0.396	6.324
Iran	0.678	0.803	0.086	2.455	1.257
Israel	1.082	0.872	1.696	0.780	0.110
Jordan	0.289	0.354	0.087	0.479	13.030
Kuwait	0.739	0.308	0.670	4.094	0.201
Lebanon	0.516	0.666	0.354	0.134	15.008
Libya	1.294	2.382	0.000	0.008	0.447
Oman	0.513	0.087	0.190	4.369	0.757
Qatar	0.845	0.028	0.168	8.412	1.420
Saudi Arabia	0.817	0.519	0.829	2.982	2.020
Syria	0.869	1.596	0.037	0.139	6.200
Turkey	0.872	1.282	0.420	0.093	3.517
UAE	0.701	0.135	0.149	6.201	2.530
Yemen	0.274	0.237	0.014	0.907	0.972
ALL MIDDLE EAST	0.844	0.728	0.571	2.517	1.942

Source: Computed from International Monetary Fund Direction of Trade Statistics.

six times larger than what would be expected, while the trade intensity indices for Bahrain, Cyprus, Jordan, and Lebanon are even higher. Overall, the intensity index for all regional intratrade is close to two, i.e., intraregional trade is about double the expected level. This observation would counter any assertion that the level of Middle Eastern intratrade is abnormally low.

Implications of the Concentration of Middle Eastern Exports

Another factor bearing on prospects for Middle Eastern intratrade concerns the range of products these countries can export or import. If the Middle Eastern countries can competitively export a wide range of diversified goods, this should be a positive factor since regional countries would not be forced to turn elsewhere for many key imports. Ideally, comparisons between export potentials and prospective partners' import needs should also attempt to consider products that might be exported competitively, but are not traded at present. Due to difficulties in securing such information, however, most analyses are based on actual trade flows.

Several trade concentration, or diversification, indices can provide useful insights concerning this issue as it relates to prospects for Middle Eastern intraregional trade.[17] One measure is simply a count of the number of 3-digit SITC products exported. This tabulation requires that some "cut-off" be used to exclude items that are marginal in trade and which may not be exported on a regular basis. UNCTAD (1995) adopted an approach to this problem that seems sensible in that it excludes items where trade was below either $100,000, or below three-tenths of a percent of total exports. The higher the numeric value of this index, the greater the diversity of products exported. This measure's maximum value is 239, which represents the number of individual 3-digit products in the SITC Revision 2 system, and its minimum (theoretical) value is zero for a country with no exports.

A second related measure used by UNCTAD is a "diversification" index, which utilizes deviations between the shares of 3-digit SITC products in a country's exports, and their corresponding shares in world trade. The rationale for this approach is that it sets the global structure of trade as a "standard" and seeks to determine how closely it is matched by a country's exports.[18] A country with a diversification index of zero has an export structure that exactly matches that of world trade. This index ranges between zero and unity, with higher values indicating more concentrated trade structures. A third measure that has been employed in the same context is the so-called concentration index. This is the Hirschman Index, computed using the shares of all 3-digit products in a country's exports.[19] The lower this index, the less concentrated are a country's exports. Table 1.14 reports 1980 and 1994 values of these indices for Middle Eastern and several comparator countries.

These statistics reveal several important points concerning the supply capacities of the Middle Eastern countries. First, in terms of the number of products, the Middle East is exporting a considerably narrower range of goods than any of the comparator countries listed in the memo item. Libya and Qatar, for example, export 76 and 33 products respectively, as opposed to over 220 items in the case of Singapore, Korea, or Japan. There have been some impressive increases in several of the Middle Eastern countries' product count indices, such as Bahrain's, which went from 59 to 117 items, or Egypt's which increased from 80 to 171. However, the data generally suggest limitations in

TABLE 1.14 Implications of Middle Eastern Countries' Export Diversification Indices

	Diversification or Concentration Index*					
	Number of Items		Diversification		Concentration	
Exporter	1980	1994	1980	1994	1980	1994
Bahrain	58	117	0.768	0.877	0.790	0.597
Cyprus	140	96	0.746	0.730	0.148	0.183
Egypt	80	171	0.672	0.732	0.575	0.265
Iran	88	171	0.738	0.863	0.814	0.806
Israel	201	196	0.681	0.561	0.264	0.268
Jordan	107	112	0.824	0.797	0.352	0.270
Kuwait	189	140	0.695	0.896	0.732	0.932
Lebanon	194	163	0.713	0.678	0.158	0.169
Libya	42	76	0.770	0.890	0.961	0.780
Oman	101	128	0.735	0.780	0.922	0.747
Qatar	3	33	0.794	0.866	0.934	0.628
Saudi Arabia	183	199	0.757	0.842	0.942	0.728
Syria	114	123	0.671	0.839	0.619	0.655
Turkey	189	216	0.734	0.644	0.230	0.113
UAE	197	205	0.732	0.782	0.870	0.683
Average of the Above	126	143	0.735	0.785	0.621	0.521
MEMO ITEM:						
United States	236	236	0.428	0.272	0.064	0.073
Japan	224	225	0.546	0.417	0.118	0.129
Singapore	232	229	0.586	0.497	0.235	0.195
Malaysia	214	225	0.640	0.521	0.303	0.165
Korea, Republic of	207	217	0.660	0.438	0.085	0.125
Taiwan, China	210	221	0.663	0.477	0.117	0.096
Average of the Above	221	226	0.587	0.437	0.154	0.131

* See endnote 18 for the definition of the diversification and concentration index.

Source: UNCTAD, *Handbook of International Trade and Development Statistics 1995* Yemen is excluded from the comparisons since UNCTAD did not compute indices for this country.

export capacity is currently an important constraint to the expansion of Middle Eastern intratrade. The results for the both the diversification and concentration indices generally reflect further evidence concerning this point.

How "Complementary" is Middle Eastern Trade?

Aside from the concentration and diversification measures, there is an additional summary index that can provide useful information on prospects for intraregional trade in that it shows how well the structure of Middle Eastern countries' imports or exports match. This "complementarity" index has the attraction that its values for countries considering the formation of a RTA can be compared with others that have formed, or tried to form, similar arrangements. Such comparisons could provide some indication of the prospects for the Middle Eastern effort.[20]

Studies employing the index argue that the higher its value, the more likely is a proposed regional trade arrangement to succeed (Michaely 1996). Yeats (1999) takes a different view, suggesting that low values may be more informative in identifying potentially unsuccessful trade arrangements and, in some cases, can be quite misleading.[21]

Table 1.15 shows complementarity index values for each Middle Eastern country and the rest of the region, which were computed using data for the mid-1990s. To assist in evaluating this information, indices for two arrangements that previously failed are shown (LAFTA and the Andean Pact) along

TABLE 1.15 Middle Eastern Countries Trade Complementarity Indices

Regional Arrangement	Index Value	Regional Arrangement	Index Value
Regional Arrangements Which Persist			
European Community (6)	53.4	Canada-United States FTA	64.3
NAFTA	56.3	EFTA	49.8
Unsuccessful Arrangements			
LAFTA	22.2	Andean Pact	7.4
Possible Middle Eastern Arrangements			
Bahrain and Middle East	17.4	Libya and Middle East	8.5
Cyprus and Middle East	31.4	Oman and Middle East	25.6
Egypt and Middle East	28.0	Qatar and Middle East	13.6
Iran and Middle East	11.2	Saudi Arabia and Middle East	13.2
Israel and Middle East	44.7	Syria and Middle East	16.8
Jordan and Middle East	25.5	Turkey and Middle East	44.4
Kuwait and Middle East	9.6	UAE and Middle East	20.6
Lebanon and Middle East	34.3	Yemen and Middle East	5.9

Source: Computed from UN COMTRADE Statistics.

with those that persist (NAFTA, EU, etc.). The general impression that emerges is that a very low degree of complementarity exists between the trade structures of most Middle Eastern countries with the exception of non-oil exporting countries like Cyprus, Israel, or Turkey. Overall, these statistics indicate that the current opportunities for expanded intraregional trade are significantly reduced by dissimilarities between what the Middle Eastern countries have the capacity to export and what others import.

Implications of Middle Eastern Countries' Comparative Advantage

What factors limit further trading opportunities among Middle Eastern countries? Trade barriers are clearly important as an UNCTAD (1987) study showed that average tariffs in Libya, Syria, and Turkey ranged between 27 to 34 percent and actually reached 100 percent in Iran. In addition, many of the Middle Eastern countries trade regimes were NTB-ridden. Over 70 percent (by value) of Turkey's imports encountered some form of nontariff measure while this ratio was 99 percent in the case of Iran. In addition, there is also evidence that transport links within the region can be an important constraint to increased trade as most established liner conference routes follow a North-South pattern. One further possibility is that the export product profiles of some Middle Eastern countries are so similar, particularly those of the oil exporters, that there are limited opportunities for intratrade.

The revealed comparative advantage (RCA) index can provide some rough indication as to where opportunities for expanded intratrade may exist. Countries with dissimilar RCA profiles could have more opportunities to trade than those whose RCA indices are similar unless there was a high potential for IIT. RCA of country i for product j is measured by the item's share in the country's exports relative to its share in world trade.[22] The index (RCA_{ij}) has a simple interpretation. A value of less than unity (which indicates that the share of product j in i's exports is less than the corresponding world trade share) implies that the country has a revealed comparative *disadvantage* in the product. Similarly, if the index exceeds unity, the country has a revealed comparative *advantage* in the item.

Table 1.16 presents RCA indices for the regional countries exports of products classified in nine broad product groups which represent sections and divisions of the SITC Rev. 1 System. According to these statistics, Egypt has a strong comparative advantage in the production and export of refined petroleum products (the RCA of 4.94 means that the share of these goods in Egypt's exports is almost five times their share in world trade) and in manufactured goods classified in SITC 6 (Manufactures Classified by Material). The latter are generally composed of relatively labor-intensive products that

TABLE 1.16 Middle Eastern Countries' 1985 and 1997 Revealed Comparative Advantage in Broad Product Groups

		RCA Indices for Products Classified by Major SITC Groups*									
Exporter	Year	Foods & Feeds	Beverages & Tobacco	Agricultural Materials	Ores & Metals	Fuels	Animal & Vegetable Oil	Chemicals	Manufactures by Material	Machinery & Transport	Misc. Manufactures
Bahrain	1985	0.01	0.00	0.25	2.87	3.72	0.01	0.28	0.17	0.14	0.61
	1997	0.10	0.09	0.82	9.98	4.94	0.23	0.62	0.38	0.15	0.46
Cyprus	1985	3.81	3.25	0.70	0.67	0.23	2.36	0.42	0.36	0.66	2.49
	1997	2.38	3.34	1.57	2.31	0.10	2.39	0.92	0.77	0.67	1.69
Egypt	1985	0.28	0.14	1.41	0.68	4.02	0.00	0.08	0.35	0.06	0.09
	1997	0.83	0.14	1.27	1.28	5.92	0.08	0.30	1.20	0.06	1.00
Iran	1985	0.16	0.01	0.18	0.05	4.89	0.00	0.14	0.12	0.01	0.01
	1997	0.64	0.04	0.63	0.29	10.17	0.01	0.19	0.32	0.01	0.04
Israel	1985	1.56	0.11	1.29	0.80	0.08	0.06	1.54	2.56	0.56	1.06
	1997	0.68	0.06	0.83	0.45	0.13	0.03	1.37	2.73	0.69	0.93
Jordan	1985	1.43	0.33	5.10	6.77	0.42	0.05	3.14	0.35	0.58	0.18
	1997	0.95	0.10	8.10	9.43	0.01	0.34	4.09	0.45	0.21	0.35
Kuwait	1985	0.03	0.01	0.13	0.17	4.84	0.00	0.18	0.09	0.04	0.05
	1997	0.01	0.00	0.16	0.15	11.39	0.02	0.16	0.01	0.02	0.04
Lebanon	1985	2.98	2.21	2.71	1.64	0.00	0.59	0.67	0.73	0.21	3.13
	1997	1.21	3.35	2.85	3.07	0.14	2.39	1.00	1.76	0.24	1.89
Libya	1985	0.00	0.00	0.01	0.00	5.03	0.00	0.16	0.00	0.02	0.00
	1997	0.10	0.00	0.07	0.10	11.17	0.00	0.45	0.08	0.00	0.00

TABLE 1.16 (continued)

		RCA Indices for Products Classified by Major SITC Groups*									
Exporter	Year	Foods & Feeds	Beverages & Tobacco	Agricultural Materials	Ores & Metals	Fuels	Animal & Vegetable Oil	Chemicals	Manufactures by Material	Machinery & Transport	Misc. Manufactures
Oman	1985	0.05	0.01	0.01	0.07	4.96	0.00	0.01	0.01	0.06	0.03
	1997	0.14	0.01	0.04	0.21	10.75	0.01	0.04	0.01	0.09	0.26
Qatar	1985	0.01	0.01	0.04	0.05	4.68	0.00	0.56	0.25	0.01	0.03
	1997	0.00	0.00	0.06	0.08	10.55	0.01	0.76	0.04	0.01	0.15
Saudi	1985	0.02	0.03	0.11	0.14	4.86	0.01	0.27	0.02	0.04	0.02
Arabia	1997	0.04	0.02	0.13	0.17	10.38	0.05	0.74	0.09	0.05	0.09
Syria	1985	0.38	0.18	2.52	0.33	3.94	0.00	0.02	0.13	0.03	0.28
	1987	1.18	0.15	2.69	0.44	8.72	0.41	0.03	0.19	0.01	0.35
Turkey	1985	2.50	0.17	1.99	1.37	0.99	1.13	0.31	1.33	0.12	1.62
	1997	1.91	2.87	1.06	1.03	0.10	1.45	0.34	2.10	0.34	2.38
UAE	1985	0.01	0.13	0.08	0.31	4.67	0.03	0.11	0.12	0.06	0.17
	1997	0.22	0.59	0.29	1.01	9.31	0.09	0.20	0.20	0.13	0.30
Yemen	1985	1.27	0.60	1.85	1.14	3.50	0.13	0.03	0.07	0.22	0.11
	1997	0.27	0.00	0.30	0.13	11.43	0.01	0.01	0.01	0.01	0.01

*In terms of the SITC (Revision 1) system the product groups are defined as follows: Foods and Feeds (0+22); Beverages and Tobacco (1); Agricultural Raw Materials (2-22-27-28); Ores and Metals (27+28+68); Fuels (3); Animal and Vegetable Oils (3); Chemicals (5); Manufactures Classified by Material (6); Machinery and Transport Equipment (7); Miscellaneous Manufactures (8).

employ materials like leather, wood, rubber, or paper as production inputs. Egypt also registers a RCA above unity in agricultural materials, ores and metals, and miscellaneous manufactures (that is, SITC 8). As expected, Egypt's RCA index is very low for the highly capital-intensive machinery and transport group (SITC 7), and is below 0.2 for beverages and tobacco (in SITC 1) and animal and vegetable oils (SITC 4).

Of the sixteen regional countries, eleven show a strong RCA for the petroleum products group. Those not having a comparative advantage in this sector are Cyprus, Israel, Jordan, Lebanon, and Turkey. An important point to note is that many of these petroleum product-exporting countries have a very limited comparative advantage outside this one sector. For example, Iran, Kuwait, Libya, Qatar, and Saudi Arabia only have RCAs above unity in refined fuels and chemicals (many of the latter utilize crude petroleum inputs). These data provide further evidence that the potential for increased intratrade is limited by the narrow range of products that these countries can produce under internationally competitive conditions.

Opportunities for increased intraregional trade may be the greatest between the "energy exporters" and countries like Israel, Lebanon, and Turkey that have relatively high RCAs for some types of manufactured goods and processed foodstuffs. Note that Syria also has an RCA above unity for foods while Egypt has a comparative advantage in four nonfuel product groups. In short, the impression that emerges from table 1.16 reinforces the evidence presented in table 1.14 (on trade concentration) and table 1.15 (on trade complementarity). Increased opportunities for intraregional trade undoubtedly exist, but any realistic assessment of their current magnitude must recognize the influence of the limited export potentials of most Middle Eastern countries in many key product sectors.

Policy Implications

Any assessment of Middle Eastern countries' recent trade performance and export prospects reveals a number of both negative and positive aspects. On the negative side, perhaps the most important aspect is the region's very high trade concentration in petroleum exports. Over the last decade, international prices for petroleum fell substantially below their level in the early 1980s, so future regional economic prospects will clearly depend on market conditions for energy products. Other essentially negative findings concern the very (product) concentrated structure of many Middle Eastern countries' exports which limits the potential for expanded intraregional trade, the fact that IIT appears to be at relatively immature levels, and the fact that most Middle Eastern countries have not yet fully engaged in international production sharing as reflected in trade in parts and components.

On the positive side, one of the most promising developments is that most Middle Eastern countries seemingly experienced a significant improvement in international competitiveness in the 1990s, which had a significant expansionary impact on their exports. Export prospects of Middle Eastern countries will clearly depend heavily on implementing national trade, fiscal, and economic policies that continue to enhance international competitiveness. As related studies show that the Middle Eastern countries generally face relatively low external foreign trade barriers in major markets (Yeats 1996), their focus should be on the adoption of internal policies that create a more favorable domestic commercial environment.

NOTES

1. Countries included in this chapter's definition of the Middle East region include Bahrain, Cyprus, Egypt, Iran, Israel, Jordan, Kuwait, Lebanon, Libya, Oman, Qatar, Saudi Arabia, Syria, Turkey, UAE, and Yemen. Iraq has been excluded from this analysis due to the effects of UN imposed sanctions on its trade. This corresponds closely to the International Monetary Fund's definition in its *Direction of Trade Statistics* except that Turkey and Cyprus are excluded from the latter.

2. Under its free trade area arrangements with the United States, the EU, and European Free Trade Association (EFTA), Israel had virtually duty free access to these markets. The Uruguay Round's average 40 percent reduction in MFN tariffs will erode Israel's FTA preferences and may result in significant trade diversion. Yeats (1996) estimates that between 5 to 8 percent of Israel's textile and clothing exports to the United States may be displaced due to preference erosion. Egypt, Turkey, and several other Middle Eastern countries have similar arrangements with the EU.

3. UNCTAD's annual *Handbook of International Trade and Development Statistics* provides more detailed information on the product composition of trade in manufactures, foodstuffs, and several other broad product groups. The *Handbook* publishes statistics on each Middle Eastern country's direction of trade for total imports and exports. The United Nations Food and Agricultural Organization's *Trade Yearbook* (published annually) provides some details on trade in foods, agricultural and forestry products, fertilizers, and agricultural machinery, but gives little information on trade in manufactured products.

4. Iran has not reported national trade statistics to the United Nations since 1983; this represents one of the most important gaps in Middle Eastern trade statistics. Aggregate IMF *Direction of Trade* data suggest that Iran originates about 10 percent of all Middle East countries' exports and receives about 6 percent of all imports. Lebanon has not reported to COMTRADE since 1983, but only appears to account for about 3 percent of regional trade.

5. A special procedure was required to generate statistics for Iran and Lebanon, as they have not reported trade data since the early 1980s. Import statistics for every reporter in the COMTRADE database were aggregated and used as a proxy for these countries' export statistics. This might incorporate some upward bias in the estimated

Lebanese and Iranian statistics since imports are normally valued c.i.f. while exports are valued on a f.o.b. basis.

6. The IMF DOT statistics report an unusually high share (25 percent) of Iran's exports going to "areas not specified," as they also do for UAE (13 percent). In part, this may be due to petroleum shipments that can be diverted "en route," loaded in tankers without any specified destinations, as ships bunkers, or sent to an intermediate destination by pipeline. In these cases, a country need not know the final destination of its exports.

7. Both countries have FTA agreements with the EU while Israel also has a FTA agreement with the United States.

8. The World Bank (1992, 45) provides a listing of labor-intensive products which may be suitable for production in low wage developing countries. Included among the products with the highest labor intensity indices are men and women's clothing, textile and yarns, leather and products, wood manufactures, and furniture.

9. The index is defined as:

$$IIT = 1 - [\Sigma\Sigma\Sigma \, |X_{ijk} - M_{ijk}| / (X_{ijk} + M_{ijk})]$$

where X_{ijk} represents the exports of products from industry i from country j to country k and M_{ijk} represents the imports of products from industry i by country j from country k. In this study, industries are defined at the 3-digit level of the SITC system. The analysis is generally confined to manufactured goods, i.e., items classified in SITC groups 5 through 8 less nonferrous metals.

10. Yeats (1998, table 1) identifies the individual component products and indicates their relative importance in global trade. Motor vehicle parts account for one quarter of all components traded, while parts of office machinery and telecommunications equipment follow with 19 percent and 18 percent respectively.

11. For example, World Bank (1999) statistics indicate that the waiting time for the installation of a new phone in Jordan and Egypt ranges between 4 to 5 years. In Egypt and Iran, there is only one fax machine per 2,000 people—as opposed to over 100 in Hong Kong and 64 in Singapore. There is also considerable evidence that governmental policies have created a serious negative business climate in some Middle Eastern countries. For example, in its economic assessment of the business climate in Syria, the *Heritage Foundation-Wall Street Journal* (1997) notes that "Private property is not safe in Syria…The strong public role in the economy and official overvaluation of the Syrian Pound has led to a thriving parallel economy. Smuggling has ensured that industry has been able to obtain vital production inputs as well as a constant flow of consumer goods."

12. A detailed description and early application of this procedure can be found in GATT (1966). The analysis also constituted a large part of Kravis (1970) classic analysis of the influence of trade on the 20th century growth of developing countries.

13. A simple illustrative example may help explain this analytical approach. Assume country i exports one product j and has a 20 percent share of the world market and exports of $20 million in 1988, and a 25 percent share with exports of $37.5 million in 1996.

During this period, world demand for *i* rose from \$100 to \$150 million. The change in *i*'s exports attributed solely to changes in demand would be:

$$\Delta E_{d,i} = .20 \cdot (\$150 - \$100) = \$10 \text{ million}$$

while the change due to the competitive factor is:

$$\Delta E_{c,i} = (.25 - .20) \cdot \$150 = \$7.5 \text{ million.}$$

This example assumes that country *i* experienced no diversification in its exports.

14. For example, Braga, Safadi, and Yeats (1994) compare the recent environment for regional integration initiatives in Latin America with that which existed several decades earlier when the failed LAFTA was formed. Erzan and Yeats (1992) analyzed the trade gains Latin American countries might experience from a free trade arrangement with the United States.

15. The figures in table 1.10 understate the importance of Cyprus, which, for political reasons, is not reporting exports to Turkey in its official trade statistics.

16. The "trade intensity" index is defined as the share of one country's exports going to a partner divided by the share of world exports going to the partner. That is:

$$TI_{ij} = [x_{ij}/X_{it}] \div [x_{wj}/X_{wt}]$$

where x_{ij} and x_{wt} are the value of *i*'s exports and world exports to *j*, X_{it} is *i*'s total exports and X_{wt} are total world exports. An index of more (less) than unity indicates a bilateral trade flow that is larger (smaller) than would be expected given the partner country's importance in world trade.

17. The underlying assumption is that the higher the level of export diversification the better the prospects for a successful regional integration initiative. The more diversified a country's exports, the greater the range of potential products that can be traded with regional partners. If only a limited number of such goods exist, members of an RTA may have to rely heavily on third countries for a high share of their key imports and this would likely reduce their commitment to, and perceived benefits from, the arrangement. There may also be important secondary effects from a high degree of export concentration. Some studies show that countries with highly concentrated exports may experience a relatively high degree of export earnings instability—a factor that makes economic planning difficult. Such instability could reduce a country's ability to consistently maintain financial commitments required by a regional arrangement. For a related discussion, see Massel (1970) or MacBean (1966).

18. The diversification index for country *j* is defined as:

$$D_j = [\Sigma|h_{ij} - h_i|]/2$$

where h_{ij} is the share of commodity *i* in the total exports of country *j* and h_i is the share of the commodity in world exports. World trade, however, is concentrated in some products like petroleum and automobiles. As a result, this measure would show that a country with equal shares in every 3-digit product (complete diversification) has more concentrated exports than another whose profile matched the (concentrated) structure of world trade.

19. The Hirschman Index for country *j* (H_j) is defined as:

$$Hj = \sqrt{\Sigma(x_i / X)^2}$$

where x_i is country *j*'s exports of 3-digit product *j*, and *X* is country *j*'s total exports. The index has been normalized to account for the number of actual 3-digit products that could be exported.

20. See Michaely (1996) for an application that attempted to use the measure to assess prospects for RTAs in Latin America. The index of trade complementarity between countries *k* and *j* (C_{ij}) is defined as:

$$Cij = 100 - \Sigma(|m_{ik} - x_{ij}|/2)$$

where x_{ij} is the share of good *i* in the global exports of country *j* and m_{ik} is the share of good *i* in all imports of country *k.* The index is zero when no good exported by one country is imported by the other, and 100 when the export-import shares exactly match.

21. This index has some limitations. First, it takes the existing structure of exports as a given and determines how well it matches a potential partner's imports. This assumes that existing exports can be diverted to a regional partner or that exports can be expanded at constant costs. Also, the approach assumes that there is something optimal about the existing structure of trade, which need not be the case. Third, the complementarity index treats all exports as having the same priority, yet some may have very different national policy objectives. Fourth, both the influence of distance and transport costs are neglected in the index.

22. That is, if x_{ij} is the value of country *i*'s exports of *j*, and X_{tj} is the country's total exports, its RCA index is:

$$RCA_{ij} = (x_{ij}/X_{tj}) \div (X_{iw}/X_{tw})$$

where the *w* subscripts refer to world totals.

CHAPTER 2

Agricultural Trade and Rural Development in the Middle East and North Africa

Dean A. DeRosa

Situated at important crossroads between Africa, Asia, and Europe, the countries of the MENA region form one of the largest groups of developing countries in the world economy.[1] In addition, with the initiation in recent years of a peace process between Israel and its Arab neighbors, the region has increasingly moved to the foreground of the world economy as private businessmen and government officials have begun to look more earnestly to the region's potential for enjoying higher sustained growth and greater economic development.[2]

Although MENA includes a number of oil-rich countries such as Kuwait, Qatar, Saudi Arabia, and UAE, it comprises mainly middle-income developing countries whose per capita income levels and economic performance, including with regard to indicators of social welfare, fall appreciably below the mean levels of countries in other regions at similar rungs of the development ladder globally (table 2.1 and appendix table 2.1). Moreover, the circumstances and lackluster economic performance of the populous low- to lower-middle-income countries in MENA—Iraq, Syria, and Yemen in the Middle East, and Egypt, Morocco, and Sudan in North Africa—are the subject of considerable international concern, one measure being the large shipments of international food aid to some MENA countries.[3]

Notwithstanding the prominence of petroleum in the region, agriculture remains important to most economies in MENA. Agricultural and rural populations still account for 40 to 60 percent of inhabitants in the MENA countries and for a substantial share of aggregate employment, belying the often much lower recorded share of agriculture in gross domestic output.[4] Thus, the livelihood and social welfare of the largest segments of the populations of the

MENA countries are still deeply rooted in agriculture and the rural economy. As a consequence, like in most less developed countries worldwide, agriculture and rural development have potentially significant—and mutually reinforcing—roles to play in achieving higher sustained growth and economic development in MENA.

For the last decade or more, however, many MENA countries have failed to achieve positive growth on a per capita basis (table 2.1). This observation applies particularly to such populous countries as Iran and Syria in the Middle East and Algeria in North Africa.[5] Although agricultural growth has widely kept pace with general economic growth in MENA, agriculture in less developed countries must grow by 2 to 3 percentage points above the rate of population growth in order to contribute significantly to not only national economic growth but also rural development and welfare. By this rule of thumb, the lackluster performance of the MENA economies is discernibly mirrored in the less than robust performance of the agricultural sector.

Agriculture and Economy-wide Policies in Economic Development[6]

That agriculture can contribute significantly to the transition of many if not most less developed countries to higher levels of growth and economic development is a pertinent and insightful theme developed by, among others, Johnston and Mellor (1961), Mellor (1966, 1995), and Johnston and Kilby (1975).[7] More specifically, this theme contends that sustained industrial development and economic growth in low to middle income countries requires policies for economic development that yield incentives for efficient expansion of not only industry but also agriculture and the rural sector, despite the expected long-term decline in the relative importance of agriculture in growing economies.

Increases in agricultural output stimulate the demand for industrial inputs such as fertilizer and farm equipment ("backward linkage") as well as expand the supply of agricultural goods used as inputs to nonagricultural production ("forward linkage"). Agricultural crop and livestock production is generally characterized by a "weak" backward linkage and "medium-strong" forward linkage (Hirschman 1958, 110).

Agricultural growth, however, also raises the real income of farm households and hence their demand not only for food and other agricultural products but also, and likely more so, for industrial goods and services. For instance, Mellor and Lele (1973) and, more recently, Ranis, Stewart, and Reyes (1989) show that such "consumption linkage" effects are critical to the influence of agricultural growth on the overall growth performance of the rural and national economy. In particular, a wider sharing of agricultural income growth among rural households leads to a greater incremental consumption demand for the labor-intensive products of rural industries. Rural industry growth in turn provides "additional impetus for further increases in agricultural productivity, leading to a mutually supportive cycle of agricultural and industrial growth" (Ranis and Stewart 1987, 140).

Beyond the reinforcing effects on industrialization and economic growth, broadly based agricultural growth has significant "spillover" effects that go to the heart of improving social welfare as part of the development process. Because poor households in most low-income countries reside mainly in rural areas, economic development strategies that recognize the importance of ensuring agricultural and rural development along with industrialization offer the promise of reducing poverty directly and, more generally, the disparity of access in rural areas relative to urban areas to social services, such as education and health care. Such development strategies can also be expected to increase access to many privately provided services, such as banking and retailing of consumer goods, in rural areas.

Particularly inhibiting greater contribution by agriculture to sustained economic growth and rural development are inappropriate economic regimes governing trade and macroeconomic policies, or so-called economy-wide policies, in many less developed countries. These regimes have given rise to what has been termed the "bias against agriculture."[8] Most often manifest in import-substitution policies and pursuit of inflationary monetary and fiscal policies (under fixed exchange rates), these regimes tend to distort the real exchange rate between nontraded and traded goods and, consequently, to distort price incentives against agriculture, with the frequent objective of promoting more rapid industrialization. This causes agriculture and other exportable goods sectors, including the small-scale rural enterprise sector, to be smaller and less internationally competitive than otherwise, and accordingly causes exports of agricultural and other labor-intensive goods to be lower than they would be under more neutral and open policy regimes. As emphasized by Bautista and Valdés (1993), the bias against agriculture also causes the purchasing power of rural populations to be lower than otherwise, adding to the demand-side constraint on economic growth in less developed countries.

In sum, more even-handed policies towards agriculture and the rural sector, associated with greater equality of access to economic opportunities, physical infrastructure, and social-service facilities in rural areas, should be expected to result in greater agricultural and rural incomes, increasing the effective demand for manufactured producer and consumer goods.[9] Such policies might also be expected to promote rural small-scale industries that can meet part of the industrial needs of agriculture while also significantly adding to the employment of the rural labor force. Finally, increased national food security (achieved through either increased domestic production of food staples or increased food imports financed by higher export earnings) and reduced pace of urbanization represent two additional social benefits of more neutral government policies in less developed countries.

TABLE 2.1 Economic Growth and Other Indicators of Social Welfare 1993 (percent)

	Average Annual Growth 1980-93 in:					Other Indicators				
	GDP (per capita)	Agriculture (per capita)	Industry	Exports	Population	Rural population (%)	Agricultural employment (%)	Adult Literacy	Life Expectancy (years)	Infant mortality per thousand births
Middle East										
Cyprus	… (…)	2 (1)	…	…	1	47	20	…	77	9
Iran	3 (-1)	5 (1)	5	4	4	42	24	46	68	48
Iraq	… (…)	2 (-1)	…	…	3	24	21	40	66	56
Israel	4 (2)	1 (-1)	…	8	2	10	4	…	77	8
Jordan	1 (-4)	4 (-1)	…	6	5	30	5	20	70	33
Kuwait	… (…)	… (…)	…	-6	2	3	1	27	76	12
Lebanon	… (…)	4 (3)	…	…	1	14	6	20	69	33
Oman	8 (3)	7 (2)	9	8	5	88	39	…	70	19
Qatar	… (…)	6 (...)	…	…	…	9	1	…	71	19
Saudi Arabia	0 (-4)	12 (8)	…	-4	4	21	33	38	69	27
Syria	… (…)	1 (-3)	…	…	4	48	23	36	67	35
Turkey	5 (3)	3 (1)	6	9	2	34	41	19	67	63
UAE	0 (-4)	10 (6)	-2	6	4	17	2	…	74	17
Yemen	… (…)	1 (-3)	…	1	4	68	…	62	53	104

TABLE 2.1 continued)

North Africa											
Algeria	2 (-1)	5 (2)	1	3	3	46	23	43	69	37
Egypt	4 (2)	1 (-1)	2	1	2	56	38	52	62	55
Libya	... (...)	3 (-1)	...	...	4	15	14	36	63	66
Mauritania	2 (-1)	2 (-1)	4	6	3	49	66	66	52	99
Morocco	4 (2)	4 (2)	3	4	2	53	34	51	65	58
Sudan	... (...)	3 (0)	...	...	3	76	54	73	53	76
Tunisia	4 (2)	5 (3)	3	7	2	44	23	32	68	42
Developing Countries										
Low-income	6 (4)	3 (1)	8	6	2	72	...	41	62	64
Middle-income	2 (0)	2 (0)	2	...	2	40	...	17	68	39
Sub-Saharan Africa	2 (-1)	2 (-1)	1	3	3	70	68	50	52	93
East Asia and Pacific	8 (6)	4 (2)	10	11	2	69	56	24	68	36
South Asia	5 (3)	3 (1)	6	7	2	74	63	54	60	84
Europe and Central Asia	0 (-1)	0 (-1)	1	...	1	35	...	5	69	25
Middle East, North Africa	2 (-1)	4 (1)	...	-1	3	45	33	41	66	52
Lat. America, Caribbean	2 (0)	2 (0)	1	3	2	29	27	15	69	43
Industrial Countries	3 (2)	... (...)	...	5	1	22	4	...	77	7

Notes: Economic growth rates are in real terms; per capita figures in parentheses.
Sources: USDA (1996) and World Bank (1995b, 1995d, and 1996b).

Greater dynamism in agriculture led by expanded trade is required to achieve higher sustained economic growth and greater rural development in MENA. The remainder of this chapter explores this issue in three sections. The first considers the current commodity structure of agricultural production and trade in MENA and investigates the comparative advantage in agriculture of the countries in the region revealed in profiles of their recent international and intraregional exports. The next section then considers the policy environment in which the MENA countries must look to improving their agricultural and trade performance, emphasizing especially the structure of protection in MENA countries that gives rise to the bias against agriculture in the region. The final section concludes with some final remarks on the importance of agricultural trade for increasing rural development and welfare.

Production, Trade, and Comparative Advantage

Agriculture in MENA has a long recorded history, rivaling that of Western civilization. In fact, the region is the center of origin of the cultivation of wheat, barley, lentils, and chickpeas, and of the domestication of sheep and goats. Though fertile areas are found in MENA along the Euphrates, Nile, and other rivers and tributaries, the region is characterized by low and erratic rainfall, limited arable land, some of the world's largest and harshest deserts, and limited water resources for irrigation (Nordblom, Goodchild, and Shomo 1995). Along with the preferences of inhabitants for a Mediterranean diet rich in cereal starches and olive oil (Spiller 1991), the physical characteristics of the region go a long way toward determining the composition of MENA agricultural production and trade.

Table 2.2 provides an overview of agricultural production in MENA during 1990-92.[10] In the aggregate, agricultural production in the region, about 230 million tons, is comparable to that in Southeast Asia (262 million tons), Sub-Saharan Africa (270 million tons), and the Southern Cone of Latin America (302 million tons). However, it amounts to only a small share (5 percent) of world output and is dwarfed by agricultural production in China, South Asia, and the major industrial countries. The largest agricultural producing countries in MENA are Iran, Iraq, Syria, and Turkey in the Middle East and Egypt, Morocco, and Sudan in North Africa.

Three-quarters of agricultural production in MENA are devoted to two product categories: cereals (38 percent) and fruits and vegetables (38 percent). Meat and dairy products—chiefly milk (9 percent) and poultry (1 percent)—account for about 12 percent of total output, followed by roots and tubers (6 percent) and sugar (2 percent).[11] Wheat is the dominant cereal crop. Barley is the second largest cereal crop in the region; in fact, it is produced in larger quantities in MENA than all other developing regions combined. In a similar vein, fruits and vegetables, which tend to be relatively high-valued products, command a larger share of total agricultural output in MENA than in all other regions of the world.

For each commodity group, the largest quantities produced by individual MENA countries are highlighted in bold typeset in table 2.2. Typically, the seven largest agricultural producing countries are also the largest producers in each commodity group. For instance, Iran is among the top one-third of MENA countries producing meat and dairy products, wheat and other cereals, fruits and vegetables, and so on. What is more noteworthy is that three smaller agricultural producing countries stand out among the major producers in certain commodities groups. First, Israel is among the top MENA producers of fruits and vegetables (2,975 million tons). Second, Saudi Arabia is among the top producers of cereals (4,501 million tons), especially wheat (3,894 million tons). Third, Algeria is among the top producers of meat and dairy products (1,570 million tons), wheat (1,422 million tons), and barley (1,350 million tons).

The composition of agricultural production varies appreciably from country to country for fundamental climatic and geographic reasons. In several small-size Middle East countries along the eastern shores of the Mediterranean (Israel, Jordan, and Lebanon), production of fruits and vegetables tends to "dominate" production of cereals, whereas the distribution of production between the two categories of agricultural products tends to be more balanced in most other MENA countries. Also, production of irrigation-intensive crops, such as rice and sugar, is limited to three countries with prime access to the waters of the Nile and Euphrates: Egypt, Iran, and Turkey. Finally, it should be emphasized that agricultural production in MENA is concentrated mainly in staple foods and some higher-valued food crops (i.e., fruits and vegetables). Comparatively little production of agricultural raw materials, such as natural fibers and animal hides and skins, takes place.

Foreign Trade

The merchandise trade of Middle East and North Africa countries amounts to between 15 percent (based on exports) and 18 percent (based on imports) of GDP (see table 2.3). This compares favorably to the "openness" of other middle-income developing countries but not to the openness of the fast-growing middle-income developing countries of East Asia, whose trade is estimated at about 25 percent of GDP. During 1992-94, merchandise exports of the MENA countries averaged about $180 billion, while merchandise imports averaged about $183 billion.

Agricultural products account for a large share of the merchandise exports of several MENA countries: Cyprus (32 percent), Lebanon and Turkey (about 25

TABLE 2.2 Agricultural Production 1990-92

			Cereals							
	Total	Meat and Dairy Products	Total	Wheat	Rice	Barley	Maize	Fruits and Vegetables	Roots and Tubers	Sugar
	Average annual value in thousands of metric tons									
Middle East										
Cyprus	991	220	119	9	...	110	...	464	189	...
Iran	39,902	4,808	15,015	9,101	2,279	3,450	173	15,654	2,643	792
Iraq	8,090	724	3,057	1,226	199	1,377	243	4,030	186	4
Israel	4,937	1,361	253	241	...	8	2	2,975	206	...
Jordan	1,343	195	155	89	...	62	4	916	65	...
Kuwait	81	35	2	...	...	1	1	44	...	...
Lebanon	2,707	297	80	56	...	19	3	2,039	254	1
Oman	452	103	4	1	...	...	...	348	5	...
Qatar	75	35	4	1	...	3	...	36	...	...
Saudi Arabia	7,816	977	4,501	3,894	...	390	6	2,320	54	...
Syria	9,632	1,593	3,584	2,419	...	952	207	3,165	423	76
Turkey	79,357	9,799	30,129	19,919	215	7,333	2,127	27,997	4,468	1,985
UAE	641	103	8	3	...	2	4	535	4	...
Yemen	2,244	498	675	136	...	49	61	841	160	...

TABLE 2.2 (continued)

North Africa										
Algeria	8,331	**1,570**	2,861	**1,422**	2	**1,350**	2	2,859	870	...
Egypt	**34,797**	**2,986**	**13,809**	**4,456**	**3,508**	157	**4,997**	**13,836**	**1,904**	**1,033**
Libya	1,908	411	290	143	...	144	1	1,041	148	...
Mauritania	455	334	95	1	37	...	2	26	6	...
Morocco	**14,635**	**1,574**	**5,966**	**3,372**	17	**2,157**	329	**5,142**	**970**	482
Sudan	**10,796**	**4,188**	**3,827**	601	1	...	51	1,613	144	463
Tunisia	5,294	619	2,130	1,497	...	590	...	2,250	218	23
Developing Countries										
Sub-Saharan Africa	269,509	23,033	64,874	3,872	9,718	1,183	24,397	51,924	107,537	6,117
China	774,972	44,896	397,475	98,590	186,455	2,333	96,991	135,211	143,053	7,899
Southeast Asia	261,989	9,229	131,138	132	114,133	...	16,455	46,130	49,493	9,017
South Asia	523,414	83,820	256,393	69,681	147,955	1,773	11,620	100,313	25,425	15,593
MENA Countries	228,981	29,138	85,354	49,662	6,580	18,350	8,559	87,976	13,018	4,397
Latin America	381,153	63,942	104,131	19,556	16,055	1,704	55,859	95,512	45,493	20,205
Industrial Countries										
European Union	438,734	126,266	146,927	74,751	2,194	37,979	25,037	101,304	36,120	13,344
North America	644,897	112,287	368,869	96,408	7,449	21,738	217,184	59,652	22,241	6,741
World	4,410,923	721,843	1,903,741	556,801	521,497	159,702	497,492	806,410	567,975	110,285

Source: USDA (1996).

TABLE 2.3 Exports and Imports of MENA Countries by World Regions 1992-94

Partner Countries and World	All Products	Manuf. Products	Mineral Fuels	Agri-cultural Products	Selected Agricultural Categories and Products: Food, Live Animals	Livestock Meats, Dairy	Cereals, Cereal Products	Wheat	Rice	Barley	Fruits, Vegs.	Sugar	Agr. Raw Mats.
	Average annual value in $ millions (Share of total trade with region in percent)												
	Exports												
Developing Countries													
Sub-Saharan Africa	502	379	49	65	55	0	10	1	3	0	10	1	6
	(100)	(75)	(10)	(13)	(11)	(0)	(2)	(0)	(1)	(0)	(2)	(0)	(1)
East Asia	17,633	3,863	13,414	140	74	3	27	26	0	0	23	1	52
	(100)	(22)	(76)	(1)	(0)	(0)	(0)	(0)	(0)	(0)	(0)	(0)	(0)
South Asia	1,180	859	85	73	40	0	8	8	0	0	27	2	31
	(100)	(73)	(7)	(6)	(3)	(0)	(1)	(0)	(0)	(0)	(2)	(0)	(3)
Europe, Central Asia	3,588	2,007	581	888	692	15	171	73	12	10	226	122	97
	(100)	(56)	(16)	(25)	(19)	(0)	(5)	(2)	(0)	(0)	(6)	(3)	(3)
MENA	16,042	6,881	5,222	3503	2,568	673	447	120	68	72	1,034	117	303
	(100)	(43)	(33)	(22)	(16)	(4)	(3)	(1)	(0)	(0)	(6)	(1)	(2)
Latin America,	1,002	500	390	65	31	0	5	1	0	2	14	0	26
Caribbean	(100)	(50)	(39)	(6)	(3)	(0)	(1)	(0)	(0)	(0)	(1)	(0)	(3)
Industrial Countries													
European Union	29,481	15,797	9,153	3,972	2,912	63	45	4	13	1	2,197	43	657
	(100)	(54)	(31)	(14)	(10)	(0)	(0)	(0)	(0)	(0)	(7)	(0)	(2)
Other OECD	18,533	7,190	10,198	936	629	21	20	0	1	0	274	5	78
	(100)	(39)	(55)	(5)	(3)	(0)	(0)	(0)	(0)	(0)	(2)	(0)	(0)
World	179,711	46,809	116,203	11,756	8,475	779	952	442	77	75	4,690	325	1,808
	(100)	(26)	(65)	(7)	(5)	(0)	(1)	(0)	(0)	(0)	(3)	(0)	(1)

TABLE 2.3 (continued)

	Imports												
Developing Countries													
Sub-Saharan Africa	829	171	77	562	291	118	16	0	0	0	12	2	248
	(100)	(21)	(9)	(68)	(35)	(14)	(2)	(0)	(0)	(0)	(2)	(0)	(30)
East Asia	10,951	9,337	42	1,523	833	18	147	1	120	0	176	91	275
	(100)	(85)	(0)	(14)	(8)	(0)	(1)	(0)	(1)	(0)	(2)	(1)	(3)
South Asia	2,424	1,508	2	879	778	52	344	3	337	0	131	6	75
	(100)	(62)	(0)	(36)	(32)	(2)	(14)	(0)	(14)	(0)	(5)	(0)	(3)
Europe, Central Asia	6,582	4,110	845	1,426	664	292	139	59	2	41	170	13	589
	(100)	(62)	(13)	(22)	(10)	(4)	(2)	(1)	(0)	(1)	(3)	(0)	(9)
MENA	16,042	6,881	5,222	3,503	2,568	469	260	120	68	73	1,034	117	302
	(100)	(43)	(33)	(22)	(16)	(4)	(2)	(1)	(0)	(0)	(6)	(1)	(2)
Latin America,	2,320	691	6	1,349	993	260	100	30	32	1	126	192	171
Caribbean	(100)	(30)	(0)	(58)	(43)	(11)	(4)	(1)	(0)	(0)	(5)	(8)	(7)
Industrial Countries													
European Union	65,983	54,429	934	8,249	5,860	1,990	1,975	675	62	529	439	572	1,551
	(100)	(82)	(1)	(13)	(9)	(3)	(3)	(1)	(0)	(1)	(1)	(1)	(2)
Other OECD	32,475	26,450	330	4,916	3,077	549	2,067	1,092	114	219	158	16	789
	(100)	(81)	(1)	(15)	(9)	(2)	(6)	(3)	(0)	(1)	(0)	(0)	(2)
World	182,994	138,013	9,532	28,057	18,887	5,046	6,476	2,318	1,169	848	2,185	1,662	4,374
	(100)	(75)	(5)	(15)	(10)	(3)	(4)	(1)	(1)	(0)	(1)	(1)	(2)

Source: UN Trade Data System (1996).

percent), and Jordan and Syria (about 20 percent) in the Middle East, and Sudan (95 percent), Mauritania (49 percent), and Morocco (28 percent) in North Africa. They account for a large share of the merchandise imports of a somewhat different group of MENA countries in the two subregions: Iraq (65 percent), Yemen (30 percent), and Jordan, Lebanon, and Oman (20 to 25 percent), and Algeria (33 percent) and Egypt, Mauritania, and Sudan (about 24 percent).

Exports

The exports of most MENA countries are dominated by mineral fuels (i.e., crude petroleum) and manufactures. Mineral fuels account for 65 percent of total MENA exports, while manufactures account for just over 25 percent. Indeed, no country in the Middle East and only Mauritania and Sudan in North Africa are predominantly agricultural-exporting countries.[12]

The agricultural exports of the MENA countries reflect the structure of the region's agricultural production considered previously. The largest single product category is fruits and vegetables (3 percent of merchandise exports) followed by wheat and other cereal grains (1 percent) and agricultural raw materials (1 percent). The largest exporters of fruits and vegetables include Iran, Israel, and Turkey in the Middle East and Egypt and Morocco in North Africa. With respect to cereals, Saudi Arabia and Turkey are the predominant exporters in the first subregion, and Egypt and Sudan are the predominant exporters in the second subregion.

Notwithstanding the limited significance of agricultural products in MENA exports, agricultural products enjoy a somewhat higher profile in exports to MENA's largest trading partner, the EU (14 percent of merchandise exports), developing Europe and Central Asia (25 percent), and the MENA region itself (22 percent). With regard to intraregional trade, intra-MENA trade accounts for 30 percent of MENA exports of agricultural products to all regions and for exceptionally high proportions of total MENA exports of some prominent categories of agricultural products—barley (96 percent), rice (88 percent), livestock, meats, and dairy products (87 percent), and cereals (47 percent).

Imports

Manufactured products, principally from the EU and other major industrial countries, comprise three-quarters of MENA merchandise imports. The largest share of imported agricultural products consists of food products (10 percent of MENA merchandise imports), including not only cereals (4 percent) but also higher value-added products such as livestock and dairy products (3 percent) and fruits and vegetables (1 percent). Agricultural raw materials are also among the largest categories of agricultural products in MENA imports (2 percent).

MENA imports of agricultural products by country appear determined to a large extent by such fundamental factors as per capita income levels and population. For instance, particularly large volumes of livestock, meats, and dairy products are imported by higher-income countries such as Israel, Saudi Arabia, and UAE and by particularly populous countries such as Iran and Egypt. Also, large international food aid recipients such as Egypt, Jordan, and Morocco appear to import exceptionally large amounts of wheat and other cereals. Finally, countries with relatively large manufacturing sectors, such as Egypt, Israel, Morocco, and Turkey are among the largest importers of natural fibers and other agricultural raw materials used to produce textiles and other material manufactures.

MENA imports of agricultural products originate from mainly the major industrial countries (about 50 percent). Intraregional trade accounts for only about 10 percent of total agricultural imports. Remarkably, however, intraregional trade in MENA accounts for nearly 50 percent of all fruits and vegetables imported by the countries in the region.

Revealed Comparative Advantage

The commodity patterns of MENA international and intraregional trade can be employed to examine the RCA of the Middle East and North Africa countries. The RCA indicator employed here is one commonly specified in applied analyses of international trade relations (e.g., Balassa 1979). It relates the importance of each MENA country as a supplier of agricultural and other products to the world market (and alternatively to markets in MENA) relative to all competing exporting countries. In symbols, the indicator is computed as *International Trade:*

$$RCAj(i,w) = [Xj(i,w)/ TX(i,w)] / [Xj(w,w)/TX(w,w)] \quad (1)$$

and *Intraregional Trade:*

$$RCAj(i,m) = [Xj(i,m)/ TX(i,m)] / [Xj(w,m)/TX(w,m)] \quad (2)$$

where $Xj(i,.)$ represents exports of commodity j by country i to the world (w) or MENA (m), $Xj(w,.)$ represents exports of commodity j by the world (that is, exports of the commodity by all competing producers) to the same two markets, and $TX(i,.)$ and $TX(w,.)$ represent total exports of all commodities by country i and the world, respectively. Broadly speaking, RCA values greater than unity indicate comparative advantage, and RCA values of less than unity indicate com-parative disadvantage.[13]

International Trade

The exceptional comparative advantage in crude petroleum of the majority of countries in the MENA region is apparent in the computed RCA statistics in table 2.4. Although many MENA countries export substantial amounts of manufactured products, comparative advantage in a wide range of manufactures appears significant for only one MENA country, Israel. The comparative advantage of other MENA countries in manufactures is typically in products requiring mainly unskilled labor, such as clothing and other apparel. With respect to this important category of trade in manufactures for many less developed countries, several MENA countries are identified as competitive producers of "light" manufactures: Cyprus, Lebanon, and Turkey in the Middle East, and Egypt, Morocco, and Tunisia in North Africa.

The comparative disadvantage of the MENA countries in agriculture stands in contrast to their strong comparative advantage in crude petroleum. The one important exception is fruits and vegetables. With the exception of Iraq and Kuwait in the Middle East and Algeria and Libya in North Africa, most MENA countries exhibit strong comparative advantage in fruits and vegetables.

Individual MENA countries also exhibit substantial comparative advantage in selected agricultural categories and products. Jordan, Syria, and Sudan evidence international competitiveness in livestock, meats, and dairy products. Similarly, Saudi Arabia and Turkey are revealed to be competitive exporters of wheat; Jordan and particularly Egypt of rice; Cyprus, Syria, Turkey, and Tunisia of barley; Cyprus, Egypt, Lebanon, Sudan, and Turkey of sugar; and Egypt, Syria, and Sudan of agricultural raw materials.

Intraregional Trade

The intraregional RCA statistics gauge the competitiveness of the MENA countries as exporters to one another. As might be expected, the competitiveness of the MENA countries as suppliers of not only crude petroleum but also light manufactures is reduced, reflecting the similarity of mineral fuel deposits and labor resources in most MENA countries. Of greater interest here is the evidence that the MENA countries have appreciable intraregional comparative advantage in agriculture, led in particular by strong comparative advantage in livestock, meats, and dairy products, and fruits and vegetables. This may reflect not only some sharp differences in agricultural resources and production capabilities between the MENA countries but also natural barriers to trade with countries outside MENA, including transportation and handling costs, and general or possibly religious preferences of consumers for regional varieties of agricultural products.[14] In sum, under current economic and other circumstances the com-parative advantage of most countries in the MENA region differs depending upon whether their exports are destined for world markets or markets in neighboring countries.[15]

Trade Regimes and the Bias against Agriculture

The previous section demonstrated that although agriculture in MENA is not broadly competitive in international markets, particular subsectors of agriculture in many MENA countries are competitive, both internationally and intraregionally. Under such circumstances, improvement of the international terms of trade for agriculture resulting from the milestone, albeit modest, Uruguay Round agreement on agriculture should be expected to benefit the agricultural and rural economies of the MENA countries that have sizable agricultural sectors and rural populations.[16]

Two recent studies have attempted to assess the broad implications of the Uruguay Round agreement for the MENA countries. The first, a partial equilibrium analysis by Yeats (1996), estimates that the liberalization of trade regimes in the EU, Japan, and United States under the agreement will expand Middle East exports by $800 million annually. Unfortunately, the study does not indicate the magnitude of the underlying impacts on agricultural production and exports by Middle Eastern countries.

The second study is a compendium devoted to the implications of the Uruguay Round for Arab countries, edited by El-Naggar (1996). It includes an analysis by Goldin and Kherallah (1996) focused specifically on the Uruguay Round's impacts on agriculture in MENA. Unfortunately, the analysis provides little by way of quantitative estimates of the expected impacts on agricultural production or trade. Nonetheless, it usefully relates econometric estimates of the impacts of the Uruguay Round agreement on international prices of agricultural products to the principal agricultural exports of eight MENA coun-tries classified as oil exporters (Algeria and Saudi Arabia), diversified exporters (Egypt, Jordan, Morocco, Syria, and Tunisia), and primary com-modity exporters (Sudan). The findings point to potential gains to agricultural producers in several of the countries considered, especially producers of fruits and vegetables and natural fibers but also producers of vegetable oils, meats, and grains (except rice). However, in interpreting their findings, Goldin and Kherallah emphasize that, to be realized, the expected gains for MENA agri-culture must be accompanied by reforms to economy-wide trade and macroeconomic policies in order to ensure that the higher international prices for agricultural products are received by farmers.[17]

Protection in MENA

The last point brings to the fore the issue of the repression of agriculture in MENA by inappropriate economy-wide policies. Despite the importance of agriculture and, more generally, the rural economy in the region, protection

TABLE 2.4 Revealed Comparative Advantage of MENA Countries in International and Intraregional Trade 1992-94

	Manuf. Products	Clothing Apparel	Mineral Fuels	Agri-cultural Products	Selected Agricultural Categories and Products: Food, Live Animals	Livestock Meats, Dairy	Cereals, Cereal Products	Wheat	Rice	Barley	Fruits Vegs.	Sugar	Agr. Raw Mats
Middle East							**International Trade**						
Cyprus	0.80	4.97	0.26	2.68	3.45	0.80	0.79	0.39	0.44	8.42	13.67	1.40	0.31
Iran	0.10	0.02	9.90	0.47	0.61	0.06	0.01	0.00	0.01	0.00	2.29	0.10	0.33
Iraq	0.01	0.00	11.29	0.07	0.10	0.02	0.04	0.06	0.00	0.00	0.39	0.00	0.01
Israel	1.16	1.07	0.13	0.61	0.69	0.25	0.15	0.00	0.02	0.00	2.33	0.30	0.68
Jordan	0.68	0.63	0.02	1.62	2.04	2.84	0.27	0.00	1.33	0.00	5.35	0.22	0.23
Kuwait	0.06	0.08	10.82	0.03	0.03	0.02	0.05	0.00	0.05	0.00	0.03	0.07	0.03
Lebanon	0.93	3.15	0.07	2.03	2.52	0.60	0.52	0.01	0.50	0.00	9.29	2.19	1.03
Oman	0.20	0.47	9.26	0.33	0.23	0.14	0.22	0.33	0.33	0.01	0.17	0.07	0.01
Qatar	0.22	0.46	9.50	0.02	0.03	0.13	0.01	0.00	0.01	0.00	0.00	0.00	0.01
Saudi Arabia	0.11	0.00	10.36	0.08	0.11	0.07	0.49	1.62	0.00	0.00	0.06	0.04	0.03
Syria	0.09	0.96	8.42	1.59	1.19	2.08	0.58	0.23	0.00	9.34	2.22	0.44	3.23
Turkey	0.95	7.16	0.18	1.99	2.43	0.85	2.28	3.13	0.06	4.80	6.64	4.68	0.63
UAE	0.20	0.61	9.18	0.25	0.23	0.16	0.15	0.01	0.56	0.04	0.46	0.17	0.06
Yemen	0.03	0.01	10.75	0.31	0.42	0.15	0.05	0.00	0.07	0.00	0.01	0.29	0.17
North Africa													
Algeria	0.03	0.00	9.94	0.06	0.08	0.01	0.01	0.00	0.00	0.00	0.34	0.00	0.01
Egypt	0.43	1.63	6.41	0.84	0.88	0.41	1.13	0.00	10.47	0.04	2.57	1.22	1.05
Libya	0.06	0.01	10.96	0.02	0.01	0.00	0.00	0.00	0.00	0.00	0.02	0.00	0.06
Mauritania	0.01	0.04	0.05	4.10	6.56	0.01	0.01	0.00	0.00	0.00	0.01	0.01	0.16
Morocco	0.80	8.44	0.21	2.35	3.45	0.03	0.14	0.07	0.00	0.45	8.09	0.41	0.74
Sudan	0.04	0.01	0.00	7.92	4.37	6.93	8.41	0.00	0.03	0.00	2.64	9.46	19.05
Tunisia	0.99	11.47	1.36	1.01	0.70	0.25	.058	0.02	0.01	1.26	1.14	0.12	0.19
MENA Countries	0.35	1.47	7.45	0.54	0.63	0.24	0.47	0.75	0.39	0.66	1.62	0.59	0.32

TABLE 2.4 (continued)

	Manuf. Products	Clothing Apparel	Mineral Fuels	Agri-cultural Products	Selected Agricultural Categories and Products: Food, Live Animals	Livestock Meats, Dairy	Cereals, Cereal Products	Wheat	Rice	Barley	Fruits Vegs.	Sugar	Agr. Raw Mats
					Intraregional Trade								
Middle East													
Cyprus	0.87	2.59	0.18	2.10	1.44	1.28	1.04	0.29	0.00	4.68	3.99	0.50	0.52
Iran	0.14	0.14	13.29	1.23	1.60	0.47	0.02	0.00	0.02	0.00	10.67	0.11	0.96
Iraq	0.00	0.00	19.04	0.04	0.07	0.02	0.00	0.00	0.00	0.00	0.52	0.00	0.00
Israel	0.91	0.30	3.52	0.70	0.12	0.17	0.01	0.00	0.01	0.00	0.25	0.03	3.76
Jordan	0.70	0.49	0.07	2.79	3.26	4.85	0.22	0.00	0.51	0.00	15.41	0.12	0.52
Kuwait	0.78	0.56	5.73	0.39	0.43	0.26	0.31	0.00	0.08	0.00	1.02	0.25	0.36
Lebanon	0.85	6.29	0.05	2.14	2.92	0.68	0.20	0.00	0.01	0.00	21.91	0.47	0.76
Oman	0.67	1.22	5.00	1.30	0.65	0.55	0.41	0.52	0.34	0.00	1.08	0.15	0.05
Qatar	0.96	0.13	4.60	0.19	0.24	0.86	0.04	0.00	0.00	0.00	0.00	0.00	0.18
Saudi Arabia	0.33	0.03	12.49	0.46	0.54	0.71	0.45	1.00	0.00	0.00	0.95	0.11	0.24
Syria	0.19	3.35	4.63	3.90	4.45	6.43	0.92	0.39	0.00	5.88	19.98	0.26	5.48
Turkey	0.81	1.85	0.22	2.42	2.97	2.93	2.05	1.99	0.03	3.50	7.57	3.27	0.58
UAE	0.60	0.49	4.82	1.48	1.21	0.99	0.43	0.01	0.81	0.04	5.00	0.46	0.28
Yemen	0.10	0.00	0.28	5.02	6.69	3.89	0.03	0.00	0.00	0.00	0.25	3.87	1.68
North Africa													
Algeria	0.14	0.00	16.57	0.10	0.13	0.08	0.00	0.00	0.00	0.00	0.41	0.00	0.06
Egypt	0.54	0.95	5.98	1.76	2.27	1.36	1.60	0.00	8.14	0.03	9.88	0.89	1.04
Libya	0.35	0.26	13.67	0.15	0.09	0.04	0.01	0.00	0.00	0.00	0.30	0.01	0.56
Mauritania	0.03	0.23	0.00	5.98	6.41	0.00	0.00	0.00	0.00	0.00	1.81	0.15	10.04
Morocco	1.02	1.55	1.04	1.05	0.95	0.05	0.60	0.22	0.00	0.93	1.98	0.08	2.44
Sudan	0.02	0.00	0.00	6.36	6.73	17.19	3.69	0.00	0.00	0.00	5.69	1.43	11.75
Tunisia	1.08	0.56	0.11	1.04	1.17	1.02	1.51	0.05	0.00	1.62	2.00	0.16	0.21
MENA Countries	0.57	0.91	6.25	1.42	1.55	1.52	0.79	0.59	0.67	0.98	5.40	0.81	0.79

Sources: Average annual ratios of country to world commodity trade shares in international and MENA markets for merchandise imports, based on data compiled from the UN Trade Data System (1996).

TABLE 2.5 Import Restrictions in MENA Countries by Product Category 1984-93

	International Trade Imports	Ad Valorem Tariff Rates		NTB Frequency Rates		International Trade Imports	Ad Valorem Tariff Rates		NTB Frequency Rates	
	1992	1984-87	1991-93	1984-87	1991-93	1992	1984-87	1991-93	1984-87	1991-93
	$ Millions	Percent				$ Millions	Percent			
Middle East Countries		**Cyprus ($10,380)**					**Iran ($2,120)**			
Primary Products	901	10.3	...	40.8	...	2,175	16.8	...	99.0	...
Food	534	16.5	...	68.4	...	1,188	21.4	...	97.9	...
Cereals	55	0.0	...	69.2	...	528	2.2	...	69.2	...
Agricultural raw materials	39	7.9	...	15.8	...	224	16.7	...	100.0	...
Crude fertilizers, mineral oils	14	1.9	...	9.0	...	N/A	10.0	...	100.0	...
Mineral fuels	282	1.0	...	48.1	...	253	7.9	...	100.0	...
Nonferrous metals	33	6.1	...	5.7	...	N/A	10.2	...	100.0	...
Manufactured Products		20.3	...	28.6	...	11,133	22.2	...	99.4	...
Chemicals	231	8.6	...	30.3	...	1,234	15.4	...	97.2	...
Iron and steel	92	3.1	...	23.3	...	N/A	11.9	...	100.0	...
Machinery and equipment	1,066	11.7	...	47.0	...	7,131	12.3	...	100.0	...
Other manufactures	967	30.9	...	19.3	...	2,768	31.3	...	100.0	...
Textiles and apparel	299	43.5	...	34.0	...	313	31.8	...	100.0	...
All Products	3,290	17.5	...	32.2	...	13,501	20.7	...	99.3	...
		Kuwait ($20,140)					**Saudi Arabia ($7,570)**			
Primary Products	1,222	2.9	...	6.8	...	4,187	11.7	12.0	4.4	...
Food	968	1.5	...	10.2	...	3,319	11.3	11.9	8.9	...
Cereals	90	0.0	...	7.7	...	322	7.4	6.5	0.0	...
Agricultural raw materials	154	3.9	...	0.0	...	168	12.0	12.0	0.8	...
Crude fertilizers, mineral oils	12	4.1	...	5.2	...	183	12.1	12.1	0.0	...
Mineral fuels	34	4.4	...	0.0	...	59	12.0	12.3	0.0	...
Nonferrous metals	54	3.8	...	13.2	...	459	12.3	11.8	0.0	...

TABLE 2.5 (continued)

	International Trade Imports 1992	Ad Valorem Tariff Rates 1984-87	Ad Valorem Tariff Rates 1991-93	NTB Frequency Rates 1984-87	NTB Frequency Rates 1991-93	International Trade Imports 1992	Ad Valorem Tariff Rates 1984-87	Ad Valorem Tariff Rates 1991-93	NTB Frequency Rates 1984-87	NTB Frequency Rates 1991-93
	$ Millions	Percent				$ Millions	Percent			
Manufactured Products	5,970	4.7	...	1.8	...	18,227	12.4	12.2	3.4	...
Chemicals	359	5.2	...	2.2	...	2,226	12.4	11.9	5.6	...
Iron and steel	350	4.1	...	1.3	...	824	12.3	13.2	4.0	...
Machinery and equipment	3,072	4.1	...	1.1	...	8,990	12.1	11.8	5.0	...
Other manufactures	2,189	4.8	...	2.1	...	6,187	12.5	12.4	1.4	...
Textiles and apparel	611	4.3	...	0.0	...	2,149	12.2	12.2	0.0	...
All Products	7,259	4.2	...	3.5	...	24,069	12.2	12.1	3.9	...
	Syria ($1,750)					**Turkey ($2,970)**				
Primary Products	896	13.1	...	30.7	...	7,299	18.7	8.2	93.9	...
Food	746	20.4	...	44.4	...	1,357	24.6	11.8	92.2	...
Cereals	268	7.3	...	84.6	...	156	6.3	11.0	84.6	...
Agricultural raw materials	44	7.7	...	31.1	...	1,080	12.8	4.4	99.3	...
Crude fertilizers, mineral oils	9	5.9	...	14.9	...	734	11.3	4.1	98.5	...
Mineral fuels	72	8.8	...	11.8	...	3,782	13.9	4.6	70.6	...
Nonferrous metals	26	6.2	...	1.1	...	346	16.7	7.3	100.0	...
Manufactured Products	1,480	15.5	...	38.7	...	15,500	24.2	9.3	97.3	...
Chemicals	324	7.3	...	32.1	...	3,059	12.4	8.2	92.3	...
Iron and steel	260	3.8	...	25.3	...	1,307	11.5	6.9	100.0	...
Machinery and equipment	475	11.5	...	28.9	...	8,037	21.7	8.0	99.1	...
Other manufactures	421	22.7	...	48.3	...	3,097	32.3	10.8	98.3	...
Textiles and apparel	169	28.0	...	75.7	...	745	35.7	11.8	100.0	...
All Products	2,400	14.8	...	36.6	...	22,871	22.7	9.0	96.4	...
	Algeria ($1,780)					**Egypt ($660)**				
Primary Products	3,031	17.1	18.6	79.3	26.8	3,340	50.4	23.4	43.8	...
Food	2,465	27.9	29.1	86.3	57.2	2,438	98.6	32.2	70.1	...
Cereals	494	0.0	6.4	100.0	0.0	883	5.7	8.7	100.0	...
Agricultural raw materials	252	11.0	9.8	78.6	0.0	519	9.9	12.5	10.5	...
Crude fertilizers, mineral oils	65	8.3	8.3	65.7	0.0	152	8.0	11.3	10.4	...
Mineral fuels	125	1.5	3.2	61.1	0.0	116	7.4	11.9	78.6	...
Nonferrous metals	125	3.5	13.6	79.2	0.0	116	11.5	16.7	16.4	...

TABLE 2.5 (continued)

	International Trade Imports 1992	Ad Valorem Tariff Rates 1984-87	Ad Valorem Tariff Rates 1991-93	NTB Frequency Rates 1984-87	NTB Frequency Rates 1991-93	International Trade Imports 1992	Ad Valorem Tariff Rates 1984-87	Ad Valorem Tariff Rates 1991-93	NTB Frequency Rates 1984-87	NTB Frequency Rates 1991-93
	$ Millions	Percent				$ Millions	Percent			
Manufactured products	5,611	23.4	24.6	63.6	2.8	4,951	27.1	29.2	45.6	...
Chemicals	922	11.0	14.2	50.7	1.2	1,079	10.2	14.4	55.9	...
Iron and steel	824	4.0	12.3	88.7	0.0	388	9.8	17.4	17.3	...
Machinery and equipment	2,647	9.6	16.3	58.8	0.2	2,173	18.1	18.7	29.5	...
Other manufactures	1,218	38.2	34.9	68.8	5.2	1,312	40.2	41.8	52.5	...
Textiles and apparel	133	53.0	44.2	79.5	0.0	202	59.6	56.5	75.2	...
All Products	8,648	21.7	22.9	67.8	9.5	8,293	33.5	27.9	45.2	...
	Libya ($5,700)					**Morocco ($1,040)**				
Primary Products	1,448	14.2	...	15.0	...	2,924	18.2	18.9	43.0	...
Food	1,269	17.2	...	29.2	...	1,038	27.7	27.8	73.9	...
Cereals	269	0.0	...	0.0	...	294	8.8	10.0	98.7	...
Agricultural raw materials	106	15.4	...	4.8	...	414	9.5	11.5	13.6	...
Crude fertilizers, mineral oils	14	9.3	...	2.2	...	248	8.4	8.3	4.5	...
Mineral fuels	20	9.1	...	0.0	...	1,125	10.3	12.5	65.0	...
Nonferrous metals	39	8.2	...	0.0	...	99	11.9	12.3	0.9	...
Manufactured Products	3,891	19.7	...	8.4	...	4,431	25.6	24.4	21.8	...
Chemicals	408	6.8	...	1.6	...	747	18.7	18.4	13.0	...
Iron and steel	401	1.7	...	1.3	...	396	8.3	7.8	3.1	...
Machinery and Equipment	1,813	19.4	...	6.7	...	2,072	20.8	19.7	11.8	...
Other manufactures	1,269	27.7	...	13.2	...	1,215	33.2	31.3	33.0	...
Textiles and apparel	353	27.2	...	24.6	...	387	39.1	35.1	63.7	...
All Products	5,358	18.3	...	10.3	...	7,356	23.5	22.8	27.6	...

TABLE 2.5 (continued)

	International Trade Imports 1992	Ad Valorem Tariff Rates		NTB Frequency Rates		International Trade Imports 1992	Ad Valorem Tariff Rates		NTB Frequency Rates	
		1984-87	1991-93	1984-87	1991-93		1984-87	1991-93	1984-87	1991-93
	$ Millions	Percent				$ Millions	Percent			
	Sudan ($350)					**Tunisia ($1,190)**				
Primary Products	211	56.6	...	12.0	...	1,474	22.3	25.7	77.4	37.3
Food	128	70.9	...	25.1	...	534	31.8	32.6	95.4	62.3
Cereals	84	36.9	...	0.0	...	140	17.6	22.0	100.0	100.0
Agricultural raw materials	13	50.3	...	0.0	...	237	14.5	19.7	47.1	9.4
Crude fertilizers, mineral oils	N/A	38.3	...	0.7	...	141	13.4	19.5	74.6	17.1
Mineral fuels	35	25.4	...	0.0	...	486	8.5	13.5	91.7	26.7
Nonferrous metals	N/A	54.2	...	0.9	...	76	17.6	23.9	55.7	17.4
Manufactured Products	532	56.4	...	9.4	...	4,949	24.7	28.2	75.5	30.5
Chemicals	93	31.4	...	3.3	...	523	17.2	23.1	48.3	14.5
Iron and steel	N/A	53.5	...	0.0	...	434	11.0	18.5	93.8	8.5
Machinery and equipment	260	42.1	...	3.8	...	1,951	20.1	24.2	70.9	18.8
Other manufactures	179	75.1	...	15.9	...	2,040	32.0	33.7	87.8	46.1
Textiles and apparel	32	92.9	...	22.2	...	1,249	36.5	36.9	93.8	70.6
All Products	752	56.6	...	10.0	...	6,432	24.0	27.5	76.2	32.7

Notes: Tariff and NTB frequency rates are unweighted averages of protection measures for the countries indicated. Tariffs are inclusive of customs duties and other fiscal charges on imports. NTB frequency rates refer to the percentage of national tariff lines affected by NTBs. Leaders (...) denote not available. Mid-1980s protection statistics for Kuwait and Turkey refer to 1988, and for Egypt and Saudi Arabia refer to 1989. Early-1990s protection statistics for Egypt refer to 1995. Values in parentheses are per capita GNP levels in 1993, and import levels for Iran and Sudan refer to average annual values of imports during 1992-94.

Sources: UNCTAD (1994, 1995), World Bank (1995c, 1996c), and computations based on data compiled from the UN Trade Data System (1996).

from imports of manufactures and other products remains high in many countries in MENA, contributing significantly to overvaluation of the real exchange rate (the relative price of nontraded goods to traded goods), and thereby to repression of domestic relative prices in subsectors of agriculture that are internationally competitive.

Table 2.5 indicates the magnitude of protection during the last decade in the MENA countries for which data on import tariffs and NTBs are available.[18] The data on tariffs reveal the combined magnitude of ad valorem customs duties and other fiscal charges on imports (so-called para-tariffs). The NTB data, on the other hand, indicate the percentage of national tariff schedule lines in each product category affected by quantitative restrictions and other NTBs, as compiled by UNCTAD for its inventory of trade control measures in industrial and developing countries (UNCTAD 1994a).

The most open countries in MENA are the high-income Arabian Gulf countries (Kuwait and Saudi Arabia), with average tariff rates not exceeding about 10 percent and average NTB rates not exceeding about 5 percent. Most other countries in the region are inward looking, with average tariff rates widely exceeding 20 percent and average NTB rates widely exceeding 30 percent. This is true of low-income countries such as Egypt and Sudan, but also middle-income countries such as Algeria, Iran, and Turkey. The high NTBs are particularly costly in economic terms because, unlike ad valorem tariffs, NTBs limit the extent to which the price system allocates resources among alternative uses. They also tend to be associated with discretionary administered systems for authorizing imports that encourage "socially unproductive" rent-seeking activities.[19] Finally, it should be noted that such extensive reliance on administered protection is similar mainly to the broad enforcement of NTBs at high frequency rates in the low-income countries of South Asia and Sub-Saharan Africa (Erzan et al. 1989, DeRosa 1992). In the more open trade regimes of East Asia, administered protection is enforced much more selectively and at much lower average frequency rates (e.g., DeRosa 1988, 1995b).

The MENA countries tend to enforce higher rates of protection for manufactures, especially light manufactures comprising the category of other manufactures in table 2.4, than for traditionally internationally-competitive subsectors of agriculture such as agricultural raw materials. This structure of protection is a fundamental determinant of the bias against agriculture, distorting domestic price incentives in favor of shifting resources to production of nontraded goods and import-competing manufactures.

The MENA countries also tend to enforce high rates of protection for food, frequently by administered protection measures that include state trading. This protection reflects national concerns for food security, and it is often enforced in conjunction with direct controls on domestic food prices.[20]

However, efforts to achieve food security and especially food self-sufficiency drain resources from more internationally competitive subsectors of agriculture. Considerations for comparative advantage suggest that expanded production and exports in the internationally competitive subsectors of not only agriculture but also industry and other natural resource-based sectors would increase national food security more than protection of inefficient domestic food producers, by providing foreign exchange earnings for increased imports of food at lower domestic resource cost.

Finally, it is noteworthy that some MENA countries, such as Algeria and Tunisia, have significantly reformed their trade regimes during the last decade, succeeding particularly in reducing their average levels of administered protection. These reforms should be expected to improve export performance. To the extent, however, that the trade regimes of these and other MENA countries continue to protect manufacturing and other subsectors favored by the government and domestic special interests, a significant bias against agriculture will remain and continue to inhibit the potential of agriculture to contribute more significantly to domestic output and exports.

Regional Cooperation

With the commencement of a peace process in the Middle East between the Arab countries and Israel, renewed interest in the implications of closer economic relations has swept the greater MENA region and has spawned a series of regional economic summits, with the most recent summit held in Cairo, Egypt in November 1996 (table 2.6).[21]

Past and Present

Among Arab countries, economic cooperation efforts have a history dating back to the Alexandria Protocol of 1945, which established the League of Arab States. A number of formal agreements have been signed to foster closer economic relations, but with little lasting success (Lakhoua 1993). Today, among the most active organizations devoted to expanding trade and other economic relations among Arab countries are the Council of Arab Economic Unity (CAEU) and the GCC.[22]

Both organizations have the objective of establishing customs unions, with accommodations for expanded preferential trade in agricultural as well as manufactured products. Indeed, the Arab Common Market (ACM) formed in 1965 by several CAEU countries (Egypt, Iraq, Jordan, Syria, and Yemen) and the Unified Economic Agreement ratified in 1981 by the GCC countries specifically prescribe the liberalization of customs duties on trade in agriculture, including animal products.[23]

Bilateral trading arrangements also feature prominently in the history of intra-MENA trade relations. As indicated in table 2.6, Jordan, Lebanon, Syria, and several North African countries (especially Morocco and Tunisia) have established a number of bilateral trading accords over the last two decades.

TABLE 2.6 Economic Cooperation in MENA

	Arab Common Market (1964)	Gulf Cooperation Council (1981)	Economic Cooperation Org. (1985)	Arab Maghreb Union (1989)	Bilateral EMA Trading Arrangements * (1987-96)	MENA Economic Summits (1994-96)
	Organization members, summit participants					
Middle East						
Cyprus (CYP)						X
Iran (IRN)			X			
Iraq (IRQ)	X				TUN	
Israel (ISR)						X
Jordan (JOR)	X				LEB, MOR, SYR, TUN, EMA	X
Kuwait (KUW)		X			TUN	X
Lebanon (LEB)					JOR, SAU, SDN, SYR, EMA	
Oman (OMN)		X				X
Qatar (QTR)		X				X
Saudi Arabia (SAU)		X			LEB, TUN	X
Syria (SYR)	X				JOR, LEB, LBY, MOR, TUN	
Turkey (TUR)			X		EMA	X
United Arab Emirates (UAE)		X			TUN	X
Yemen (YEM)	X					X
North Africa						
Algeria (ALG)				X	LBY, MOR, TUN	
Egypt (EGY)	X				SDN, EMA	X
Libya (LBY)				X	ALG, MOR, SYR, TUN	
Mauritania (MAU)	X			X		X
Morocco (MOR)				X	ALG, LBY, JOR, SDN, SYR, TUN, EMA	X
Sudan (SDN)					EGY, LEB, MOR, TUN	
Tunisia (TUN)				X	ALG, IRQ, JOR, KUW, LBY, MOR, SAU, SDN, SYR, UAE, EMA	X

Notes: Dates in parentheses indicate commencement year of the cooperation agreement. Bilateral trading arrangements between MENA countries are those in operation, circa 1987.
*EMA arrangements refer to partnership agreements with the EU under the Euro-Mediterranean Agreement. In 1996, Turkey entered into a custom union agreement with the EU.
Sources: Kirmani et al. (1994), Hoekman and Djankov (1996b), UNCTAD (1987), and WEF (1994, 1995, 1996).

Whether tariff barriers and NTBs to intraregional trade have been substantially lowered in MENA under the various accords for regional and bilateral economic cooperation is problematical. Although tariff concessions may have been widely exchanged, it is likely that NTBs in MENA have continued to be enforced against imports from all countries. Therefore, although framework agreements and other pacts for closer economic relations among Arab countries in MENA have been adopted, effective implementation of these agreements may be far from a reality today—not unlike the early experiences with regional economic cooperation schemes among developing countries in other regions.[24]

The new process of MENA economic summits may eventually succeed in overcoming this situation, e.g., by eventually establishing a MENA free trade area.[25] Indeed, the process is the only regional economic "arrangement" that includes not only Israel but also a large number of countries from both the Middle East and North Africa. It also has the strong political endorsement and financial backing of the international community, including Russia and the United States.

Finally, some MENA countries are also currently negotiating, or have concluded, so-called partnership agreements with the EU under its Mediterranean free trade initiative.[26] These agreements offer the MENA countries expanded preferential access to markets in the EU, though not significant expansion of MENA agricultural exports restricted by the EU's Common Agricultural Policy (CAP) before January 1, 2000, in exchange for both reciprocal trade concessions and general economic policy reforms by the MENA countries. The first EU partnership agreement was signed by Tunisia in July 1995, followed by Morocco in October 1995; in January 1996, Turkey entered into a comprehensive custom union agreement with the EU.[27] Other MENA countries that have begun the process of entering into EU partnership agreements include Egypt, Jordan, and Lebanon.

Against the background of the "hub and spoke" design of the EU partnership agreements, a MENA free trade area might be viewed as necessary to ensure that incentives for not only expanded trade but also expanded investment are distributed efficiently between the MENA countries and the EU. A MENA free trade area might also be viewed as a means of maintaining the focus of MENA countries on their mutual economic interests, amid competing incentives for expanding relations with developing countries outside of the region, e.g., the increasing interest of Iran and Turkey in expanding their economic relations with Pakistan and the newly independent countries in Central Asia (see table 2.6).

Economic Considerations

While inclusion of considerations for agriculture in the establishment of any future MENA economic cooperation schemes seems secure,[28] the extent of the benefits to be derived from such schemes are less certain.

Of fundamental importance for determining the implications of regional trading arrangements for both agriculture and national economic welfare is the underlying complementarity of natural and accumulated resources, including human capital, among the countries forming a free trade area. If preferential trading arrangements result in little or no improvement in the terms of trade facing agriculture in the region, then it is unlikely that the regional arrangements will substantially overcome distortions to domestic price incentives against agriculture arising from protection and other inappropriate economy-wide policies. A particular danger is that where countries are very similar in their (relative) resource endowments, national import substitution policies to promote industrialization or protect favored industries will essentially be replaced by regional import substitution policies that succeed in liberalizing trade between neighboring countries but result in increased protection against imports from the world's most efficient producers.

Regional trade liberalization among less developed countries most often takes the form of reduced barriers to intraregional trade in manufactures. To the extent that policy-based disincentives to agriculture have their origins mainly in industrial protection, such trade liberalization would be a positive step. Greater economic integration of neighboring lower-income countries would tend to lower the domestic terms of trade for industrial products, as the output of manufactures in the region operating at high unit costs is gradually supplanted by output of manufactures in the region operating at lower unit costs. This eventuality should also be expected to release productive resources to internationally competitive subsectors of agriculture and industry, as the domestic terms of trade of these subsectors improve vis-à-vis those of import-competing sectors.

The more difficult question is whether the expected improvement in the domestic terms of trade of the competitive sectors in agriculture will be sufficient to eradicate or substantially reduce the bias against agriculture. Beyond the prospect of some rationalization of industrial output and possibly agricultural output with the region,[29] the likelihood of substantial relative price adjustments is limited where the resource endowments of the less developed countries forming the free trade area are mainly competitive rather than complementary.

Ultimately, the extent to which RTAs might be counted upon to reduce the bias against agriculture is an empirical question. No quantitative studies of this issue have been undertaken for the MENA region. A recent study of the issue by DeRosa (1995b, 1996b) for the new free trade area among the Association of Southeast Asian Nations (ASEAN) uses a CGE model to trace the adjustment of key variables determining the extent of the bias against agriculture, including the real exchange rate and other relative prices. The study finds that the expected gains to agriculture and national welfare under the ASEAN Free Trade Area are modest. On the other hand, general trade liberalization following the most-favored-nation principle underlying the General Agreement on Tariffs and Trade (GATT) and the new WTO generally yields significant gains for both agriculture and national welfare because it substantially expands ASEAN trade with the major industrial countries (the principal trading partners of ASEAN), whose natural and accumulated resources are highly complementary to the abundance of labor, tropical land, and other natural resources found in the countries of Southeast Asia.

These results suggest that agriculture might be expected to benefit in some measure from regional economic cooperation in MENA, including under schemes that would emphasize greater regional cooperation for infrastructure development, management of water resources, or other aspects of "deeper" economic integration (Lawrence 1996). However, with respect to goods markets alone, trade liberalization in MENA that encompasses trade with the EU and the region's other principal trading partners is likely to hold the promise of substantially larger and dependably significant gains to MENA agriculture and surrounding rural economies. Moreover, this conclusion is likely to hold regardless whether the EU or other major trading partners offer any reciprocal trade concessions, including reforms to the CAP or other trade-distorting farm policies in the major industrial countries. Essentially, so long as there is some price-sensitivity to international markets for the agricultural products and other goods exported by the MENA countries, effective reduction of the protection in these countries that gives rise to the bias against agriculture should be expected to reduce the overvaluation of real exchange rates in MENA, reallocate resources to more efficient uses in internationally competitive subsectors of agriculture and industry in the region, and stimulate greater agricultural production and exports from the region to international markets wherever they may be found abroad.

Summary and Conclusion

Along with achieving higher sustainable growth and greater national economic development, accelerated rural development remains a major objective of most countries in MENA, to provide not only disadvantaged groups but also other inhabitants of rural areas in MENA with higher living standards and more equitable access to the private and public services found in urban areas.

Agriculture is the nucleus of productive activities in the rural economy of most countries in MENA. Moreover, agriculture still accounts for an appreciable-to-large share of domestic output and especially employment in both the low-income countries and middle-income countries of the region. Under such circumstances, agriculture can be expected to contribute significantly to achieving higher sustainable growth and greater economic development in general and to achieving greater economic development and welfare in rural areas in particular, as predicted in economic theory and recorded in the experiences of developing countries in other regions.[30] Indeed, that agricultural growth has failed to surpass population growth by desirable margins of 2 to 3 percentage points during the last decade in many if not most less developed countries in MENA indicates that more dynamic and robust growth of agriculture can contribute significantly to achieving development goals in the region for both the national and rural economies of MENA countries.

Expanding agricultural trade by MENA countries is an appropriate and natural avenue for pursuing more dynamic and robust performance in agriculture, involving likely adjustments within as well as outside the sector as considerations for comparative advantage are increasingly called upon to allocate arable land, labor, water, and other resources (including financial and physical capital) to more efficient uses. Indeed, some MENA countries might face higher rather than lower bills for their imports of cereals and other food staples. These countries, however, might also realize higher foreign exchange earnings from expanded exports of other agricultural products, such as livestock, fruits and vegetables, or agricultural raw materials, or from expanded exports of internationally competitive manufactures.

High levels of protection, particularly for manufactures and some food products, provide a clear indication that a substantial "bias against agriculture" exists in many countries in MENA. Improvement of the global trading environment for agriculture—through adherence to the Uruguay Round agreement on agriculture in the nearer term and possible further reforms to farm policies in the EU and other major industrial countries in the longer term—will expand world demand for MENA agricultural exports. However, reforms to trade and other economy-wide policies in the MENA countries themselves to eliminate the bias against agriculture and to establish more neutral or even-handed public policies toward agriculture would result in equal if not much larger gains in MENA agricultural production and trade.

Trade liberalization and other economic policy reforms in MENA to promote agriculture and rural development might be pursued through regional cooperation in MENA, as envisioned by the Arab organizations for economic cooperation and the new, more inclusive process of MENA economic summits. Considerations for comparative advantage, however, suggest that agricultural trade and rural development would be served best by thoroughgoing trade liberalization in MENA on a nondiscriminatory basis. This would ensure that the region's trade relations would be expanded with its largest trading partners and that import-substitution policies inhibiting greater agricultural production and trade in the region would be curbed most effectively. Unilateral trade liberalization following the MFN principle underlying the

WTO is one important avenue for achieving such thoroughgoing trade liberalization. However, pursuit of "open regionalism" in MENA, following the example of the Asia-Pacific Economic Cooperation (APEC) Forum, is another avenue for achieving largely the same end.[31] Pursuit of open regionalism to achieve nondiscriminatory trade liberalization in MENA and, more fundamentally, higher sustainable growth and greater rural development would also have the advantage of prominently preserving the ongoing process of regional dialogues on economic policies and the promulgation of regional economic accords that is expected by all parties concerned to yield substantial political as well as economic dividends for the countries in the greater MENA region.

APPENDIX TABLE 2.1 The MENA Economies 1993

	Population (millions)	Arable Land Area (km^2 (%))	Population Density (Pers./ $km.^2$)	Education Index	Per Capita Income ($)	Structure of Production (Employment): Agriculture	Industry	Mfg.	Merchandise Trade (Agricultural Trade): Exports	Imports
						------- Percent of GDP (Labor force, Total trade)				----------
Middle East										
Cyprus	1	9 (21)	111	...	10,380	7 (14)	... (30)	...	... (32)	... (14)
Iran	64	1,648 (39)	39	87	2,120	24 (40)	29 (23)	14	16 (6)	29 (14)
Iraq	19	438 (27)	43	116	1,750	... (16)	... (18)	...	... (1)	... (65)
Israel	5	21 (36)	248	247	13,920	... (4)	... (29)	...	21 (7)	32 (9)
Jordan	4	89 (14)	46	...	1,190	8 (15)	26 (23)	15	28 (20)	80 (23)
Kuwait	2	18 (8)	100	179	20,140	0 (1)	55 (25)	9	30 (1)	49 (16)
Lebanon	4	10 (39)	400	...	1,750	... (...)	... (...)	...	... (25)	... (23)
Oman	2	212 (5)	9	69	4,850	3 (45)	53 (24)	4	46 (4)	35 (20)
Qatar	1	11 (5)	91	...	15,030	... (3)	... (32)	...	... (1)	... (15)
Saudi Arabia	17	2,150 (41)	8	107	7,570	... (19)	... (20)	...	23 (1)	22 (15)
Syria	14	185 (76)	76	153	1,750	28 (33)	... (24)	...	... (19)	... (18)
Turkey	60	779 (50)	77	114	2,970	15 (53)	30 (18)	19	10 (24)	19 (10)
UAE	2	84 (3)	21	107	21,430	2 (8)	57 (27)	8	59 (3)	56 (10)
Yemen	13	528 (34)	25	...	280	21 (61)	24 (17)	11	5 (4)	20 (30)

APPENDIX TABLE 2.1 (continued)

North Africa										
Algeria	27	2,382 (16)	11	114	1,780	13 (26)	43 (31)	11	26 (1)	20 (33)
Egypt	56	1,001 (5)	56	179	660	18 (40)	22 (22)	16	6 (10)	23 (24)
Libya	5	1,760 (9)	3	...	5,700	... (18)	... (37)	...	... (1)	... (20)
Mauritania	2	1,026 (38)	2	...	500	28 (55)	30 (10)	12	52 (49)	78 (24)
Morocco	26	447 (71)	58	89	1,040	14 (45)	32 (25)	18	15 (28)	25 (19)
Sudan	27	2,506 (50)	11	14	350	30 (70)	... (9)	...	... (95)	... (23)
Tunisia	9	164 (58)	53	83	1,190	18 (28)	31 (33)	19	30 (12)	49 (12)
Developing Countries										
Low-income	3,093	39,093 (...)	79	38	380	28 (...)	35 (...)	25	16 (...)	19 (...)
Middle-income	1,596	62,452 (...)	26	140	2,480	... (...)	... (...)	...	17 (...)	19 (...)
Sub-Saharan Africa	559	24,274 (41)	23	28	520	20 (67)	33 (...)	16	23 (20)	22 (15)
East Asia & Pacific	1,714	16,369 (40)	105	71	820	17 (58)	41 (...)	30	24 (12)	26 (8)
South Asia	1,194	5,133 (65)	233	62	310	30 (65)	26 (...)	17	11 (18)	14 (9)
Europe & Central Asia	495	24,242 (...)	20	...	2,450	... (...)	... (...)	...	15 (...)	18 (...)
MENA	263	11,015 (31)	24	130	...	14 (35)	... (...)	...	... (7)	... (15)
Latin America & Caribbean	466	20,507 (43)	23	133	2,950	... (26)	... (...)	...	10 (23)	12 (11)
Industrial Countries	812	32,145 (42)	25	305	23,090	... (4)	... (...)	...	16 (10)	16 (5)

Sources: USDA (1996), World Bank (1995a, 1995d, 1996c), and UN COMTRADE database.

Notes: Education index is the secondary enrollment rate plus five times the university enrollment rate, both calculated in their respective age cohorts for 1989.

NOTES

This chapter is based on a paper presented to the Fourth Annual World Bank Conference on Environmentally Sustainable Development, "Rural Well-Being: From Vision to Action," September 25-27, 1996, Washington, DC. Helpful comments by John M. Underwood and Inder K. Sud, among other conference participants, are gratefully acknowledged.

1. The countries comprising MENA are indicated in the tables accompanying this section. In the main, the countries are those specified in the World Bank's *World Development Report* series, with the addition of four countries: Cyprus and Turkey in the Middle East, and Mauritania and Sudan in North Africa.

2. Fischer et al. (1993), for instance, estimate that reduced military expenditures in the Middle East would release productive resources amounting to about 10 percent of GDP per annum and yield an increase in economic growth of 1 to 2 percentage points in the countries of the region. See also Fishelson (1989) and Fischer (1993).

3. In 1993, Egypt received international food aid shipments of cereals amounting to nearly 500 thousand metric tons, followed by Jordan, Morocco, and Sudan with shipments of between 200 and 250 thousand tons each. See FAO (1994).

4. The share of agriculture in low-income and middle-income developing countries is often biased downward by the economic policy related repression of prices for agricultural commodities in these countries. Thus, the contribution of agriculture to total employment in such countries is frequently a more reliable indicator of the economic importance of agriculture to the national economy.

5. It is likely that the availability of reliable data on economic growth during 1980-93 for more countries in MENA would reveal that additional countries in the region experienced negative per capita growth rates during the last decade.

6. The subsection draws heavily on Bautista and DeRosa (1996).

7. Also see Johnson (1995) for a general discussion of the appropriate role of government in agriculture and rural development in more developed countries as well as less developed countries. For a recent analysis of the strategic impacts on growth and other economic variables that improved agricultural performance would have in Egypt under economic policy reforms, see John Mellor Associates et al. (1995).

8. See Krueger, Schiff, and Valdés (1988, 1992) and Bautista and Valdés (1993) for in-depth case studies involving a wide range of countries, including selected countries in MENA.

9. The importance of physical and social infrastructure for agricultural growth and rural development in low-income countries is reviewed recently by Ahmed and Donovan (1992). In the context of MENA, among the most important aspects of the social infrastructure to the region, in addition to individual countries, is the efficient development and utilization of limited water resources. See, for instance, World Bank (1995c).

10. The discussion here focuses solely output volumes of major crops and other agricultural products, including meats and dairy products. Important considerations for the utilization of arable lands and pastures, production yields, and production input

requirements are beyond the scope of the present analysis. For more in-depth review of agriculture and farm systems in MENA, see Nordblom, Goodchild, and Shomo (1995). See also Khaldi (1984).

11. Among other major agricultural crops and products are pulses (2 percent), cotton and sunflower seeds (1 percent), and natural fibers and other agricultural raw materials (1 percent).

12. The World Bank (1995d) classifies Egypt, Sudan, and Yemen as service exporting countries owing to the large number of overseas "remittance" workers in the Middle East and elsewhere from the three countries. As classified by the Bank, diversified exporters include Bahrain, Kuwait, Morocco, Syria, Tunisia, and Turkey; manufactured exporters include Israel and Lebanon; and petroleum exporters include all other MENA countries.

13. RCA values reflect not only fundamental factors such as natural resource endowments but also trade-distorting factors, such as foreign and domestic protection and also foreign and domestic subsidies to production and trade. Thus, for example, the RCA values computed for MENA trade in agriculture will reflect trade-distorting farm policies in the major industrial countries and the MENA countries themselves, including pricing of scarce water resources for irrigation and other agricultural uses at below their financial cost, let alone their opportunity cost, in many MENA countries (World Bank 1995a).

14. DeRosa (1995a) finds similar differences between computed international and intraregional values of revealed comparative advantage for the MENA countries during 1987-89. Moreover, he finds that the differences between the two sets of RCA values are statistically significant for most MENA countries, based on the results of a rank correlation analysis.

15. While this finding holds possible implications for the formulation of policies governing the multilateral versus regional relations of MENA countries, it does not provide guidance to the relative benefits of pursuing one set of economic relations over the other. DeRosa (1995a) provides an exploratory investigation of the relative benefits of expanding intraregional versus international trade in staple food commodities. Other recent studies have investigated the merits of closer economic relations between MENA countries and the EU, with limited focus on the economic impacts on agricultural production and trade. See, for instance, Rutherford, Rutström, and Tarr (1993), Brown, Deardorff, and Stern (1995), and Harrison, Rutherford, and Tarr (1997).

16. At the same time, higher prices for food commodities should be expected to place a burden on food-importing countries in MENA. However, the impacts of the Uruguay Round agreement on agriculture must be weighed against the impacts of other aspects of the overall Uruguay Round agreement, many of which are generally expected to be positive for less developed countries. For example, many developing countries, including those in MENA, might realize higher export earnings from the multilateral liberalization of trade in non-food agricultural sectors and manufacturing sectors such as textiles and apparel. For an overview of the Uruguay Round agreement and its implications for agriculture and other sectors in less developed countries, see Martin and Winters (1996) and Hathaway and Ingco (1996).

17. More generally, the total gains from the Uruguay Round to individual MENA countries will be bounded by the extent of their own commitments to trade liberaliza-

tion under the Uruguay Round agreement. Notably in this regard, only 10 MENA countries are members of the WTO and are signatories to the Final Act of the Uruguay Round: Bahrain, Egypt, Kuwait, Israel, Mauritania, Morocco, Qatar, Tunisia, Turkey, and UAE. See Zarrouk (1996).

18. The discussion here focuses on protection in output markets for agricultural and other products. Although protection for production inputs is also important, estimates of effective rates of protection are beyond the scope of the present analysis. Notably however, computed effective rates of protection are often highly correlated with nominal rates of protection.

19. On the economics of rent-seeking and so-called directly unproductive profit-seeking activities, see Tullock (1967, 1980), Krueger (1974), and Bhagwati (1982).

20. Food products in table 2.6 include processed foods as well as food primary commodities. Thus, the high rates of protection for food in table 2.6 reflect protection for domestic food processing industries in addition to protection for domestic cultivation of food crops.

21. The first MENA economic summit was held in Casablanca, Morocco in 1994, and the second in Amman, Jordan in 1995.

22. At this writing, comparatively little is known by the author about the two other organizations for regional economic cooperation in MENA included in table 2.6, the Economic Cooperation Organization and the Arab Maghreb Union.

23. In 1970, the League of Arab States established the Arab Organization for Agricultural Development, with headquarters in Khartoum. The objectives of the organization, to which more than 15 Arab states belong, include increasing intra-regional trade in agricultural products among Arab countries (UIA 1987).

24. See, among others, Langhammer and Hiemenz (1990) and de Melo and Panagariya (1993).

25. Fischer (1993) sets out an early vision of the forms that economic cooperation in MENA could take to promote greater flows of trade, capital, and labor throughout the region, including the possible establishment of a regional development bank and the necessary involvement in planning cooperation efforts of both private business leaders and government officials. A similar vision is set forth in the Casablanca Declaration, the official communiqué of the 1994 MENA economic summit.

26. See Hoekman and Djankov (1996b).

27. For overview and quantitative analyses of these agreements, see Rutherford, Rutström, and Tarr (1993), Page and Underwood (1996), Brown, Deardorff, and Stern (1996), Harrison, Rutherford, and Tarr (1997), and Togan (1996). A compendium of studies analyzing the macroeconomic and sectoral implications of an EU partnership agreement for Egypt, among other MENA countries, is presented in Galal and Hoekman (1997).

28. The agenda of the recent MENA economic summits have prominently included sessions on enhancing the role of agriculture in MENA, including as a priority sector for expanded growth of exports in order to promote general economic growth and rural development. See WEF (1994, 1995, 1996).

29. As discussed previously in this section, in addition to protecting industry many developing countries also protect production of staple food commodities and processed

foods. In doing so, governments distort price incentives for subsectors of agriculture that have considerable comparative advantage. Reducing high rates of protection then can lead to expansion of *intra-industry* trade as well as *interindustry* trade favoring internationally competitive subsectors of agriculture.

30. See, for instance, Mellor (1995) and Bautista and DeRosa (1996).

31. Under open regionalism, trade concessions negotiated between regional trading partners would be extended on an unconditional basis to all trading partners, including trading partners located outside the region. On open regionalism in East Asia and the still uncertain degree of conditionality to be observed in the "nondiscriminatory" free trade area envisioned for the APEC region, see Drysdale and Garnaut (1993) and APEC (1994). On forms of regional economic cooperation in other developing areas, see De Melo and Panagariya (1993).

CHAPTER 3

Intra-Industry Trade of Arab Countries: An Indicator of Potential Competitiveness

Oleh Havrylyshyn and Peter Kunzel

The recent signing and ongoing discussions of bilateral agreements to liberalize trade between the EU and several Arab countries raise the question as to how the latter will fare in a more competitive environment.[1] Most Arab countries have traditionally been dependent on their natural resources. As a consequence, they have had fewer pressures to diversify and specialize their industrial base. As Nsouli, Bisat, and Kanaan (1996) point out, some Arab countries are more able to adapt to new trade opportunities, whereas others have less flexibility to adjust to new market opportunities and increased competition. In the trade literature, the amount of intra-industry trade (IIT), or trade that a country does in similar goods, is often taken as a measure of the diversity, degree of specialization, and degree of technical sophistication of its industrial sector. This can be used to infer the country's ability to compete in a changing environment. This chapter analyzes the evolution of IIT over the period 1984-94 to shed light on the level of industrial specialization for Arab countries and the implied potential to compete with industrialized economies in a more open trade setting.

IIT Theory and Competitiveness Implications for Arab Countries

The factor proportions theory as posited by Heckscher and Ohlin predicts that patterns of trade will be based on the relative abundance and intensity of factors used in the production process. Trade flows between countries occur in complementary goods, owing to the comparative advantage based on differing factor endowments in a perfectly competitive trading environment. Grubel and Lloyd

(1975) first observed and analyzed an apparent anomaly: a high proportion of industrial country trade is a two-way exchange within the same group of goods, presumably with the same factor intensity. This trade, which they labeled IIT, describes trade in similar but slightly differentiated products, based on imperfect competition, or trade in close substitutes demanded from consumers in different countries who may have distinct tastes or preferences.

Early critics of this analysis argued that IIT was merely a statistical artifact, representing aggregation of Heckscher-Ohlin trade. This implies that if SITC product categories were disaggregated to further levels, all resulting trade would simply reflect original products based on unique factor ratios. However, this view-point has been countered both theoretically and empirically. Most recently, Bhagwati (1994), starting from the Heckscher-Ohlin model, has considered IIT from a production position as two-way trade in commodities that are similar in factor intensity. The explanation for this new theory relies on scale economies at the firm level and imperfect competition as opposed to factor endowments or intensities. Bhagwati demonstrates that it is always possible to find endowments for which 100 percent of trade is intra-industry so that large shares of IIT may not be contradictory to the factor endowments theory. Furthermore, it can be shown that trade in differing products is in commodities with the same factor intensity and hence also non-Heckscher-Ohlin trade. As to empirical tests, Gray (1979) demonstrates that whereas calculations of more disaggregated IIT data show decreased values, the IIT phenomenon does not disappear.

Many studies after Grubel and Lloyd have found that the more advanced and developed an economy, the more specialized its trade structure will be.[2] Thus, industrialized countries tend to have greater levels of IIT than developing countries, with a rough continuum where middle-level income countries show IIT levels higher than low-income ones but below those of industrial countries. Also, successful exporters (e.g., East Asia, other Newly Industrialized Countries) exhibit a speedy and substantial increase in the levels of IIT. From this it can be inferred that higher IIT levels reflect a greater ability to compete in a changing trading environment and that large changes in IIT also reflect flexibility in adapting to competition. Thus, simplifying this interpretation, one could say that those potential signatories of a liberalizing agreement with the EU,[3] which have a relatively high or at least recently increased levels of IIT, are perhaps better positioned to be successful in adapting to a new trading environment. For those Arab countries with still low levels of IIT, the gap between their IIT levels and those of the EU is a measure of the opportunity and challenge of establishing the necessary policy background which would stimulate new investment, greater efficiency, and hence higher IIT.

IIT is a result or effect of increased specialization, not a cause thereof. The underlying determinants of a country's preparedness to compete internationally and to adapt to changing circumstances are influenced by fiscal and monetary policy, factor markets, investment, and international trade and trade restrictions such as tariffs and quotas.[4] However, significant advantages to specialization exist in the context of trade liberalization. In particular, adjustment based on specialization within the same industry may be less costly than new industrial investment and, by reducing the need for labor mobility, imposes less social costs. Moreover, increased specialization enhances competitiveness and acts as a catalyst for new innovations, technologies, and growth. These considerations are relevant for policy formulation that aims to minimize social and economic costs in the process of trade liberalization. This chapter will focus only on the IIT index as an indicator reflecting broadly the degree of competitiveness of Arab countries.

Caution is required in interpreting the IIT as an indicator of preparedness. On the one hand, a high level of IIT is broadly indicative of a greater flexibility to compete internationally and hence of better preparation for trade liberalization. On the other hand, a reverse causation could be argued: liberalization, even only vis-à-vis the EU, can stimulate investment and efficiency improvements, which in turn would be reflected in an increased IIT index. The proposition that trade liberalization generates increased IIT is posited in the literature, although it remains, in fact, unresolved. Globerman and Dean (1990) argue against this proposition by analyzing the Canada-U.S. FTA. They present results of a survey of Canadian firms which concludes that these do not plan to specialize more. Their study also indicates that there appears to be a "topping out" or even reversal of increasing IIT levels, suggesting that product specialization is not an expected outcome of the FTA between the United States and Canada. Similarly, Hamilton and Kniest (1990) examine whether a change in the level of protection has consequences for IIT levels in Australia and New Zealand. They find no support for this hypothesis. However, one must be cautious about inferences regarding these studies as they analyze the effects of liberalization or protectionism on IIT for industrialized countries, where the notion of topping out may be more applicable. Nevertheless, most studies agree that the impact of trade liberalization on IIT is inconclusive.

Summing up, the analysis that follows does not ask whether the EU Agreements will lead to increased specialization. Given that Arab countries face liberalization, a more relevant question is how well can they compete and adjust to a new environment. The objective of the analysis is therefore to assess how specialized Arab economies are relative to other countries at present, how well they might adapt in the future, what determines the level of specialization, and finally, in what products Arab countries are competitive. IIT is used as an indicator of these characteristics.

Methodology of Calculating the IIT Index

The IIT index we use stems from the original work of Grubel and Lloyd (1975). All data used for the calculation of the indices are at the 3-digit SITC level and are subsequently aggregated. In addition, and for the purpose of obtaining more meaningful results, we utilize primarily import rather than export data, as it is more reliable and complete. Furthermore, as trade data may be distorted or simply not reported for a given year, we take averages over two time periods, 1984-86 and 1992-94.

Inter-industry trade (*INTE*), i.e., trade in different products, is defined as:

$$INTE_i = | X_i - M_i | \tag{1}$$

where X_i are total exports in product category i and M_i are total imports in product category i. Thus it is clear that *IIT* is simply all trade that is not inter-industry, or:

$$IIT_i = (X_i + M_i) - | X_i - M_i | \tag{2}$$

Equivalently, we can normalize *IIT* to get a measure of the share of *IIT* for each commodity:

$$IIT_i = \frac{[(X_i + M_i) - | X_i - M_i |]}{(X_i + M_i)} \tag{3}$$

Hence if there is no *IIT*, one of X_i or M_i will be zero so that the IIT index will be zero. Similarly if all trade is intra-industry, $X_i = M_i$, and the IIT index will take a value of 1.

As we must determine an aggregated IIT index (*AIIT*) for each country and region, we follow Grubel and Lloyd by aggregating the IIT index for each commodity at the 3-digit SITC code level, using the weighted mean:

$$AIIT = \frac{\sum_{i=1}^{n}(X_i + M_i) - \sum_{i=1}^{n} | X_i - M_i |}{\sum_{i=1}^{n}(X_i + M_i)} \tag{4}$$

This aggregation measure has often been criticized as being biased downward by the degree of trade imbalance, i.e., the larger the trade imbalance, the larger the net trade, hence the smaller the IIT index. Although adjustments to IIT indices do exist, previous studies have shown that they do not clearly yield significant changes from the unadjusted index. In addition, Lee and Lee (1993) argue that no adjustment to the imbalance has conclusively been calculated, without presenting shortcomings of their own. Subsequently, we will use the unadjusted aggregation measure as presented in equation (4).

A final issue that must be kept in mind when considering IIT involves re-exports, which do not reflect increased specialization but merely flow through a country. Re-exports do not account for significant amounts of total IIT for most countries, with the exception of economies that are natural ports or routing ways such as Hong Kong and Singapore.

IIT in the Arab Region

Table 3.1 provides an indication of IIT developments for Arab countries over the last decade and in relation to comparator groups and countries. If one considers the level of IIT as indicative of the level of industrial development, the data clearly suggest that Arab countries as a group, with an IIT level ranging from below 10 percent to 41.4 percent and averaging 25 percent, do not have highly advanced industrial bases.

The Arab region compares unfavorably with other regions. For example, NAFTA registers an IIT level of 77.3 percent in 1992-94, while the APEC region has an IIT level exceeding 90 percent for the same period. IIT levels are

TABLE 3.1 IIT Indices in Manufactures: Total Trade

Country	1984-86	1992-94
Algeria	0.051	0.052
Bahrain	0.107	...
Djibouti	0.055	0.026
Egypt	0.102	0.172
Jordan	0.207	0.248
Kuwait	0.192	0.131
Morocco	0.158	0.204
Oman	0.164	0.414
Qatar	...	0.076
Saudi Arabia	0.047	0.096
Syria	0.143	0.125
Tunisia	0.238	0.301
United Arab Emirates	0.074	0.081
Arab Countries*	0.159	0.250
Comparator Countries		
Israel	0.469	0.584
Turkey	0.159	0.284
Regional Averages *		
Industrial Countries	0.876	0.878
EU	0.860	0.886
Andean Pact	0.237	0.290
APEC	0.874	0.903
Mercosur	0.428	0.519
NAFTA	0.687	0.773

* Weighted Averages.

Source: Trade Analysis and Reporting System (TARS).

considerably lower even when comparing the Arab region to one with comparable PCI levels, such as Mercosur. At the same time, Arab countries show positive signs of more rapidly increasing IIT levels over the period 1984-86 to 1992-94, relative to a less successful trade agreement such as the Andean Pact.[5] The two comparator countries, Israel and Turkey, have among the highest IIT levels for the region. With an IIT index of 58.4 percent for 1992-94, Israel is the most specialized economy in the region.

Within the Arab region, relatively high IIT indices are observed for Oman and Tunisia, followed by Egypt, Jordan, and Morocco.[6] Somewhat lower IIT indices in the region are recorded in Kuwait and Syria, whereas the rest of the Arab countries' IIT levels fall below 10 percent. Marked increases in IIT levels have occurred for Oman, the two comparator countries Israel and Turkey, and to a lesser extent Egypt, Jordan, Morocco, Saudi Arabia, and Tunisia.

Oman in particular has more than doubled its IIT; at over 40 percent, it is second only to Israel. However, this may reflect the re-export problem mentioned earlier. Oman's strategic location at the entrance of the Arabian Gulf makes it a likely candidate for re-exports to Iran, Iraq, Qatar, Saudi Arabia, and UAE. When analyzing Oman's trade data more carefully, it appears that tobacco manufactures, representing close to 7 percent of total trade, has substantially increased both on the import and on the export side. Domestic absorption, representing the difference between imports and exports, is roughly 45 percent of total imports. This indicates that over half of total imports in tobacco manufactures are re-exported. A review of other categories however shows that re-exports are not the only cause for increased IIT levels. Other commodities including metals, and textiles, and articles show increased IIT indices and at the same time increased domestic exports. Nevertheless, a portion of the large IIT increase in Oman is certainly attributable to re-exports. Saudi Arabia has also doubled its IIT, but at 9.6 percent remains amongst the least specialized. Countries for which IIT indices have actually fallen include Djibouti, Kuwait, and Syria; perhaps the drop in IIT for Kuwait is a consequence of the Gulf War. Indeed, IIT levels for Kuwait were back up to 17.3 percent in 1994.

Overall, one should expect that countries exhibit larger amounts of IIT within a unified trade or geographical area for proximity reasons. As Balassa and Bauwens (1987) explain, the cost of information for trading differentiated products is higher than for standardized products and increases with distance. This hypothesis is confirmed for the Arab region, as depicted in table 3.2. IIT levels for the Arab region as a whole for the 1992-94 period is higher for intraregional than for global trade. IIT is 21.1 percent for Arab trade with other Arab countries and is virtually the same for IIT trade with developing countries, which is 20.5 percent. IIT indices are highest for trade within the Arab region versus trade with other regions for Egypt, Qatar, UAE, and in particular Saudi Arabia, which has an intraregional IIT index of 42.6 percent. Whereas trade for these countries appears to be specialized within the Arab region, their share of Arab trade as a percentage of world trade is below 10 percent. IIT levels are lowest for trade within the Arab region relative to other regions as expected for Israel (which does less than 1 percent of total trade with the other Arab countries), Oman, and Turkey.

In contrast, it appears that only 13 percent of trade in similar products is generated between the Arab region and the EU. One can perceive this low level of IIT from two directions. On one hand, it is true that these levels are very low, especially in comparison to IIT of over 88 percent for EU trade (see table 3.2). It is also possible to argue that these low levels represent further opportunity for IIT creation, perhaps in the context of EU Association Agreements. Nevertheless, it is evident that more open economies with higher IIT levels to the EU are in a better position to exploit trade creation opportunities. These countries include Oman, Saudi Arabia, Tunisia, UAE, and two important comparator countries in the Mediterranean region, Israel and Turkey.

Seven of the thirteen countries representing the Arab region are oil-exporting economies, which influences the IIT levels in commodities other than oil. Historically, oil-rich countries have had less of an incentive to diversify their economies as they rely more on their oil-generated revenues. The simple average calculations in table 3.1 confirm somewhat, but not significantly, lower overall

TABLE 3.2 Direction of Trade: IIT Trade Indices in Manufactures 1992-94

Trade with:	World	Developing countries	European Union	EU trade (% of world trade)	Arab Countries	Arab trade (% of world trade)
Algeria	0.052	0.107	0.047	67.7	0.097	2.8
Bahrain	...	...	...	8.0	...	15.6
Djibouti	0.026	0.050	0.044	32.9	...	9.6
Egypt	0.172	0.250	0.113	41.9	0.278	4.8
Jordan	0.248	0.254	0.100	25.6	0.220	0.4
Kuwait	0.131	0.256	0.081	26.9	0.191	3.8
Morocco	0.204	0.281	0.158	57.6	0.216	8.4
Oman	0.414	0.365	0.204	12.3	0.063	15.4
Qatar	0.076	0.071	0.080	16.4	0.111	9.9
Saudi Arabia	0.096	0.138	0.205	27.5	0.426	6.6
Syria	0.125	0.212	0.056	47.5	0.203	7.7
Tunisia	0.301	0.380	0.243	75.4	0.268	4.4
UAE	0.081	0.093	0.199	18.4	0.248	6.2
Arab Countries*	0.161	0.205	0.128	35.2	0.211	8.1
Oil-exporting	0.142	0.172	0.136	25.3	0.189	8.6
Non-oil-exporting	0.179	0.238	0.119	46.8	0.237	7.5
Comparator Countries:						
Israel	0.584	0.322	0.425	43.6	0.190	0.0
Turkey	0.284	0.455	0.232	47.7	0.119	3.6

* Simple averages

Source: Trade Analysis and Reporting System (TARS).

IIT levels for oil-exporting countries than for non-oil-exporting Arab countries. IIT levels for non-oil-exporting countries are 17.9 percent in trade with the world, whereas IIT levels for oil-exporting countries are only about 4 percentage points lower. A possible explanation for the small difference between IIT levels for oil- and non-oil exporting countries is that oil-exporting countries generate derivative products and industries that in turn are quite specialized, such as chemicals. The fact that IIT levels for Oman and Saudi Arabia have risen quite dramatically suggests that these countries are increasing their trade in differentiated products, indicating that their trade is becoming more specialized. IIT levels for Algeria and UAE have not changed. The situation of Kuwait, as discussed, is somewhat in doubt, but based on the 1994 data, we can infer that the IIT level has not changed or may even have fallen somewhat. Due to lack of data we cannot make the same comparison for two other oil economies, Bahrain and Qatar.

Several Arab countries today face the prospects of trade liberalization with the EU. IIT values for Arab countries are, not surprisingly, significantly lower than those of EU countries, reflecting the fact that Arab countries are not nearly as specialized as the EU countries. In addition, IIT levels are lower in trade with the EU than within the Arab region for all countries in the region, with the exception of Israel, Oman, and Turkey. The potential gain from IIT within the region is quite high as compared to the EU, especially for Arab countries that have low IIT levels with the EU at present. The implication is that there is less flexibility in trade with the EU, and it will take a longer time to adjust to a more competitive trade environment. Arab countries with the lowest EU IIT levels include Algeria, Djibouti, and Syria, which have IIT levels between 4 and 6 percent. Other Arab countries with EU IIT levels under 15 percent include Egypt, Jordan, Kuwait, and Qatar. All of these countries, except Qatar, have a large gap between IIT levels when comparing EU trade to intraregional trade. Thus, whereas potential IIT opportunities lie within the region, their level of specialization in IIT has not attained the level of EU countries. Furthermore, IIT levels for Arab countries in trade with developing countries are also substantially higher than in trade with the EU and more closely resemble IIT indices registered intraregionally. Arab countries appear to be more able to compete in IIT intraregionally and with developing countries than with the EU. This supports the argument that trade liberalization with the EU needs to be accompanied by regional, or even more, multilateral trade liberalization.

Determinants of IIT

Since the pioneering work done by Grubel and Lloyd in the mid-1970s, an abundant amount of empirical work has been undertaken to examine the determinants of IIT. Cross-country models of IIT have long been used to explain the level of sophistication of the trade structure and the level of development of countries. Grubel and Lloyd (1975) showed that the majority of trade in industrial countries was intra-industry; with some qualification, that conclusion remains valid in more recent studies such as Globerman and Dean (1990). The notion that the degree of specialization in IIT is correlated with the stage of development has led to a substantial empirical literature. The purpose of what follows is not to add to that literature but to examine the position of Arab countries in a global comparison of IIT and to draw inferences about their ability to adjust their trade structure. As discussed previously, trade liberalization does not appear to particularly encourage increased specialization and greater trade in similar but heterogeneous products. If this is the case, what does? This is the question we aim to answer.

The approach taken is to estimate a cross-sectional model of IIT, using data on the key determinants of IIT suggested by the literature.[7] The variables used and their expected signs are shown below:[8]

$$\underset{}{IITj} = F\,[\,\underset{(+/-)}{GDPj},\ \underset{(+)}{PCIj},\ \underset{(+)}{MFTXj},\ \underset{(-)}{TIMBj},\ \underset{(+)}{TOj},\ \underset{(+)}{ARAB1j},\ \underset{(+)}{EUj},\ \underset{(+)}{LAFTAj}\,] \qquad (5)$$

(i) The effect of gross domestic product, *GDP*, or the size of the economy on *IIT* is somewhat unclear from a theoretical point of view. Scale effects would likely increase the amount of IIT. However, smaller countries that are in closer geographic proximity can be expected to do more IIT than larger ones, as trade between them can be viewed as a continuation of internal trade.

(ii) The effect of the stage of development as measured by per capita income *(PCI)* is expected to be positive, reflecting enhanced demand for differentiated products.

(iii) The variable *MFTX* represents export concentration of manufactures, and is a proxy for the level of industrial development. It is simply the share of manufactures in exports, an indicator of the degree of product diversification. A higher concentration of manufactures in exports implies higher diversity, hence higher IIT. As noted previously, more industrialized countries tend to have higher ratios of IIT, assuming they have not reached the threshold level.[9] However, as Arab countries are developing, the expected sign of *MFTX* is positive.

(iv) As discussed earlier, measures of IIT may be biased by the degree to which total trade is unbalanced. Following Lee and Lee (1993), we control for the trade imbalance, *TIMB*, which is defined as:

$$TIMB_j = | X_j - M_j | / (X_j + M_j) \qquad (6)$$

where Xj is defined as total exports of country *j*, and Mj is defined as total imports of country *j*. Thus, the variable represents net trade as a share of total trade. It takes a value of zero when there is no imbalance and a value of one if there are either no exports or imports to a country (i.e., complete imbalance).

(v) The level of IIT may be affected by trade barriers. However, as tariff level data are both difficult to obtain and change frequently, we employ a proxy measure of the degree of openness, trade orientation (TO), similar to what was proposed by Balassa and Bauwens (1988). The trade orientation variable is constructed by estimating the following equation:

$$\log(X_j/P_j) = \beta_0 + \beta_1 \log(Y_j/P_j) + \beta_2 \log(P_j) + \beta_3 (X\,SUB_j^m / Y_j) + \varepsilon_j \quad (7)$$

where X_j represents exports of country j, Y_j is GDP, P_j is population, X^m_j represents mineral resources availability or exports of mineral resources, and ε_j is the residual term. We estimate the equation to determine a hypothetical value of per capita exports. The trade orientation variable is then determined as the difference between actual and hypothetical values of per capita exports. If the trade orientation variable is positive (negative), this suggests a low (high) level of restrictiveness. Thus, TO and IIT are expected to be positively correlated.

The results of the estimation of the trade orientation variable for a sample of 78 countries are reported in box 3.1. All variables have the expected sign, the overall fit is significant at the 1-percent level, and, with the exception of the mineral resource variable, all coefficient estimates are statistically significant. The results of the deviations of actual from hypothetical values are as expected: very open economies such as Hong Kong and Singapore have the highest positive deviations and more restrictive economies such as Argentina have the highest negative deviations. Among the Arab countries, this trend can also be observed, in that large negative deviations of actual from hypothesized values are observed for economies with high average tariff rates (e.g., Algeria, Morocco, Oman, and Syria). Syria has the highest negative deviation, at -3.14 standard deviations, and Saudi Arabia has the highest positive deviation at 0.77 standard deviations. Regional countries with low trade barriers, such as Israel and UAE, have positive trade orientation estimates.

(vi) Three dummy variables are included for regional agreements: ARAB1, EU, and LAFTA. These dummies take on a value of one if countries belong to the Arab League, the EU, or LAFTA, and zero otherwise. It is hypothesized that regional integration schemes such as the EU and LAFTA should be positively

Box 3.1 Regression for Trade Orientation Derivation

$$\log(X_j/P_j) = -0.507452 + 1.0432 \log(Y_j/P_j) - 0.176216 \log(P_j) + 0.394778 \log(X^m_j/Y_j)$$
$$(3.074) \qquad (25.136) \qquad (5.064) \qquad (1.592)$$

$R^2 = 0.90864$ $\quad F(3,74) = 245.32$ [0.0000]

RSS = 3.41112 for 4 variables and 78 observations

Note: t-statistics in parentheses

correlated with IIT reflecting increased possibilities of intraregional IIT. Similarly, the use of a common language and similarity in culture in the Arab region is hypothesized to be positively correlated with the level of IIT.

Model Methodology

Most previous analyses of IIT determinants use ordinary least squares estimation techniques. This has the problem that predicted values may fall outside the range of the dependent variable, which varies between 0 and 1. To address this issue we use logit techniques and follow Balassa and Bauwens (1988) in transforming the dependent variable:

$$\ln\left[\frac{IIT}{(1 - IIT)}\right] = \beta' Z + \omega \tag{8}$$

where β is the coefficient vector, Z is the vector of explanatory variables, and ω is the disturbance term. The transformation allows all theoretical values to be assumed, but it is not defined for critical values of zero (complete interindustry trade), or one (all trade is intra-industry). While IIT values of one do not arise in practice, it is possible for IIT to equal zero. To account for this we redefine IIT and estimate the equation as follows:

$$IIT = \frac{e^{\beta' Z}}{(1 + e^{\beta' Z})} + \xi \tag{9}$$

Tests for homoscedasticity could not be rejected at the 5 percent level of confidence, so that we proceeded with a nonlinear least squares estimation. The results of the cross-sectional regression (model 1) are reported in box 3.2. All variables except for the LAFTA and ARAB1 dummies have the anticipated sign. Overall explanatory power is quite high at 70 percent,[10] and the overall fit is significant at the 1-percent level. The t-statistics indicate that all the variables are significant at least at the 2.5-percent level, with the exception of the trade imbalance and LAFTA coefficients. To test for exclusion of these two variables, we make use of the Wald test and determine that the hypothesis that the null of these coefficients being equal to zero cannot be rejected with a 77 percent confidence level. We therefore proceed to reduce the model.

The revised model (model 2) which excludes the trade imbalance and LAFTA variables has similar coefficient estimates. The F-statistic for overall fit is well above the 1-percent confidence level, and all coefficients are statistically significant. The hypotheses put forth in previous studies regarding determinants of IIT are confirmed. The positive coefficient on GDP indicates that scale effects may dominate proximity effects. Furthermore, the significance level of this variable implies strong effects of GDP on the level of IIT.

The PCI variable has the expected positive contribution. A scatter plot of IIT ratios against the log of PCI reveals that, with the exception of Oman and Tunisia, all Arab countries lie below the expected levels of IIT.[11] On average, the two regional comparator countries, Israel and Turkey, have significantly higher IIT levels than Arab countries. Whereas Turkey lies only slightly below the expected levels, Israel significantly "outperforms" all countries in the region. Arab countries are clearly not as IIT intensive as Asian or industrialized countries, and are more similar to the Western Hemisphere distribution. Only Israel and Oman have high IIT levels. IIT levels for Egypt, Jordan, Morocco, and Turkey appear fairly close to what be expected given their PCI levels, whereas the remaining countries have IIT levels well below the norm. Overall, given their PCI, Arab countries fall below their expected level of IIT.

The results indicated in the scatter diagram are mostly confirmed when IIT levels are normalized by regression analysis. Table 3.3 gives an indication of deviations of actual from predicted IIT levels for Arab and comparator countries. It appears that IIT levels for Syria and Kuwait are perhaps not as low (relative to the mean) as the scatter plot suggests, whereas Turkey falls lower than what is implied by plotting per capita GDP against IIT. More important, however, is that the results corroborate the findings that, with the exception of Oman and Tunisia, all Arab countries' IIT regressions fall well below the predicted level.

Box 3.2 IIT Regressions

Model 1

$$IIT_j = -2.9246 + 0.3638 \log(GDP_j) + 0.3275 \log(PCI_j) + 0.9179\,(MFTX) - 0.9802\,(TIMB)$$
(4.74) (3.47) (2.046) (2.334) (0.706)

$$+\ 1.0567\,(TO) - 0.8577\,(ARAB1) + 0.4905\,(EU) - 0.0194\,(LAFTA)$$
(2.494) (2.446) (2.313) (0.081)

$R^2 = 0.70295$ $F(8,69) = 20.411$ [0.0000]

RSS = 1.18771 for 9 variables and 78 observations

Model 2 (reduced model)

$$IIT_j = -3.129 + 0.3714 \log(GDP_j) + 0.3529 \log(PCI_j) + 0.9564\,(MFTX) + 1.1615\,(TO)$$
(5.82) (3.579) (2.279) (2.464) (3.107)

$$-\ 0.8609\,(ARAB1) + 0.4634\,(EU)$$
(2.465) (2.272)

$R^2 = 0.70067$ $F(8,69) = 27.699$ [0.0000]

RSS = 1.19685 for 9 variables and 78 observations

The values below the coefficients are the t-statistics.

The manufactures export concentration coefficient estimate is slightly below unity, indicating that the more industrial a country, the more trade is specialized. As expected, the trade orientation variable is positive and highly significant, suggesting that the lower the degree of restrictiveness, the more IIT occurs. The regional dummies take on opposite signs. The EU coefficient is positive, as expected, confirming common country characteristics effects. However, the Arab

FIGURE 3.1 Summary Regression Plots for Selected Arab and Sample Countries 1994

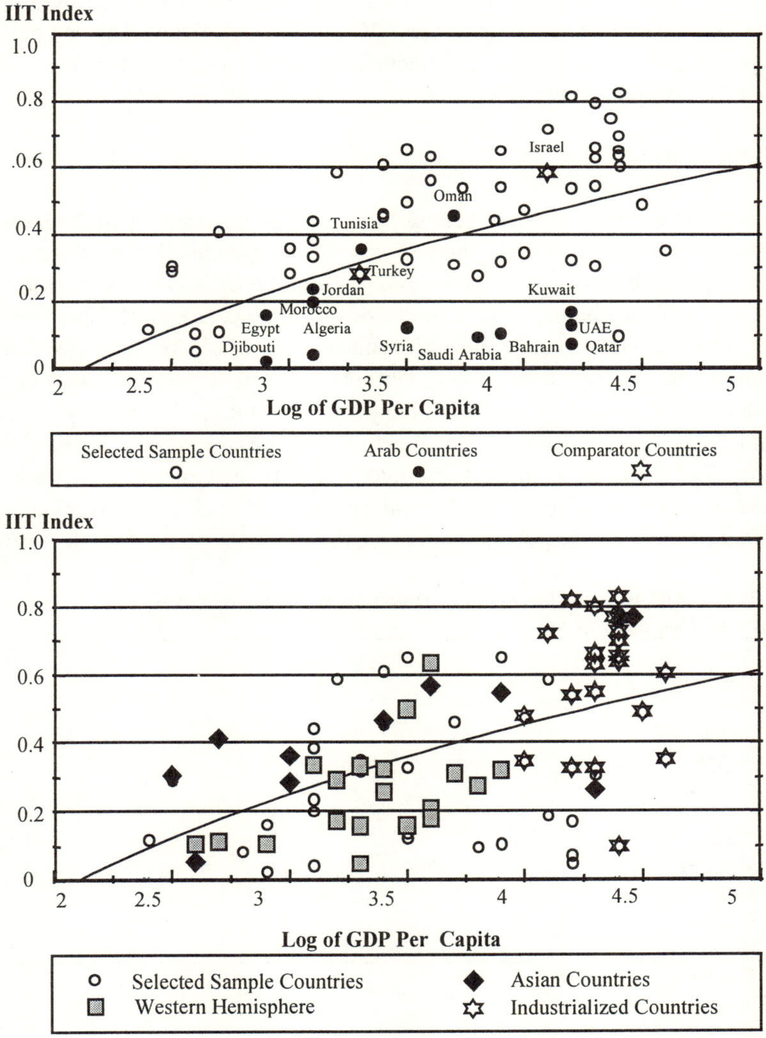

coefficient is negative and significant, possibly reflecting the economic separation among the countries in the region. Indeed, trade amongst Arab countries represents only 8 percent of their total world trade.[12]

To some extent the model identifies characteristics of economies that enhance the degree of their trade specialization. A number of inferences can be drawn for the stage of a country's development and its capacity to adapt to a more competitive economic environment. Among the explanatory variables, the largest effects on IIT are attributable to the degree of industrial development (as measured by the share of manufactures in exports variable) and the degree of nonrestrictiveness (as measured by the trade orientation variable). It is interesting to note that, relative to previous studies, *PCI*, is less significant. This is perhaps attributable to the fact that the manufactures exports variable and *PCI* are both proxies for the level of development.

Products in IIT

Early work in the 1970s undertaken by Lloyd and Grubel found that the highest degree of IIT for industrialized countries was observed in chemical products. This also emerges in the analysis of Arab countries and the EU as shown in table 3.4, where IIT levels in chemicals are respectively 45.7 percent and 91.6 percent for the period 1992-94. Even though Arab countries as a whole have increased their IIT levels for all categories during 1992-94 relative to 1984-85, it remains apparent that their IIT levels fall well below those of the EU, especially in basic manufactures (SITC category 6) and machinery and transport equipment (SITC category 7). Trade in chemicals averaged only 18 percent of total trade in manufactures for the period 1992-94, but that trade, as well as in miscellaneous manufactures (SITC category 8), has a greater tendency to be trade in similar

TABLE 3.3 IIT Regression Fit: Deviations from Predicted Levels (in standard deviations)

Algeria	-1.5
Djibouti	-1.2
Egypt	-1.1
Jordan	-1.3
Kuwait	-0.5
Morocco	-0.5
Oman	1.9
Qatar	-1.2
Saudi Arabia	-1.5
Syria	-0.6
Tunisia	0.0
United Arab Emirates	-2.8
Comparator countries:	
Israel	0.5
Turkey	-1.5

products. This suggests that the degree of specialization in these categories is more advanced or that these industries are relatively more developed and present potential gains for increased trade. Although it is equally possible that there is more room for specialization in other categories, indices in machinery and transportation equipment lag far behind those in the EU. Clearly, the Arab region overall has not yet reached a high degree of sophistication in this category of products.

Notwithstanding the overall lower IIT indices, it is encouraging to view the increase that has occurred in IIT in all product categories. While the Globerman and Dean's (1990) evidence of slowing IIT in most product categories for North America and Australasia is confirmed for the EU, this is clearly not the case for Arab countries. The EU, having already extremely high IIT indices, appears to be reaching a saturation point in most categories. The Arab region, on the other hand, not having attained the same stage of development, shows impressive increases in IIT indices across all product categories.

Table 3.5 presents more disaggregated IIT indices for Arab countries for commodities that reflect a high degree of specialization and those products that show large increases in IIT. The overall simple average IIT level for the products in table 3.5 increased from 24.9 percent in 1984-86 to 49.6 percent in 1992-94. This represents almost a doubling of IIT levels for the Arab region in this specialized group of products and confirms the potential for competitiveness in these commodities. Higher levels of IIT are again observed in chemicals, particularly organic chemicals. Although basic manufactures and machinery and transportation equipment are least specialized in general, this is clearly not true for all products within these respective categories. Levels of IIT in metals such as aluminum and lead, as well as in leather manufactures, are also relatively high.

More importantly, significant increases have occurred in IIT levels for many basic manufactures such as crafts and textiles as well as for several machinery products, which as a group have the lowest IIT levels for the Arab region. Many products in these two SITC categories have evolved quite dramatically from IIT levels below 10 percent. These products include glassware, iron and steel shapes, railway rails, iron and steel castings, electrical distributing machines, and

TABLE 3.4 Intra-Industry Trade by Product Group

		Arab Countries		EU	
SITC code	Product Group	Average	Average	Average	Average
		1984-86	1992-94	1984-86	1992-94
5	Chemicals	0.311	0.457	0.890	0.916
6	Basic Manufactures	0.161	0.266	0.865	0.891
7	Machinery and transport. equipment	0.049	0.103	0.846	0.879
8	Miscellaneous manufactured goods	0.200	0.437	0.883	0.878

Source: TARS.

electrical machinery. From almost nonexistent IIT in these commodities in the mid-1980s, increased industry specialization led to substantial IIT levels in less than a decade. The high levels of IIT in so many 3-digit SITC products suggests that the degree of specialization attained enables Arab countries to be competitive in a world market setting.

Conclusion

The Arab region overall does not have a highly advanced industrial base. IIT levels for Arab countries are lower than those registered in other regions such as NAFTA, APEC, or Mercosur. However, the Arab region does show positive signs of rapidly increasing IIT levels over the last decade. IIT levels for oil-exporting

TABLE 3.5 Arab Countries: Intra-Industry Trade Indices in Manufactures for Selected Commodities

	Average (1984-86)	Average (1992-94)
512 Organic chemicals	0.744	0.964
513 Inorganic elements, oxides, etc	0.670	0.636
521 Coal, petroleum, etc	0.076	0.444
554 Soaps, cleaning, etc	0.277	0.699
571 Explosives	0.062	0.416
581 Plastic materials, etc	0.117	0.639
611 Leather	0.128	0.632
612 Leather, etc, manufactures	0.853	0.795
642 Articles of paper, etc	0.146	0.447
656 Textile products, etc	0.119	0.435
657 Floor covering, tapestry, etc	0.247	0.407
661 Cement etc, building products	0.115	0.373
665 Glassware	0.027	0.287
666 Pottery	0.064	0.263
673 Iron and steel shapes	0.040	0.397
676 Railway rails, etc, iron, steel	0.001	0.239
677 Iron, steel, wire excluding wire rod	0.103	0.454
679 Iron, steel castings	0.005	0.168
684 Aluminum	0.759	0.846
685 Lead	0.954	0.856
722 Electrical power machines, switches	0.033	0.115
723 Electrical distributing machines	0.058	0.525
729 Electrical machinery	0.028	0.163
735 Ships and boats	0.163	0.488
831 Travel goods, handbags	0.132	0.338
841 Clothing not of fur	0.577	0.841
851 Footwear	0.215	0.527
Simple Average	0.249	0.496

countries are only marginally lower than those of non-oil-exporting countries. This may be because although oil-exporting countries have less incentive to diversify their economies, these countries generate derivative products and industries like chemicals, which tend to have high levels of IIT.

In addition to having low overall IIT levels in their global trade, Arab countries also have lower IIT levels in trade with the EU as compared to intra-regional trade or in trade with other developing countries. No Arab country has higher IIT levels in trade with the EU than with other Arab countries or other developing countries. This suggests that Arab countries have more similar levels of industry specialization and that they compete more effectively in the intra-regional or multilateral setting than specifically with the EU. Those countries that have relatively high levels of IIT with the EU and can be expected to be better able to compete effectively with EU firms include Oman, Saudi Arabia, Tunisia, UAE, and the two regional comparator countries, Israel and Turkey. Nevertheless, the simple average of this more specialized group is still only 25 percent, well below IIT levels of over 85 percent recorded by EU countries. That even the more specialized countries have IIT levels that fall well below those registered in the EU indicates that adjusting to a more competitive environment will take time. That Arab countries' IIT levels are higher for trade within the Arab region and with developing countries than with the EU suggests that bilateral trade agreements between Arab countries and the EU should be accompanied by regional and multilateral liberalization.

The cross-country econometric analysis of IIT determinants reveals that IIT levels for the Arab region are significantly lower than one might expect given their level of PCI. Our coefficient estimates for trade orientation and exports of manufactures are larger than obtained in previous studies. Overall, the results imply that if Arab countries take measures to increase liberalization and diversify their industrial production, IIT levels would be much higher. If Arab countries can specialize in existing industries through greater IIT, significant economic gains might be expected while at the same time adjustment costs are minimized.

The results also reveal that the most advanced degree of specialization and potential for effective competition lies in chemicals. However, specific commodities in the other manufacturing categories have reached equally high levels of specialization, comparable to that of EU countries. These products include a variety of items in basic manufactures, leather articles, and metals. Furthermore, significant increases have occurred in IIT levels for many basic manufactures and machinery products. These findings suggest that Arab countries can compete effectively in such types of commodities.

Finally, what are the broader implications for global integration of Arab economies? Arab countries' efforts to liberalize depend upon numerous macroeconomic, social, and political factors. The benefits from opening economies and pursuing outward-oriented development strategies depend on their ability to compete in a new environment. The agreements with the EU are unique and unprecedented in that two distinct regions with very different economic structures are to enter in a free trade zone. The willingness to do so rests upon the premise that both sides are to gain from this arrangement. Studies conducted by Nsouli, Bisat, and Kanaan (1996) and Havrylyshyn (1997) suggest that some countries are more ready than others, but the consensus appears to be that potential gains are significant. Both increased specialization and IIT can reduce adjustment costs as well as increase potential competitiveness in trade. The analysis undertaken in this chapter indicates that increased specialization has been achieved over the last decade in Arab countries, but that a considerable potential remains to be exploited. With the appropriate mix of market-oriented and open economy policies, this potential could be fulfilled through increased specialization and higher IIT levels. This conclusion holds both for those countries that are or will be engaged in the EU Mediterranean initiative and for those that pursue global integration outside this initiative.

Notes

The authors wish to thank the Middle Eastern Department of the International Monetary Fund for making possible the preparation of this paper. We are grateful to Mohamed El-Erian, Klaus Enders, Nuri Erbas, Adnan Mazarei, Thomas Helbling, and Volker Treichel for their comments, and to Isabelle Tavernier for providing the trade data.

1. In this chapter, we look only at a subset of thirteen countries for which data was available to conduct the research. These countries include Algeria, Bahrain, Djibouti, Egypt, Jordan, Kuwait, Morocco, Oman, Qatar, Saudi Arabia, Syria, Tunisia, and UAE. In addition, we will frequently use two other regional countries for comparison, Israel and Turkey, which are committed to trade liberalization with the EU.
2. See Havrylyshyn and Civan (1983), Balassa and Bauwens (1988), and Stone and Lee (1995).
3. EU Agreements have already been signed with Morocco and Tunisia. Other potential signatories are principally Southern Mediterranean countries, including Egypt, Jordan, and Lebanon. We have extended the country scope to include other Arab countries, as we regard this study in a more global context of trade liberalization. Both Israel and Turkey have concluded Association Agreements as well.
4. These issues are discussed more broadly for the region in the aforementioned papers of Nsouli, Bisat, and Kanaan (1996), and Havrylyshyn (1997b).
5. Successful trade arrangements denote those that are trade creating rather than trade diverting.
6. Morocco's IIT levels may be somewhat understated, as the TARS data that is used does not include trade under the "admission temporaire" regime. Therefore some manufactured goods—particularly textiles—which are traded directly to and from the EU are not recorded. Since these traded manufactures represent specialized trade, it is likely that the absence of this data yields IIT levels that are lower than actual IIT levels for Morocco. Calculations of IIT for Morocco utilizing EU trade data show that IIT levels for trade with

the EU are 18.7 percent, above the IIT level of 15.8 percent obtained using Moroccan import data. Given that EU trade represents 57.6 percent of total trade, it is possible to estimate that IIT for Morocco with the world is 22.1 percent using EU trade data. This differs only slightly from the 20.4 percent IIT level obtained using Moroccan import data.

7. See Havrylyshyn and Civan (1983), Balassa and Bauwens (1988), Stone and Lee (1995).

8. Seventy-eight countries are used in all regression analysis (see endnote 11). The source of the data is TARS and IMF, *World Economic Outlook.*

9. Globerman and Dean (1990) argue that product specialization can "top out" or even reverse after a certain level of industrialization has been achieved. However, as noted in Havrylyshyn and Civan (1983), the definition of IIT constrains it to the range 0-1.0. Hence, if the level of development is a key determinant, it is likely there will be a flattening of the curve at the high end and before 1.0 is reached. Whereas the upper constraint of unity provides a basis for IIT to "top out," reversion of IIT is less straightforward to explain. A possible interpretation of reversion is that highly sophisticated countries reach a stage of development when the service sector takes on a larger share of the economy, thereby reducing manufacturing activity, and hence IIT.

10. The R^2 value of 0.70 is high especially for cross-sectional data. In relation to previous studies, the degree of explanatory power of this model falls in the high range. In comparison, Balassa and Bauwens (1987) and Lee and Lee (1993) find R^2 values of 0.57 and 0.43 respectively, whereas Havrylyshyn and Civan (1983) and Globerman and Dean (1990) find R^2 values ranging from the 0.73 to 0.82. The reason for the high R^2 may be attributed to the large and diversified sample that includes countries from the highest to the lowest stage of development.

11. Western countries included in the bottom panel of the scatter diagram include Argentina, Barbados, Bolivia, Brazil, Chile, Columbia, Costa Rica, Ecuador, El Salvador, Guatemala, Honduras, Mexico, Nicaragua, Panama, Paraguay, Peru, Trinidad, and Tobago. The industrialized countries include Australia, Austria, Belgium, Canada, Denmark, Finland, France, Germany, Greece, Iceland, Ireland, Italy, Japan, the Netherlands, New Zealand, Norway, Portugal, Spain, Switzerland, Sweden, the United Kingdom, and the United States. The Asian countries include People's Republic of China, Hong Kong, India, Indonesia, the Republic of Korea, Malaysia, Pakistan, the Philippines, Singapore, and Thailand.

12. See El-Erian et al. (1995).

PART TWO

Quantifying the Gains from Liberalization

CHAPTER 4

Assessing the Implications for Lebanon of Free Trade with the European Union

Will Martin

A key component of the proposed EMA between Lebanon and the EU is liberalization of their bilateral trade. This liberalization parallels the proposals for liberalization between the EU and other Mediterranean countries (Hoekman and Djankov 1996b). Completion of all of these agreements would lead to a "hub and spoke" system of FTAs between the EU and its Mediterranean partners, a pattern that is likely to both reduce the gains relative to a free trade area involving all of the Mediterranean countries and to give a larger share of these diminished gains to the EU hub (Wonnacott 1996). The proposed agreement provides for—and the EU explicitly encourages—the negotiation of complementary FTAs around the Mediterranean rim, a process that could lead to the construction of a free trade area extending from the Baltics to the Mediterranean rim.

While unilateral trade liberalization by a small country is unambiguously beneficial in the long run, it is not necessarily the case that discriminatory liberalization of the type proposed will be beneficial for either or both of the partners. Whether such liberalization will be beneficial to a small country like Lebanon depends heavily upon a number of factors such as the protection rates applied by Lebanon and its trading partners, the pattern of trade, and the structure of production and consumption.

This chapter will examine the factors that influence whether Lebanon will gain from the proposed preferential trade liberalization, make a preliminary assessment of the potential gains or losses, and consider some policy alter-natives in the implementation of such an agreement. This task is complicated by the special features of Lebanon's reconstruction economy, particularly the massive imbalance between imports and exports currently being financed by financial flows from abroad. Since this imbalance may have affected the pattern of trade, we examine evidence on trade patterns and balances from the pre-civil war period to provide a crosscheck on the reliability of the most recent data.

The chapter begins with a review of the economic issues involved in assessing a preferential agreement and an examination of the direction and composition of Lebanon's trade flows. This is followed by an a description of the pattern of protection applied by Lebanon, and an assessment of the incentives it creates for distorting industrial output, and the implications of these distortions for adjustment costs following liberalization. The final part of the chapter considers the consequences of different forms of trade liberalization for the Lebanese economy using a simple, illustrative general equilibrium model of the Lebanese economy. The details of the model that is used are reported in the appendix to this chapter. The approach used is quite general and can be used for any small developing economy for which there are only limited data available.

Economic Impacts of FTAs

This section outlines the framework used to evaluate the proposed FTA between Lebanon and the EU. To do this, the effects of changes in the rates of protection that Lebanon levies on its imports must first be considered. Then, we consider the implications of changes in the protection imposed by Lebanon's trading partners.

We follow Armington in assuming that Lebanese consumers distinguish between imported and domestic goods and between imports by country of origin (Armington 1969). For simplicity, and because of Lebanon's small size in world markets, it is assumed to be a price taker in the markets for its imports and exports. This specification considerably simplifies the analysis of the trade diversion and trade creation that are central to the evaluation of discriminatory trade liberalization. A very simple diagrammatic approach is used in this section; however, this approach can be shown to provide a second order approximation to a rigorous estimate derived from the balance of trade function approach (Martin 1996).

The market for goods imported by Lebanon from the EU is illustrated in figure 4.1. In this market, the elimination of tariff barriers creates additional trade and contributes positively to welfare. In the diagram, the elimination of the tariff reduces the price within Lebanon of goods from the EU from p_d to p_w. This reduces tariff revenues by $p_d abp_w$. However, the gains to consumers are greater than this loss because they are able to increase the quantity of European goods that they purchase. Following the decline in the domestic price, consumers move down the (compensated) demand curve for European goods, D_{EU}, from initial quantity Q_0 to final quantity Q_1. The gain to consumers is given by area $p_d acp_w$. The net gain to Lebanon in this market is the gain to consumers less the loss of tariff revenue and is represented in the figure by the area *abc*. This gain might be viewed as resulting from trade creation.

If there were no other distortions, the welfare impacts of liberalizing imports from the EU could be analyzed solely in that market. However, since formation of a FTA liberalizes imports only from partner suppliers, there are likely to be continuing distortions against imports from other suppliers. Thus, what happens in the market for imports from non-partner countries must be considered. The impact on other markets could be described as trade diversion and will generally lead to welfare losses when trade barriers are lowered to zero.[1] These welfare impacts of this trade diversion are represented in very simple, diagrammatic terms in figure 4.2. The initial demand for imports from non-EU countries is shown by the curve D_0. Following the fall in the price of imports from the EU, the demand for imports from partner countries (generally assumed to be substitutes) falls to D_0'. The welfare loss to Lebanon is the loss in tariff revenues, shown by the area *abcd* in figure 4.2. This loss arises because of the difference between the marginal value of the good in Lebanon, given by p_d, and the cost of that good to Lebanon, p_w, times the change in the quantity imported.

This consideration of the import markets helps to identify a number of the factors relevant to the welfare impact of a FTA. Clearly, the higher the price reduction associated with cutting protection and the more responsive the demand to the reduction in protection, the larger the gains from trade creation.

FIGURE 4.1 The Market for Goods Imported from the EU

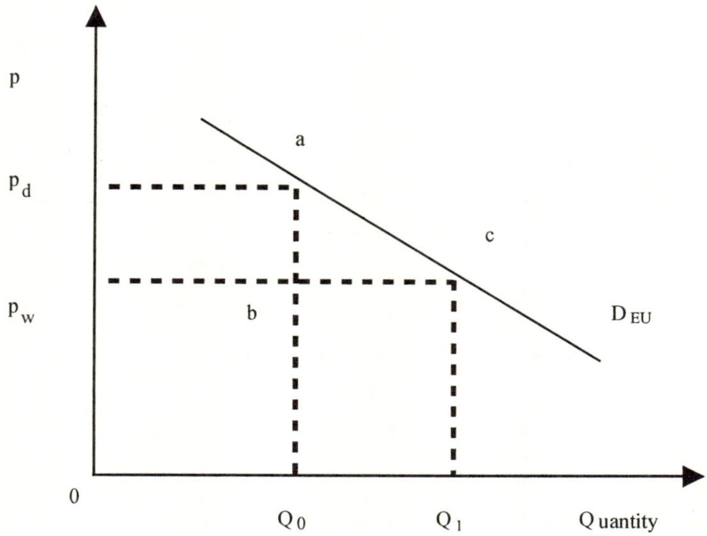

The price responsiveness of import demand will be higher based on the levels of the substitutability between domestic and imported goods, the substitution between imports from different sources, and the initial trade volume (if the size of increase in trade is proportional to the initial trade volume). Trade diversion costs are likely to be greater the higher the tariffs applied in the non-partner markets and the greater the reduction in the quantity of imports from these markets. Two comparisons that are likely to be instructive are the relative heights of trade barriers against the partner and the rest of the world (ROW) and the substitutability of imports relative to domestic goods (that determines net trade creation) versus the substitutability between imports from different sources (that determines trade diversion).

On the export side, countries entering FTAs typically benefit from the improved market access provided by reductions in their partners' trade barriers. Since we treat Lebanon as a small country in its export markets, this benefit takes a very simple form. The price received by Lebanon rises from the price within the partner country less the tariff to the full domestic price within the partner country. The benefits to Lebanon arise from both the improvement in the price it receives for its existing exports to the partner country and from its ability to respond by increasing supplies to that country.

The export market faced by Lebanon in its partner is represented diagrammatically in figure 4.3. The supply of exports from Lebanon to its partner is shown by the supply curve, S_X. Prior to the formation of the FTA, the price received by Lebanon was the price in the partner country, *pf,* less the

FIGURE 4.2 The Market for Goods Imported from Non-EU Suppliers

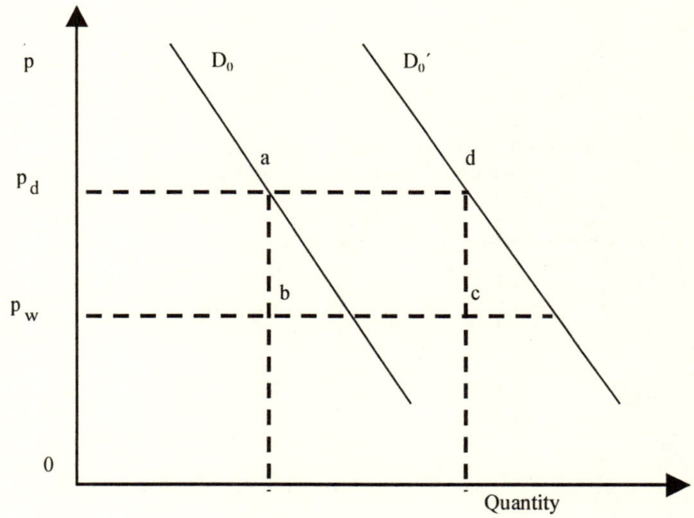

tariff applied by the partner country *t,* so the net price was $(p_f - t)$. This price is equal to the world price p_W of the good since the domestic price is assumed equal to the world price plus the tariff. With the agreement, the price received by Lebanon is p_f. The benefit to Lebanon is given by the increase in the price, *t,* times the initial quantity of exports, Q_0, plus the gains resulting from Lebanon's ability to increase its export supply to this market, shown by area *abc* in figure 4.3. In the figure, the total gains to Lebanon are represented by tQ_0 + *abc*. As long as Lebanon imposes no other distortions in its export markets, this terms of trade gain is a net gain to Lebanon. In contrast with the case of trade creation on the import side, no offsetting loss must be considered.

The specification of the gains to Lebanon from increased access to its partner markets assumes that the partner's external trade barriers remain the same and that the additional exports supplied by Lebanon and any other countries given preferential access to this market are not sufficient to reduce the price in the partner market below $p_W + t$. If sufficiently large suppliers obtain access to this market, this price will fall, reducing the gains to Lebanon.

Clearly, this analysis of the export side suggests that what happens to trade barriers in Lebanon's trading partners should be an important part of the evaluation of the proposed FTA. The gains are clearly positively related both to the size of the initial barriers imposed against Lebanon, the price responsiveness of Lebanon's exports, and possibly also to the magnitude of the initial trade flows between partners. Thus, each of these factors should be taken into account in the assessment.

FIGURE 4.3 The Market for Exports from Lebanon to the Partner Country

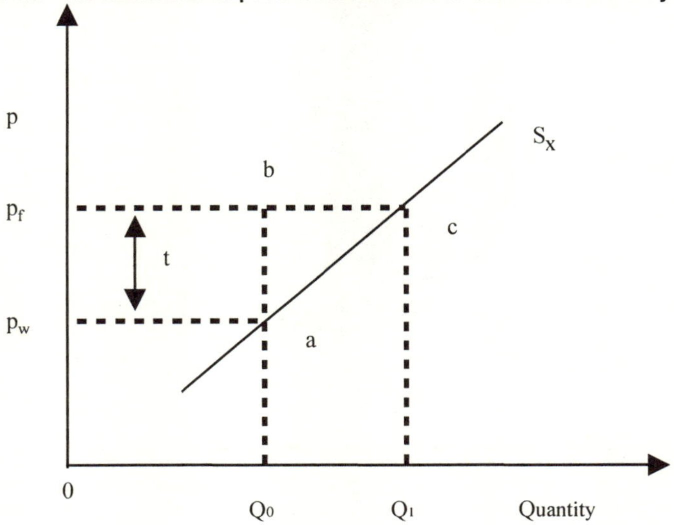

The Direction of Lebanon's Trade

In this section, we use data on merchandise trade for the first half of 1996 obtained from Lebanon's Customs Statistics to obtain an indication of the importance of trade with the EU and with its other trading partners. Both import and export trade flows are considered, and particular attention is given to the trade flows with the EU and with other potential free-trade partners in the region.

Imports

On the import side, figure 4.4 shows the importance of various regions as sources of Lebanon's imports. While the data on which these shares are based are extremely detailed and appear to be very comprehensive, there is some possibility that the current trade flows reflect either seasonal factors or the particular pattern of trade during reconstruction. However, these shares appear to be broadly consistent with data for 1974, the last year before the civil war, shown in figure 4.5, and so it seems unlikely that the biases involved in using

FIGURE 4.4 Lebanon: Sources of Imports 1996

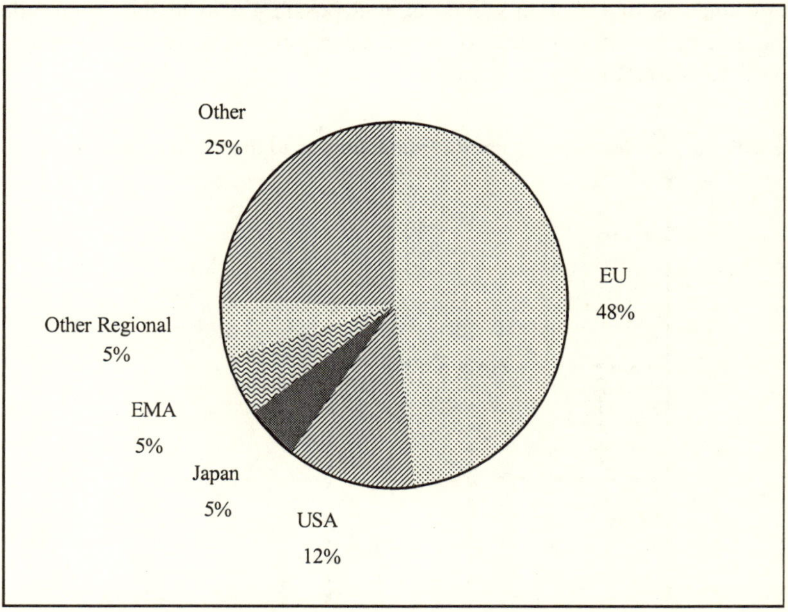

Note: The EMA countries are Algeria, Egypt, Israel, Jordan, Lebanon, Morocco, Syria, and Tunisia (Nsouli, Bisat, and Kanaan 1996). The Other Regional trading partners are Bahrain, Cyprus, Kuwait, Saudi Arabia, Turkey, UAE, and Romania.
Source: Lebanese Customs data for January-June 1996.

current data are particularly large. However, comparison of figures 4.4 and 4.5 does highlight the relatively rapid growth of countries other than the EU, the United States, Japan, and the Middle East as sources of imports—the share of the ROW rose from 16 to 25 percent over the period from 1974 to 1996.

The share of Lebanon's imports obtained from the EU is quite high and has declined only slightly since the prewar period. Europe's share of imports is slightly above the shares reported for two other countries evaluating or entering into FTAs with the EU—45 percent for Egypt (Konan and Maskus 1997a) and 44 percent for Turkey (Harrison, Rutherford, and Tarr 1997). Importantly, however, the share is not nearly as high as in some of the other countries covered by the EU's Mediterranean Strategy. In Tunisia, for example, close to 70 percent of imports are sourced from the EU (Jbili and Enders 1996), while roughly 65 percent of Morocco's imports come from the EU (Winters 1996a).

Since the EU encourages the formation of preferential trading arrangements between countries entering into EMAs and since it is likely to be in Lebanon's interests to avoid the "hub and spoke" problem associated with introducing free trade with Europe alone, consideration must be given to the consequences of establishing FTAs around the rim of the Euro-Mediterranean area. The trade shares of the other EMA countries are therefore of particular

FIGURE 4.5 Lebanon: Sources of Imports 1974

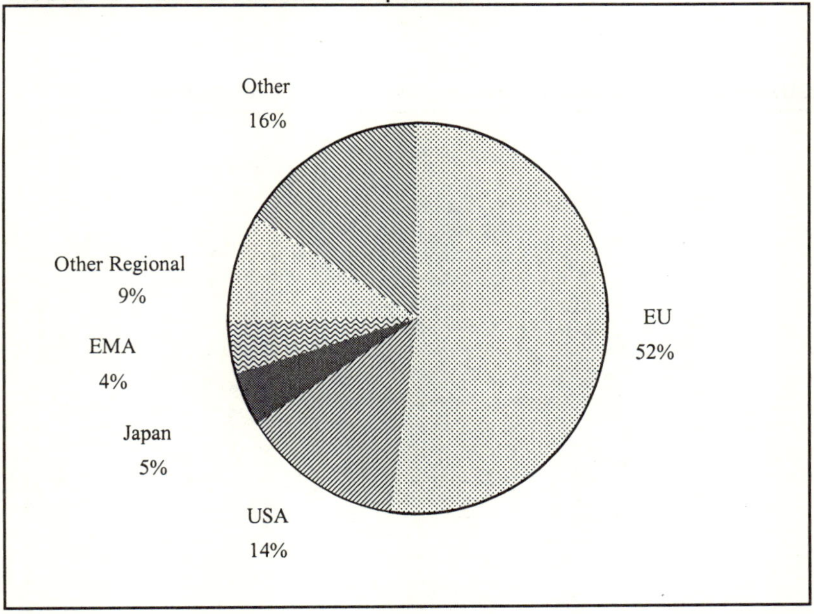

Source: UN COMTRADE statistics.

interest. With only a 5 percent share, these countries are relatively small suppliers of Lebanon's imports. Other important regional suppliers accounted for a further 5 percent.

Exports

Because of Lebanon's heavy reliance on financial flows from abroad to augment domestic savings during the reconstruction of its economy, recorded imports of goods and services are very large relative to GDP (estimated at $13.405 billion in 1996) and greatly exceed exports. The World Bank projects imports of goods and nonfactor services of $8.587 billion in 1996 and exports to be $1.334 billion, or just over 15 percent of the value of imports. The direction of these exports is shown for major destinations in figure 4.6.

Clearly, the direction of Lebanon's merchandise exports is considerably different from that of its imports. The EU accounts for only 17 percent of total Lebanese exports, compared to 48 percent of its imports. This share is much lower than in some of the other EMA countries, such as Egypt, which directs 45 percent of its exports to the EU (Konan and Maksus 1997a), or Tunisia, which sends 80 percent of its exports to the EU (Jbili and Enders 1996). The United States and Japan are also much less important than on the import side, with 3 percent and 1 percent respectively of Lebanon's exports. In contrast, the EMA countries and other countries in the region, with 17 and 37 percent of

FIGURE 4.6 The Direction of Lebanon's Merchandise Exports 1996

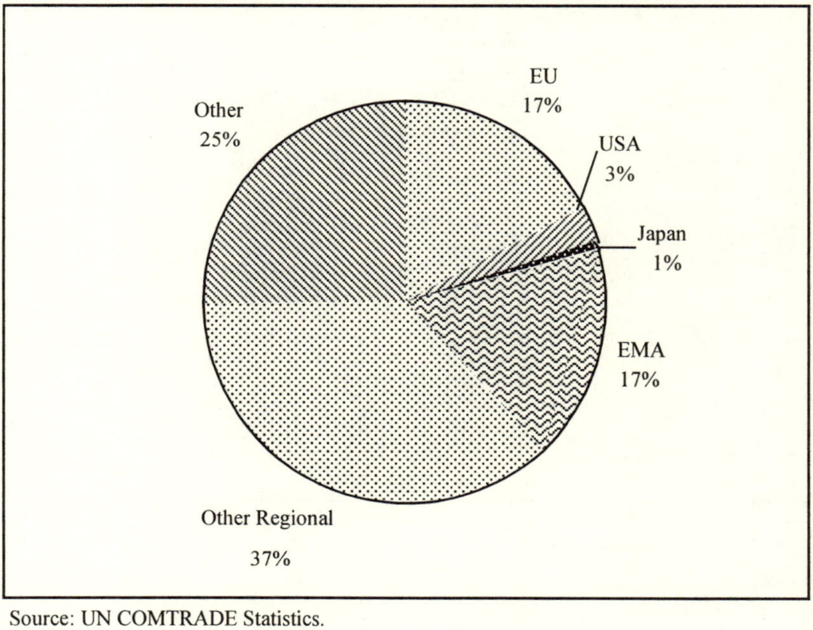

Source: UN COMTRADE Statistics.

exports respectively, account for much higher shares of Lebanon's exports than of its imports. Given the potentially very large gains obtainable from reciprocal liberalization with countries that are large export markets, it seems likely that Lebanon should pay particular attention to the possibility of forming FTAs with some of its regional trading partners.

Given Lebanon's current very large trade imbalance and low level of exports, it seems reasonable to question any inferences about the direction of trade based on current data. To obtain some indication of the reliability of these data, we compared them with estimates of prewar trade flows obtained from the UN COMTRADE system. The results are summarized in figure 4.7.

The pattern of exports in figure 4.7 is broadly consistent with that presented in figure 4.6, allaying some of the potential concerns about the representativeness of the available data on current exports. The share of exports to the EU15 has remained strikingly stable, while the share from the United States has declined and that from Japan risen from a very low level. Exports to the EMA partner countries have increased their share very slightly, from 16.2 to 17 percent. In contrast, the share of exports going to other regional trading partners has declined substantially, from 44 to 37 percent. As in the case of imports, the countries outside the region (other than the United States and Japan) have increased their shares of exports substantially.

FIGURE 4.7 Export Destinations for Lebanon 1974

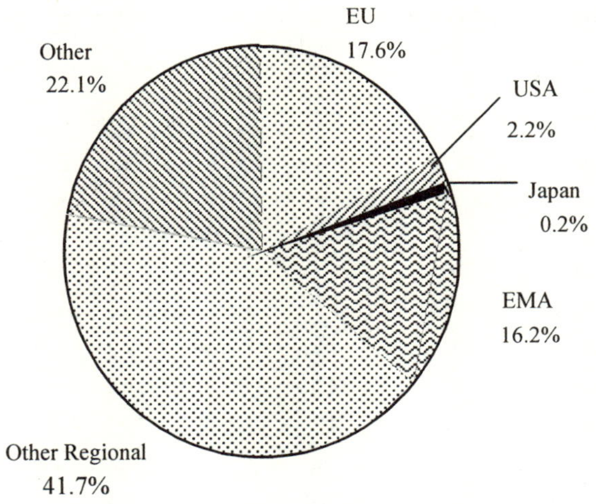

Source: UN COMTRADE statistics.

The Composition of Lebanon's Imports

To obtain some indication of the differences between imports from the EU and those from ROW, each has been aggregated up from the finely disaggregated tariff line level into broader aggregates defined in appendix table 4.1. These broader aggregates were chosen to allow more meaningful interpretation of the data and to provide a basis for the calculation of effective rates of assistance in the following section. Using these aggregates, the commodity composition of imports from the EU and the ROW are shown in table 4.1.

A striking feature of Lebanon's import pattern, evident in the first column of table 4.1, is the importance of the three broad categories of transport equipment, other machinery and equipment, and other heavy manufactures. These three categories alone account for over half of total imports. This may be to some degree a transitional phenomenon, reflecting the very heavy investments in rebuilding associated with reconstruction. However, part of it probably reflects an underlying comparative advantage of the Lebanese economy in light industry and services rather than in heavy industry.

The importance of the commodity aggregates in EU and ROW exports to Lebanon varies considerably. Within agriculture, exports of grain and non-grain crops are less important for the EU than for other suppliers, while livestock products are more important to the EU. There is a striking difference in transport equipment, which accounts for a far higher share of EU than ROW exports. In contrast, petroleum and coal products are predominantly sourced outside the EU.

TABLE 4.1 The Commodity Composition of Lebanon's Imports by Source

	World	EU	ROW
Grains	2.2	0.2	4.1
Non-grain crops	3.7	1.2	6.0
Livestock products	4.9	6.0	3.8
Processed food	8.0	5.7	10.2
Natural resources	1.8	2.1	1.5
Textiles	3.5	3.0	4.0
Apparel	2.7	3.1	2.2
Light manufactures	5.0	5.4	4.7
Transport equipment	17.8	18.4	17.3
Machinery and equipment	16.9	20.3	13.9
Petroleum and coal products	6.5	5.8	7.1
Chemicals, rubber, and plastics	10.6	14.5	7.0
Other heavy manufactures	16.3	14.4	18.1
TOTAL	100.0	100.0	100.0

Europe is more important than other regions as a source of heavy industrial products such as chemicals, rubber, and plastics and other heavy manufactures.

From the table, it is clear that the differences in the composition of exports from the EU and from the world as a whole are relatively minor, suggesting that analysis can usefully proceed at a relatively highly aggregated level, particularly if the products are assumed to be differentiated by country in Lebanon's import market.

Protection on Imports from the EU and the ROW

Weighted average tariff rates for each of the commodities considered in table 4.1 are reported in table 4.2. These rates presented are trade-weighted averages of the nominal rates, expressed in ad valorem terms. In most of the cases covered by table 4.2, the average nominal rates applying to the individual commodity aggregates are similar for imports from the EU and imports from other sources. Exceptions are non-grain crops, where the EU faces a substantially lower tariff than the world as a whole, and light manufactures and machinery and equipment where the tariff on the EU is lower than average. The overall average for imports from the EU is 0.6 percentage points below the tariff imposed on imports from the ROW.

The weighted average tariff rates presented in table 4.2 are based on the statutory rates levied in the schedule except in those few cases (chicken, banana, gasoline [benzine], and tiles) in which rates are based on the maximum of an ad valorem or a specific rate and collections were substituted to obtain an

TABLE 4.2 Nominal Tariff Rates on Imports from the EU and the World

	World	EU	ROW
Grains	2.0	2.0	2.0
Non-grain crops	12.0	7.7	12.8
Livestock products	3.1	3.0	3.2
Processed food	18.3	16.8	19.0
Natural resources	4.1	3.8	4.6
Textiles	14.5	14.2	14.8
Apparel	29.5	29.8	29.2
Light manufactures	14.6	17.0	12.3
Transport equipment	18.5	19.6	17.4
Machinery and equipment	10.3	8.4	12.8
Petroleum and coal products	60.4	61.8	59.3
Chemicals, rubber, and plastics	8.1	7.8	8.6
Other heavy manufactures	8.6	10.4	7.3
TOTAL	15.4	15.1	15.7

ad valorem rate. Average tariff rates based on estimated collections were also calculated, but proved to be almost identical to the numbers presented in table 4.2. Unfortunately, these collections data are based on assessments made early during the somewhat tortuous process of customs clearance in Lebanon, and it appears that adjustments to the customs assessments are made frequently. Estimates of actual, final collections were only available on a more aggregated and fragmentary basis. However, these estimates appeared consistent with a very small degree of slippage in customs collections after the initial assessment stage. Thus, it seems reasonable to take the average tariffs presented in table 4.2 as broadly indicative of the effective tariffs levied.

Another important feature of the protection regime relevant to evaluation of the free trade proposal is the variation in average tariffs across supplying countries. Although Lebanon's tariffs on individual products do not discriminate by country of origin, the average rates applied to each trading partner may vary substantially because of differences in the composition of each country's exports to Lebanon. These differences are very obvious in table 4.3, which shows the weighted average tariffs applied by Lebanon on its imports from a range of major trading partners.

The relatively high rates applied against imports from a number of other EMA countries, such as Syria and Tunisia, will tend to increase the trade diversion losses from Lebanon entering a FTA with the EU (see fig. 4.2). These high rates would also tend to increase the gains from trade creation should Lebanon enter into FTAs with these countries.

The simple average tariff provides another measure of the height of the barriers imposed by a tariff regime. While seriously defective in not taking into account the relative importance of particular tariff lines, it is not vulner-

TABLE 4.3 Tariffs Imposed by Lebanon on Imports from Supplying Countries

	Average Tariff		Average Tariff
EU15	15.1	Syria	58.7
Switzerland	2.1	Tunisia	24.3
Japan	16.1	Turkey	11.2
United States	14.8	UAE	7.8
Canada	8.9	Romania	6.2
Algeria	3.9	Russia	7.6
Bahrain	7.8	Brazil	7.5
Cyprus	18.0	China	16.7
Egypt	14.1	Hong Kong	16.3
Jordan	15.0	Singapore	16.1
Kuwait	11.5	Thailand	15.7
Morocco	12.0	ROW	10.8
Saudi Arabia	10.5	TOTAL	15.4

able to a problem that plagues trade-weighted averages in countries with high trade barriers: if the barriers are sufficiently high on a particular good, the trade weight for that good will approach zero. Simple (unweighted) average tariffs applied on the goods exported by the EU average 11.3 percent, and 11.0 percent on all goods. These rates are slightly below the weighted average tariff rates presented in table 4.2 because of the importance of relatively high tariff rates on some large import categories. This, in turn reflects the importance of the tariff as a means of raising revenue in Lebanon and the relatively modest rates levied on most goods; because of the modest rates, few goods are face effectively prohibitive tariffs. In countries with more restrictive tariff regimes, simple average tariffs are typically higher than weighted average tariffs because of the induced reductions in the volumes of imports facing higher tariff rates.

Nontariff Barriers

NTBs are far more difficult to measure compared to the relatively transparent barriers imposed by tariffs. While the formal protection structure in Lebanon includes very few NTBs, there appear to be some important nontariff barriers to trade. One of the most obvious of these barriers is the costs imposed by the very complex and relatively expensive "formalities" involved in clearing goods through customs. Other costs appear to be introduced through the sole agency system, which may allow accredited agents to exclude even second-hand goods and to restrict competition in the sale of wide ranges of goods. While shipping and insurance costs appear to be quite low, additional handling costs arise from the obsolescence of much of Lebanon's trade infrastructure following destruction and lack of investment during the civil war period.

A very rough indication of the magnitude of the NTBs to trade in Lebanon can be obtained by comparing the prices of standardized goods within Lebanon with the prices of the same goods in world markets. This approach has been implemented by comparing the prices of a range of goods in Lebanon with the prices of the same goods in Qatar, a relatively open economy, and, as an additional check, with the average of the nine Middle Eastern economies covered by the United Nations/World Bank International Comparisons Project (ICP).[2] A great deal of effort has been devoted to specifying products con-sistently in this project, thus mitigating one of the problems that typically plagues use of the price comparison approach to inference about trade barriers. To avoid comparing prices of nontraded goods, a subset of 140 goods judged to be traded goods was selected from the 214 goods included in the surveys conducted in late 1995.

Since weighting factors appropriate to evaluation of trade policy are not available for the commodities considered, simple averages of the percentage differences between prices in Lebanon and in the comparators were calculated. These averages are presented in table 4.4. For all commodity groups except medical supplies, prices in Lebanon were higher than in Qatar. In some cases, such as fuels, the price differentials seem readily explicable by the tariffs imposed in Lebanon. However, the overall pattern seems less easy to explain, since the average price differential observed is more than twice the weighted average tariff applied in Lebanon (15.4 percent) and over three times the simple average tariff (11 percent).

The two major factors, in addition to tariffs, that might be expected to affect the relationship between prices in Lebanon and those in Qatar are the relative income levels of each country and the war damage to infrastructure in Lebanon. The much higher average level of PCI in Qatar than in Lebanon can be expected to raise prices in Qatar relative to Lebanon.[3] Even traded goods of the type considered in this comparison typically embody a substantial quantity of domestic factor inputs in their consumer prices and, as a consequence, their prices tend to be higher in high income economies.[4] On the other hand, wartime damage to infrastructure in Lebanon might be expected to raise prices in Lebanon by raising the costs of transporting and supplying goods to consumers, although reconstruction had considerably reduced the largest of these costs (e.g., the need for private electricity generators) by the time of the ICP survey. These two factors offset each other to some degree, and it seems reasonable to take the observed price differential as a tentative indicator of the effect of NTBs on trade in Lebanon. If this estimate is accepted, it implies roughly doubling the protection implied by the weighted average tariff.

TABLE 4.4 Differentials between Lebanese Prices and Those in Qatar and the Middle East

Relative to:	Qatar (%)	Middle East Average (%)
Food	33	5
Beverages and tobacco	19	5
Clothing	68	13
Hardware	23	-1
Medical supplies	-28	-22
Motor vehicles	33	14
Fuel	118	37
Electronic appliances	14	2
Light manufactures	48	14
Machinery	4	-8
Transport equipment	18	8
Building supplies	62	15
AVERAGE	34	7

The comparison with the average price level for the nine Middle Eastern ICP countries is also striking. Despite the generally high average rates of protection relative to Lebanon's, the average prices of traded goods appear to be above average in Lebanon. This suggests that the range of barriers to trade and competition in Lebanon may be considerably greater than is typically supposed.

Industry Incentives and Adjustment Costs

While the rates of tariff protection applied in Lebanon are generally relatively modest, even such modest tariff rates can create substantial incentives to expand particular sectors. The effective rate of protection (ERP) provides a summary measure of the incentives created by a protection regime to expand particular sectors and to contract others. The ERP takes into account the impact of protection on the price of output and on the prices of tradable intermediate inputs in calculating the change in the returns to value adding factors in a particular sector.[5] It can be seen as a generalization of the nominal rates of protection presented in earlier tables.

Import-competing sectors benefit from the price increases in their outputs resulting from protection to their output. Their net benefit depends upon the extent to which the benefit to their output is offset by the increased costs imposed on their inputs. Export-oriented sectors do not benefit from protection granted to their output. Thus, for these sectors, the only impact of protection measured by an ERP is the increase in their costs resulting from tariffs on their inputs.

TABLE 4.5 ERPs Provided to Selected Lebanese Industries by Tariffs

	Importer (%)	Exporter (%)
Wheat	-1.4	-4.8
Non-grain crops	16.1	-3.9
Fish	3.2	-5.9
Other minerals (non-oil)	3.0	-4.7
Food products	24.1	-5.8
Textiles	18.9	-8.8
Apparel	52.1	-9.2
Leather	50.0	-9.7
Wood and products	26.9	-8.1
Pulp and paper	10.9	-8.9
Petroleum and coal products	481.8	-7.4
Nonmetallic minerals	26.6	-7.0
Fabricated metal products	13.9	-4.1
Machinery and equipment	15.8	-7.7

ERPs for selected sectors in Lebanon are presented in table 4.5. The cost structures for intermediate goods on which these calculations are based were drawn from a representative input-output table for the MENA region contained in the Global Trade Analysis Project (GTAP) model (Hertel 1997). The vitally important ratios of intermediate use to gross output were adjusted to actual Lebanese data obtained from the recent Lebanese industrial census (Ministry of Oil and Industry 1996).

The effective rates of assistance provided to import-competing producers are generally positive and sometimes quite large. Using the latest available information on tariffs and trade patterns, these effective rates range from -1.4 percent for wheat to 52 percent for apparel. The effective rate calculated for petroleum and coal products is an extraordinary 482 percent, highlighting the potentially very large costs of high tariff rates such as those applying on petroleum products in Lebanon should domestic production of petroleum products be recommenced.[6]

The effective rates of assistance applying to export-oriented producers are negative, as expected. For these producers, the protection regime provides no benefit in terms of output prices but does impose a burden through higher prices for at least some inputs. To some degree, this burden can be alleviated through Lebanon's duty suspension arrangements, but these involve additional compliance costs and do not allow complete relief, especially where export production involves indirect use of imported inputs for which duty suspension treatment is not feasible.

ERPs could potentially be calculated taking into account information on NTBs. However, the information on these barriers is not available in a form that would allow accurate calculation of effective rates on a sectoral basis. It is clear, however, that ERPs must be considerably higher in those sectors (e.g., clothing, light manufactures, and building supplies) in which prices are substantially higher than would be implied by Lebanon's tariff protection.

While the ERP is more general than the nominal rate of assistance, it does have a serious limitation in that it ignores the impact of trade barriers on the price of nontraded goods in the economy. Higher trade barriers cause consumers to shift away from imported goods towards domestically produced goods. This increase in demand raises the price of domestic nontraded goods, resulting in an increase in the price of nontraded goods relative to traded goods—a phenomenon known as a real exchange rate appreciation. This real exchange rate appreciation imposes a burden on all traded sectors, protected or not. It reinforces the burden imposed by protection on export-oriented sectors and offsets the gains to protected import-competing sectors. This problem can be overcome by using a fully-fledged general equilibrium model, in which the relative price of nontraded goods is determined endogenously. This is done later in this chapter.

Adjustment and Adjustment Costs to Industry Following Liberalization

The effective rates of protection highlight the substantial incentives provided to distort the structure of industry in Lebanon. Achieving the potential benefits of the EMA will involve some reallocation of resources. Much of this reallocation will occur within industries and firms in response to the new incentives prevailing after the agreement. Some will require the reallocation of resources between industries.

Where much trade is intra-industry in nature, as seems likely to be the case in post-reconstruction Lebanon, liberalization is likely to increase both imports and exports in many industries. Liberalization places competitive pressure on the production of import substitutes in affected industries and increases import penetration. At the same time, reductions in firms' cost structures allow the same industries and even firms to expand their production for the export market. This response to liberalization generally leads to considerably lower adjustment costs than where intersectoral shifts in employment and output are required.

In most developing countries, there is a tendency for the protected sectors to be relatively capital-intensive, and those sectors taxed by protection to be relatively labor-intensive. As a consequence, liberalization tends to have strongly positive effects on labor demand, employment, and wages (Krueger 1981). In Lebanon, the situation seems to be slightly more complex. For the limited number of industrial sectors where a comparison between labor

FIGURE 4.8 The Relationship between Labor Intensity and Effective Assistance in Lebanon 1996

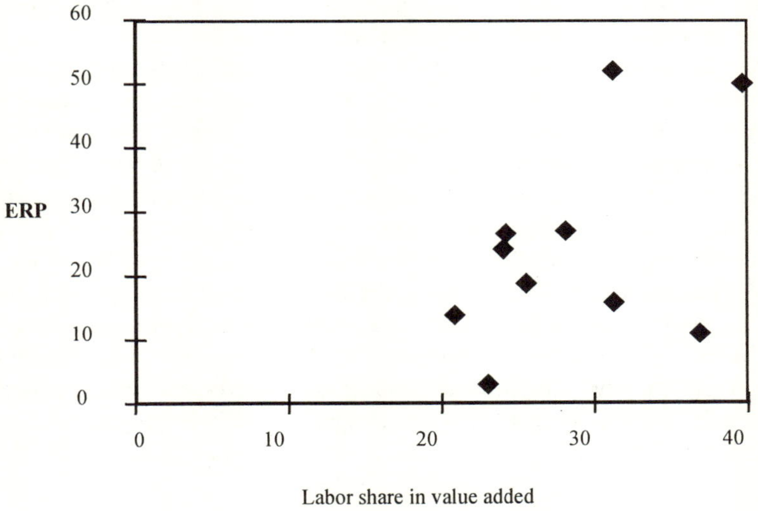

intensity and ERPs for import-competing production is feasible, there does appear to be a positive association, as shown in figure 4.8.[7] However, this relationship is heavily dependent upon the two observations with the highest rates of assistance, wearing apparel and leather products respectively. If these two observations were excluded, there would be a weak negative association between labor intensity and effective assistance.

The high labor intensity of the apparel and leather products sectors raises special issues. At this early stage of recovery, the protection provided to these two sectors probably does increase employment by allowing substitution for imports of these goods. However, providing protection to these sectors is certainly not a coherent basis for long-term restructuring. Given the small size of the domestic market, import substitution in these industries will very quickly reach its limits and become a brake on growth, rather than its source. Certainly, by the time that the reductions in effective protection proposed under the EMA come into effect, these industries will have reached the limits of the domestic market. Given the absence of restrictions on exports from Lebanon into the EU market, there are excellent opportunities for expansion of exports, and it seems undesirable to distract firms away from a focus on meeting the needs of the export market by providing profitable, but inherently limited, incentives to focus on the rather different needs of the domestic market.

The data presented in figure 4.8 are for the manufacturing sector alone—the only sector for which comparable data on factor intensities are available from Lebanese sources. An important feature of trade liberalization with Europe and within the region is likely to be a substantial increase in the export of services from Lebanon. Since exports of services from Lebanon are typically labor-intensive and frequently intensive in the skilled labor that is relatively abundant in Lebanon, the expansion of these service sectors is likely to be an important source of employment opportunities.

While the data needed to analyze the impacts of liberalization on employment by sector are not available for Lebanon, these data are available for a number of other countries contemplating similar EMAs and for Turkey which is entering a wide-ranging FTA with the EU. For Egypt, Morocco, Tunisia, and Turkey, multisectoral models have been constructed and used to assess the proportion of the workforce that must change jobs as a consequence of the reforms. Even though the trade liberalization envisaged is greater in each of these cases than in Lebanon, the percentage of workers who must move between industries is typically very small—generally around 2 percent of the workforce (see Konan and Maskus 1997a, for Egypt; Rutherford, Rutström, and Tarr 1993, for Morocco). Over the twelve-year implementation period of the agreement, this implies an annual change in employment of only one sixth of one percent per year, which is extremely small relative to the flow of workers between jobs in any normal economy and infinitesimal relative to the changes needed for other reasons during the reconstruction and the return to growth of the Lebanese economy.

The level of employment and wage rates depend critically upon the maintenance of macroeconomic stability and on microeconomic policies that allow the rapid redeployment of labor in response to a range of shocks. These shocks include the relatively small and gradual changes resulting from the trade policy reforms under consideration and the much larger continuing shocks resulting from forces such as terms of trade changes. If macroeconomic stability is maintained and the economy becomes more open, one important benefit is likely to be a sustained investment boom associated with the development of modern competitive industries; this boom will greatly facilitate adjustment and any needed reallocation of labor.

At the microeconomic level, Lebanon's policy needs to focus on maintaining the productivity of its workers and on ensuring that labor markets operate efficiently. Continuing investment in education is vital if labor productivity and hence real wages are to remain above the average for the region and to increase as the economy restructures and grows. Real wages need to be flexible both overall and for particular types of labor if unemployment problems are not to be exacerbated. Labor markets will need to become more efficient in matching workers and jobs as the economy becomes more complex and skill-matching more difficult.

The experiences of the three relatively new Mediterranean members of the EU highlight some of the macroeconomic and microeconomic adjustment needs confronting Lebanon. It appears that Spain and Portugal took most of the measures that were required to achieve macroeconomic balance and efficient performance of the role of government. Both of these countries experienced much higher growth rates following accession, although labor market rigidities in Spain contributed to a serious, continuing problem of unemployment. In Greece, the adjustments to public spending required to achieve macroeconomic balance were deferred, and Greece's economic performance since joining the EU has been extremely disappointing (Winters 1996b).

Trade Barriers Facing Lebanese Exports

The only barriers facing Lebanese exports that would be changed as a direct outcome of the current negotiations are those in the EU. Under the current agreement between Lebanon and the EU, Lebanon has essentially free access to the European market for virtually all industrial goods, albeit subject to rules of origin restrictions that some regard as restrictive (GATT 1979). Given recent changes in the WTO procedures for handling regional agreements, there is some doubt about the ability of the current agreement to withstand challenge, and the EU has suggested that it may be withdrawn if a new agreement is not reached. Thus, it seems reasonable to view the retention of the current access to the EU as a potential benefit of reaching a new agreement. While the protection levied by Lebanon's other trading partners is not on the table, the presence of an agreement may make it easier for Lebanon to reach FTAs with other EMA members and potentially with other countries in the region. For this reason, we consider both the barriers facing Lebanon in the EU and in other markets.

EU Trade Barriers

The post-Uruguay Round MFN tariff rates to be applied by the EU on non-preferential imports are given in table 4.6 together with the commodity composition of Lebanon's exports. These rates take into account the full reductions in tariff rates agreed under the Uruguay Round and are calculated assuming that the applied tariff rates for a particular tariff line would stay the same as in the base year tariff supplied to the GATT's Integrated Datebase (1988), except where a tariff binding offered is lower than the base tariff rate. The resulting post-Uruguay Round rates have been aggregated into a set of commodities broadly similar to the GTAP commodities presented in earlier tables. Two estimates of agricultural protection are presented. The first includes the protective effects of NTBs on the subset of agricultural imports to which these apply (Ingco 1996), while the second covers all agricultural trade but includes only tariff protection.

TABLE 4.6 Post Uruguay Round Tariff Rates and Lebanese Exports to the EU

	Tariff Rate	Trade Value 1988
Agriculture excluding Fish: Estimate 1	12.6	1.9
Agriculture excluding Fish: Estimate 2	2.3	12.4
Fish and fish products	0	0
Petroleum	0	0
Wood, pulp, paper, and furniture	0	3.5
Textiles and clothing	10.9	27.8
Leather, rubber, and footwear	4.4	6
Metals	2.5	26.3
Chemical and photographic supplies	4.5	6.1
Transport equipment	7.7	1.4
Non-electric machinery	1.5	2.5
Electric machinery	3.4	3.5
Mineral products, precious stones, and metal	1.2	13.6
Manufactured articles, nes.	0.1	23.6
Industrial goods (line 5-14)	4.1	114.3
TOTAL	3.9	126.7

Source: Finger, Reincke, and Ingco (1996) and U. Reincke personal communication.

The tariff rates that would be applied on Lebanese industrial exports to the EU in the absence of the current agreement are generally quite low, except on agricultural products and on textiles and clothing. Since tariff concessions do not currently apply on agricultural products and extensive liberalization does not appear to be envisaged, the protection rate on agricultural products is unlikely to be greatly affected by the result of the negotiations, although small volumes of quota-constrained access to a few protected EU markets are likely to be negotiated. The most important rate is probably the tariff of 4.1 percent applying on industrial goods since these goods accounted for over 90 percent of Lebanon's trade in 1988 and probably for a higher percentage today.

Trade Barriers in Other Markets

Estimates of the rates of protection prevailing in the most important of Lebanon's trading partners are presented in table 4.7. These estimates include both simple and trade-weighted average rates of protection.

TABLE 4.7 Protection Rates in Lebanon's Major Trading Partners

	Simple Average Tariff	Weighted Average Tariff
European Union	4.6	3.9
Switzerland	2.4	1.7
Japan	4.6	2.8
United States	4.5	2.8
Canada	6.1	2.4
Algeria	22.9	16.4
Bahrain	3.0	3.0
Cyprus	10.1	17.5
Egypt	42.2	31.0
Jordan	28.4	22.0
Kuwait	4.2	4.2
Morocco	22.8	19.0
Saudi Arabia	12.1	11.3
Syria	11.0	12.6
Tunisia	33.2	24.8
Turkey	9.0	3.9
UAE	4.5	4.5
Romania	12.3	11.7
Russia	N/A	12.0
Brazil	13.2	11.7
China	35.6	32.0
Hong Kong	0.0	0.0
Singapore	0.4	1.3
Thailand	8.5	26.1

Important features of table 4.7 are the relatively low levels of protection in the developed economies and the much higher rates of protection in many of Lebanon's regional trading partners. Given the analysis in section 1, these high rates imply that Lebanon could potentially gain from reciprocal trade liberalization with these countries, which are typically relatively more important as destinations for its exports than as sources of imports.

Trade Liberalization, Welfare, and Export Competitiveness

To evaluate discriminatory and nondiscriminatory trade liberalization, a small simulation model was developed using the very limited available data on the Lebanese economy. It was not feasible to construct a conventional multisectoral CGE model of the Lebanese economy given the absence of an IO table or even complete national accounts information. However, a very simple model in the spirit of the 1-2-3 model developed by Devarajan, Lewis, and Robinson (1993) can be developed. An initial version of the model was developed in EXCEL. The current version was developed in the GEMPACK language to allow for consideration of a wider range of trading partners, initial states of the economy, and policy experiments.[8] To obtain a realistic assessment of trade creation and export growth, both models take into account the impact of liberalization on the price of nontraded goods relative to the price of traded goods, a price change frequently referred to as the real exchange depreciation resulting from trade liberalization. [9] In the remainder of this section, the results of some key liberalization experiments are first considered. Then, the real exchange rate impacts obtained using the model are compared with estimates obtained using real-world data to provide some confirmation that the model's results are realistic for this key response. Finally, the sensitivity of the results to alternative specifications of the model parameters and initial data are considered.

TABLE 4.8 Key Consequences of Liberalization by Lebanon

	Euro-Med %	Retain EU %	FTA %	Europe + FTA %	MFN %	Total %
Imports from EU	23.4	0.2	-10.0	13.3	-0.5	0.6
Exports to EU	8.5	11.1	-1.9	17.0	16.6	21.9
Total import volume	0.5	0.2	2.2	3.4	3.5	4.6
Tariff revenues	-57.0	0.2	-26.4	-73.9	-100.0	-100.0
Consumer prices	-6.5	0.1	-3.3	-8.8	-12.6	-12.2
Exports	8.5	0.2	7.2	15.8	16.6	20.7
Nontraded good price	-5.9	0.2	-2.3	-7.2	-11.0	-10.1
Real expenditure	-0.3	0.06	0.6	0.6	0.6	0.9

Results of Liberalization Experiments

Some key results for several different forms of liberalization by Lebanon are presented in table 4.8. The first column of the results shows the consequences for Lebanon of the elimination of tariffs on imports from the EU. The second column evaluates the benefits for Lebanon of retaining its current preferential access to the EU market, assuming a counterfactual where it would be lost in the absence of an agreement. The third column deals with the abolition of trade barriers between Lebanon and its fellow EMA members. The fourth column refers to the establishment of free trade with Europe and with the other EMA countries plus Turkey, which has established free trade with all of the countries currently having FTAs with the EU (Harrison, Rutherford, and Tarr 1997). Column 5 shows the effects of unilateral elimination of all tariffs by Lebanon. The final column includes discriminatory liberalization by Lebanon, Europe, and the other EMA participants together with abolition of Lebanon's tariffs against non-EMA countries. The results in the final column could presumably only be achieved by Lebanon exchanging discriminatory tariff liberalizations and then unilaterally removing all of its non-partner tariffs.

These results for the basic EMA presented in column 1 highlight the importance of trade diversion over trade creation under the proposed agreement. While imports from the EU increase, imports from the ROW fall substantially and total imports rise by only 0.5 percent. Because of the trade diversion, tariff revenues fall by 57 percent, substantially more than would be indicated by the base share of the EU in import tariff revenues (48 percent).

The increase in total imports is very small in this simulation for two main reasons. First, the reduction in the price of imported goods causes a fall in the price of nontraded goods or a real exchange rate devaluation. The fall in the price of nontraded goods reduces the incentive for consumers to substitute away from domestic goods towards the now-cheaper imports. The second reason follows from the extremely small level of initial imports. The fall in the price of nontraded goods (relative to exports) increases the incentive to export and leads to a substantial percentage increase in exports. However, given the very small base level of exports, this increase in exports allows only a relatively small percentage increase in imports if the trade balance is to stay constant.

The combination of a fall in the price of imports and a fall in the price of nontraded goods leads to downward pressure on the overall level of consumer prices. The overall impact on static economic welfare is slightly negative, with a welfare loss of 0.3 percent of base-period expenditure or 0.5 percent of base period GDP.[10] This reflects the fact that tariffs imposed on imports from the EU were initially slightly below those imposed on other trading partners and that they were lowered all the way to zero, increasing the losses from trade diversion.

Since there is some risk that Lebanon's current access to the EU might be lost in the absence of an agreement, the retention of Lebanon's current access is a potential benefit from signing a EMA. The results in column 2 begin from a counterfactual where Europe has imposed a tariff of 4 percent on Lebanon and show the benefits to Lebanon of eliminating this tariff. As is evident from the table, the increase in the prices received for exports to the EU does stimulate a sizable increase in exports to the EU. However, given the low initial level of total exports and the small EU share, the impact on the rest of the economy is quite small. The welfare impact is positive since, as shown in figure 4.3, such an improvement in Lebanon's terms of trade is virtually certain to increase welfare.

The FTA shock in column 3 represents an exchange of tariff preferences between Lebanon and its partner EMA countries (plus Turkey) and the removal of their tariffs against exports from Lebanon.[11] The removal of the partners' tariffs against Lebanon is important because these tariffs are much higher than those levied in the EU and therefore provide larger terms of trade gain. The reductions in Lebanon's import tariffs on imports from Syria and Tunisia are likely to be welfare-enhancing because these imports are, on average, subject to higher than average tariffs. Total imports increase both because of the reduction in Lebanon's tariffs and because the improved terms of trade resulting from partner liberalization raises incomes and allows spending to increase. The reduction in import tariffs reduces the price of nontraded goods and hence increases the competitiveness of the export sector—stimulating an increase in imports. The increase in economic welfare of 0.6 percent of base expenditure (i.e., 0.9 percent of 1996 GDP) is quite sizable given the very small base level of exports from Lebanon. This result is consistent with the findings of Harrison, Rutherford, and Tarr (1997) who concluded that the formation of FTAs with its major trading partners was the largest single source of gains for Turkey from entering into a FTA with the EU.

The results in column 4 cover the situation where Lebanon reduces its tariffs against the EU, retains its preferential access to the EU, and also negotiates FTAs with its neighbors. This approach results in virtually the same increase in welfare as the previous FTA simulation; the welfare gains are much larger than the sum of the gains from the three individual experiments reported in the first three columns. The complementary liberalization with Lebanon's trading partners clearly reduces the trade diversion losses associated with granting preferences to the EU alone.

The results in column 5 refer to an experiment in which Lebanon reduces its tariffs on all its trading partners to zero on a MFN basis. This obviously reduces tariff revenues by 100 percent. It results in a static welfare increase of 0.6 percent of base period (1996) expenditure, or 0.9 percent of initial GDP. The fall in the price of imports results in a reduction in the cost of living of

12.6 percent, while the prices of nontraded goods fall by 11 percent. Suppliers of nontraded goods such as labor are clearly better off because the decline in the price of their output is less than the decline in overall consumer prices. The decline in the price of nontraded goods relative to export prices increases the competitiveness of the export sector and causes the increase in export volume of 16.6 percent. The volume of total imports increases by only 3.5 percent because the initial value of exports is so much smaller than the initial level of imports.

The final column of results in table 4.8 refers to the situation where Lebanon first undertakes mutual preferential liberalization vis-à-vis its fellow EMA members and then unilaterally lowers its barriers against the ROW. This approach, if successfully implemented, would result in greater gains in both trade and welfare than any of the other approaches. Unfortunately, there must be considerable doubt about whether these gains can be achieved on a sustainable basis since it is likely that other EMA members seeking to make their economies more open will also lower their MFN protection, reducing the benefits accruing from Lebanon's preferential access to their markets. However, if this were the case, the gains to Lebanon would become those of MFN liberalization alone—0.6 percent of GDP, a gain that is equal to the best obtainable under the FTA options considered and that is not vulnerable to erosion through the policy actions of others.

Partial Model Validation: Comparing the Real Exchange Rate Impact with Direct Estimates

The fall in the price of nontraded goods resulting from liberalization, frequently termed a real exchange rate depreciation, is an extremely important feature of the liberalization experiments and one that is perhaps the most difficult for policy makers to understand and articulate to their constituencies. It is vitally important not only because it improves the competitiveness of the export sector and increases exports but also because it reduces the cost pressures facing import competing sectors and allows many to adapt and flourish—and frequently even to become exporters—following comprehensive liberalization. While a single import-competing sector will clearly be made worse off by a cut in its own protection alone, it may be better off if protection is simultaneously reduced across the economy as a whole.

Exporters will unambiguously be better off if protection is reduced. As Clements and Sjaastad (1984) emphasize, since protection does not increase long run output, any increase that it generates in the output of import-competing sectors must cause a corresponding reduction in the output of other sectors. Usually, the adverse impact is greatest on the export sector. Since the price of nontraded goods rises as consumers shift away from importables to nontraded goods, producers in the nontraded sector are effectively able to pass much of the increase in their costs through to their customers. With the price of exports from a small country like Lebanon fixed on world prices, there is no corresponding opportunity for exporters to pass on any of the increase in their costs, so their profitability is squeezed by rising costs. In this sense, protection can be seen as a tax on exporters, even though its direct impact is on importers.

Given the importance of the impact of changes in protection on the price of nontraded goods, it seems important to compare the estimates obtained using the model with those obtained using real-world data. Estimates of the ratio of the change in the price of nontraded goods to the tariff-induced change in the price of importables have been calculated for a wide range of economies and a number of these estimates are presented in table 4.9. To compare these with the results of the MFN liberalization experiment reported in table 4.8, the ratio of the percentage change in the price of nontraded goods to the change in the price of imported goods must be calculated. The results presented in column 5 of table 4.8 imply a decline of 11.0 in the price of nontraded goods following a 13.3 percent decline in the price of imported goods.[12] This implies that the prices of nontraded goods in the model decline by 82 percent of the decline in the price of imported goods—a result very close to the middle of the range of estimates presented in table 4.9.

Considering Alternative Parameters and Base Data

The results presented in table 4.8 depend heavily upon the parameter values and the characteristics of the base data set used in the analysis. Rather than presenting an analysis of the consequences of arbitrary changes in a wide array of parameters and data values, it seems desirable to consider the implications

TABLE 4.9 Estimated Impacts of Changes in Domestic Prices of Importables for Prices of Nontraded Goods

	Estimation period	Impact (%)	Source
Chile	1959-70	55	Clements and Sjaastad (1984)
Uruguay	1966-79	53	Clements and Sjaastad (1984)
Argentina	1935-79	57	Clements and Sjaastad (1984)
El Salvador	1962-77	70	Clements and Sjaastad (1984)
Australia	1950-80	70	Clements and Sjaastad (1984)
Brazil	1950-78	70	Clements and Sjaastad (1984)
Colombia	1970-78	95	Clements and Sjaastad (1984)
Argentina	1975-88	84	Devereux and Connolly (1996)
Colombia	1973-88	90	Devereux and Connolly (1996)
Ecuador	1974-87	93	Devereux and Connolly (1996)
Venezuela	1974-87	103	Devereux and Connolly (1996)

of a smaller set to which the results are likely to be particularly sensitive. As shown by Rutherford, Rutström, and Tarr (1993), one feature of the parameter set of a standard CGE model that is likely to be of particular importance is the relationship between the elasticity of substitution between domestic and imported goods (that has a large impact on the extent of trade creation) and the elasticity of substitution between competing suppliers (that has its most direct impact on trade diversion).[13] Given the limitations of our knowledge about the magnitude of this parameter, we consider the case where it is 4.5, i.e., 50 percent higher than the base value of 3.0 used in table 4.8. With the elasticity of substitution between domestic and imported goods remaining at 1.5, this change increases the importance of trade diversion relative to trade creation, something that would not happen if both elasticities of substitution were increased together. The results of this experiment are presented in table 4.10.

The results in table 4.10 show much larger changes in trade volumes from discriminatory trade liberalization than the corresponding columns in table 4.8. In column 1, the increase in imports from the EU following discriminatory liberalization against the EU rose from 23 to 34.5 percent. This increase in trade diversion results in somewhat larger reductions in tariff revenues than were observed in table 4.8. Overall, however, the conclusions of the analysis appear to be relatively robust with respect to this parameter; while the welfare benefits of liberalization do generally increase, the qualitative implications of liberalization are not greatly affected.

Another important feature influencing the results of the analysis is likely to be the net trade position (see Schiff 1997 for a general discussion of this issue). It seems clear that Lebanon's extremely large current trade deficit reflects, to some degree, temporary factors such as the investment associated with reconstruction and the repatriation of capital formerly invested abroad. As reconstruction proceeds, and particularly as much of the current capital

TABLE 4.10 Key Consequences of Liberalization by Lebanon with High Import Substitutability

	Euro-Med %	Retain EU %	FTA %	EU + FTA %	MFN %	Total %
Imports from EU	34.5	0.2	-21.6	12.6	-5.0	-4.0
Exports to EU	9.2	11.1	-0.4	18.1	16.9	22.2
Total import volume	0.2	0.2	2.8	4.1	4.3	5.4
Tariff revenues	-62.3	0.2	-35.6	-79.0	-100.0	-100.0
Consumer prices	-6.9	0.1	-4.6	-9.7	-13.0	-12.6
Exports	9.2	0.6	8.8	16.9	16.9	21.0
Price of nontraded	-6.4	0.2	-1.1	-7.9	-11.2	-10.3
Real expenditure	-0.3	0.06	0.8	0.9	1.0	1.3

inflow begins to be serviced, the trade deficit will diminish. To gain some idea of the sensitivity of the results to the initial trade balance, the analysis was repeated with total trade (exports plus imports of goods and nonfactor services) held constant but with balanced trade imposed.

From the results presented in table 4.11, it is clear that the key consequence of moving to balanced trade is a substantial increase in the welfare gains that arise from increasing export prices. Thus, the gains from reciprocal free trade with EMA partners more than double to 1.7 percent of expenditure (and 1.7 percent of GDP in this situation). The total welfare gain from reciprocal discriminatory liberalization with the EU and Mediterranean FTA members rises to 2.0, while the gain from the negotiation of reciprocal discriminatory liberalization followed by MFN liberalization in Lebanon rises to 2.3 percent of GDP. The gain from MFN liberalization increases to 0.7 percent of a smaller level of expenditure.

The results presented in tables 4.8, 4.10, and 4.11 are all based on the assumption that Lebanon liberalizes its tariff barriers without changing the tariff equivalents associated with the apparently quite large NTBs operating in the Lebanese economy. To examine the implications of such NTBs, a new database was constructed including high NTBs of the type suggested by the price comparisons presented in table 4.4. In the absence of direct estimates of the extent of discrimination across countries, the tariff rates applied to imports from all countries were doubled (in line with the price differences between Lebanon and Qatar observed in table 4.4), and a new model database was constructed consistent with the resulting quota rents being redistributed within Lebanon in the same manner as tariff revenues. The simulations presented in table 4.12 explore the consequences of fully liberalizing both tariff barriers and NTBs in Lebanon. These simulations use the base parameter applied in table 4.8 and a datebase that differs only because of the differences in the magnitude of the trade distortions.

TABLE 4.11 Key Consequences of Liberalization by Lebanon with Balanced Trade

	Euro-Med %	Retain EU %	FTA %	EU + FTA %	MFN %	Total %
Imports from EU	26.0	0.8	-7.1	20.0	3.3	7.6
Exports to EU	3.5	10.5	-6.4	6.6	6.6	8.5
Total import volume	2.6	0.8	5.8	9.6	7.7	11.9
Tariff revenues	-56.2	0.8	-23.7	-72.4	-100.0	-100.0
Consumer prices	-5.2	0.3	-1.7	-6.1	-10.4	-8.9
Exports	3.4	0.1	2.2	5.5	6.6	7.4
Price of nontraded	-3.8	0.7	0.4	-2.4	-7.1	-4.4
Real Expenditure	-0.2	0.3	1.7	2.0	0.7	2.3

Comparing the results in table 4.12 with those in table 4.8, it is clear that the elimination of both tariff barriers and NTBs in Lebanon would have a much greater impact than the elimination of tariff barriers alone. In the case of discriminatory liberalization against the EU alone, the impacts on trade, tariff revenue, and welfare would all be substantially increased. The adverse welfare impact would be quadrupled, giving rise to serious concerns about this approach to liberalization. Reciprocal FTAs with EMA partners would, however, reverse these losses and generate more than twice the gains reported in table 4.8. However, once the elimination of NTBs is taken into account, the largest welfare gains accrue from nondiscriminatory liberalization.

Adjustment, Reconstruction, and Competitiveness

A widely expressed concern in Lebanon is that the agricultural and industrial sectors are uncompetitive and cannot survive without protection. This concern must be interpreted in relation to the very heavy reliance on financial inflows from abroad during its reconstruction phase. In 1996, financial inflows from abroad are expected to amount to 57 percent of GDP. These financial flows include foreign assistance, remittances from overseas Lebanese, domestic capital returning to Lebanon, and foreign capital attracted by high domestic interest rates.

Clearly, such large inflows are unlikely to be sustained. Once the major infrastructure reconstruction projects wind down and foreign debt service requirements increase, the net financial inflows from abroad are likely to decline substantially. They are not likely to decline to zero because of continuing remittance flows from Lebanese abroad and income from factors owned abroad. However, a substantial reduction from the current levels seems inevitable.

The large financial inflows into Lebanon and correspondingly high levels of spending create major pressures for deindustrialization that have been studied for open economies undergoing resource booms (Corden and Neary 1982).

TABLE 4.12 Consequences of Liberalizing Both Tariff and Nontariff Barriers

	Euro-Med %	Retain EU %	FTA %	FTA +EU %	MFN %	Total %
Imports from EU	43.3	0.2	-26.6	16.8	-3.9	-2.9
Exports to EU	17.8	11.1	4.9	30.7	32.5	38.5
Total import volume	-0.2	0.2	4.0	6.4	8.0	9.1
Tariff revenues	-65.6	0.2	-39.7	-81.4	-100.0	-100.0
Consumer prices	-12.7	0.09	-9.4	-18.3	-23.4	-23.0
Exports	17.8	0.6	14.6	29.4	32.5	37.1
Price of nontraded	-11.9	0.2	-7.3	-15.1	-19.7	-18.9
Real expenditure	-1.3	0.07	1.3	1.7	2.2	2.6

The resulting "Dutch Disease" almost always creates pressures for protection of the traded goods sector or at least strengthens resistance to liberalization. While these pressures are understandable, governments that succumb to them damage their economies, particularly their already hard-pressed export sectors. Such self-inflicted damage to the export sector is particularly undesirable in situations such as Lebanon's, where a vibrant export sector will be needed to service debts built up during the reconstruction phase.

The basic mechanism of adjustment to an increase in spending financed by financial inflows from abroad was first set out by Salter (1959), who provided a simple model of internal and external balance. This model considers two broad types of goods—traded and nontraded goods. The key feature of the model is that the market for nontraded goods must balance, or there will be pressures for the price of nontraded goods to change. The market for traded goods, by contrast, need not be in balance at all times. A country with access to funds from abroad may run a deficit in the market for traded goods, while a country wishing to increase its assets abroad (or pay down its debts) may run a surplus in the traded goods market.

A simple diagrammatic treatment provides a very simple way to summarize the results of the Salter model. The production side of the economy is represented by a production possibility frontier showing the combinations of traded and nontraded goods that can be produced in the economy. Consumer preferences are represented by an indifference curve between traded and nontraded goods. In the situation shown in figure 4.9, where income equals expenditure and the trade deficit is zero, the relative prices of traded and nontraded goods are determined by the tangency between the production possibility frontier and the indifference curve.

FIGURE 4.9 Determination of the Real Exchange Rate with No Trade Deficit

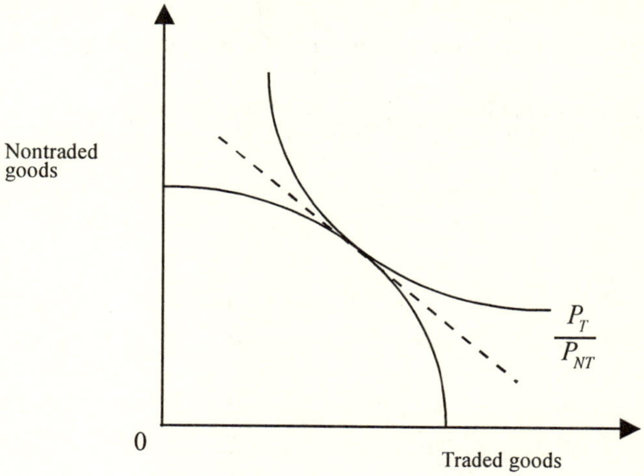

When a country has access to international capital markets, it may choose to spend more than its income for a time. In figure 4.10, this choice is shown by a move away from the origin of the community's indifference curve. In order to maintain balance in the market for nontraded goods, the supply of nontraded goods must equal the demand. In contrast, the domestic supply of traded goods need not equal the demand, since traded goods can be imported. The outcome is shown in figure 4.10. The relative price of traded to nontraded goods has adjusted so that the supply of nontraded goods is equal to the demand, and all of the imbalance between income and spending is transferred into the nontraded good relative to the traded good, or a real exchange rate appreciation. This price rise was needed to stimulate production of the nontraded good and to reduce the demand in order to bring this market into equilibrium.

The rise in the price of nontraded goods depicted in figure 4.10 is an inevitable consequence of a country spending more than its income. Attempts to thwart the process can only succeed temporarily by throwing the economy into disequilibrium and creating pressures for subsequent changes in relative prices. During a phase of high spending, such as the current reconstruction phase in Lebanon, firms in the traded goods sector will find their competitiveness reduced. These firms are being "squeezed" to provide the resources needed in the nontraded sector for activities such as infrastructure development.

As the reconstruction phase winds down, the real exchange rate can be expected to depreciate. This will increase the competitiveness of both the export sector and the import-competing sector. To gain some idea of the likely extent of the reduction in the real exchange rate, the effects of halving the

FIGURE 4.10 Determination of the Real Exchange Rate with Financial Inflows

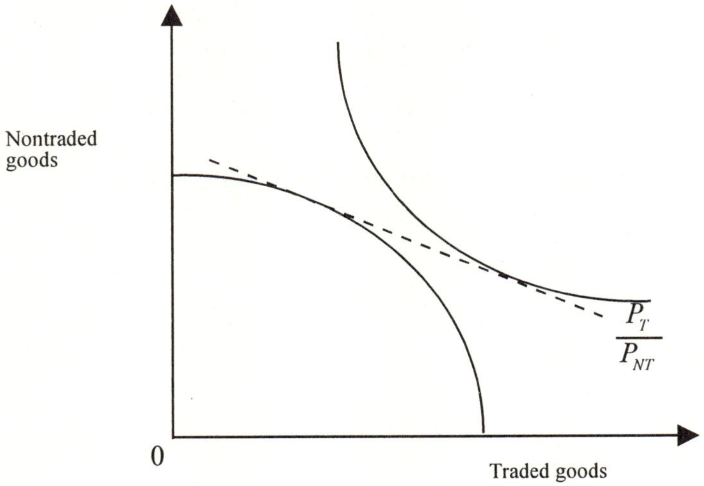

current financial inflow and the resulting trade deficit were considered using the model developed for this study. A halving of the financial flows assumes that Lebanon continues to be the beneficiary of a substantial net inflow of funds from the ROW, despite the need to service the debts incurred during reconstruction. If the balance of payments data on which the analysis is based fully reflected the flow of funds, then it would be probably be appropriate to specify complete elimination of these flows, or even a reversal. However, there are reasons to believe that the estimates on which the analysis is based overstate the magnitude of the capital inflows, particularly by inadequate measurement of services exports, and so the measured deficit on goods and services is likely to remain positive. Results of this experiment are presented in table 4.13.

The results in table 4.13 highlight the magnitude of the adjustments in Lebanon's trade position that are likely to be involved as the reconstruction process winds down. A key feature of the adjustment process is the decline in the price of nontraded goods. This real depreciation of almost 25 percent greatly increases the competitiveness of the export sector and allows exports to increase by nearly 45 percent. Import volumes decline by over 38 percent, causing a corresponding reduction in tariff revenues. The reduction in the price of nontraded goods puts downward pressure on consumer prices at a fixed nominal exchange rate, causing a 14 percent decline in overall consumer prices.

The trade implications of the winding down of reconstruction spending in Lebanon have much in common with the MFN liberalization experiment reported in table 4.8. Both result in a decline in the prices of nontraded goods and of consumer prices overall, a real exchange rate depreciation, an expansion of exports, and a decline in tariff revenues. Trade liberalization may have an important role to play in beginning the process of adjustment needed to deal with the reduction in the inflows associated with reconstruction. Certainly, it would help in the development of the competitive export industries that will be needed to pay Lebanon's way in the post-reconstruction phase.

TABLE 4.13 Consequences of Halving Financial Inflows in Lebanon

	Percent change
Export volume	44.5
Price of nontraded good	-24.6
Import volume	-38.2
Tariff revenue	-38.1
Consumer prices	-13.9

Appendix 4.1 Definitions of Commodity Aggregates used in the Study

At various points in this study, commodity trade is aggregated from the extremely fine detail found in the Customs Data into broader aggregates that allow comparison with the production structure and allow presentation of the data in more comprehensible form. These aggregations have been done using the commodity composites found in the GTAP model and a more aggregated set of commodities frequently used in work with this model. These commodity aggregates are set out in appendix table 4.1.

APPENDIX TABLE 4.1 GTAP Commodities and Broader Commodity Aggregates

Aggregated Commodity	GTAP Commodity	Aggregated Commodity	GTAP Commodity
Grains	Paddy rice Processed rice Wheat Other grains	Light manufacturing	Leather, etc. Lumber Other manufacturing
Non-grain crops	Non-grain crops	Transport equipment	Transport equipment
Livestock products	Meat products Milk products Other livestock products Wool	Machinery and equipment	Machinery and equipment
Processed food	Other food products Beverages and tobacco Fisheries	Petroleum and coal products	Petroleum and coal products
Natural resources	Forestry Coal Oil Gas Other minerals	Chemicals, rubber, and plastics	Chemicals, rubber, and plastics
Textiles	Textiles	Other heavy manufactures	Primary ferrous metals Nonferrous metals Fabricated metal Products Pulp paper, etc. Nonmetallic minerals
Apparel	Apparel		

Note: The aggregate commodities presented in this table have been defined by Hertel to allow presentation of reasonably compact and intelligible tables (Hertel 1997). The basic GTAP commodities can be related to the underlying trade data using a concordance with the Harmonized System 92 (GTAP web site at <www.agecon.purdue.edu/gtap/info/concord.htm>). This concordance was updated to the HS96 used in the Lebanese Customs data by examining the descriptions of the individual tariff line items and developing a concordance to allocate all of the HS96 commodity trade to the HS92 commodity categories.

Appendix 4.2 The Structure of the Model used in the Analysis

The structure of the model was greatly constrained by the availability of data about the structure of the Lebanese economy. In the absence of an input-output table, to represent the sectoral structure of the economy, it was not possible to develop a CGE model of the type used by Harrison, Rutherford, and Tarr (1997) for Turkey, by Rutherford, Rutström, and Tarr (1993) for Morocco, or by Konan and Maskus (1996) for Egypt. Instead, the structure of the model used for this analysis was based on the 1-2-3 model of Devarajan, Lewis, and Robinson (1993) extended to allow for trade with a range of partner countries. This modeling approach is much less demanding in terms of data requirements. Its requires only an estimate of total GDP and data on trade and tariffs at the level of disaggregation required, both of which are available. The core of the model can be summarized in six equations:

1. The expenditure function $e = e(\mathbf{p}, u)$
2. The demand equations $\partial e/\partial p_i = q_i = e_i(p,u)$
3. The revenue function $r = r(\mathbf{p}, v)$
4. The output supply functions $\partial r/\partial p_i = x_i = r_i\ (\mathbf{p}, v)$
5. The market clearing condition for the nontraded good
$$q_n = x_n$$
6. The income-expenditure condition (equivalently the balance of trade constraint)
$$e(\mathbf{p}, u) - r(\mathbf{p}, v) - (e_p - r_p).(\mathbf{p} - \mathbf{p}^*) = f$$

where $\boldsymbol{p}$ is a vector of domestic prices; u is the level of consumer utility; r is the maximum revenue generated from production in the economy given the available resources and technology, v; $\mathbf{p}^*$ is the world price vector; and f is the financial inflow from the ROW.

To deal with issues of preferential trade liberalization, an additional level was incorporated in the nest for demand and output. On the import side, this involved specifying an import expenditure function and corresponding import demand equations. On the export side, an export revenue equation and export supply functions were added:

7. The import expenditure function $em = (\mathbf{pm}, q_m)$
8. The import demand functions $q_{mi} = \partial em/\partial pm_i$
9. The export revenue function $rx = (\mathbf{px}, q_x)$
10. The export supply functions $qx_i = \partial rx/\partial px_I$

where *em* is the expenditure function for imports as a function of the aggregate quantity of imports and the prices of imports from different countries of origin; ***pm*** is a vector of the prices of imported goods; q_{mi} is the quantity of imports from origin country *i*; *rx* is the revenue generated from quantity of exports q_x ; ***px*** is a vector of prices of export goods; and qx_i is the volume of exports to destination *i*.

The model was implemented by specifying CES functions for the expenditure functions for total expenditure and expenditure on imports and CET functions for the revenue aggregators at both the total revenue and export revenue stages. The equations of the model were then differentiated and converted into percentage change form for efficient solution using GEMPACK (Codsi and Pearson 1988). Because of the large changes involved in many of the experiments, the coefficients of the model were updated and solved using a series of steps and extrapolation to ensure that the nonlinearity of the model was fully taken into account (Hertel, Horridge, and Pearson 1992).

The critical elasticity parameters were specified based on an interpretation of the extensive survey of the literature on import demand and supply elasticities provided by Goldstein and Khan (1985), together with recent econometric findings by Panagariya, Shah, and Mishra (1996) and a survey of the literature by Gunter (1995). Goldstein and Khan (1985, 1076) place the price elasticity of import demand at -0.5 to -1.0, with long-run demand elasticities (the type of interest in this study) consistently higher than short-run elasticities. On this basis, an elasticity of import demand of about -0.75 appeared reasonable. Using the CES function, the own-price elasticity of demand is related to the elasticity of substitution as $\eta = (1 - S_m).\sigma$, where S_m is the share of imports in total expenditure. Given the large share of imports in expenditure (50 percent), an elasticity of substitution between imports and the domestically produced good of 1.5 was chosen.

The base value for the elasticity of substitution between imports from different sources was specified at 3.0. This elasticity must be higher than the elasticity of demand for imports in total if imports from different sources are to be substitutes rather than complements. Further, the elasticity of demand for imports from a particular country, which includes this effect, has consistently been found to be above the elasticity of import demand. Goldstein and Khan's consensus estimate for the elasticity of export demand is more than twice the value for the elasticity of import demand. Further, Panagariya, Shah, and Mishra (1996) provide new estimates that suggest this elasticity for exports from developing countries may be much higher than has previously been thought.

The elasticity of transformation for exports is based on the evidence on export supply elasticities, which bear the same relationship to the elasticity of transformation in production as elasticities of import demand do to the elasticity of substitution. Goldstein and Khan (1985) place the elasticity of export supply in the range from 1.0 to 4.0 for industrial countries, while Gunter's survey suggests that a range from 0.8 to 2.5 might be more appropriate for developing countries. On this basis, an elasticity of transformation between domestic and exported goods of 1.5 was specified. The elasticity of transformation between markets was set at 3.0 on the assumption that the differences between the requirements of different export markets are less than the differences between those of the domestic and export markets.

Appendix 4.3 The Model Equations, Data, and Command Files

The first section of this appendix defines the sets, coefficients, and equations used in the model, together with the statements used to read in the information on coefficients contained in the data set and the formulas used to calculate the coefficients derived from this data set. The second section displays the actual data used to construct the coefficients for the base simulations. This section shows the command file that specifies the files from which coefficients and data are to be read, the choice of endogenous and exogenous variables, and the specification of the initial simulation, the elimination of tariffs on imports from the EU.

I. Model Equations

```
!--------------------------------------------------------!
!                  Set Statements                         !
!--------------------------------------------------------!
SET GOODS #All goods # (nontrad, import, export);
SET CONS #Consumer goods# (nontrad, import);
      Subset CONS is subset of GOODS;
SET PROD #Produced goods# (Nontrad, export);
      Subset PROD is subset of goods;
SET ACTIVITY #Represents Behavior by CES/T# (Cons,Prodn,Source,Destn);
SET REVEN #Sources of revenue# (prodn,tariff);
SET EXPE #Sources of expenditure# (reven,foreign);
SET ORIGIN #Import supplying countries# (EU15, SWZ, JAP, USA, CAN, ALG, BAR, CYP,
EGY, JOR, KUW, MOR, SAU, SYR, TUN, TUR, UAE, ROU, RUS, BRA, CHI, HOK, SIN,
THA,ROW);
!--------------------------------------------------------!
!                Variable Statements                      !
!--------------------------------------------------------!
VARIABLE
e #Expenditure function for Lebanon#;
u #Utility index#;
(all, i, goods)  p(i)        #Domestic Prices of composite goods#;
(all,i,CONS)     q(i)        #Demand for consumer good i #;
                 pc          #Consumer price index#;
                 em          #Expenditure on imports #;
(all,i,origin)   qm(i)       #Imports from supplying region i#;
(all,i,origin)   pcif(i)     #CIF price of imports from region i#;
(all,i,origin)   pm(i)       #Domestic price of imp from region i#;
(all,i,origin)   tau(i)      #Tariff rates from region i#;
(all,i,origin)   powtau(i)   #1 plus tariff rate#;
```

```
                px          #Price of composite output#;
                capacity    #Output capacity of the economy #;
                 r            #Revenue from production#;
(all,i,prod)    qx(i)        #Output of composite good i#;
                revx         #Revenue from exports#;
(all,i,origin)  qdx(i)       #Exports to country i#;
(all,i,origin)  pdx(i)       #Export price in country i#;
                trev         #Total tariff revenue#;
                f            #Foreign inflow#;
!--------------------------------------------------------!
!       Coefficients to be read in                       !
!--------------------------------------------------------!
COEFFICIENT:   GDP #GDP at mkt prices#;
COEFFICIENT:   (all,i,origin) M(i) #Imports at CIF prices #;
      UPDATE   (all,i,origin) M(i) = qm(i)*pcif(i);
COEFFICIENT:   (all,i,origin) TAR(i) #Tariff rate on imports from origin region i#;
      UPDATE   (all,i,origin) TAR(i) = tau(i);
COEFFICIENT:   (all,i,activity) SIGMA(i) #Subst and Transformation parameters#;
COEFFICIENT:   (all,i,origin) X(i) #Exports to region i#;
COEFFICIENT:   (all,i,CONS) C(i) #Expenditure on final consumption goods#;
!--------------------------------------------------------!
!                Read Statements                         !
!--------------------------------------------------------!
FILE LEBDATA #Data for Lebanon Model#;
Read GDP from file LEBDATA Header "GDP";
Read M from file LEBDATA Header "IMP";
Read X from file LEBDATA Header  "EXP";
Read TAR from file LEBDATA Header "TAR";
Read SIGMA from file LEBDATA Header "SIG";
!--------------------------------------------------------!
!       Coefficients to be calculated                    !
!--------------------------------------------------------!
COEFFICIENT:   PRODN #Value of output#;
FORMULA:       PRODN = GDP - SUM(j,origin,(TAR(j))*M(j));
FORMULA:       C("nontrad") = Prodn - SUM(j,origin, X(j));
FORMULA:       C("import") = SUM(j,origin,M(j)*(1 + TAR(j)));
COEFFICIENT:   (all,i,CONS) SC(i) #Share of good i in final consumption#;
FORMULA:       (all,i,CONS) SC(i) = C(i)/SUM(j,CONS,C(j));
COEFFICIENT:   (all,i,origin) SM(i) #Import shares at domestic prices#;
FORMULA:       (all,i,origin)  SM(i) = (1 + TAR(i))*M(i)/SUM(j,origin,(1 +TAR(j))*M(j));
COEFFICIENT:   (all,i,origin) TAUCONV(i) #Convert % Ch in ta to % ch in 1 + tar#;
FORMULA:       (all,i,origin) TAUCONV(i) = TAR(i)/(1+TAR(i));
COEFFICIENT:   (all,i,prod) SX(i);
FORMULA:       SX("nontrad") = C("nontrad")/(C("nontrad") + SUM (j,origin,X(j)));
FORMULA:       SX("export") = SUM(j,origin,X(j))/(C("nontrad") + SUM(j,origin,X(j)));
COEFFICIENT:   (all,i,reven) SY(i);
FORMULA:       SY("Prodn") = PRODN/GDP;
```

```
FORMULA:        SY("tariff") = SUM(i,origin,TAR(i)*M(i))/GDP;
COEFFICIENT:    TR #Total tariff revenues#;
FORMULA:        TR = SUM (i,origin,TAR(i)*M(i));
COEFFICIENT:    (all,i,origin) STR(i) #Share of origin i in total tar rev#;
FORMULA:        (all,i,origin) STR(i) = (TAR(i)*M(i))/SUM(j,origin,TAR(j)*M(j));
COEFFICIENT:    (all,i,origin) SDX(i) #Share of market i in total exports#;
FORMULA:        (all,i,origin)  SDX(i)= X(i)/SUM(j,origin,X(j));
COEFFICIENT EXPEND #Total absorption#;
FORMULA:        EXPEND = GDP + SUM(j,origin,M(j)) - SUM(j,origin,X(j));
COEFFICIENT:    (all,i,expe) SE(i) #Share of foreign inflow in total expenditure#;
FORMULA:        SE("reven") = GDP/EXPEND;
FORMULA:        SE("foreign") = (SUM(j,origin,M(j)) - SUM(j,origin,X(j)))/EXPEND;
UPDATE (CHANGE) GDP=Prodn*r/100 + TR*trev/100;
!---------------------------------------------------------!
!       Equations                   !
!---------------------------------------------------------!
EQUATION EXPFNCTN #Expenditure function#
       e = Sum(i,CONS,SC(i)*p(i)) + u;
EQUATION DEMAND #Demand Functions#
       (all,i,CONS) q(i) = u - SIGMA("CONS")*(p(i) - Sum(j,CONS,SC(j)*p(j)));
EQUATION CONPRICE #Consumer Price Index#
       pc = Sum(i,CONS,SC(i)*p(i));
EQUATION IMPEXPEND #Import expenditure function#
       em = SUM(i,origin,SM(i)*pm(i)) + q("import");
EQUATION IMPDEMAND #Qty of imports from region i#
       (all,i,origin) qm(i)=q("import") - SIGMA("source")*(pm(i)-SUM(j,origin,SM(j)*pm(j)));
EQUATION IMPRICE #Composite import price#
       p("import") = SUM(j,origin,SM(j)*pm(j));
EQUATION IMPPRICE #Changes in domestic prices of imports#
       (all,i,origin) pm(i) = pcif(i) + powtau(i);
EQUATION CHPOWTAU #Changes in the power of the import tariff#
       (all,i,origin) powtau(i) = TAUCONV(i)*tau(i);
EQUATION PRODREV #Revenue from production#
       r = SUM(i,prod,SX(i)*p(i)) + capacity;
EQUATION OUTPUT #Output of composite goods#
       (all,i,prod) qx(i) = capacity + SIGMA("PRODN")*(p(i) - SUM(j,prod,SX(j)*p(j)));
EQUATION NTCLEAR #Mkt clearing condition for NT goods#
       q("nontrad") = qx ("nontrad");
EQUATION PROUTPUT #Composite price for output#
       px = SUM(i,prod,SX(i)*p(i));
EQUATION EXPREV #Revenue from exports#
       revx = SUM(j,origin,SDX(j)*pdx(j)) + qx("export");
EQUATION EXQTY #Exports to destination i#   (all,i,origin)
       qdx(i) = qx("export") + SIGMA("Destn")*(pdx(i) - SUM(j,origin,SDX(j)*pdx(j)));
EQUATION PREXP #Composite price of exports#
       p("export") = SUM(i,origin,SDX(i)*pdx(i));
EQUATION TARREV #Changes in tariff revenues#
       trev = SUM(i,origin,STR(i)*(tau(i) + qm(i) + pcif(i)));
EQUATION INCOMEXP #Income expenditure condition#
       e =SE("reven")*(SY("prodn")*r + SY("tariff")*trev) + SE("foreign")*f;
```

II. Display of Model Data

GDP at market prices.

COLUMN	1	
ROW 1	ROW	TOTALS
	20171.0	20171.0

Exports to region i.

Next submatrix contains numbers from the X(ORIGIN) part, which are positions (1-25) of X(ORIGIN).

COLUMN	1	2	3	4	5	6
ROW 1	EU15	SWZ	JAP	USA	CAN	ALG
	362.310028	44.580040	14.136049	62.033718	11.558180	4.076928
COLUMN	7	8	9	10	11	12
ROW 1	BAR	CYP	EGY	JOR	KUW	MOR
	31.175228	26.229221	47.663734	124.783836	141.829300	0.887512
COLUMN	13	14	15	16	17	18
ROW 1	SAU	SYR	TUN	TUR	UAE	ROU
	302.917877	183.712860	2.845081	41.325035	200.403000	27.676888
COLUMN	19	20	21	22	23	24
ROW 1	RUS	BRA	CHI	HOK	SIN	THA
	25.140749	8.253618	0.554712	11.987265	0.753450	1.293765
COLUMN	25	ROW				
ROW 1	ROW					
	429.871674	2107.999756				

Imports at CIF prices.

Next submatrix contains numbers from the M(ORIGIN) part, which are positions (1-25) of M(ORIGIN).

COLUMN	1	2	3	4	5	6
ROW 1	EU15	SWZ	JAP	USA	CAN	ALG
	6508.231445	424.705475	673.692383	1619.747314	91.284927	10.042952
COLUMN	7	8	9	10	11	12
ROW 1	BAR	CYP	EGY	JOR	KUW	MOR
	8.707051	41.158096	106.207359	84.523247	11.878446	11.915149
COLUMN	13	14	15	16	17	18
ROW 1	SAU	SYR	TUN	TUR	UAE	ROU
	190.187912	529.396667	8.888326	280.221832	51.087238	90.334663
COLUMN	19	20	21	22	23	24
ROW 1	RUS	BRA	CHI	HOK	SIN	THA
	199.711	125.789	400.456	24.5164	64.7600	117.380
COLUMN	25	ROW				
	ROW					
ROW 1	1893.18	13568.0				

Next submatrix contains numbers from the SIGMA(ACTIVITY) part, which are positions (1-4) of SIGMA(ACTIVITY).

COLUMN	1	2	3	4	ROW
ROW 1	Cons	Prodn	Source	Destn	
	1.500000	1.500000	3.000000	3.000000	

Next submatrix contains numbers from the TAR(ORIGIN) part, which are positions (1-25) of TAR(ORIGIN).

COLUMN	1	2	3	4	5	6
ROW 1	EU15	SWZ	JAP	USA	CAN	ALG
	0.151000	0.020900	0.161000	0.148000	0.089000	0.039000
COLUMN	7	8	9	10	11	12
ROW 1	BAR	CYP	EGY	JOR	KUW	MOR
	0.078000	0.180000	0.1410001	0.150000	0.115000	0.120000
COLUMN	13	14	15	16	17	18
ROW 1	SAU	SYR	TUN	TUR	UAE	ROU
	0.105000	0.587000	0.243000	0.112000	0.078000	0.062000
COLUMN	19	20	21	22	23	24
ROW 1	RUS	BRA	CHI	HOK	SIN	THA
	0.076000	0.075000	0.167000	0.163000	0.161000	0.157000
COLUMN	25					
ROW 1	ROW					
	0.108000					

III. The Command File for the EU Liberalization Experiment

```
    !Command file for simulating Lebanon Model
Auxiliary files = Lebanon;
    !Data files
File lebdata = lebdata.dat;
    !Equations file information
Equation file = Lebanon; Model = Lebanon; Version = 1; Identifier = Basic Lebanon-EU Model
    !Display file;
Display file = Lebanon.dis; Simulation = Yes;
    !Closure;
Exogenous pcif tau capacity pdx f; Rest endogenous; Shock tau = uniform -100;
    !Solution method
Method = Euler; Subintervals =10; steps = 2 4 6; Verbal description = MFN Scenario;
Solution file = Lebanon;  Log file = Lebanon.log;  Updated file lebdata= lebdata.upd;
```

NOTES

Superb research assistance by Emiko Fukase is gratefully acknowledged.

1. Bhagwati and Panagariya (1996) show that, beginning with equal tariffs on imports from partner and non-partner countries, the marginal welfare impact of reducing the tariff on the partner will initially be positive but will decline as the tariff on the partner declines.

2. These economies are Bahrain, Egypt, Jordan, Lebanon, Oman, Palestine, Qatar Syria, and Yemen.

3. The *World Development Report 1996* estimates per capita income in Qatar at $12,820 in 1994 dollars.

4. Kravis and Lipsey (1988) found that prices of tradable goods were 40 percent higher in their highest real GDP group than in their lowest. Since their highest income group had an average income 16 times higher than their low income group, this difference overstates the likely difference between Qatar and Lebanon, where the income difference is more in the order of four times. A more likely plausible estimate of the predicted difference would be in the order of 10 percent.

5. The Effective Rate of Assistance is defined as:

$$ERP = \frac{VA^1 - VA^*}{VA^*}$$

where VA^1 is the value added per unit of output at distorted prices, while VA^* is the value added at world prices. VA^1 is known, while VA^* must be calculated to make the approach operational.

6. The import tariff on petroleum is equivalent to an excise tax in the absence of domestic production. If, as seems to be the case, a tax on domestic production would be levied in the event of domestic production resuming, then the current duty is equivalent to an import duty. The effective rate presented is relevant should domestic production resume but be untaxed.

7. Only industrial sectors are included since data on the share of wages in value added is available from the Lebanese industrial census only for these sectors. The petroleum products sector is excluded because of its extremely high effective rate of assistance.

8. The structure of the model and the choice of parameter values are discussed in appendix 4.2. The equations of the model, the data used and an illustrative command file used to specify which variables are exogenous and the shocks are presented in appendix 4.3.

9. This price change is purely a real phenomenon and is completely independent of the exchange rate mechanism used. It will arise even in a purely dollarized economy.

10. According to World Bank projections, expenditure in Lebanon was 1.57 times GDP in 1996.

11. The countries actually considered were Algeria, Egypt, Jordan, Morocco, Syria, Tunisia, and Turkey. As part of its agreement with the EU, Turkey is entering into FTAs with a range of other countries having FTAs with the EU. Ideally, this experiment would also have included liberalization with respect to Israel and Palestine, but there was essentially no recorded trade with these economies in the base period.

12. The percentage change in the price of imported goods is given by the impact of the tariff change on the price of imported goods divided by the initial price of imported goods. For a good with a world price of unity, this change is -0.154/(1+0.154), or 13.3 percent.

13. For this purpose, a standard CGE model is one containing a two-level nested CES structure where consumers choose between a domestic good and a composite of imports from all sources, and then choose between competing suppliers of imports.

CHAPTER 5

A Free Trade Agreement between the European Union and a Representative Arab Mediterranean Country: A Quantitative Assessment

Thomas F. Rutherford, Elisabet E. Rutström, and David Tarr

During the 1980s, the foreign trade policies of many Arab Mediterranean countries began to move from inward-looking import substitution toward outward-looking export promotion. As of the mid-1990s, average collected tariff rates in countries such as Tunisia had fallen to about 10 percent in manufacturing and resource industries, while in Egypt average tariffs were approaching 20 percent, down from some 35 percent in the early 1980s. Despite this progress, in many countries tariff surcharges of various types and NTBs remain prevalent, and total protection including the surcharges and the tariff equivalent of the NTBs remains relatively high compared to many export-oriented economies in East Asia, Eastern Europe, and Latin America.

Countries in the region are in the process of implementing or negotiating FTAs with the EU. The importance of European trading partners has been growing during the 1980s and 1990s. For example, in 1996 over 50 percent of Tunisian and Moroccan trade was with European trading partners, dominated by France, Germany, and Italy. The prior existence of the cooperation agreements with the EU imply that Arab Mediterranean countries already enjoyed free access to European markets in almost all industrial products and raw materials on a non-reciprocal basis. Exceptions include some textile and clothing goods that are covered by voluntary export restraint agreements and restrictions in agricultural products, especially in fruits and vegetables.

The Euro-Mediterranean FTAs will eliminate tariffs and NTBs against imports from the EU. In exchange, Arab Mediterranean nations will receive some improved access to EU markets, primarily in agricultural products, although less was achieved in opening EU markets to agricultural exports than was hoped. Harmonizing health and technical regulations with the standards of the EU will further result in lower costs and higher revenues for exporters. Adopting a standardized system (such as EN 29000 or ISO 9000) will facilitate accreditation in the EU. Some financial aid from the EU will be included in order to facilitate the economic restructuring that will result from the FTA. Additional beneficial effects on trade and growth can also be expected from more favorable access to credit and information activities, as well as improved telecommunications. Policies to encourage tourism are also suggested as part of the agreement.

In this chapter, the impact of the EMAs is quantitatively assessed. Rather than dealing with a specific country, a benchmark dataset that reflects the characteristics of countries in the region has been constructed. Thus, the "country" may be considered a representative small economy in the Arab Mediterranean region. What is somewhat innovative about this analysis is that all of the aspects of the agreements discussed above are quantitatively assessed, i.e., the focus is not simply on the tariff changes in the representative country.[1] Moreover, the impacts of the various elements of the agreements are decomposed, so that the relative importance of the various components of the agreements can be assessed.

Estimates of the aggregate impacts on national welfare and sectoral impacts in terms of production and employment suggest that a typical country should expect to gain between 3 percent to 5 percent of GDP per year from a FTA with the EU, depending on the assumptions that are made regarding the coverage of the agreement. It is also estimated that tariff liberalization with respect to the rest of the world would provide additional benefits with very little additional adjustment costs. In the long run, there is a significant expansion of labor-intensive light manufactures such as textiles and clothing, primarily at the expense of tourism services and petroleum and natural gas.

Given the industry adjustments that will be necessary as a result of the FTAs, many Arab Mediterranean countries are concerned about appropriate industrial restructuring policies. The final section of the chapter departs from the model and draws from the literature on industrial restructuring to provide suggestions of appropriate industrial restructuring policies for Arab Mediterranean countries adapting to the FTAs with the EU.

A Small Open Economy Model

General Model Structure

The Small Open Economy (SOE) model used in this chapter is designed for trade policy analysis with a large number of sectors. The model is a "generic" general equilibrium model of a single economy along the lines of De Melo and

Tarr (1992), Harrison, Rutherford, and Tarr (1993, 1996) and Rutherford, Rutström, and Tarr (1997). The most important extension embodied here is a detailed treatment of trade sectors and trading partners in a way that is consistent with more aggregated production structures. In particular, both imports and exports of each sector are decomposed into imports and exports from and to the EU and imports and exports from and to the ROW. This extension allows for consistent modeling of the detailed impacts of trade agreements, despite not being able to model the full production detail corresponding to those policies due to lack of data.

Goods are produced using primary factors and intermediate inputs. Primary factors include labor and capital. In the short-run model, it is assumed that labor is fully mobile across sectors and that capital is sector-specific. In the alternative long-run formulation, both factors are allowed to be mobile across sectors. The short-run model is expected to generate smaller welfare gains from liberalization, since resources are constrained in their ability to reallocate to more productive uses. On the other hand, the short-run model is also expected to exhibit less extreme changes in production structure since the sector specificity of capital generates less elastic supply schedules.

Production exhibits constant returns to scale and individual firms behave competitively, selecting output levels such that marginal cost at those output levels equals the given market price. Output is differentiated between goods destined for the domestic and export markets. Exports are further distinguished according to whether they are destined for the EU or the ROW. This relationship is characterized by a two-level CET frontier. Composite output is an aggregate of domestic output and composite exports; composite exports are aggregates of exports for the EU and ROW markets.

Final demand by private households arises from nested CES utility functions. This allows consumer decision-making to occur in the form of multistage budgeting. At the top level, goods from different sectors compete, subject to the budget constraint of the consumer, and all income elasticities are unity. In the second stage, the consumer decides how much to spend on domestic or imported goods in each sector, subject to income allocated to spending in that sector in the first stage. Finally, having decided how much to spend on imports as a whole, the consumer allocates this expenditure on EU and ROW imports. Each allocation decision is modeled as a CES function.

The model allows tariff rates to differ depending on whether the imports are from the EU or the ROW. Exports can be sold at different prices depending on whether they are destined for EU or ROW markets. The same is possible on the import side. The small country assumption is employed regarding both imports and exports with respect to both the ROW and the EU. The exogenous export price to the EU is allowed to change as a result of trade policy concessions by the EU to the representative economy, and the reduction of trade

TABLE 5.1 Key Sectoral Data for the Typical Arab Mediterranean Country

							TRADE BY SECTOR			TARIFF RATE	
	(1)	(2)	(3)	(4)	(5)	(6)	(7)	(8)	(9)	(10)	(11)
	Output	Labor	Capital	Imports	% from EU	Exports	% from EU	Imports	Exports	EU	ROW
AGRICULTURE											
Agriculture and fishery (AGF)	11	3	26	5	21	3	85	11	6	23	8
MANUFACTURING	39	19	15	82	-	55	-	-	-	-	-
Food products (FOP)	10	3	4	5	36	5	70	15	9	15	15
Nonmetal mineral prod (NMM)	3	2	2	1	187	2	30	15	14	18	12
Electromechanical ind (EMI)	7	4	2	37	76	9	80	68	25	11	12
Chemicals (CHM)	6	2	1	12	59	11	36	48	36	13	10
Textiles (TEX)	9	7	5	19	90	27	94	54	58	23	12
Misc. manufacturing (MIS)	4	2	1	7	60	2	50	34	10	14	12
MINING AND RELATED	8	3	12	8	-	13	-	-	-	-	-
Mining (MIN)	1	2	1	-	24	1	71	17	18	10	2
Petroleum and natural gas (PNG)	6	1	10	8	30	12	99	39	42	12	1
Electricity (ELE)	1	1	1	0	-	-	-	-	-	-	-
Water (WAT)	-	1	-	0	-	-	-	-	-	-	-
SERVICES	42	74	48	5	-	29	-	-	-	-	-
Construction (CON)	7	12	2	0	-	-	-	-	-	-	-
Trade (TRD)	5	3	13	0	-	-	-	-	-	-	-
Transport and com (TRC)	6	11	6	3	60	8	33	16	27	1	-
Tourism (TOU)	8	5	6	0	-	18	54	-	-	-	-
Financial/insurance svcs. (FIN)	2	4	4	-	-	-	-	5	2	-	-
Private services (PRS)	6	5	17	2	-	3	-	6	8	-	-
Public services (PUB)	8	34	0	-	-	-	-	-	-	-	-

and transport costs from the EU is accommodated by reducing the exogenous import price from the EU. These distinctions allow for the study of several policy options that are part of the FTA with the EU that result in improved market access for exports as well as imports and also allows for the assessment of some policy options not typically analyzed in modeling exercises.[2]

Government expenditures and investment demand are exogenous. Funding of government expenditures is provided by tax revenues and tariff revenues. In addition to tariffs, the government also derives income from indirect taxes (net of subsidies). These are modeled as Value Added Taxes (VAT). Since private consumption equals the income from primary factors plus net transfers to the consumer by the government (from domestic and foreign trade taxes), Walras law is satisfied. Public consumption is balanced with revenue.

World market import and export prices are fixed, so there are no endogenous changes in the TOT. In other words, import supplies and export demands are infinitely elastic at given world prices. In some scenarios, the price of exports to the EU is exogenously increased to represent improved market access to the EU, or the price of EU imports is decreased, reflecting lowered costs of trading with the EU. The current account balances the value of exports and imports taking into account exogenously fixed capital inflows.

Empirical Implementation of the Model

The Input-Output (IO) table, which distinguishes 18 production sectors, provides a consistent set of IO relationships showing intermediate, final demand, and value added transactions. The IO table is representative of the structure of an Arab Mediterranean economy, which relies on tourism and natural resources (mining, primarily oil and gas) for much of its foreign exchange earnings. Table 5.1 summarizes some of the most important industry data employed in the model, and displays the names of each of the 18 sectors along with a 3-letter acronym for later reference.

Columns 1 to 3 of table 5.1 show the value share of output, employment, and capital by sector, derived from the IO table. About 40 percent of the output, 50 percent of the capital stock, and 75 percent of the labor force is found in the service sectors. Manufacturing sectors are responsible for another 40 percent of output while utilizing only about 15 percent to 20 percent of primary factors. The agriculture and mining sectors deliver the remaining 20 percent of output. The agricultural sector is the largest single user of capital in the economy (26 percent), which reflects a heavy reliance on irrigation for many crops, and the treatment in the IO table of payments to owner-occupiers as operating surplus.[3] The public services sector is the most important employer of labor.

Columns 4 and 6 display the sectoral decomposition of imports and exports, where the share accounted for by EU imports and exports is displayed in columns 5 and 7. Textiles, tourism, and petroleum and natural gas account for almost 60 percent of all exports. The electromechanical products sector has the largest share of imports (35 percent), followed by textiles and chemicals. Trade with the EU comprises a dominant share of both exports and imports in almost every sector. It is only in chemicals that exports to other trading partners are important. This sector accounts for over 10 percent of all exports, and over 60 percent of that goes to non-EU destinations. On the import side, non-EU sources are primarily important in the petroleum and natural gas sector, which accounts for almost 8 percent of all imports, 70 percent of which originate in non-EU countries. Columns 8 and 9 show the importance of trade for each sector. Only in the electromechanical and the textiles sectors are import shares more than 50 percent. On the export side, there is a heavy dependence on trade for textiles and, of course, for tourism.

The protection rates displayed in the table reflect import tariffs and NTB ad valorem tariff equivalents. The latter pertain to certain agricultural and food sectors. These aggregate to ad valorem rates of 18 percent on imports from all regions. The NTB ad valorem equivalents reflect, among other things, import certificate requirements of the type discussed in GATT (1994). However, for most product categories, it is assumed that these certificates do not represent barriers to trade.

The only domestic tax is assumed to be a uniform VAT levied on domestic value-added. The VAT is imposed at a rate (about 20 percent) such that the government derives twice as much revenue from VAT collections than it derives from duty collections in the benchmark. In counterfactual simulations, the impact of eliminating exemptions in the VAT is examined.

Estimates of elasticities of substitution must be assumed for nested CES functions of various types. Output is a CES aggregate of value added and intermediate inputs, where we typically assume a zero elasticity of substitution at this top level, i.e., Leontief production. Labor and capital in each sector combine in a CES aggregate to produce value added with elasticity of substitution (see table 5.2). Substitution of intermediate inputs in production is also Leontief. On the export side, output is transformed between goods for domestic and export markets with a transformation elasticity of 2.0 and further transformed across destinations (the EU and ROW) with an elasticity of 4.0.[4]

In demand, all goods are a CES (Armington) aggregate of domestic and imported varieties. The elasticity of substitution between aggregate composite goods is unity, i.e., Cobb-Douglas. The elasticity of substitution between imported and domestic goods in the Armington aggregate is set at a value of 2.0 for all goods. Imported goods are also a CES aggregate of varieties from the EU and ROW with elasticity of substitution set at 4.0.

The SOE model is generated with GAMS software developed by Brooke, Kendrick, and Meeraus (1988) and solved with the MPS/GE software developed by Rutherford (1989, 1992).

Results

Overall Results: Short and Long Run Models

In this section, the overall impacts of a FTA with the EU and related policy scenarios are examined. The complete set of simulation scenarios is listed in box 5.1. The FTAs with the EU involve a sequential reduction in import barriers, with 40 percent of all imports liberalized early and the remainder backloaded. Therefore, elimination of NTBs in food and agriculture, liberalization of tariffs on 40 percent of all imports from the EU, and complete tariff elimination against imports from the EU are separately investigated.

Following the proposed FTA, the impact from improved market access to the EU for agricultural exporters is also simulated. This is modeled through improved terms-of-trade (TOT) for the agricultural sector. This TOT effect is expected to have the opposite effect on the agricultural sector compared to the elimination of NTBs. Some possible effects from harmonizing health and technical standards with the EU and from improvements in the trading environment through more efficient telecommunications and financial services are also investigated. The latter scenarios are expected to manifest themselves as TOT improvements. Also included is a scenario designed to illustrate the effects of a FTA with the EU in the context of a stylized representation of tariff liberalization resulting from the Uruguay Round. A scenario which extends the FTA beyond the Uruguay Round context and sees the country engage in complete liberalization of import tariffs on all trading partners is also examined. Given the possible exclusion of the agriculture and food sectors from the FTA, EXAG looks at tariff liberalization exempting agriculture and food.

TABLE 5.2 Elasticities of Substitution between Labor and Capital Use

Industry	Elasticity	Industry	Elasticity
AGF	0.945	ELE	1.884
FOP	0.945	WAT	1.884
NMM	0.4256	CON	1.988
EMI	0.9808	TRD	1.283
CHM	1.009	TRC	1.884
TEX	0.9266	TOU	2.055
MIS	1.189	FIN	2.055
MIN	0.4256	PRS	2.055
PNG	0.293	PUB	1.988

Finally, the scenario NEWVAT investigates the impact of eliminating exemptions and making the VAT uniform across sectors of the economy.[5] This is simulated as a reintroduction of distortionary VAT rates from the benchmark uniform rates.

The impacts of each scenario on welfare and other aggregate measures are shown in table 5.3. For convenience, all tables employ the scenario acronyms defined in box 5.1 and the sector acronyms defined in table 5.1. Some sectoral impacts are presented in the following sections.

In table 5.3, welfare is measured as the equivalent variation in income for the private household that would just offset the change in welfare brought about by the counter-factual scenario. It is measured as a percentage of benchmark GDP (WELFARE%). For the purpose of reporting welfare changes as a percent of GDP, we alternatively divide by private consumption rather

BOX 5.1 Simulation Scenarios

EU-40 Elimination of tariffs on 40 percent of import value from the EU, corresponding to the least protected sectors.

EU-TAR Elimination of tariffs on all imports from the EU.

EU-NTB Elimination of NTBs in food and agriculture imports from the EU.

EU-AGR Improved access to agricultural markets in EU, corresponding to an assumed 8 percent improvement in the agricultural export prices to the EU.

EU-STD Harmonization of standards assumed to improve export prices for all tradable sectors to the EU by 2 percent.

EU-TEL Improvements in trade related activities such as telecommunications and financial services assumed to result in higher export prices and lower import prices of 1 percent each for all tradable sectors relative to the EU.

LIB-EU *All* expected effects from a free-trade agreement with the EU, including tariff and NTB elimination, and changing terms-of-trade due to improved agricultural market access, harmonization of standards, and more efficient trading environment.

LIB-UR Free-trade agreement with the EU *plus* 30 percent across-the-board tariff liberalization, reflecting effects from the completion of the Uruguay Round.

LIB Free-trade agreement with the EU *plus* 100 percent across-the-board tariff liberalization.

EXAG Elimination of tariffs on all imports from the EU, excluding agriculture.

NEWVAT Changing the uniform VAT assumption to a distortionary VAT system.

than full GDP (GDP/CONS%). As we do not allow investment or government demand to vary with import prices, the use of private consumption as the denominator for welfare gains as a percent of GDP is appropriate given the modeling assumptions. The numeraire, PU, the price of the composite utility good, which is a broad basket of consumption goods, is essentially analogous to a consumer price index (CPI). The percentage change in the real exchange rate is denoted by PFX/PU. It is best interpreted as a measure of the purchasing power of domestic production; it can be informally interpreted as the real price of foreign exchange. One measure of the extent of resource adjustment brought about by the scenario, hence of the possible transition costs of adjustment, is provided by the percentage of the total labor force that moves from one industry to another (LAB.ADJ%). Another component of adjustment costs is reported in table 5.3 as the losses in returns to capital in declining industries

TABLE 5.3 Aggregate Effects (% indication percentage change from base)

Short-Run Results (sector-specific capital model)						
	EU-40	EU-TAR	EU-NTB	EU-AGR	EU-STD	EU-TEL
WELFARE %	-0.2	0.5	0.1	0.2	1.1	1.2
GDP/CONS%	-0.2	0.4	0.1	0.2	1.1	1.2
PFX/PU%	0.9	4.4	0.8	-0.3	-1.0	-0.4
LAB.ADJ%	0.2	1.7	0.2	0.1	0.3	0.2
CAP.ADJ%	0.5	2.2	0.4	0.2	-	1.1
TAU	1.1	1.4	1.0	1.0	1.0	1.0
TRADE INT%	70.5	73.8	70.1	69.9	69.8	69.7
	LIB-EU	LIB-UR	LIB	EXAG	NEWVAT	
WELFARE %	3.1	3.3	3.7	0.4	-3.0	
GDP/CONS%	3.0	3.2	3.6	0.3	-3.7	
PFX/PU%	3.7	4.1	5.1	3.8	-1.6	
LAB.ADJ%	2.1	2.2	2.3	1.7	5.2	
CAP.ADJ%	1.1	1.4	2.1	7.6	-	
TAU	1.3	1.4	1.4	1.3	2.3	
TRADE INT%	73.9	74.1	74.6	73.6	72.8	
Long-Run Results (mobile capital model)						
	EU-40	EU-TAR	EU-NTB	EU-AGR	EU-STD	EU-TEL
WELFARE %	-0.1	1.6	0.2	0.1	1.3	1.3
GDP/CONS%	-0.1	1.2	0.2	0.1	1.3	1.3
PFX/PU%	0.6	-0.1	0.4	-	-1.2	-0.6
LAB.ADJ%	0.2	7.0	0.2	0.1	0.9	0.7
TAU	1.1	1.3	1.0	1.0	1.0	1.0
TRADE INT%	70.8	82.0	70.3	69.6	70.5	70.2
	LIB-EU	LIB-UR	LIB	EXAG	NEWVAT	
WELFARE %	4.7	4.9	5.3	1.5	-9.7	
GDP/CONS%	4.2	4.4	4.8	1.1	-12.5	
PFX/PU%	-2.1	-1.8	-1.2	-0.5	-2.8	
LAB.ADJ%	8.8	8.9	9.2	6.9	9.9	
TAU	1.3	1.3	1.4	1.3	2.7	
TRADE INT%	84.2	84.5	85.7	81.6	78.4	

in terms of the numeraire, measured as percent of the benchmark capital stock value (CAP.ADJ%). We explain the methodology for these measures in more detail in the following sections. The scalar change of the uniform VAT rate that is required to ensure constant real government expenditures (TAU) is reported.[6] Finally, a standard measure of "trade intensity," defined as the sum of the value of imports and exports divided by twice GDP and then expressed as a percentage (TRADE INT%), is reported.

Welfare Gains

First consider the scenario LIB-EU, which is the most encompassing version of the FTA with the EU. This scenario results in improvements in annual welfare and GDP of about 3.1 percent in the short run and 4.7 percent in the long run. If, in addition, the liberalization that will be undertaken as part of Uruguay Round (LIB-UR) is taken into consideration, the welfare gain increases to 3.3 percent in the short run and 4.9 percent in the long run. The largest welfare gain is found for the complete unilateral tariff liberalization scenario (scenario LIB) which is about 3.7 percent in the short run and 5.3 percent in the long run.

The scenario EU-40 deserves special attention because it produces a reduction in welfare. It involves eliminating tariffs against EU imports for sectors with the lowest tariffs such that 40 percent of the value of EU imports are affected. This was a feature of both the Moroccan and Tunisian agreements (Hoekman and Djankov 1997a). The EU-40 scenario reflects a strategy which is designed to minimize adjustment costs in the short run and defer until later in the implementation period of the FTA reductions in tariffs that are likely to lead to more disruption of production. The EU-40 scenario reduces welfare (or real income) because although the average tariff falls (thus reducing the anti-trade bias of the economy), the variance of the tariff is increased; relatively speaking, the sectors already receiving the highest protection and which have too many resources gain at the expense of the less protected sectors. The sector distortion, along with trade diversion costs of regionally discriminatory liberalization, dominates the benefits of lowering the average level of the tariff.

Finally, the scenario EXAG is of particular interest given that the FTAs exempt the agricultural and food sectors. Tariff elimination on all remaining sectors is still expected to be beneficial and the magnitudes slightly smaller than EU-TAR, i.e., around 0.4 percent in the short run and 1.5 percent of GDP in the long run.

The reason for the increase in gains in the long run derive from the fact that the greater capital mobility implies that the elasticity of supply is greater for all firms in the long run model.[7] With greater elasticity of supply, the gains to the economy from tariff removal (in terms of removed production deadweight loss) will be higher. At the same time, the greater elasticity of supply in the long run implies that there is a greater output adjustment in response to the change in tariffs and more movement of factors of production including labor.

Adjustment Costs

In table 5.3, we have endogenously estimated the adjustment or "restructuring" costs associated with the policy changes. Those losses have been decomposed into labor adjustment costs and capital adjustment costs. As labor is forced to shift industries, it will require real resources to move and retrain workers for the new employment. These costs are estimated by a proxy: we assume that for each worker that must change jobs, there are costs of adjustment equal to one year of average wages. The results are presented in the row labeled LAB.ADJ%.[8] In the long run with mobility, capital moves to the point where the rate of return is equalized across sectors; in the short run with fixed capital, there is a return to capital in each sector which differs in general from that in other sectors. Thus, mobile capital results in greater movement of capital across sectors but less variation in the rental rate on capital.

From the parameter LAB.ADJ%, it is evident that in the short run 2.1 percent of the labor force will have to change jobs due to the FTA (the scenario LIB-EU), whereas over four times as many (8.8 percent) must change jobs in the long run. This corresponds to 2.1 percent and 4.8 percent of private consumption GDP in the short and long run, respectively. The reason that there is less movement of labor in the specific capital version of the model is that the rent on capital varies in response to a change in demand. But an increase in the rent on sector specific capital reduces the output expansion in response to an increase in demand for the output of the sector. This in turn mutes the increased demand for labor.

The second component of adjustment costs that we estimate is capital adjustment cost. As a result of changes in relative prices, some plant and equipment may become redundant in their industries. Some may be used in other industries with little adjustment costs, e.g., trucks. But other equipment may not be easily adapted to use in other industries. In the latter case, the economy will have to expend resources to adapt the capital to the new industry or it will have to save more to invest in new capital that is capable of producing the products that are now in demand. These effects are estimated by a proxy, which is the sum of the losses to specific capital owners, a measure that is meaningful only in the short-run model.[9] In the case of the FTA, the capital adjustment costs are equal to 1.1 percent of the value of the capital stock, or 0.95 percent of private consumption GDP.

In sum, the short-run total adjustment or restructuring costs are expected to correspond to 3 percent of the benchmark export value, or 2 percent of the GDP in the benchmark. The labor adjustment costs are based on the assumption that these costs are equal to one year's average wage. It would only be half of that if adjustment costs of one-half year's wages were assumed instead. It is also important to recognize the fact that the welfare changes recur annually, as they represent permanent increases in the standard of living, but that the adjustment costs are a once-and-for-all phenomenon. Thus, the ratio of welfare gains to adjustment costs increases if we take the present value of the benefits and costs over time.

Adjustment costs as measured here tend to be positively correlated with larger welfare gains. This just reflects that fact that, in general, the way the economy reaps the benefits of comparative advantage and specialization is by reallocating resources from less productive activities to more productive activities. As such, resource reallocation is a necessary component of the traditional benefits of liberalization; there is no "free lunch" in these regards.

The second conclusion concerns the incremental benefits of extending the liberalization occasioned by the FTA to engage in complete, across-the-board tariff liberalization (LIB). In addition to the large increment in welfare that results from this unilateral step, what is also noteworthy is that the adjustment costs, either in the short or long run as captured by the LAB.ADJ% measure, increase less than proportionally with welfare. This result derives from the fact that liberalization only with the EU leads to a reallocation of resources based on a new set of relative prices that will not be an efficient reallocation in the case of trade diversion. When liberalization occurs with all the world, the adjustment costs deriving from trade diversion are avoided.

Revenue and Tax Impacts

In all scenarios, we estimate the fiscal impact of the change. When tariffs are lowered, government revenue declines, and we estimate the amount by which the VAT must increase in order to maintain an unchanged government fiscal deficit. The scenarios explicitly incorporate the required increase in the VAT and the loss in welfare as a result of the increase in the VAT. In the case of the FTA (scenario LIB-EU), assuming no change in the structure or exemptions of the VAT, the loss of tariff revenue is expected to require an increase in the VAT by 30 percent (this can be seen from the variable TAU, which increases, to 1.3). In the model, an increase in the uniform VAT rate from around 20 percent to around 26 percent would keep the real value of government revenues unchanged.[10] The implications for all scenarios on the rate of VAT are shown in the row labeled TAU.

Reform of the VAT

If we assume the VAT is not applied in a uniform manner across sectors, we can simulate the impact of a reform of the VAT structure. In the scenario labeled NEWVAT in table 5.3, the VAT is applied in a non-uniform manner, where some sectors are exempt from VAT and the VAT rates are not equal for sectors where the VAT applies. The simulation shows that moving from a uniform VAT to a more "real world" VAT results in a dramatic loss in welfare of 3 percent of GDP in the short run and 9.7 percent in the long run. Conversely, we interpret this simulation as indicating that the economy could expect to achieve a welfare gain of 9.7 percent of GDP by moving to a uniform VAT. This is a substantial increase in welfare that, in the long run, is larger than any of the trade liberalization scenarios. At the same time, the adjustment costs associated with the reform of the VAT system are quite high (5.2 percent of the labor force must change jobs in the short run and 9.9 percent in the long run).

The variable TAU shows that the consequences of eliminating exemptions and moving to a uniform VAT has a considerably stronger revenue impact than tariff reduction through the FTA of general liberalization of trade. Thus, if the government moved to eliminate exemptions and make the VAT uniform, it could lower the VAT rate, even if it lowered tariffs. A similar result has been found by Maskus and Konan (1997).

The Exchange Rate and the Balance of Payments

As expected, the results show that trade liberalization depreciates the real exchange rate. The reduction of tariffs induces an increase in imports, which requires a depreciation of the real exchange rate in order to restore equilibrium in the balance of payments. Examining the scenario LIB-EU, the row labeled PFX/PU% shows that the real exchange rate would have to depreciate by 3.7 percent in the short run in order to avoid an increase in the deficit in the balance of trade. With the greater trade liberalization under the scenario LIB, the required depreciation of the real exchange rate in order to avoid an increase in the deficit in the balance of trade is larger (equal to 5.1 percent).

We have also estimated the impact on the balance of payments (in the long-run model) if the government were to attempt to avoid the necessary real exchange rate devaluation and hold the exchange rate fixed. (This is not shown in the table). In the case of LIB-EU, we find that the balance of trade would move into deficit by 12.3 percent of the value of exports. With the larger trade liberalization of the LIB scenario, the balance of trade would move into deficit by 17.6 percent with a fixed exchange rate. A balance of payments deficit of this magnitude would not be sustainable in the long run. The government would be forced to allow the exchange rate to depreciate or reverse the trade liberalization with the imposition of exchange or import controls. Permitting the exchange rate to depreciate to market determined levels is clearly the preferred policy path.

We conclude that the FTA will give rise to important welfare improvements, even when taking into account the transitional adjustment costs. In the

TABLE 5.4 Percentage Change in Exports and Imports (Short Run)

	Exports										
	EU-40	EU-TAR	EU-NTB	EU-AGR	EU-STD	EU-TEL	LIB-EU	LIB-UR	LIB	EXAG	NEWVAT
AGF	1.3	5.1	4	11.2	0.2	-0.4	22.5	23.1	25.2	3.3	3.3
CHM	3.8	11.7	-	-0.2	-0.3	0.6	11.9	13.5	17.8	11.4	-12.1
EMI	2.9	3.6	-0.2	-0.1	1.3	0.9	5.6	6.1	7.6	3.5	-6.7
FIN	0.1	-2.9	-	-0.2	-1.2	-1.1	-5.2	-5.3	-5.4	-3	-26.5
FOP	1.1	2.5	3.1	-1.1	-	-0.3	5.4	5.9	7.3	1.2	7.7
TOU	0.5	-0.6	0.7	-0.4	-1	-0.9	-1.9	-1.7	-0.9	-1.4	10.5
MIN	0.4	-1.1	-	-0.2	-0.1	-0.4	-1.7	-1.7	-1.6	-1.3	9.9
MIS	1.4	3.6	-	-0.1	-0.3	-	3	3.5	4.8	3.4	-87.9
NMM	0.6	2.1	0.1	-0.2	-0.8	-0.5	0.9	1.7	4.1	2	7.9
PNG	0.1	2.2	0.1	-0.1	1	0.6	3.9	4	4.1	2.2	0.1
PRS	0.8	1.2	0.5	-0.5	-1.2	-1.2	-0.8	-0.8	-0.4	0.9	6.7
TEX	0.4	17.6	0.1	-0.2	2.3	1.7	21.5	21.6	22.2	17.4	0.8
TRC	0.3	-	-2	-0.2	-1.7	-1.2	-5	-5.1	-5.1	-2.1	25.5
	Imports										
	EU-40	EU-TAR	EU-NTB	EU-AGR	EU-STD	EU-TEL	LIB-EU	LIB-UR	LIB	EXAG	NEWVAT
AGF	-0.4	-1.8	14.3	1.7	3.2	2.7	26.1	27	29	-4.3	-0.9
CHM	1.6	5.2	-0.3	0.2	1	1.3	7.3	8.1	10.2	5.3	-9.2
EMI	1.1	2.3	-0.2	0.1	0.8	0.9	3.9	4.1	4.6	2.4	-1.7
FIN	-0.2	2.4	-0.1	0.2	3	2.9	8.6	8.7	8.8	2.5	28
FOP	0.5	2.9	-1.7	0.9	3.1	2.8	7.4	10.6	19.2	-3.7	-2.7
MIN	1.8	9.8	-0.1	0.1	1.8	1.9	13.7	14.8	17.6	9.8	-20.9
MIS	1	7.3	-0.3	0.3	2	2.1	11.5	12.3	14.4	7.6	58.5
NMM	-0.5	3.5	-0.2	0.2	1.7	1.3	6.5	9.6	17.8	3.7	-5.9
PNG	-0.2	1.4	-0.2	0.1	1.4	1.1	3.9	3.9	4	1.6	-1
PRS	-1.2	-4	-0.8	0.7	3.5	3.5	2.2	2	1.3	-3.4	-4.7
TEX	-0.3	18.3	-0.3	0.2	2.2	2.2	23	23.1	23.3	18.5	-1.7
TRC	0.4	-0.1	-0.4	0.4	2.8	2.9	5.3	5.3	5	0.2	-12.4

short run, the gross welfare gains are small, and it is necessary to incur adjustment costs that reduce the net welfare gains. In the long run, however, the gross welfare gains are larger, and the adjustment costs are incurred only in the first year, so that the subsequent annual gross welfare gains of 4.7 percent per year are also the net welfare gains.

The Short-Run Model: Sectoral Impacts

Although the detailed impacts of the FTA can be seen most clearly in terms of employment and production changes in table 5.6, the primary channel of influence in this model is through the effects of each component of the FTA on trade volume and input prices. Thus, we begin with a discussion of the impact of the FTA on the percentage change in gross trade volumes shown in table 5.4 and the percentage changes in input prices in table 5.5. In each case, we focus on the LIB-EU column, and then work back to the earlier columns to see which component of the FTA contributes to which change.

The main result from table 5.4 is the expansion of the value of imports and exports that comes from liberalizing tariffs.[11] The expansion of imports is always expected, as foreign goods compete more favorably with domestic products, but the intriguing outcome is to see how much exports expand. The reason for this export expansion is simple enough: tariff liberalization results in large reductions in the input prices of some intermediate inputs into production, making local producers in certain sectors more competitive on both domestic and export markets. Moreover, the depreciation of the real exchange rate results in increased returns to exports. Thus, in an explicit general equilibrium sense, it is the case that import tariffs act as export taxes.

Substantial declines in price are observed in table 5.4 for TEX, EMI, CHM, MIS, and AGF. For all of these sectors except AGF, the tariff reduction on EU imports (EU-TAR) accounts for the largest component of the price decline; for AGF, it is the elimination of NTBs on EU imports (EU-NTB). For TEX, the 40 percent reduction in tariffs (EU-40) has virtually none of the beneficial price effects of the complete tariff liberalization case, implying that piecemeal compromises may be imposing additional adjustment costs.

The structural impacts are significant for some sectors, as can be seen in table 5.6, but due to the sector-specificity of capital, only about 2 percent of the labor force is being relocated. The textile sector (TEX) is the greatest beneficiary from liberalization of imports, and employment is expected to expand by over 25 percent in this sector. Most of the labor will come from PRS, MIS, AGF, TRC, EMI, and TOU. It is interesting to observe that in the scenario EU-40 there is very little in the way of shifts in production across sectors, i.e., the industrial structure remains essentially unchanged. Thus, we should not expect much in the way of benefits from this scenario. In fact, the little adjust-

TABLE 5.5 Percentage Change in Prices (Short Run)

	EU-40	EU-TAR	EU-NTB	EU-AGR	EU-STD	EU-TEL	LIB-EU	LIB-UR	LIB	EXAG	NEWVAT
AGF	0.1	1.5	-2.2	0.7	0.4	0.5	-0.1	-	-0.1	2.1	-2.5
CHM	-1.0	-1.9	0.8	-0.3	-0.7	-0.7	-2.5	-2.9	-3.8	-2.4	-1.2
CON	0.2	3.2	0.8	-0.2	0.1	0.1	4.3	4.3	4.6	2.6	6.1
ELE	0.4	2.8	0.7	-0.2	-	0.1	3.6	3.9	4.8	2.2	19.2
EMI	-1.9	-2.3	0.8	-0.3	-0.8	-1.0	-3.3	-3.4	-3.8	-2.8	-1.2
FIN	0.8	5.7	0.8	-0.2	0.4	0.5	7.6	8.0	9.2	5.2	12.1
FOP	0.1	1.8	-0.2	0.1	0.2	0.3	2.1	1.9	1.2	2.7	-3.7
TOU	0.4	3.4	0.3	-	0.7	0.7	5.3	5.5	6.1	3.2	-5.3
MIN	1.2	5.3	0.8	-0.3	-	0.2	6.3	6.8	8.3	4.7	-8.3
MIS	-0.3	-0.9	0.7	-0.3	-0.3	-0.3	-0.8	-0.9	-1.3	-1.3	44.3
NMM	0.6	2.5	0.7	-0.2	-0.2	-	3.0	2.4	1.1	2.0	-4.5
PNG	0.8	1.7	0.8	-0.3	-0.4	-0.3	1.8	2.1	3.0	1.2	-1.8
PRS	0.4	3.1	0.5	-0.1	0.6	0.6	4.9	5.2	6.0	2.7	-4.2
PUB	0.5	4.7	0.7	-0.2	0.4	0.4	6.5	6.8	7.8	4.2	-10.4
TEX	0.7	-10.6	0.7	-0.3	-0.6	-0.9	-11.3	-11.1	-10.6	-11.1	-1.9
TRC	0.5	4.4	0.7	-0.2	0.2	0.2	5.6	6.0	7.0	3.9	-8.8
TRD	1.0	7.4	1.1	-0.3	1.1	0.9	10.6	11.0	12.2	6.9	-27.7
WAT	0.5	4.1	0.7	-0.1	0.5	0.6	6.0	6.3	7.2	3.6	74.5

TABLE 5.6 Short-Run Percentage Changes in Labor Use and Production

	Labor Use										
	EU-40	EU-TAR	EU-NTB	EU-AGR	EU-STD	EU-TEL	LIB-EU	LIB-UR	LIB	EXAG	NEWVAT
AGF	-0.8	-5.2	-2.4	1.8	-	-	-6.5	-6.8	-7.8	-4.4	19.0
CHM	3.6	9.9	-0.2	-0.1	-0.7	0.4	9.2	10.7	14.8	9.6	-21.4
CON	-	-0.1	-	-	-	-	-	-	-	-0.1	-0.3
ELE	0.3	-0.3	-0.4	0.3	0.6	0.9	0.7	0.8	1.0	-0.1	-24.1
EMI	-0.3	-4.6	-0.4	-	-0.2	-0.5	-5.5	-5.6	-5.6	-4.7	-8.5
FIN	-	-0.9	-0.1	-	-0.4	-0.3	-1.8	-1.8	-1.9	-0.9	-9.1
FOP	-0.4	-3.8	2.6	-0.6	0.3	0.3	-0.5	-0.9	-2.1	-3.0	8.4
TOU	0.9	-2.8	1.4	-0.9	-1.9	-1.7	-5.1	-4.7	-3.2	-4.4	25.2

TABLE 5.6 (continued)

MIN	1.4	1.8	-0.1	-0.1	-0.7	-0.3	0.4	0.9	2.3	1.6	-5.1
MIS	-0.6	-5.9	-0.4	0.2	-0.4	-0.2	-6.9	-7.3	-8.4	-5.7	-89.2
NMM	0.2	-1.3	-0.1	-	-0.6	-0.4	-2.5	-3.0	-4.5	-1.3	4.7
PNG	-	-0.8	-	-	-	-0.1	-0.9	-0.9	-1.0	-0.8	-4.9
PRS	-1.1	-7.4	-0.9	0.4	-	0.2	-8.1	-8.3	-9.1	-6.9	8.2
PUB	-	-0.2	-	-	-	-	-0.1	-0.1	-0.2	-0.2	0.4
TEX	0.5	20.7	-	-0.2	3.1	2.3	26.0	26.2	27.0	20.4	0.6
TRC	-0.4	-3.6	-0.3		-1.2	-0.9	-5.9	-6.0	-6.3	-3.5	21.7
TRD	0.5	4.2	0.7	-0.3	1.2	0.9	6.8	6.8	7.0	4.4	-48.2
WAT	-0.6	-4.1	-0.6	0.4	0.6	0.7	-3.4	-3.4	-3.6	-3.7	-50.3

Production

	EU-40	EU-TAR	EU-NTB	EU-AGR	EU-STD	EU-TEL	LIB-EU	LIB-UR	LIB	EXAG	NEWVAT
AGF	-0.1	-0.4	-0.2	0.1	-	-	-0.5	-0.5	-0.6	-0.3	1.3
CHM	1.8	4.8	-0.1	-0.1	-0.3	0.2	4.4	5. 1	7.1	4.6	-11.2
CON	-	-0.1	-	-	-	-	-	-	-	-	-0.3
ELE	0.1	-0.1	-0.1	0.1	0.2	0.3	0.2	0.3	0.3	-	-8.1
EMI	-0.2	-2.6	-0.2	-	-0.1	-0.3	-3.1	-3.1	-3.2	-2.6	-4.8
FIN	-	-0.4	-	-	-0.1	-0.1	-0.7	-0.7	-0.7	-0.3	-3.4
FOP	-0.2	-1.4	0.9	-0.2	0.1	0.1	-0.2	-0.3	-0.7	-1.1	2.8
TOU	0.3	-1	0.5	-0.3	-0.7	-0.6	-1.9	-1.7	-1.2	-1.6	8.9
MIN	1	1.2	-0.1	-0.1	-0.5	-0.2	0.3	0.6	1.6	1.1	-3.6
MIS	-0.3	-2.6	-0.2	0.1	-0.2	-0.1	-3.1	-3.3	-3.7	-2.5	-58.6
NMM	0.1	-0.5	-	-	-0.3	-0.1	-1	-1.3	-1.9	-0.5	1.8
PNG	-	-	-	-	-	-	-	-	-	-	-0.2
PRS	-0.2	-1.2	-0.1	0.1	-	-	-1.3	-1.4	-1.5	-1.1	1.3
PUB	-	-0.2	-	-	-	-	-0.1	-0.1	-0.2	-0.2	0.4
TEX	0.2	9.2	-	-0.1	1.4	1	11.4	11.5	11.8	9	0.3
TRC	-0.2	-1.8	-0.1	-	-0.6	-0.4	-3	-3.1	-3.2	-1.8	10.7
TRD	0.1	0.6	0.1	-	0.2	0.1	0.9	0.9	0.9	0.6	-8
WAT	-0.3	-1.9	-0.3	0.2	0.3	0.3	-1.5	-1.5	-1.6	-1.7	-25.1

TABLE 5.7 Changes in Prices of Sector-Specific Capital and Labor (Short Run)

	EU-40	EU-TAR	EU-NTB	EU-AGR	EU-STD	EU-TEL	LIB-EU	LIB-UR	LIB	EXAG	NEWVAT
AGF	-1.2	-4.9	-1.8	1.8	0.9	0.9	-3.7	-3.9	-4.7	-4.2	20.3
CHM	3.2	10.5	0.6	-0.2	0.3	1.3	12.8	14.5	19.1	9.9	-21.2
CON	-0.4	0.6	0.8	-0.1	0.9	0.9	3.3	3.5	3.8	0.3	-0.1
ELE	-0.2	0.5	0.6	-	1.3	1.4	3.7	4	4.4	0.3	-13.6
EMI	-0.7	-4	0.4	-0.1	0.8	0.4	-2.5	-2.3	-2.1	-4.4	-8.6
FIN	-0.4	0.2	0.8	-0.1	0.7	0.7	2.5	2.6	2.9	-0.1	-4.5
FOP	-0.8	-3.4	3.6	-0.7	1.3	1.2	2.8	2.5	1.5	-2.8	8.9
TOU	-	-0.7	1.5	-0.5	-	-	0.8	1.2	2.2	-1.8	11.6
MIN	3	4.9	0.6	-0.4	-0.8	0.1	4.4	5.8	9.5	4.2	-11.5
MIS	-0.9	-4.3	0.5	-	0.6	0.7	-2.7	-2.8	-3.5	-4.4	-84.6
NMM	0.2	-2.4	0.5	-0.1	-0.6	-	-2.6	-3.7	-6.7	-2.7	11.3
PNG	-0.2	-2.1	0.7	-0.2	1	0.6	0.2	0.3	0.5	-2.4	-15.9
PRS	-0.9	-3.1	0.4	0.1	1	1	-0.8	-0.7	-0.9	-3.1	4
PUB	-0.2	0.5	0.5	0.2	1.1	1.1	3.5	3.7	4.1	0.2	-3.1
TEX	0.2	23.3	0.8	-0.4	4.3	3.3	32.6	33.1	34.4	22.6	0.7
TRC	-0.6	-1.3	0.6	-0.1	0.3	0.4	0.1	0.2	0.3	-1.5	11
TRD	-	3.9	1.3	-0.4	1.9	1.6	8.8	9	9.5	3.8	-40.1
WAT	-0.7	-1.5	0.4	0.1	1.3	1.3	1.5	1.7	1.9	-1.6	-30.9
LABOR	-0.4	0.7	0.8	-0.1	0.9	0.9	3.4	3.5	3.9	0.4	-

ment that does occur is partly perverse (since the dispersion of protection is increased), so there are slight losses. For example, ELE and TOU expand under EU-40 but eventually contract under either EU-TAR or LIB-EU. We conclude that the strategy of reducing tariffs on the sectors where it will have the least impact first will result in losses of welfare and additional adjustment costs because some industries will expand that do not have comparative advantage and will contract as a result of implementation of the full FTA.[12]

The changes in the rate of return to capital across sectors as shown in table 5.7 serves as an indicator of which sectors might increase their profitability as a consequence of the trade liberalizations. The structure of these changes on the expansion side mirror the changes in employment structure, with textiles (TEX) and chemicals (CHM) showing the largest increases in profitability. In terms of declining industries, the structure is somewhat different compared to the changes in employment structure, due to differences in capital/labor intensities across industries. The biggest losers on the capital side are found in AGF, MIS, NMM, EMI, and PRS.

The Long-Run Model: Sectoral Impacts

In table 5.8 we consider the long run, where capital is mobile across sectors. This model is particularly important for the impacts on sectoral production and employment. The reason for the increase in gains in the long run that were discussed above derive from the fact that the greater capital mobility implies that the elasticity of supply is greater for all firms in the long run model. With greater elasticity of supply, the gains to the economy from tariff removal (in terms of removed production deadweight loss) will be higher.

In the long run, the sectoral impacts are substantially different. Consider the scenario LIB-EU. In the long run, only sectors TEX and TRD expand, attracting resources out of all other sectors. Recall that in the short run CHM also expanded, but this is not the case in the long run. Given full mobility of all factors of production, resources move in greater proportion to those sectors in which the country enjoys comparative advantage. The expansion is dominated by TEX that more than doubles its output and employment. Most of these resources come from TOU, PNG, MIN, EMI, and TRC.

Industrial Restructuring

General Principles

We have shown that implementation of the FTA or a more general trade liberalization will result in adjustment costs in the short run and important changes in industry structure in the long run. Given the long run benefits of a reoriented industrial structure based on comparative advantage, what reforms,

TABLE 5.8 Long-Run Percentage Changes in Labor Use and Production

	Labor Use										
	EU-40	EU-TAR	EU-NTB	EU-AGR	EU-STD	EU-TEL	LIB-EU	LIB-UR	LIB	EXAG	NEWVAT
AGF	-0.8	-10.4	-1.8	1.6	-0.6	-0.4	-13.2	-13.6	-14.9	-9.5	16.9
CHM	4	-6.6	-0.1	-0.3	-1.6	-0.1	-12.3	-11.6	-9.5	-6.5	-48.2
CON	-0.1	-2.6	-0.2	0.1	-0.1	-0.1	-3.3	-3.3	-3.5	-2.5	-0.3
ELE	0.3	-8.3	-0.3	0.2	-0.5	-0.2	-10.3	-10.4	-10.8	-8	-17.1
EMI	-0.3	-13.2	-0.1	-0.1	-0.6	-0.7	-16.9	-17.1	-17.8	-13.1	-29.2
FIN	-0.2	-7	-0.4	0.3	-0.6	-0.5	-9.1	-9.3	-9.8	-6.7	-6.3
FOP	-0.6	-11	0.7	0.4	-0.7	-0.5	-11.3	-11.7	-13	-10.2	13.1
TOU	-0.4	-42.5	2.2	-0.5	-8.7	-6.8	-50	-50	-50.3	-43.3	143.2
MIN	3	-10.2	0.1	-0.4	-1.9	-0.7	-16.4	-16	-14.8	-10.2	-40.2
MIS	-0.3	-6.2	-0.1	-	-0.1	-	-7.9	-8.2	-9.2	-6	-89.3
NMM	0.2	-6.6	-	-0.1	-1.1	-0.7	-9.2	-9.9	-11.8	-6.6	-3.9
PNG	0.3	-19.4	0.3	-0.7	-1.2	-1.5	-24.6	-24.8	-25.5	-19.4	-39.4
PRS	-0.7	-12.8	-0.6	0.3	-0.8	-0.6	-15.5	-15.8	-16.7	-12.4	1.4
PUB	-	-0.2	-	-	-	-	-0.2	-0.2	-0.2	-0.2	-
TEX	1.3	99.9	0.3	-0.9	12.3	9.2	124.5	125.9	130.7	98.3	-48.3
TRC	-0.5	-12.9	-0.3	-	-1.8	-1.4	-17.2	-17.4	-18.1	-12.7	10.4
TRD	0.1	3.6	-0.2	0.2	1.1	0.8	4.3	4.2	4.1	3.8	-26
WAT	-0.3	-10.2	-0.4	0.3	-0.6	-0.3	-11.8	-11.9	-12.5	-9.9	-25.7

TABLE 5.8 (continued)

	Production										
	EU-40	EU-TAR	EU-NTB	EU-AGR	EU-STD	EU-TEL	LIB-EU	LIB-UR	LIB	EXAG	NEWVAT
AGF	-0.6	-6.1	-1.5	1.3	-0.3	-0.2	-8	-8.3	-9.3	-5.4	16.5
CHM	4.1	-4	0.1	-0.4	-1.4	-	-9.3	-8.4	-6.1	-4	-48.3
CON	-	-	-	-	-	-	-	-	-	-	-0.5
ELE	0.6	-1.7	0.1	-0.2	-0.1	0.2	-2.1	-2.1	-2	-1.7	-17.6
EMI	-0.2	-11.1	-	-0.2	-0.5	-0.6	-14.4	-14.6	-15.2	-11.1	-29.4
FIN	-0.3	-	-	-	-0.1	-0.1	-0.8	-0.8	-0.8	-0.3	-6.8
FOP	-0.5	-8	0.9	0.2	-0.5	-0.3	-7.6	-7.9	-9	-7.3	12.8
TOU	-0.1	-38.3	2.6	-0.8	-8.3	-6.5	-45.3	-45.3	-45.3	-39.3	141.9
MIN	3	-9.6	0.1	-0.4	-1.9	-0.7	-15.7	-15.2	-14	-9.6	-40.2
MIS	-0.2	-2.8	0.1	-0.1	0.1	0.2	-3.6	-3.9	-4.6	-2.7	-89.3
NMM	0.3	-5.4	-	-0.1	-1	-0.6	-7.7	-8.4	-10.2	-5.4	-4
PNG	0.4	-18.2	0.4	-0.8	-1.1	-1.4	-23.2	-23.4	-24	-18.3	-39.5
PRS	-0.4	-4.4	-	-0.1	-0.2	-	-5.1	-5.2	-5.5	-4.3	0.7
PUB	-0.2	-	-	-	-0.2	-0.2	-0.2	-0.2	-	-	-
TEX	1.4	105.2	0.5	-1.1	12.5	9.4	132	133.6	139.1	103.4	-48.4
TRC	-0.3	-8.4	-	-0.3	-1.5	-1.1	-11.8	-11.9	-12.2	-8.4	10
TRD	0.3	9.9	0.1	-0.1	1.5	1.2	12.4	12.5	12.9	9.9	-26.3
WAT	-0.1	-5.1	-0.1	-0.2	-	-5.4	-5.4	-5.5	-4.9	-26	-

policies, or instruments should be employed to best achieve the reoriented industrial structure? The general principle from both industrial restructuring surveys (Leiberman 1990, Atiyas et al. 1992) and our model is that it is crucial for the government to provide a stable macroeconomic environment conducive to business development with neutral incentives to all firms and industries. Neutral incentives (those which do not distinguish by sector or firm) are crucial so that entrepreneurial innovation is rewarded more highly than rent-seeking activities. The economy must provide its most talented members with the incentive to engage in entrepreneurial activities such as starting or expanding firms, developing new products, and lowering costs. If the economy provides extensive subsidies or tax exemptions to industries or firms, or presents a difficult regulatory framework within which to do business, talented people will find it more profitable to engage in the socially wasteful activity of lobbying the government for subsidies, protection, and tax or regulatory relief.[13] This socially wasteful lobbying is especially harmful because it attracts the entrepreneurs who would otherwise be helping the economy grow.

Models such as those used here provide information on which sectors can be expected to expand and contract in response to the changed market signals after a FTA or similar reform. Expanding industries are likely to be those in which the country has comparative advantage. These shifts in resources, however, will occur over time as a result of market forces. Targeting particular industries for special assistance, on the other hand, involves a number of risks that are potentially very costly. First, there is the risk that the wrong industries will be identified. The market is a more reliable indicator of the industries that have comparative advantage than any economic model. Over time, this is particularly true as comparative advantage changes with technological development. Moreover, targeting industries as "winners" will generate rent seeking, i.e., industries will spend resources to obtain government subsidies rather than attempt to compete more effectively on the market. Thus, experience in most countries has shown that a government policy of attempting to "pick winners" is highly counterproductive.

Results from the Model

With respect to the model, we have elaborated two types of policy reform that could be undertaken to provide more neutral incentives and facilitate effective industrial restructuring: reform of the VAT and the design of tariff liberalization.

Reform of the VAT

First, the results show that exemptions to the VAT and its uneven rate of application in sectors that do pay VAT distort the allocation of resources. The government could help to assure efficient resource allocation and restructuring by eliminating exemptions to the VAT and reducing different applied rates across sectors. With the non-neutral VAT structure in place, resources will flow toward industries with relatively low rates of VAT, which are not necessarily the industries in which the country has comparative advantage. Based on our static model, we have shown that in the long run, VAT reform would result in substantial benefits, indicating that the VAT structure induces resource allocation away from the economy's comparative advantage.

Reform of the Tariff Structure

The EU-40 scenario shows that a policy of non-uniformity of tariffs would result in a loss in welfare. A structure that provides uniform protection to industries would instead reduce distortions. Moreover, experience has shown that a policy of non-uniformity increases rent-seeking pressures on the government. Industries or firms that find it in their interest to obtain protection specific to their industry will often judge it not in their interest to obtain a general industry-wide increase in protection. With a uniform tariff structure, industries that would expend resources lobbying for general industry-wide tariff protection suffer from a free-rider problem in that they can capture only a small portion of the benefits of protection. In either event, a uniform tariff structure discourages wasteful petitioning of the government and encourages valuable entrepreneurial talent to make their industries more efficient and competitive.[14]

Providing a Stable, Neutral Environment Conducive to Entrepreneurial Talent

Studies of appropriate industrial structuring by the World Bank have concluded that in order to facilitate effective industrial restructuring, governments should provide a stable macroeconomic environment conducive to business development with neutral incentives to all firms and industries. Leiberman (1990) notes that such an environment would include the following main elements.

Sound Macroeconomic Policies to Provide a Stable Business Environment

This includes avoiding overvalued exchange rates, which discourage exports and make import-competing sectors vulnerable. Fiscal deficits should be avoided in part because they crowd out private investment and because they lead to inflation which makes price signals less transparent. Regulatory regimes that are pervasive, frequently changed, and not transparent should be avoided since they encourage rent seeking for regulatory relief.

Sound Competition Policies

This includes first and foremost an open trade regime so that firms produce according to comparative advantage and are forced to compete. Constraints on foreign investment, including restraints on repatriation of profits and royalties as well as inadequate protection of intellectual property, limit access to state-of-the-art production technology and to marketing networks. Barriers to entry and exit (including licensing of capacity expansion and limits on firm size) as well as discretionary subsidies prevent industrial development and constrain the ability to respond to new competition. Complex licensing requirements often exclude small firms for whom the costs of dealing with the bureaucracy are excessive. Protection of state-owned monopolies—including special pricing arrangements, subsidies, and credits—reduces the incentive to the state-owned enterprise to restructure and inhibits competition from new, more efficient competitors (who are often private and often an effective means of privatizing the industry). Price controls prevent the transmission of market signals to firms and should be avoided.

Sound Labor Market Policies

Policies, which facilitate labor mobility, are crucial in effective restructuring. Estimates have shown that labor adjustment costs are often larger where labor adjustment is restricted (Leiberman 1990). Therefore layoffs should not be restricted or penalized by law. Strong unions sometimes act as an important barrier to effective labor mobility. Retraining programs may play a useful role in facilitating labor mobility.

Adequate Infrastructure

Inadequate or inefficient infrastructure in ports, roads, telecommunications, water, and electricity can hinder industrial competitiveness. At the same time, costly public projects in these areas will increase the fiscal burden, crowd out private investment, and similarly hinder industrial competitiveness. Infrastructure projects should therefore target bottleneck areas for efficiency and attempt innovative financing and participation solutions that involve the private sector.[15]

Technical assistance in the form of information and marketing, technology transfer, and training programs may also be useful. These programs would include those that help firms develop an effective export-marketing strategy, that focus on adapting foreign technology to local conditions, and that are designed to develop a flexible labor force. Industry associations and efficient banks are likely to be the best agents for identifying and arranging appropriate technical assistance. Restructuring assistance from the EU might be sought for a number of these activities.

The benefits of cooperative standards arrangements between the EU and Arab Mediterranean countries are likely to lead to substantial benefits. The estimates noted earlier assume that as a result of increased quality control and standardization with the EU market, exporters should be able to sell their goods more effectively and at a higher price in the EU market. It would thus be helpful for Arab Mediterranean governments to cooperate with the EU to assure that appropriate testing and approval facilities (accepted by the EU) are available to exporters. These facilities may be developed privately, but the FTA would be improved from the perspective of partner countries if the EU accepts conformity assessments performed by local laboratories.

Conclusions

In terms of aggregate welfare gains, which are the most important summary measure we have of the overall impact on the economy, our estimates imply that the most important component for Arab Mediterranean countries of a FTA with the EU does not concern the liberalization of tariffs and NTBs. However, this result depends on how accurate our assessment is of the magnitude of the TOT improvement that is caused by the agreement. Traditional improvements in market access and trade policies generate smaller aggregate welfare gains compared to less traditional improvements in market access via harmonization and mutual recognition of standards.[16]

The most important conclusion is that bilateral FTAs with the EU set the policy stage for even greater improvements in welfare if accompanied by an across-the-board liberalization of tariffs that can be undertaken unilaterally. Moreover, movement to a uniform VAT that applies to all sectors would also increase welfare significantly and serve to compensate the government for the loss of tariff revenue occasioned by the FTA.

Notes

The authors are grateful to Robert Beekman for research assistance and to Glenn W. Harrison, Bernard DeCaluwe, Julie Stanton, and Linda Likar for valuable comments. We thank Minerva Patena and Maria Kasilag for logistical support.

1. A similar approach is taken in Harrison, Rutherford, and Tarr (1997).
2. Ibid.
3. In some CGE models, the share of operating surplus allocated to capital in agricultural sectors is re-allocated to payments to labor. We interpret these payments as a rent earned by the primary factor land instead. Payments to "capital" in agriculture therefore include a payment to land as well as traditional working capital.
4. Harrison and Vinod (1992) and Harrison, Rutherford, and Tarr (1993) demonstrate the role of systematic sensitivity analysis of models such as these with respect to plausible ranges of uncertainty about key elasticities. However, such sensitivity analysis is not performed here.
5. Also reported in the text are the results of three scenarios replicating the policy simulations for LIB-EU, LIB-UR, and LIB, but allowing the trade balance to change in response to a fixed real exchange rate. These simulations need to be interpreted with care as discussed later in this chapter.

6. For example, a value of TAU of 1.04 means that VAT rates need to be scaled up by 4 percent in order to compensate for tariff revenues lost when the scenario is applied. A value of TAU of 0.99 implies that VAT rates need to be scaled down by 1 percent. We keep the government budget constant so as to isolate the impact from the FTA itself on the economy. The uniform VAT rate employed in our base model also isolates the distortionary impact from the trade regime from other distortionary taxes.

7. This follows from the Le Chatelier Principle, which implies that the elasticity of supply will increase with the number of variable factors. See Varian (1984), 56-57. See De Melo and Tarr (1992), 130-134 for an elaboration that includes a graph.

8. One could also interpret these as one year of unemployment costs.

9. Our model is not well adapted to measure the costs of these effects. In the long-run model, we assume that capital is perfectly malleable between sectors; and in the short-run model, we assume that the price of capital changes sufficiently such that all capital remains fully employed in its original sector.

10. The VAT is not increased on imports, but as we do not model exemptions for exports either, these two features will generally tend to cancel each other out in the aggregate.

11.Trade occurs in both directions for the "same good" here. We adopt the Armington assumption that products are distinguished by country of origin or destination, so these are not in effect the same good.

12. For some sectors (ELE), tariff liberalization alone results in a decline, but the impact of harmonization of standards and improved telecommunications, which is part of the FTA, results in an expansion of these sectors.

13. See Murphy, Shleifer, and Vishny (1991).

14. See Harberger (1990) and Panagariya and Rodrik (1993).

15. For example, Venezuela has recently privatized its telecommunications sector with a reported considerable increase in efficiency.

16. An alternative way of modeling harmonization of product standard is proposed in Harrison, Rutherford, and Tarr (1996).

CHAPTER 6

Rents, Red Tape, and Regionalism: Economic Effects of Deeper Integration

Bernard Hoekman and Denise Konan

Most of the literature on the economics of preferential trade agreements (PTAs) focuses on the impact of discriminatory liberalization on members of such agreements. Recently, analysts have begun to emphasize the role of PTAs as instruments that can be used by governments in the pursuit of "deep integration" (e.g., Lawrence 1996). This can be defined as cooperation among countries that is aimed at reducing the market-segmenting effect of domestic (non-border) regulatory policies. Examples of such policies are health and safety-related product standard regulations, national competition policies, professional licensing and certification regimes, prudential supervision requirements imposed on financial services providers, environmental policies, and administrative procedures and requirements that are associated with the enforcement of regulation (e.g., conformity assessment procedures and customs clearance practices). These types of policies affect goods and services, production processes, and legal and natural persons. They may have effects analogous to NTBs, even though the underlying intent may not be to discriminate against foreign suppliers of goods and services. Indeed, the regulations concerned may apply equally to domestic and foreign products, in contrast to standard NTBs. Nonetheless, they can act to segment markets and reduce competition.

The regulatory barriers and measures that figure on the deep integration agenda often impose real resource or frictional costs on international exchange or prohibit entry by foreign suppliers altogether. Deep integration initiatives to remove such costs can have substantial beneficial impacts. This may require decisions by governments to recognize a partner's policies or to harmonize regulatory policies. Thus, deep integration can have far-reaching consequences in terms of "sharing" of sovereignty. A key question in evaluating the justification for PTAs from a multilateral trading system perspective is the extent to which formal agreements are technically necessary to achieve deep integration. The more this is so, the stronger the potential case for pursuit of regional integration. Another question that is relevant in evaluating the case for regionalism is to what extent actions taken in the PTA context to reduce the prevalence of market segmentation due to regulations can be and are applied on a nondiscriminatory basis. If PTA-based policy innovations to reduce transactions or market access costs are applied to nonmembers as well as members of a PTA, this increases the attractiveness of regionalism as an instrument of trade and investment policy reform.

This chapter investigates the potential importance of deep integration for Egypt in the context of trade agreements with the EU. It is sometimes argued that FTAs between Mediterranean countries and the EU will be detrimental to the former because they already have duty-free access to EU markets for manufactures (Schiff 1997). But to the extent that a EMA reduces regulatory impediments in the EU, partner countries may gain in market access terms. The greater the share of frictional NTBs in a Mediterranean country's policy mix, the higher are frictional costs imposed on trade; the greater the extent to which abolition of such costs applies on a nondiscriminatory basis, the greater the potential welfare gains resulting from a "deep" PTA.

The implications of considering these distinctions is explored by evaluating the economic impact of alternative trade liberalization and policy integration scenarios for Egypt using a CGE model. The case of Egypt is considered for illustrative purposes, largely driven by the fact that a significant amount of analytical work on Egypt already exists (Maskus and Konan 1997). The government is far-advanced in negotiations with the EU to establish a FTA, [1] and in 1997, agreement was reached in the Arab League to establish a FTA over a 10-year period starting in 1998.[2] Neither agreement does much to pursue a deep integration agenda, although the EMA has the potential to do so. This chapter makes an attempt to quantify the magnitude of the opportunity costs of not doing so, taking into account that unilateral elimination of some regulatory barriers on a nondiscriminatory basis may not be feasible. The primary purpose of the analysis is to assess the possible orders of magnitude of the economic effects of alternative policy initiatives that aim at reducing "red tape" as well as traditional border barriers such as tariffs on both a discriminatory or a nondiscriminatory basis. Data constraints severely restrict what is feasible, and the analysis should be regarded as exploratory in nature.

Conceptual Issues

As tariffs and related "traditional" trade barriers decline in importance, industries have started to focus on the consequences of differences in regulatory regimes across countries for their ability to compete. Regulatory regime differences may have consequences for the degree to which the contestability of markets is enhanced following a significant reduction or the complete elimination of trade control measures. Commonly mentioned examples concern the prevalence of state-owned or controlled industries/firms, the extent to which governments subsidize the activities of domestic industry, and the competition policy (antitrust) regime that applies. The greater the role of the state in the economy and the more tolerant a government is of anticompetitive business practices such as cartels, bid rigging, and other horizontal restraints, the less impact a formal elimination of trade barriers may have on the contestability of markets.

Although the market-segmenting effects of regulatory policies may be intentional, in many cases this simply is a side effect. For example, the enforcement of health and safety standards requires testing and conformity assessment procedures for products. These presumably will apply equally to domestic and imported goods. But exporters may already be subject to equivalent controls in their home country, so that testing is duplicative, leading to higher compliance costs for foreign firms. Customs procedures may also be duplicative insofar as paperwork and data requirements have already been demanded by authorities in the home country or are not relevant to the needs of customs. Such policies may therefore be largely resource wasting and redundant.

It has been estimated that over 60 percent of U.S. exports are subject to mandatory health, safety, and related standards. For exports to the EU, government-issued certificates were required for 45 percent of these goods, private, third-party certification was accepted in 15 percent of cases, and for the remainder manufacturer's self-certification sufficed (Wilson 1998). Within the EU, some 75 percent of the value of intra-EU trade in goods is subject to mandatory technical regulations (European Commission 1996).[3] Conformity assessment policies may therefore constitute an important technical barrier to trade. Their prevalence has risen rapidly. Unter (1998) estimates that in the case of the Hewlett-Packard Company, redundant testing and conformity assessment procedures increased six-fold between 1990 and 1997.

The EU now requires third-party testing, certification, or quality system registration for certain regulated sectors by organizations designated, or "notified," to the Commission by the member states as technically competent. Only these bodies can approve goods for circulation in European markets and affix the European "CE Mark" to certified products. The requirement that final assessments be performed by European notified bodies—in limited cases, the

EU has authorized subcontracting by notified bodies to allow certification by foreign firms—raises the costs of testing and certification to non-EU manufacturers in many sectors and was a prime motivation for the mutual recognition agreement (MRA) negotiations between the EU and the United States, which concluded in 1997. In total, these MRAs cover over $40 billion of bilateral trade. The MRA on telecommunications and information technology products alone could result, when fully implemented, in an approximately $1.4 billion savings to consumers and manufacturers (Wilson 1998), implying that the frictional costs that are abolished were equivalent to a 5 percent "tax" on the value of the goods traded. While this is a significant cost reduction, the MRAs are regarded as a second best solution by U.S. industry, which would prefer to rely much more heavily on supplier self-certification instead of third-party conformity assessment.

Similar situations apply to services producers, where the need for licensing and certification of suppliers and prudential supervision may be duplicated across countries. Often such requirements are complemented by outright market access restrictions for foreign providers. The result is generally higher cost supply and the creation of rents for domestic suppliers.

The major options for dealing with the market segmenting and/or anti-competitive effects of regulatory regimes are harmonization and acceptance (or "recognition") of foreign regulatory policy regimes. Each of these options may be pursued unilaterally or in a concerted manner.

Harmonization may involve adoption by one country of another country's set of rules or the negotiation of a common set of disciplines that imply changes for both (or all) countries. Examples abound of unilateral or independent harmonization to the standard of a trading partner. These are often driven by market size disparities. One example was a 1992 decision by Canada to adopt the U.S. emission standards for automobiles that were specified in the U.S. Clean Air Act of 1990 so as to ensure that auto makers located in Canada could realize economies of scale (i.e., avoid having to set up separate production lines for the Canadian and U.S. markets). Another example driven by market access considerations was a decision by Switzerland to adopt the EU regime on technical regulations and industrial standards (in effect, the *acquis communautaire*). This ensured that Swiss goods could enter and circulate in the EU on the same basis as EU-produced goods (Messerlin 1998).[4] Numerous developing countries have pursued a unilateral harmonization strategy. Often this was done by maintaining systems inherited from a colonial past or military occupation, but more deliberate efforts have also been made. South Korea, for example, adopted many German and U.S. technical product regulations in the 1950s as part of a strategy to upgrade the quality of industrial production and foster exports.

Harmonization may also be based on intergovernmental cooperation and agreement or may involve a decision to cede sovereignty to common or supranational institutions. The latter is often regarded as a necessary condition for economic integration to occur—Robson (1988) defines integration as "the assignment of particular economic functions and instruments to the union or community and their exercise at that level rather than at the level of the member states." Supranational institutions may be involved in the process of setting the rules of the game (as in the case of the EU, where the Commission has been delegated the power of proposing directives and regulations) and/or the enforcement of negotiated commitments (e.g., acceptance by PTA member states of binding, independent third-party adjudication or arbitration in NAFTA, or, more far-reaching, the creation of a supra-national institution such as the Court of Justice in the EU).

A complement of unilateral harmonization to the standards of a trading partner or international norms is unilateral recognition of foreign regulatory regimes. Thus, a government may decide that the professional qualifications of doctors trained and certified in certain countries are sufficient for them to practice (although nationality constraints and economic needs tests may still prohibit entry by foreign service providers). Similarly, a government may accept foreign certificates of safety for certain imports as sufficient proof of quality (e.g., the Underwriters Laboratories "UL" mark is accepted in many countries). However, the ability of unilateral recognition to reduce transaction costs is inherently limited to the jurisdiction of the government concerned. In some cases, a government or regulatory body may not be familiar with or trust foreign certification systems or may consider foreign standards to be unacceptable. If so, products will be subjected to testing and certification at point of entry into its jurisdiction, imposing additional costs on imports.

Negotiation of MRAs is a mechanism through which transactions costs can then be reduced further. MRAs may be required even if a harmonization strategy is pursued by a country, as the trading partner whose standards are emulated may not accept foreign test results or conformity assessment systems as equivalent to its own, even if the formal standards are identical. Conversely, mutual recognition may require some degree of harmonization, especially in areas where mandatory standards or regulations apply, so as to ensure that the underlying norms satisfy certain basic, minimum standards.

A major advantage of mutual recognition is that allowances can be made for differences in standards across countries. Subject to a "minimal equivalence" norm in those cases where public interest considerations are important, mutual recognition can ensure that existing idiosyncrasies in national requirements that do not affect health or safety objectives are accepted by trading partners. Although significant time and energy may still be required to achieve agreement on what the "minimum standards" should be in cases where these are considered necessary, this should be easier to achieve than complete harmonization.

An important empirical question is to determine the size of the potential benefits of deep integration initiatives. Relatively little work has been done on this, almost all of it focusing on the EU's Single Market Programme. One conclusion that emerges from this work is that the welfare impact of deep integration will be greater the more the restrictions being addressed waste real resources rather than generate rents that are captured by interest groups (e.g., Winters 1992; Baldwin 1995). In such cases, there is no rent or revenue for a country to lose by removing the restriction, unlike the losses that occur as tariffs or import quotas are abolished. Thus, it is important to determine whether regulatory barriers create rents or not. Estimates of frictional costs range between 2 and 3 percent of the value of trade (European Commission 1996). In the APEC context, estimates are somewhat higher, reflecting greater "red tape." It is also important to determine to what extent regulatory reform can be achieved unilaterally as opposed to requiring formal, international agreements. Unilateral reforms may be sufficient to realize a significant share of the total potential gains. However, it can only affect domestic transactions, while formal agreements may have an impact in facilitating both imports and exports as market access becomes less costly.

Finally, it is necessary to determine whether formal agreements to reduce the incidence of regulatory costs for importers and exporters can be extended to third parties. Non-members may gain if the reductions in regulatory barriers apply on a nondiscriminatory basis. If so, trade diversion will be less of a concern, although supply switching from a low to a higher cost provider may still arise under deep integration initiatives. Both recognition agreements and harmonization decisions may be inherently discriminatory with respect to outsiders. For the former, discrimination may be implied if recognition is not extended to some countries. Harmonization may increase barriers to trade for third parties if their national standards or norms differ from the common norm applied in the PTA. Consequently, it cannot be assumed that reductions in real costs associated with actions to reduce the market-segmenting effect of differences in regulatory regimes will benefit nonmembers.

The standard policy prescription for reducing the opportunity costs associated with trade diversion is to lower trade barriers on ROW imports. While this is straightforward if the barriers are of the traditional type (e.g., tariffs, quotas), once attention shifts to domestic regulatory regimes it may not be possible to unilaterally "multilateralize" liberalization actions that have been implemented in a PTA context. Much depends in this connection on the types of barriers that are involved. Some reductions in trade costs can be extended to all sources of imports. An example are customs clearance procedures and associated documentary requirements (in the EMA context, this could include adoption of the EU's Single Administrative Document). Other liberalization actions may not automatically extend to third countries. Examples include decisions to link computer systems of customs, to accept self-declaration for purposes of enforcement of mandatory product standards and related testing and certification procedures, or to recognize professional qualifications.

Summing up, the impact of a PTA on members and the rest of the world depends on the extent to which the regulatory barriers that are eliminated are frictional in nature, whether reforms can be pursued unilaterally, and whether policy integration benefits extend on a nondiscriminatory basis. The greater the share of frictional barriers in the total set of barriers that is removed by the PTA and the greater the extent to which barrier removal extends to nonmembers, the more beneficial it will be for the member countries. These are empirical questions or issues that should figure in any evaluation of a PTA. Unfortunately, little information tends to be available regarding the type of barriers that are subject to elimination in the PTA context or the extent to which nonmembers are able to benefit from them. What follows makes an attempt to determine the possible quantitative importance of some of these factors using a CGE model of the Egyptian economy.

Egypt: Trade Policy and the Pattern of Trade

Given the recent decision to establish an Arab League FTA and ongoing negotiations on a FTA with the EU, bilateral Egyptian trade flows are separated into four regions: the EU (including Turkey), the United States, the Arab League, and ROW.[5] The EU is Egypt's largest trading partner, accounting for roughly 40 percent of merchandise imports in 1995 and absorbing 45 percent of Egypt's exports. The United States comes second in terms of imports, accounting for 19 percent of total imports, while the Arab League is the second most important export market for Egypt, absorbing 16 percent of all exports of goods in 1995. As shown in table 6.1, in many product categories including processed food-stuffs, wood products, paper and printing, glass and mineral products, and transport equipment, more than 50 percent of total Egyptian exports go to Arab markets. In contrast, Egypt imports relatively little from the Arab League region. The most important in terms of import shares are petroleum products, beverages, and textiles and clothing. Despite their relatively large presence in production, vegetable foodstuffs and food processing are major import goods, as are machinery and chemicals. On the export side, Egypt's trade flows are dominated by transport services (largely because of the Suez Canal), oil, tourism, and textiles and clothing.

TABLE 6.1 Benchmark Output and Trade Shares

		Import				Export			
SECTOR	Output	Total	EU*	USA	MENA**	Total	EU*	USA	MENA**
AGRICULTURE	(1)	(2)	(3)	(4)	(5)	(6)	(7)	(8)	(9)
1. Vegetable products, foodstuffs (VG1)	12.4	13.3	11.7	47.9	2.2	2.6	27.0	1.5	63.5
2. Vegetable products, non-foodstuffs (VG2)	1.7	0.0	36.9	16.5	1.2	0.1	49.3	13.4	14.1
3. Animal products (ANI)	8.0	0.8	82.7	0.0	9.6	0.3	35.2	2.3	53.0
MINING AND QUARRYING									
4. Crude petroleum and natural gas (OIL)	2.7	1.2	52.0	7.0	24.4	18.5	30.6	4.6	1.0
5. Other extractive industries (MIN)	.09	2.0	17.7	14.8	3.5	0.2	56.8	9.2	21.4
MANUFACTURING									
6. Food processing (FOO)	7.7	15.1	40.3	10.6	2.3	1.3	20.1	4.5	49.3
7. Beverages (BEV)	0.6	0.0	41.7	16.3	28.5	0.0	1.2	0.0	87.6
8. Tobacco products (TOB)	1.9	1.0	27.0	27.4	2.5	0.0	0.4	0.7	45.3
9. Cotton ginning and pressing (TX1)	1.2	0.5	36.9	0.3	0.9	4.2	33.7	0.2	1.4
10. Cotton spinning and weaving (TX2)	5.2	2.4	33.4	7.1	3.7	10.3	72.4	10.9	6.1
11. Clothing: assembled and pieces (CLO)	1.4	0.0	12.4	0.9	19.1	1.2	34.7	49.1	8.6
12. Leather products, excluding shoes (LEA)	0.2	0.0	25.7	0.9	13.8	0.1	48.8	1.5	30.9
13. Shoes (SHO)	0.4	0.0	16.0	2.9	12.0	0.0	20.5	1.9	60.5
14. Wood products, excluding furniture (WOO)	1.1	5.0	39.8	1.4	0.4	0.1	1.5	0.1	86.1
15. Furniture (FUR)	1.4	0.0	57.0	34.7	1.4	0.5	14.9	10.6	58.5
16. Paper and printing (PAP)	1.5	3.3	46.8	17.1	2.9	0.9	1.6	0.8	91.7
17. Chemicals, excluding petroleum (CHE)	3.1	10.8	62.6	12.2	7.9	1.8	31.3	3.5	39.4
18. Petroleum refining (PET)	2.7	1.2	48.4	6.2	28.9	3.3	58.5	0.6	7.2

TABLE 6.1 (continued)

		Import				Export			
SECTOR	Output	Total	EU*	USA	MENA**	Total	EU*	USA	MENA**
MANUFACTURING (continued)	(1)	(2)	(3)	(4)	(5)	(6)	(7)	(8)	(9)
19. Rubber, plastics, and products (RPL)	0.8	2.3	42.8	20.4	9.8	0.3	41.3	0.7	45.3
20. Porcelain, china, pottery (POR)	0.3	0.4	47.4	7.8	11.5	0.1	42.2	1.5	32.4
21. Glass and products (GLA)	0.3	0.5	63.3	5.3	3.6	0.1	9.3	5.5	62.1
22. Mineral products, n.e.i. (MPD)	1.7	0.4	61.6	3.8	2.2	0.0	4.8	2.0	80.9
23. Iron, steel, other base metals (MET)	2.8	2.6	35.5	11.8	9.0	0.8	68.3	1.9	24.3
24. Machinery and appliances (MAC)	3.5	23.1	59.4	17.4	2.4	4.6	9.5	3.9	58.0
25. Transportation equipment (TRA)	1.0	5.9	33.8	12.1	0.7	0.4	3.6	0.3	89.8
26. Other manufacturing (OMF)	0.1	0.5	47.6	11.2	3.5	0.1	25.4	3.2	62.5
SERVICES AND OTHER									
27. Electricity, gas, and water (ELE)	1.7	0.2	44.6	16.8	4.3	0.7	25.0	7.0	40.0
28. Construction (CON)	5.5	0.2	44.6	16.8	4.3	0.8	25.0	7.0	40.0
29. Trade (TRD)	7.1	0.3	44.6	16.8	4.3	5.6	25.0	7.0	40.0
30. Restaurants, hotels, coffeehouses (RES)	2.3	0.0	44.6	16.8	4.3	5.0	25.0	7.0	40.0
31. Transport and storage (TRN)	6.0	1.3	44.6	16.8	4.3	31.9	44.7	6.7	20.2
32. Communications (COM)	0.8	0.1	44.6	16.8	4.3	0.4	25.0	7.0	40.0
33. Financial establishments (FIN)	1.5	1.1	44.6	16.8	4.3	0.0	25.0	7.0	40.0
34. Insurance (INS)	0.3	0.0	44.6	16.8	4.3	0.5	25.0	7.0	40.0
35. Real estate, housing services (HSG)	2.8	3.9	44.6	16.8	4.3	0.0	25.0	7.0	40.0
36. Social and community services (SER)	6.0	0.1	44.6	16.8	4.3	0.2	25.0	7.0	40.0
37. Recreational and cultural services (REC)	0.5	0.2	44.6	16.8	4.3	3.2	25.0	7.0	40.0
38. Personal services (PER)	0.9	0.0	44.6	16.8	4.3	0.0	25.0	7.0	40.0

* Including Turkey
** Excluding Israel
Source: Modified from Konan and Maskus 1997.

We draw two conclusions from these statistics. First, although the EU is by far the largest trading partner of Egypt, trade flows are rather diversified. The non-Arab, non-EU, non-U.S. ROW provides 34 percent of imports and takes 25 percent of exports. These numbers suggest that the potential for trade diversion from a "classic" PTA with just one of Egypt's major trading partners is significant. Second, services play an important role in Egypt's current account. As there are no disaggregated data available on services trade or its breakdown by region, for purposes of the modeling exercise that follows it is assumed that the Arab League region has a 40 percent export share, the EU 25 percent, and the United States 7 percent (see table 6.1).[6]

Although tariffs have been declining in recent years at around 20 to 25 percent (the maximum tariff was recently reduced to 50 percent), the import weighted average tariff is still relatively high. Tariffs on inputs are often lower than those applied to final goods, leading to effective rates of protection that are often a multiple of nominal rates.[7] With the exception of those on imports of textile products, all quantitative restrictions have been abolished, and the textile bans are scheduled to be eliminated in the coming years as part of Egypt's commitments under the Uruguay Round.[8]

As tariffs and quotas have declined in importance, administrative control of the import process has become more prominent and important. Such controls and "red tape" are reflected in customs clearance procedures, in the enforcement of national health and safety standards, and in the logistics involved in moving shipments to, through, and from ports. These controls impose real trade costs on the private sector, both directly in terms of financial charges and indirectly through the opportunity costs of delays incurred in customs clearance (Kheir-El-Din 1998). Customs valuation and classification practices are problematic. Assessed values are frequently reported to exceed invoice values, and applied tariffs may be a multiple of the statutory rate.[9] Invoices are frequently rejected; in the case of one large foreign firm, 200 out of some 600 declarations in 1996 were rejected or contested. The Egyptian system of standards and technical regulation is a major bottleneck for importers. The General Organization for Export and Import Control (GOEIC) is one of a number of bodies that inspects consignments of goods entering Egypt that are subject to quality control standards.[10] As of 1994, some 1,550 tariff lines (25 percent of the tariff schedule) were subject to such controls.[11] As is the case for tariff rates, many of which escalate sharply, fees for goods that are intended for retail sale were generally at least twice as large as those that applied if further processing occurred in Egypt. Nathan Associates (1996) estimate that the direct and indirect costs of the system of standards and technical product regulations increased costs for traders and producers by between

5 and 90 percent, depending on the industry, with the highest costs for food products and imported final consumer goods.

An absence of competition in key service sectors also imposes excess costs on business. Only Egyptian nationals may import. Fees charged by the public companies providing port services for handling and storage of goods are some 30 percent higher than in neighboring countries or nations with which Egypt competes, while these companies do not provide quality service in return. Maritime shipping is a monopoly of the state-owned Egyptian Maritime Navigation Company. A 1994 survey revealed that the cost of shipment and handling in Egypt of a standard container was 27, 22, and 19 percent higher than in Jordan, Syria, and Turkey respectively (Mohieldin 1997). Foreign firms seeking to advertise their goods pay a multiple of the rates charged for domestic producers. Low quality and high cost telecommunications impose additional costs on the private sector. The telecommunications provider is an inefficient public monopoly; waiting times for new lines, revenue per line, and percentage of completed calls are among the lowest in the Middle East. National and international communications are a multiple of cost, reflecting a policy of cross-subsidizing local calls. The company manufactures telephone sets and small switches itself. It has been estimated that adopting a more competitive regulatory regime for telecommunications would generate a net welfare gain that is equivalent to the total current sales of the company (some $800 million; see Galal 1998). Insurance is dominated by three public sector firms that have 85 percent of the general insurance market and over 90 percent of the life insurance market. Foreign ownership is only allowed in free zones, although the government committed to allow foreign presence in domestic market through joint ventures by 1999, subject to a maximum equity stake of 49 percent.

No comprehensive estimates exist of the total cost and incidence of the various regulatory barriers that confront Egyptian producers and traders. The standards regime alone has been estimated to have a negative direct impact equivalent to one percent of GDP (Nathan Associates 1996). Indirect effects (e.g., through discouraging investment) will increase total costs. A number of initiatives have been taken in recent years to study and reduce red tape costs. Documentary requirements have been simplified, the incidence of stamp duties reduced, and fees for port and related services lowered. The shipping monopoly is in the process of being abolished.[12] While these initiatives have improved the situation, much more remains to be done. In principle, implementation of a EMA could help to achieve a reduction in red tape costs through a process of simplification and abolition of administrative controls and harmonization and mutual recognition of standards. The following analysis explores this issue further.

The Model and Benchmark Data

Egypt is modeled as a price taker on world markets; policy changes are assumed not to significantly alter prices in other regions of the world.[13] Egypt's MFN tariffs are applied to each region in the benchmark case, weighted across sub-sectors by global import shares. To take into account existing preferential trade within the Arab region, some of the simulations reduce applied tariffs on intra-Arab trade by 40 percent.[14] Production exhibits constant returns to scale and, as firms operate in a perfectly competitive environment, prices equal marginal costs of output. Following standard practice, final outputs are produced according to a Leontief function using intermediate inputs and real value added (fig. 6.1).[15] A constant elasticity of substitution (CES) production function describes the substitutability between labor and capital inputs in producing real value-added. Intermediate inputs and final goods are differentiated by country of origin according to the Armington assumption, so that export and import prices differ across regions.[16] In each sector, demand for domestically produced and imported goods is represented by a CES function, and intermediate imports are also differentiated by region of supply in a CES structure. Similarly, Egyptian industries supply regionally differentiated goods to both domestic and foreign markets (exports). Production follows a nested two-stage constant elasticity of transformation (CET) function. Total output is first calculated as the sum of domestic supply and total exports, with the latter then being allocated across regions (EU, United States, Arab League, and ROW) according to a sub-CET function.

Capital is assumed to be partially mobile in the sense that there are a number of resource-constrained sectors which we take to be agriculture (VG1, VG2, ANI)), mining (OIL, MIN), utilities (ELE), and transport (TRN). In all other sectors, capital is freely mobile. The intention underlying this assumption is to capture the strong possibility in Egypt of resource constraints that limit intersectoral factor flows and output changes. In particular, Egyptian experts seem concerned about the ability to expand agricultural production in the face of significant water scarcities. There are also constraints on output in crude petroleum and the Suez Canal. To address the latter problem, transportation exports are held constant in the counterfactuals.

A representative consumer maximizes a nested CES utility function with a corresponding multi-staged budget constraint. In the first stage, the consumer decides how much to spend on goods from each sector, given the budget constraint. Income elasticities across sectors are set at unity as given by a Cobb-Douglas (CD) utility nest. In the second nest, the consumer determines domestic and aggregate import expenditures in each sector according to a CES function. Then given a budget for imports, the consumer selects purchases of imports from each region. These latter functions also characterize the split between government consumption and investment spending on domestic and imported goods and services. The representative consumer receives income from primary factors (production labor, non-production labor, and capital), net transfers from the government, and the current-account deficit as well as any net economic rents from the operation of NTBs to trade.

FIGURE 6.1 Structure of the Model

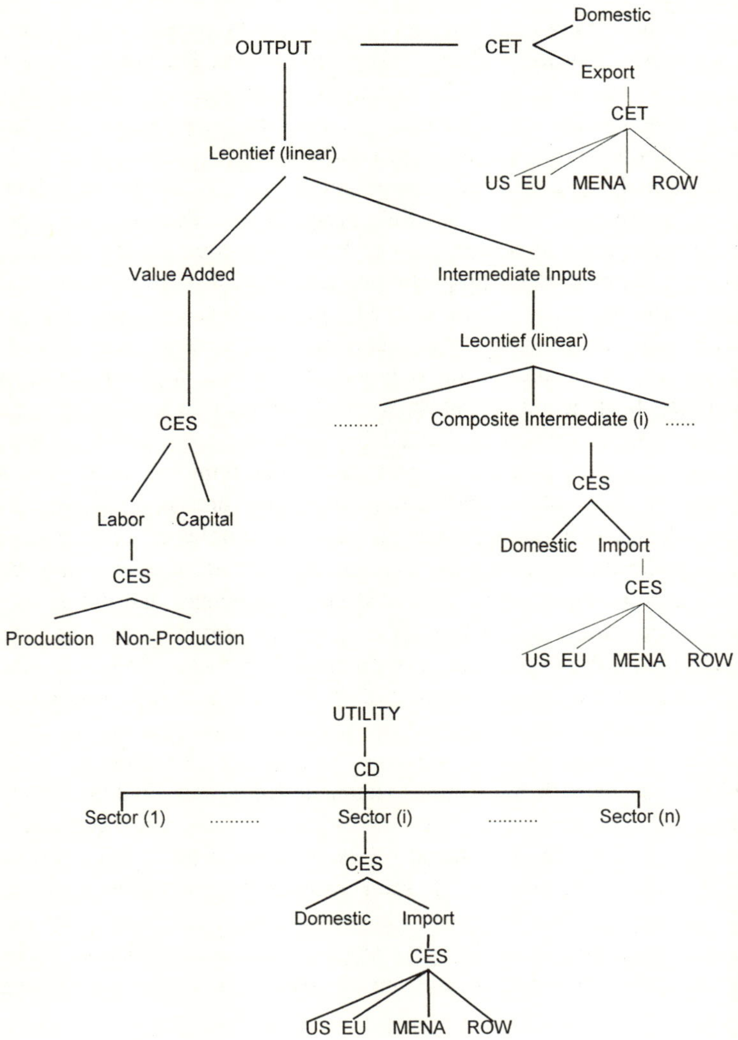

As tariff reform will have a direct impact on government finances—import duties constitute over 15 percent of tax revenues and over 10 percent of total current revenues (including transfers from public firms)—some care is taken to consider government revenue.[17] The government is held to operate under a fixed deficit constraint in that any change in tariff collections is compensated by an endogenous domestic tax change that makes any trade policy change revenue neutral. Public collections may rise or fall in response to the removal of a tariff, as domestic activity may increase in sectors that are more heavily taxed domestically.[18] Required changes in domestic tax collections are achieved by changing the Goods and Service Tax (GST), a sales tax that applies to final consumption and capital investment of domestic goods and imports but which does not apply to exports. The numerous sectoral deviations from the average GST rate and exemptions and evasion of this tax are taken into account by calibrating tax rates to measures of government revenue from indirect taxes in the benchmark year.[19]

The formal equations and notation of the model are presented in the appendix. Intermediate inputs are disaggregated into domestic sources and imports to incorporate importing costs and tariffs in purchases for the production sector. Sector-specific proportionate import costs (u_i) and export costs (v_i) capture the impact of NTBs, or "red tape." As discussed previously, import NTBs will be of four types, depending on whether formal bilateral agreements are a precondition for removal and whether they are frictional or rent-creating. Insufficient data exists to allow a breakdown of the existing set of NTBs into these categories, but all four types of costs are prevalent and significant in Egypt. Examples of costs that can be removed on an "unconditional" basis include administrative procedures and time-related costs due to inspection delays or monopoly port services. Examples of costs that could require formal bilateral agreements may include product standards and certification regimes, recognition of national licensing schemes, and recognition of qualification requirements for professional service providers. In the absence of information on the distribution of such benefits between the EU and ROW, in the simulations we assume that half of the red tape cost reduction on goods imports is "bilateral" or "conditional" on the negotiation of a MRA. In terms of goods sectors, import barriers are approximated as a 15 percent excess cost.

NTBs also vary in their implementation from being frictional to being resource-using and rent-seeking, and the simulation exercises consider both possibilities. In the case of frictional NTBs, we assume that a reduction in import NTBs shifts "rent revenues" to the consumer (representative agent) in the form of increased purchasing power. In contrast, resource-using NTBs impose further costs on society as they employ resources wastefully. That is, NTBs are directly unproductive and their rents are dissipated. In either case, changes in aggregate consumption are a direct measure of "equivalent variation," with the cost of living index associated with the utility function chosen as numeraire.

One of the impacts of deeper integration with the EU will potentially be greater competition in service markets by Egyptian firms, foreign suppliers, and FDI. To appropriately model the service sector would require information on the nature of present market imperfections and the potential form that an open market might take. The current environment is approximated with either a conservative 7.5 or 15 percent markup on service production, where the rents generated are collected by the representative agent.[20] In addition, import barriers are assumed to add a 10 percent increment in cost to construction, 30 percent in transport (excluding Suez Canal activities) and communications, and 15 percent in the remaining service markets. Service import barrier removal is assumed to require a MRA (i.e., to be discriminatory) in construction, business, financial, insurance, real estate and housing services, social and com-munity services, recreational and cultural services, and personal services (CON, INS, FIN, HSG, SER, REC, and PER). For the remaining service sec-tors, liberalization is assumed to be applied strictly on a MFN basis (ELE, TRD, RES, TRN, and COM). Throughout the counterfactuals, service import barriers are rent-creating.

A distinctive feature of the approach taken is that we do not impose any export NTBs on Egyptian producers. In past work (e.g., Maskus and Konan 1997, Hoekman, Konan, and Maskus 1998), this was done to account for inefficiencies and higher costs incurred by exporters. The direct imposition of "cost wedges" on service sector inputs, along with the various NTBs applied to imports of goods and services, should allow us to better account for the anti-export bias implied by status quo policies.

Two standard closure rules are imposed: the savings-investment balance equation (12) and a fixed current account balance equation (14) (see the appendix for all equations). The savings-investment balance is based on the assumption that the capital stock is exogenously fixed at the benchmark level. This stock is financed through forced consumer savings which acts as a direct (lump-sum) tax. A capital good is modeled as composite goods of fixed composition. Firms buy composite capital according to their preferences. The interest rate (an index price of the composite capital stock) is endogenous and determined by factor demand conditions.[21] The current-account imbalance is held constant at its benchmark level throughout the simulations. Foreign currencies are scaled so that the appropriate GDP deflator ("world" price index) is one. Given the small-economy assumption, the world price index is held constant throughout the analysis. Because the benchmark current account is in deficit, it represents an addition to the representative agent's income through exogenous capital inflows, as noted in equation (12). To hold B fixed while international prices are constant requires a balancing item in equation (14). This is accomplished by means of a change in the home "real exchange rate," which refers implicitly to a change in the home price index (generated by changes in the prices of home-produced goods) sufficient to sustain a constant current-account deficit measured at world prices.[22] Thus, B is held fixed along with the price terms, requiring e to change as import and export volumes change.

The government budget deficit is a deduction in available income for the representative agent, constituting a transfer to government consumption. As indicated earlier, we hold D fixed during our simulations. Thus, if a policy reform causes prices to fall, thereby reducing the tax revenues required to finance government expenditures, this tax saving is transferred to the representative agent. At the same time, if trade liberalization results in lost tariff revenues, the revenues are recouped by means of allowing GST tax rates (τC_i) to vary. The GST is applied on sales of goods and services at rates ranging from zero to 25. The standard tax rate is 10 percent (see table 6.2 for benchmark GST rates).[23] Taxes paid by firms on their intermediate input purchases are recoverable through a tax credit, with the exception of purchases of investment goods and some service inputs. In the absence of sufficient information on these tax credit exceptions, we choose to model the tax as a levy solely on final goods purchases, assuming that taxes on all inputs are credited back to purchasing firms.

The data for the model consist of a Social Accounting Matrix (SAM) and other parameters, such as elasticities of substitution and transformation,[24] import and export trade flows by region, and tax and tariff rates. These data are assembled into a consistent set of relationships between intermediate demand, final demand, and value-added transactions using the 1989-1990 IO table for Egypt, updated to incorporate trade and tax policies and trade shares as of 1994.[25] Trade and tariff data by 8-digit HS line were aggregated to the IO sectoral basis using import weights consistent with the concordance between the IO table and the tariff classification. From these data, regional trade shares for 1994 were applied to 1990 trade volumes on the IO basis. Egypt does not realize the full revenue that would be obtained if statutory tariff rates were applied to all imports because of various exemptions for duty-drawback provisions and investment incentives. Thus weighted legal tariff rates were scaled downward (by some 20 percent) to ensure consistency with total import duty collections in 1994. To take into account the existence of the quantitative restrictions on imports of textiles and clothing, the statutory MFN rates for this sector have been doubled. Finally, it is assumed that the cost impacts of "red tape" on imports from Arab countries are half those facing other trading partners reflecting past integration efforts within the region.

TABLE 6.2 Government Policy and Elasticity Parameters (percent)

SECTOR	GST-94*	K Tax-94	Egypt Tariff 1994	MENA Tariff	ESUB
	(2)	(3)	(4)	(5)	(6)
AGRICULTURE					
1. Vegetable products, foodstuffs (VG1)	0.0	0.0	2.5	6.3	0.95
2. Vegetable products, non-foodstuffs (VG2)	10.0	0.0	6.7	28.9	0.95
3. Animal products (ANI)	0.0	0.0	4.4	6.7	0.95
MINING AND QUARRYING					
4. Crude petroleum and natural gas (OIL)	0.0	18.0	8.2	2.9	0.43
5. Other extractive industries (MIN)	10.0	18.0	7.0	15.6	0.43
MANUFACTURING					
6. Food processing (FOO)	0.0	18.0	6.8	18.3	0.95
7. Beverages (BEV)	10.0	18.0	953.2	14.8	0.95
8. Tobacco products (TOB)	10.0	18.0	65.5	83.1	0.95
9. Cotton ginning and pressing (TX1)	10.0	18.0	17.3	24.9	0.93
10. Cotton spinning and weaving (TX2)	10.0	18.0	23.3	17.4	0.93
11. Clothing: assembled and pieces (CLO)	10.0	18.0	53.7	32.5	1.19
12. Leather products, excl. shoes (LEA)	10.0	18.0	34.8	44.6	0.75
13. Shoes (SHO)	10.0	18.0	51.8	36.9	0.75
14. Wood, excl. furniture (WOO)	5.0	18.0	8.1	28.1	0.93
15. Furniture (FUR)	10.0	18.0	46.9	34.9	0.93
16. Paper and printing (PAP)	0.0	18.0	13.3	18.6	1.00
17. Chemical, excl petroleum (CHE)	5.0	18.0	8.9	17.6	1.01
18. Petroleum refining (PET)	0.0	18.0	7.1	20.0	0.43
19. Rubber, plastics and products (RPL)	10.0	18.0	15.6	24.7	0.97
20. Porcelain, china, pottery (POR)	10.0	18.0	43.5	21.3	0.93
21. Glass and products (GLA)	10.0	18.0	29.6	17.2	0.97
22. Mineral products, n.e.i. (MPD)	5.0	18.0	18.1	12.7	0.43
23. Iron, steel, other base metals (MET)	10.0	18.0	17.2	32.6	0.43
24. Machinery and appliances (MAC)	25.0	18.0	17.9	19.9	1.20
25. Transportation equipment (TRA)	25.0	18.0	41.2	56.6	1.88
26. Other manufacturing (OMF)	10.0	18.0	19.3	24.9	1.19
SERVICES AND OTHER					
27. Electricity, gas, and water (ELE)	2.5	23.0	0.0	0.0	1.88
28. Construction (CON)	10.0	23.0	0.0	0.0	1.99
29. Trade (TRD)	8.0	23.0	0.0	0.0	1.28
30. Restaurants, hotels, coffeehouses (RES)	8.0	23.0	0.0	0.0	1.99
31. Transport and storage (TRN)	0.0	23.0	0.0	0.0	1.88
32. Communications (COM)	5.0	23.0	0.0	0.0	1.99
33. Financial establishments (FIN)	8.0	23.0	0.0	0.0	1.99
34. Insurance (INS)	0.0	23.0	0.0	0.0	1.99
35. Real estate and housing services (HSG)	8.0	23.0	0.0	0.0	1.99
36. Social and community services (SER)	10.0	23.0	0.0	0.0	1.99
37. Recreational and cultural services (REC)	8.0	23.0	0.0	0.0	1.99
38. Personal services (PER)	10.0	23.0	0.0	0.0	1.99

* Adjusted to be consistent with the real value of the 1990 government deficit. MENA tariff is trade weighted.

Source: Based on World Bank data and authors' calculations.

Preferential Trade Liberalization: Simulations and Results

Various preferential trade liberalization scenarios for Egypt are analyzed with the model, involving different combinations of FTAs with the EU and the Arab region. The first, tables 6.3 and 6.4, columns 1, is a shallow partnership agreement with the EU in which Egypt preferentially removes all tariffs on EU goods

TABLE 6.3 Impacts of Egyptian-EU Trade Agreement with Service NTBs Fixed

	Shallow Integration (NTBs fixed)	Deep Integration with Frictional Import NTBs		Deep Integration with Rent-Generating NTBs	
		MFN	MRA	MFN	MRA
	(1)	(2)	(3)	(4)	(5)
Macroeconomic Variables (% change)					
Welfare (EV)	0.153	1.239	1.785	0.363	0.292
Exchange Rate	2.342	2.858	3.050	3.258	3.701
Goods and Service Tax	-3.937	-4.422	-2.992	-3.790	-1.833
Average Tariff	4.516	4.444	4.122	4.449	4.128
Tariff Revenue	-1.705	-1.693	-1.748	-1.701	-1.760
Production Wage	1.988	2.728	3.066	2.772	3.163
Non-production Wage	2.366	3.142	3.508	3.331	3.871
Interest Rate	1.879	2.688	2.972	2.729	3.040
Trade Creation ($ million)	125	135	153	133	150
Trade Diversion ($ million)	141	138	154	140	158
Export Value Share (%)					
EU	40.5	40.6	40.5	40.5	40.4
USA	5.6	5.6	5.6	5.6	5.6
MENA	22.9	22.9	23.0	23.1	23.2
Import Value Share (%)					
EU	56.1	56.3	58.7	56.4	58.8
USA	14.3	14.3	13.6	14.2	13.5
MENA	3.1	3.0	2.8	3.0	2.8
Export Value (change $ billion)					
EU	.342	.357	.370	.402	.445
USA	.027	.028	.030	.036	.043
MENA	.133	.142	.152	.179	.215
Import Value (change $ billion)					
EU	1.050	1.170	1.409	1.142	1.360
USA	-.200	-.172	-.204	-.184	-.224
MENA	-.052	-.057	-.067	-.059	-.070
Export Quantity (% change)					
EU	19.5	20.3	21.0	22.9	25.3
USA	10.3	10.8	11.5	13.6	16.2
MENA	12.6	13.5	14.4	17.0	20.4
Import Quantity (% change)					
EU	36.7	40.9	49.3	39.9	47.6
USA	-16.3	-13.9	-16.6	-14.9	-18.1
MENA	-18.4	-20.3	-23.9	-20.9	-24.9

but does not liberalize NTBs or service barriers.[26] The EU responds by providing somewhat improved access to its markets assumed to be equivalent to a 1 percent increase in export price for all commodities except agriculture and clothing, where a 2-percent TOT improvement occurs (VG1, VG2, ANI, TX1, TX2, CLO). These improvements are assumed to reflect the removal by the EU of frictional NTBs. Egypt already enjoys duty-free access to EU markets for manufactures and is not likely to obtain significantly better market access terms for agricultural produce.[27]

The draft EMA devotes some attention to the reduction of administrative NTBs to Egyptian trade. There are articles dealing with technical assistance to ensure greater harmonization and upgrading of customs and standards-related institutions, and financial assistance is available for improvements in infrastructure. If these provisions are implemented and trade procedures and institutions are modernized, this may have a substantial impact in reducing trade costs. Several possibilities for deep integration are considered in table 6.3 (service barriers fixed) and table 6.4 (service barriers liberalized). We suspect that most of the NTBs on goods are frictional as they relate to "quality control" and red tape at the borders, reported in table 6.3, columns 2 and 3 and table 6.4, columns 2 to 5. Yet, there is no firm evidence on this score and thus we also model the possibility that NTBs are rent-creating, table 6.3, columns 4 and 5 and table 6.4, column 6 to 9. In each case, we consider two levels of service liberalization: elimination of a 7.5 percent and a 15 percent domestic price wedge, respectively.

There is also a MFN and a MRA scenario in each case. In the case of NTBs on goods, we assume that one-half of the import barriers are nondiscriminatory and are fully eliminated on a MFN basis once they are removed in the context of a FTA with the EU. The remaining NTBs are assumed to be "standards-related" in that their removal is on a discriminatory basis, benefiting only the EU. In the context of the prospective EMA, the MRA scenario combines MFN liberalization of nondiscriminatory barriers and removal of standards NTBs on imports from the EU (so that standards liberalization does not extend to the rest of the world). On the services side, we distinguish between sectors where liberalization will apply on a MFN basis and those where it cannot. In the latter case, the MRA results are additional to the MFN scenario. The MFN scenario, e.g., table 6.3, columns 2 and 4, liberalizes barriers on a nondiscriminatory basis. The reduction of "standards-related" services regulations is assumed to require a formal MRA with the EU, so that these barriers are eliminated on a discriminatory basis, e.g., table 6.3, columns 3 and 5.

The next set of scenarios focuses on an EU agreement against the backdrop of the FTA with the Arab League nations. The Arab League agreement is a "classic" FTA under which only tariffs are removed. As

TABLE 6.4 Impacts of Egyptian -EU Trade Agreement with Service NTBs Liberalized

		Deep Integration with Frictional Import NTBs				Deep Integration with Rent-Generating NTBs			
	Shallow Integration	Service Barriers 7.5 %		Service Barriers 15%		Service Barriers 7.5 %		Service Barriers 15.0 %	
	(NTBs fixed)	MFN	MRA	MFN	MRA	MFN	MRA	MFN	MRA
	(1)	(2)	(3)	(4)	(5)	(6)	(7)	(8)	(9)
Macroeconomic Variables (% change)									
Welfare (EV)	0.153	1.397	1.935	1.544	2.074	0.512	0.431	0.648	0.546
Exchange Rate	2.342	3.122	3.411	3.097	3.389	3.506	4.000	3.483	3.982
Goods and Service Tax	-3.937	-4.386	-3.001	-4.438	-3.040	-3.694	-1.658	-3.720	-1.640
Average Tariff	4.516	4.443	4.121	4.443	4.120	4.448	4.127	4.447	4.126
Tariff Revenue	-1.705	-1.694	-1.750	-1.693	-1.749	-1.702	-1.761	-1.701	-1.760
Production Wage	1.988	2.956	3.689	3.035	3.785	3.022	3.855	3.110	3.970
Non-production Wage	2.366	3.203	3.639	3.130	3.563	3.427	4.119	3.365	4.066
Interest Rate	1.879	2.845	3.138	2.755	3.040	2.880	3.192	2.786	3.086
Trade Creation ($ million)	125	135	153	135	153	133	150	133	150
Trade Diversion ($ million)	141	138	155	138	155	140	158	140	158
Export Value Share (%)									
EU	0.405	0.406	0.405	0.405	0.404	0.405	0.403	0.405	0.403
USA	0.056	0.056	0.056	0.056	0.056	0.056	0.057	0.056	0.057
MENA	0.229	0.230	0.232	0.231	0.232	0.232	0.235	0.232	0.235
Import Value Share (%)									
EU	0.561	0.562	0.595	0.562	0.595	0.563	0.596	0.563	0.596
USA	0.143	0.143	0.133	0.143	0.133	0.143	0.133	0.143	0.133
MENA	0.031	0.030	0.027	0.030	0.027	0.030	0.027	0.030	0.027

TABLE 6.4 (continued)

		Deep Integration with Frictional Import NTBs				Deep Integration with Rent-Generating NTBs			
	Shallow Integration	Service Barriers 7.5 %		Service Barriers 15%		Service Barriers 7.5 %		Service Barriers 15.0 %	
	(NTBs fixed)	MFN	MRA	MFN	MRA	MFN	MRA	MFN	MRA
	(1)	(2)	(3)	(4)	(5)	(6)	(7)	(8)	(9)
Export Value (Change $ billion)									
EU	0.342	0.429	0.460	0.430	0.461	0.474	0.530	0.475	0.531
USA	0.027	0.040	0.045	0.040	0.046	0.047	0.057	0.047	0.057
MENA	0.133	0.190	0.220	0.192	0.223	0.227	0.283	0.229	0.285
Import Value (change $ billion)									
EU	1.050	1.194	1.535	1.197	1.538	1.166	1.488	1.170	1.491
USA	-0.200	-0.163	-0.210	-0.161	-0.209	-0.174	-0.229	-0.173	-0.228
MENA	-0.052	-0.055	-0.069	-0.055	-0.069	-0.057	-0.072	-0.057	-0.072
Export Quantity (% change)									
EU	19.462	24.391	26.158	24.448	26.212	26.959	30.187	27.008	30.223
USA	10.259	15.102	17.160	15.212	17.249	17.918	21.759	18.005	21.803
MENA	12.633	18.017	20.906	18.264	21.136	21.559	26.878	21.776	27.054
Import Quantity (% change)									
EU	36.713	41.745	53.683	41.870	53.808	40.777	52.013	40.893	52.122
USA	-16.261	-13.196	-17.061	-13.063	-16.937	-14.147	-18.563	-14.025	-18.459
MENA	-18.419	-19.669	-24.765	-19.580	-24.681	-20.280	-25.697	-20.196	-25.624

mentioned previously, little is known regarding the tariffs that are effectively applied on intra-Arab trade flows. As the Arab region is a major destination of Egyptian exports and tariff levels in the region are significantly higher than those that are applied in the EU and U.S. markets, in principle liberalization of Arab trade barriers can have a major impact on Egyptian welfare. In the scenarios, an attempt is made to assess the sensitivity of the results to different levels of applied tariffs in the Arab region. We compute the applied tariff rates in the benchmark case as a function of actual trade weights, i.e., the Arab region's TOT adjusted as a percentage of the weighted average tariff rates (table 6.2.)[28]

Table 6.3 reports results for Egypt-EU FTA scenarios holding services barriers fixed. If the agreement is restricted to a shallow FTA, an estimated welfare gain of 0.15 percent is generated over benchmark 1994 levels. The real exchange rate (ERATE) or shadow price of foreign currency increases by 2 percent in order to maintain the benchmark current account deficit. The goods and services tax (GST) falls by about 4 percent. As the reformed tariffs become more efficient tax collection tools, the GST can be lowered, implying a gain in welfare for the representative agent. Despite a decrease in tariff collections, government budget neutrality implies a *reduction* in the GST as resources and consumption flow into highly domestically-taxed sectors in response to the fall in tariffs.[29] Real returns to both factors, production and non-production labor (PLWAGE and NLWAGE), increase by around 2 percent, reflecting enhanced efficiency in the economy. EU exports to Egypt increase by 34 percent by value. Trade diversion exceeds trade creation, resulting in the very small positive impact of the PTA.

A deep integration scenario has a substantially larger impact in terms of welfare, ranging from 0.3 to 1.8 percent of GDP depending on whether NTBs are assumed to be frictional or not. If NTBs are modeled as frictional, welfare gains are not surprisingly the largest. All deep integration scenarios involve elimination of nondiscriminatory NTBs. Whether a MRA is reached to eliminate EU standards-related NTBs is important and in a surprising fashion. When import barriers are treated as frictional (as we largely suspect), an EU MRA raises welfare by 44 percent over what is obtained from elimination of the nondiscriminatory merchandise NTBs. In comparison, if NTBs are treated as rent-creating, a MRA with the EU results in lower trade creation, higher trade diversion, and a smaller reduction in the GST. Instead of increasing welfare, in this case an EU MRA lowers welfare by about 20 percent. In extensive sensitivity analysis (not reported), this pattern is remarkably robust; extending NTB liberalization to European standards on a discriminatory basis (MRA scenario) is welfare-enhancing with frictional barriers but is worse than only eliminating nondiscriminatory barriers when such barriers generate economic rents. This suggests that there are "nontraditional" trade diversion costs associated with MRAs, in that the welfare impact of preferential liberalization depends on the type of barrier that is being removed.

If services barriers and the domestic service markups are also removed (table 6.4), welfare gains expand from between 8 percent in column 3 to 87 percent in column 9 over scenarios in table 6.3. Elimination of high services barriers with frictional NTBs has a moderate effect—welfare is 25 percent higher under MFN liberalization (column 4) and 16 percent higher under the MRA scenario (column 5). In the case of rent-creating NTBs for goods, the contribution of service liberalization is substantially greater, and welfare gains

TABLE 6.5 Sectoral Impacts of Egyptian-EU Trade Agreement and Frictional Import NTBs

Sector	Shallow (NTBs fixed)			MRA - Service NTBs fixed			MRA - Services liberalized		
	Output (1)	Exports (2)	Imports (3)	Output (4)	Exports (5)	Imports (6)	Output (7)	Exports (8)	Imports (9)
AGRICULTURE									
VG1	-0.27	9.63	-2.61	-0.38	10.36	2.30	-0.37	9.83	2.53
VG2	0.39	1.79	7.26	0.26	2.24	14.69	0.39	0.20	15.85
ANI	-0.40	12.10	3.14	-0.24	9.89	13.95	-0.23	9.57	14.09
MINING AND QUARRYING									
OIL	0.20	0.48	6.96	0.17	0.76	13.47	0.36	0.89	14.01
MIN	-0.06	11.85	-0.99	-0.20	25.22	-0.12	-0.17	22.38	0.88
MANUFACTURING									
FOO	-1.45	5.48	3.02	-1.66	7.46	9.62	-1.35	8.70	9.57
BEV	0.33	9.39	-3.19	1.81	14.60	-2.47	2.18	16.63	-2.70
TOB	-0.14	8.96	75.63	0.49	10.16	93.74	2.03	15.71	93.19
TX1	0.01	1.71	38.51	-0.18	2.00	49.55	-0.36	1.02	51.16
TX2	1.68	17.51	47.07	1.88	18.81	60.04	2.40	20.16	60.05
CLO	1.62	13.82	116.36	2.16	14.62	139.96	2.63	16.74	139.01
LEA	0.86	13.34	25.16	2.13	18.28	34.97	2.83	20.83	34.82
SHO	-0.41	8.37	35.53	0.53	11.03	47.53	0.86	13.08	47.13
WOO	-1.60	8.60	1.17	-4.19	11.75	3.59	-3.70	13.51	3.67
FUR	0.02	8.08	74.82	1.42	13.20	92.03	1.84	15.01	91.80
PAP	-2.71	7.77	5.80	-4.57	9.95	10.17	-3.67	13.26	10.08
CHE	-1.60	10.88	4.19	-2.72	15.77	8.88	-1.94	17.77	9.24
PET	3.24	11.68	3.02	4.63	15.49	9.72	5.28	17.61	8.91
RPL	-2.50	10.00	7.76	-3.29	13.79	13.27	-2.75	17.22	12.59
POR	-8.73	-1.16	46.61	-9.88	1.32	56.09	-9.57	3.20	55.57
GLA	-8.69	-0.75	30.09	-10.98	-1.80	38.15	-10.56	0.16	37.85
MPD	-1.19	4.53	21.82	-1.05	7.86	31.64	-0.96	8.81	31.35
MET	-3.81	6.99	7.42	-5.92	6.87	12.21	-5.39	9.11	12.08
MAC	-5.50	7.95	8.11	-7.96	9.24	11.87	-7.04	11.93	11.84
TRA	-8.95	27.01	15.64	-10.84	33.51	19.49	-10.75	34.53	19.22
OMF	1.90	16.12	13.44	2.65	21.54	20.27	6.43	30.66	20.87

increase by between 41 and 87 percent. As in the no service reduction case, when deep integration is extended to EU standards-related barriers by a MRA, welfare rises if NTBs are frictional and falls in the case of rent-generating barriers.

Sectoral impacts for the case of frictional merchandise NTBs and MRA-based elimination (which includes abolition of the 50 percent of NTBs assumed to apply on a MFN basis) reveal that deep integration has significant

TABLE 6.6 Egyptian-EU Trade Agreement with Arab League FTA and Service NTBs Fixed

		Deep Integration with Frictional Import NTBs		Deep Integration with Rent-Generating NTBs	
	(NTBs fixed)	MFN	MRA	MFN	MRA
	(1)	(2)	(3)	(4)	(5)
Macroeconomic Variables (% change)					
Welfare (EV)	1.372	2.525	3.094	1.820	1.684
Exchange Rate	-4.387	-4.311	-4.486	-4.106	-4.103
Goods and Service Tax	-0.973	-1.410	0.197	-1.088	0.892
Average Tariff	4.365	4.331	4.037	4.349	4.070
Tariff Revenue	-1.593	-1.562	-1.610	-1.561	-1.608
Production Wage	10.201	11.671	12.593	11.907	13.098
Non-production Wage	5.497	6.565	7.127	6.631	7.267
Interest Rate	6.772	7.863	8.377	7.999	8.660
Trade Creation ($ million)	522	569	620	584	652
Trade Diversion ($ million)	78	69	84	69	83
Export Value Share (%)					
EU	0.259	0.252	0.245	0.250	0.241
USA	0.033	0.032	0.031	0.032	0.030
MENA	0.478	0.491	0.502	0.495	0.511
Import Value Share (%)					
EU	0.555	0.559	0.583	0.560	0.585
USA	0.138	0.137	0.131	0.137	0.130
MENA	0.049	0.046	0.043	0.046	0.043
Export Value (Change $ billion)					
EU	-0.557	-0.588	-0.613	-0.581	-0.602
USA	-0.110	-0.115	-0.119	-0.114	-0.118
MENA	1.161	1.229	1.290	1.283	1.400
Import Value (Change $ billion)					
EU	1.602	1.790	2.114	1.784	2.103
USA	-0.082	-0.043	-0.071	-0.051	-0.087
MENA	0.124	0.118	0.101	0.117	0.098
Export Quantity (% change)					
EU	-31.664	-33.419	-34.848	-33.056	-34.262
USA	-41.873	-43.705	-45.143	-43.429	-44.727
MENA	110.235	116.674	122.455	121.955	133.095
Import Quantity (% change)					
EU	56.034	62.611	73.951	62.382	73.545
USA	-6.691	-3.473	-5.801	-4.142	-7.086
MENA	44.088	42.212	36.000	41.587	34.841

impacts on the output of many sectors, including beverages, tobacco, clothing, leather, shoes, and furniture (table 6.5). Exports rise substantially for food, beverages, leather, wood products, and furniture. The same sectors where output tends to expand following abolition of the NTBs are also among the industries that benefit most from services liberalization. Elimination of the services wedges has virtually no additional impact on output or trade, however, relative to the deep integration case without services liberalization.

Adding a FTA between Egypt and the members of the Arab League results in substantially larger welfare gains for Egypt, even if there is no deep integration associated with the EU FTA (1.4 percent instead of 0.15 percent) (table 6.6). This is not surprising given that intra-Arab trade barriers are much higher than those applying to Egypt's exports to the EU. The Arab League FTA could give rise to large increases in intraregional trade: exports to the Arab region rise by more than $1 billion, while the value of imports from the region rise by $124 million relative to the 1994 benchmark. Implementation of the Arab FTA results in large reductions in exports to the EU and the United States, as Egyptian producers reorient their goods to the region. The Arab FTA greatly increases the payoff to deep integration with the EU as well; depending on assumptions regarding MFN versus MRA and frictional or rent-creating barriers, welfare could rise by up to 3 percent of GDP. Adding in services liberalization as well could further increase the benefits of the PTAs by another 20 to 25 percent (table 6.7). These are quite high numbers for the type of static, competitive model that is used and largely reflect the high MFN tariff levels that apply in the Arab region.

Concluding Remarks

The positive welfare implications of a shallow EU FTA for Egypt are very small, reflecting the fact that Egypt already has duty-free access to the EU. The loss in tariff revenues that will be incurred is about equal to the efficiency gains that will result. Substantial welfare gains from an EU FTA are conditional upon the elimination of regulatory barriers and red tape. If deep integration can deliver such an improvement in the business environment, gains will at least double and may rise up to ten-fold. The variance in these impact results indicates that it is important to have a good sense of whether elimination of regulatory barriers can be applied on a nondiscriminatory basis and whether the barriers create rents or are largely frictional in nature. In the case of Egypt, a case can be made that frictional costs are likely to be large, to represent a major share of the total costs imposed by the regulatory regime, and not to require MRA-type formal agreements as a condition of their abolition. But the fact remains that we do not have reliable information on any of these key parameters.

TABLE 6.7 Egyptian-EU Trade Agreement with Arab League FTA Service NTBs Liberalized

		Deep Integration with Frictional Import NTBs				Deep Integration with Rent-Generating NTBs			
	Shallow Integration	Service Barriers 7.5 %		Service Barriers 15.0 %		Service Barriers 7.5 %		Service Barriers 15.0 %	
	(NTBs fixed)	MFN	MRA	MFN	MRA	MFN	MRA	MFN	MRA
	(1)	(2)	(3)	(4)	(5)	(6)	(7)	(8)	(9)
Macroeconomic Variables (% change)									
Welfare (EV)	1.372	2.968	3.514	3.451	4.027	2.278	2.127	2.775	2.665
Exchange Rate	-4.387	-4.153	-4.218	-4.245	-4.313	-3.954	-3.845	-4.048	-3.945
Goods and Service Tax	-0.973	-1.809	-0.571	-2.147	-0.943	-1.497	0.103	-1.847	-0.291
Average Tariff	4.365	4.339	4.053	4.336	4.050	4.357	4.086	4.353	4.083
Tariff Revenue	-1.593	-1.556	-1.601	-1.553	-1.598	-1.555	-1.598	-1.552	-1.595
Production Wage	10.201	12.085	13.528	12.162	13.623	12.326	14.049	12.404	14.149
Non-production Wage	5.497	6.411	6.862	6.184	6.609	6.473	6.995	6.239	6.726
Interest Rate	6.772	8.075	8.694	7.917	8.525	8.208	8.973	8.045	8.795
Trade Creation ($ million)	522	583	647	584	648	599	680	599	681
Trade Diversion ($ million)	78	67	81	66	80	67	80	66	79
Export Value Share (%)									
EU	0.259	0.252	0.244	0.252	0.244	0.250	0.240	0.250	0.240
USA	0.033	0.032	0.031	0.033	0.031	0.032	0.031	0.032	0.031
MENA	0.478	0.491	0.506	0.491	0.505	0.496	0.515	0.495	0.514
Import Value Share (%)									
EU	0.555	0.558	0.592	0.558	0.591	0.559	0.594	0.559	0.593
USA	0.138	0.138	0.128	0.138	0.128	0.137	0.127	0.137	0.127
MENA	0.049	0.046	0.042	0.046	0.042	0.046	0.042	0.046	0.042

TABLE 6.7 (continued)

		Deep Integration with Frictional Import NTBs				Deep Integration with Rent-Generating NTBs			
	Shallow Integration	Service Barriers 7.5 %		Service Barriers 15.0 %		Service Barriers 7.5 %		Service Barriers 15.0 %	
	(NTBs fixed)	MFN	MRA	MFN	MRA	MFN	MRA	MFN	MRA
	(1)	(2)	(3)	(4)	(5)	(6)	(7)	(8)	(9)
Export Value (Change $ billion)									
EU	-0.557	-0.553	-0.573	-0.546	-0.566	-0.546	-0.563	-0.539	-0.555
USA	-0.110	-0.109	-0.112	-0.107	-0.110	-0.108	-0.111	-0.106	-0.109
MENA	1.161	1.297	1.401	1.308	1.413	1.351	1.512	1.362	1.525
Import Value (Change $ billion)									
EU	1.602	1.839	2.294	1.851	2.307	1.834	2.283	1.846	2.298
USA	-0.082	-0.027	-0.074	-0.021	-0.068	-0.035	-0.089	-0.029	-0.083
MENA	0.124	0.121	0.099	0.123	0.100	0.120	0.096	0.121	0.097
Export Quantity (% change)									
EU	-31.664	-31.440	-32.604	-31.032	-32.186	-31.074	-32.021	-30.663	-31.597
USA	-41.873	-41.436	-42.623	-40.670	-41.842	-41.157	-42.211	-40.388	-41.423
MENA	110.235	123.147	133.045	124.155	134.184	128.452	143.792	129.468	144.999
Import Quantity (% change)									
EU	56.034	64.324	80.219	64.324	80.219	64.109	79.827	64.538	80.337
USA	-6.691	-2.176	-5.994	-2.176	-5.994	-2.834	-7.252	-2.353	-6.742
MENA	44.088	43.284	35.285	43.284	35.285	42.671	34.157	43.132	34.635

The results suggest that the additional impact of services liberalization is not trivial but is less significant than expected. This appears to reflect the fact that excess service costs impact relatively more on imports and domestic production than on exports. Given low trade barriers in the EU and the relatively high tariffs maintained by Egypt and other Arab countries, it is not surprising that there are potentially large gains associated with intra-Arab trade liberalization. Here again much depends on the availability of accurate information on the actual trade policies of the Arab countries vis-à-vis each other. These are also difficult to come by. To the best of our knowledge, no comparable cross-country empirical analyses have been undertaken to estimate the tariff equivalents are of the various NTB-related trade costs that currently exist in Egypt and the Arab region more generally. Without such empirical work—which should span both product and service markets—computational work of the kind attempted in this chapter will necessarily be subject to large margins of error.

Further work is also required to improve the modeling of the impact of regulatory costs and deeper integration initiatives. In related work (Hoekman and Konan 1999), we allow for the fact that frictional costs are also imposed on Egyptian exports, e.g., arising from redundant testing of goods in trading partners and from the non-zero probability that exports may confront various instruments of administered protection in major markets such as the EU. We also consider that the impact of protection of service sectors will result in inefficiencies that raise costs for all firms located in Egypt. Incorporating these two factors into the analysis results in much greater welfare gains from liberalization and deeper integration, ranging to over 10 percent of GDP. This analysis is based on the same perfectly competitive model used in this chapter and illustrates that the gains from deeper integration may indeed be very significant. Of course, assuming perfect competition is unlikely to be appropriate for all services sectors, and a more realistic assessment should consider different market structures and allow for entry through foreign direct investment. This is the subject of ongoing work (e.g., Markusen, Rutherford, and Tarr 1999). In coming years, much better tools and methodologies are likely to be developed that are more appropriate to assess the issues raised in this chapter.

Although there are clearly weaknesses in existing datasets and modeling approaches that result in large differences in estimates of the economic effects of deeper integration, the conclusions that emerge from current CGE-based analyses are robust in the sense that they are consistent with the policy prescriptions that emerge from economic theory and analytical models. FTAs that are limited to the elimination of tariffs for merchandise trade flows are of limited value at best, as they may as easily be welfare-reducing as welfare-enhancing. It is important that FTAs go beyond elimination of tariffs and quotas to include NTBs and red tape costs as well as efforts to open service markets to foreign competition. Both policy makers and analysts must take into account that some types of "red tape" stemming from the enforcement of regulatory regimes cannot be eliminated on a MFN basis. To the extent that this is the case, account must be taken of the possibility of nontraditional trade diversion effects. A comparison of the scenarios that assume either MFN or MRA-based liberalization of merchandise NTBs suggests that the effects of MRA-type discriminatory liberalization may be detrimental if merchandise NTBs are of the rent-creating type. This finding may be a function of the modeling approach taken in this chapter, and further research into this result is clearly required. Nonetheless, it suggests that greater attention needs to be devoted to determine what share of "deep" integration benefits has been or can be extended on a nondiscriminatory basis.

Appendix 6.1 Model Equations and Notation

Production

1. Labor Aggregator	$L_i = [b_{1i}L_{1i}^{(\sigma L-1)/\sigma L} + b_{2i}L_{2i}^{(\sigma L-1)/\sigma L}]^{\sigma L/(\sigma L-1)}$
2. Value Added Function	$V_i = [a_{Li}L_i^{(\sigma i-1)/\sigma i} + a_{Ki}K_i^{(\sigma i-1)/\sigma i}]^{\sigma i/(\sigma i-1)}$
3. Imported Intermediates	$M_{iN} = [\Sigma_r\delta_{ri}m_{riN}^{(\eta i-1)/\eta i}]^{\eta i/(\eta i-1)}$
4. Composite Intermediate	$z_{ji} = [\gamma_{di}d_{ji}^{(\eta j-1)/\eta j} + \gamma_{mi}m_{ji}^{(\eta j-1)/\eta j}]^{\eta j/(\eta j-1)}$
5. Final Goods Technology	$Y_i = \min[z_{1i}/a_{1i},..,z_{ni}/a_{ni}, V_i/a_{VA}]$
6. Domestic & Foreign Sales	$Y_i = [\alpha_{Di}D_i^{(\varepsilon i-1)/\varepsilon i} + \alpha_{Xi}X_i^{(\varepsilon i-1)/\varepsilon i}]^{\varepsilon i/(\varepsilon i-1)}$
7. Export Allocation	$X_i = [\Sigma_r\beta_{ri}X_{ri}^{(ei-1)/ei}]^{ei/(ei-1)}$
8. Marginal Cost Condition	$c_iY_i = \Sigma_j(1+v_i)p_jd_{ji} + \Sigma_j\Sigma_r(1+u_j+t_{rj})p_{rj}^{m}m_{rji}$ $+ \Sigma_i(1+\tau_{Ki})w_KK_i + w_LL_{1i}$

Utility

9. Utility Function	$U = \Pi_iC_i^{\lambda i}\ ;\ \Sigma_i\lambda_i = 1$
10. Domestic & Import Consumption (applies also to G_i and I_i^F)	$C_i = [\phi_{Di}D_{iC}^{(\psi i-1)/\psi i} + \phi_{MiC}M_{iC}^{(\psi i-1)/\psi i}]^{\psi i/\psi i-i}$
11. Import Allocation (applies also to M_{iG} and M_{iI}^F)	$M_{iC} = [\Sigma_r\delta_{ri}M_{ric}^{(\eta i-1)/\eta i}]^{\eta i/\eta i-1}$

Constraints and Balancing Items

12. Agent's Budget Constraint ($u_i = 0$ if NTBs are frictional)	$\Sigma_i \tilde{p}_i^C C_i = w_K \bar{E}_K + w_L \bar{E}_L + eB - \Sigma_i \tilde{p}_i^{IF} I_i^F - \Sigma_ip_iI_i^I$ $D + \Sigma_i \Sigma_r u_ip_{ri}^{m}M_{ri} + \Sigma_i v_iY_i$
13. Government Budget Constraint	$\Sigma_i \tilde{p}_i^G G_i = D + \Sigma_i\tau_{Ki}w_{Ki}K_i + \Sigma_i\tau_{Ci}(\tilde{p}_i^C C_i + \tilde{p}_i^{IF} I_i^F)$ $+ \Sigma_i\Sigma_r(1+\tau_{Ci})t_{ri}p_{ri}^{m}(M_{riC}+M_{riI}^F)$
14. Current Account Balance	$B = \Sigma_r\Sigma_i(1/e)(p_{ri}^{m}M_{ri} - p_{ri}^{x}X_{ri})$
15. Product Market Clearance	$S_i = \Sigma_ja_{ij}Y_j + G_i + I_i^F + I_i^I + C_i$
16. Factor Market Clearance	$\Sigma_iK_i = \bar{E}_K\ ;\ \Sigma_iL_{1i} = \bar{E}_{1L}, \Sigma_iL_{2i} = \bar{E}_{2L}, K_j = \bar{E}_{Rj}$
17. Zero Profits	$p_i D_i + \Sigma_rp_{ri}^{x} X_{ri} = c_iY_i$
18. Supply Value Balance	$\tilde{p}_i S_i = \tilde{p}_i^Z \Sigma_ja_{ij}(1+v_i)Y_j + (1+\tau_{Ci})(\tilde{p}_i^C D_{iC} + \tilde{p}_i^{IF} D_{iI}^F) +$ $\tilde{p}_i^G D_{iG} + \tilde{p}_i^{IF} I_i^I + \Sigma_r(1+\tau_{Ci})(1+u_i+t_{ri})p_{ri}^{m}(M_{riC} + M_{riI}^F)$ $+\Sigma_r(1+u_i+t_{ri})p_{ri}^{m}M_{riG}$

Price Relationships and Identities

19. Components of Domestic Sales	$D_i = D_{iC} + D_{iI}^F + I_i^I + D_{iG}$
20. Components of Import Sales	$M_i = M_{iN} + M_{iC} + M_{iI}^F + M_{iG}$
21. Domestic Price of Intermediate Imports (holds also for imports for G)	$p_{ri}^N = (1 + u_i + t_{ri})p_{ri}^{m}$
22. Domestic Price of Imports for C (holds also for imports for I^F)	$p_{ri}^C = (1 + \tau_{Ci})(1 + u_i + t_{ri})p_{ri}^{m}$
23. Consumer Price of Domestic Goods (holds also for purchases for I^F)	$p_i^C = (1 + \tau_{Ci})(1 + v_i)p_i$
24. Capital-Market Equilibrium	$\tau_{K1} + w_{K1} = ... = \tau_{Kn} + w_{Kn}$ (mobile capital sectors)

Notes

We are grateful to Joe Francois and Keith Maskus for helpful comments and suggestions on an earlier version and to Sandy Yeats and Francis Ng for data.

1. Such FTAs have already been concluded between the EU and Israel, Jordan, Morocco, the Palestinian Authority, and Tunisia. Discussions are ongoing with Algeria, Egypt, Lebanon, and Syria. See Galal and Hoekman (1997) for assessments of the Tunisian and Moroccan agreements and analysis of the issues for Egypt.

2. The recent Arab League FTA may to some extent have been motivated by a desire to avoid the negative implications of an emerging "hub and spoke" network of bilateral EMAs.

3. One-third of total intra-EU flows benefit from mutual recognition; another third are subject to "harmonization" directives (the old approach) and one fifth are covered by the EU's "new" approach (which specifies minimum standards—essential requirements) (European Commission 1996, 22-23).

4. However, it did require a number of MRAs as well. Switzerland was put into a special situation because other EFTA members either joined the EU or the EEA. Under the EEA, EFTA members agreed to adopt the acquis, which automatically implied accepting to apply EU standards.

5. Turkey is included in the EU grouping because Turkey has recently concluded an agreement to form a customs union with the EU, implying that any FTA with the EU will automatically be extended to Turkey. This section draws on Maskus and Konan (1997) and Hoekman, Konan, and Maskus (1998).

6. The Arab share is assumed to be higher than for merchandise reflecting the similarity in language, the importance of proximity for service delivery, and the prevailing policy of favoring Arab services-related investment. In earlier work (Konan and Maskus 1997a; Maskus and Konan 1997), it is assumed that services trade is closely complementary to merchandise trade in terms of its sources so that regional shares of services trade equal each region's share in total merchandise trade. In this chapter, this is assumption is only maintained for export shares of the Suez Canal.

7. However, if the fact that services are heavily protected is taken into account, average effective rates of protection for manufacturing are much smaller. See Hoekman and Djankov (1997a). It is also the case that total tariff revenue collections are less than what should be collected if all tariffs were fully applied, reflecting a variety of exemptions including Arab League preferences as well as circumvention.

8. See Kheir-El-Din and El-Sayed (1997).

9. The variance in valuation and applied rates can be significant. Data provided by importers in 1995 suggest that assessed values for capital equipment may exceed invoice values by 25 percent or more, while applied tariffs may exceed the applicable statutory rates by an even wider margin. See World Bank (1995b).

10. Up to five different agencies may independently test and inspect a single consignment (Nathan Associates 1996).

11. Consignments that were rejected in 1993 included bolts and nuts, spare parts for cars, transformers, pressure cookers, filters, brake shoes, ceramic tiles, light bulbs, ballpoint pens, washing machines, wheat, fresh fruit, dried fruit, sesame, frozen meat, and frozen fish. Estimates of the economic impact of the testing system do not exist. However, anecdotal evidence suggests the effect can be significant (World Bank 1995b). For example, in 1993 hundreds of tons of frozen beef were rejected on the basis that the relevant Egyptian standard (no. 1522 of 1991) was violated. It has been claimed that this standard is excessively strict. It requires that frozen beef have a fat content of 7 percent or less if for retail sale, and once defrosted, have a drip content of no more than 1 percent by weight.

12. *Financial Times*, September 25, 1997, 8.

13. See Maskus and Konan (1997) for a fuller description of the model.

14. As discussed further below there is very little information available regarding the preference margins that actually apply.

15. A CES structure for production, assuming a substitution elasticity of 0.5, leads to very similar results.

16. This assumption may seem inconsistent with the small open economy notion that Egypt is a price taker on world markets. However, this approach is quite standard, and there is no obvious way to address this issue given the data at hand. De Melo and Robinson (1989) show that models that allow product differentiation are well behaved under a small open economy assumption; in effect, the economy is a price taker at the level of aggregate trade flows, and each region's aggregation is sufficiently distinctive to support the Armington assumption.

17. International Monetary Fund (1994).

18. This occurs in many counterfactuals. See Konan and Maskus (1997b).

19. An additional important tax in Egypt is the corporate tax or tax on operating surplus. This tax also varies across sectors; for example, it is not applied in agriculture. We hold the tax structure fixed in our policy analyses.

20. Comprehensive estimates of the cost-raising effects of regulatory regimes that restrict competition in service markets are lacking. However, many case studies of individual sectors suggest that excess costs are more than 15 percent. See section 2 of this chapter, World Bank (1995b), and the contributions in Galal and Hoekman (1997) for a discussion.

21. No distinction is made between domestic capital and capital inflows from FDI. The impact of trade liberalization on the volume of FDI is generally ambiguous. Tariff reduction will lower the incentive of foreign firms to service Egyptian markets with "tariff jumping" FDI. In contrast, lower tariffs on intermediate imports may encourage export-oriented FDI. These issues are beyond the scope of the present analysis. See Brown, Deardorff, and Stern (1997) for an exploration of the issue in the context of the EU-Tunisia agreement.

22. A rise in the "real exchange rate" is consistent with a depreciation of home currency in that the per-unit price of foreign exchange rises.

23. Tax rates on capital are held constant. Effective corporate tax rates calculated for 1990 are reported in table 6.2. Legislated corporate tax rates are considerably higher than these effective rates, which reflect tax holidays, depreciation schedules, and other exemp-

tions. Available information indicates that there is no tax on agriculture, approximately 23 percent effective tax on services, and approximately 18 percent tax on manufactures, which we apply also to the mining and crude oil sectors. These rates have been incorporated into the 1990 SAM to calibrate the benchmark economy.

24. As there is also little empirical evidence on Egyptian elasticities, labor-capital substitution is allowed to vary across industries, using estimates from Harrison, Jones, Kimbell, and Wigle (1992). Labor-labor substitution is set at a conservative 0.50 (see table 6.2). Benchmark trade elasticities are drawn from Rutherford, Rutström, and Tarr (1993). The various trade elasticities are 2.0 for substitution between domestic and imported goods, 5.0 for substitution among regional imports and for transformation between domestic output and exports, and 8.0 for transformation among regional export destinations. These parameters are consistent with the ranges of elasticities reported in Lofgren (1994). Results of sensitivity analysis with respect to the various trade elasticities are reported in Maskus and Konan (1997).

25. See Maskus and Konan (1997) for a detailed discussion of the updating procedure, which involved re-calibrating the model on the basis of the 1994 policy parameters.

26. Throughout the counterfactual simulations, the beverage tariff is not changed to reflect Egypt's social policy for maintaining rigorous barriers on imported alcoholic beverages. Similarly, tariffs on tobacco products are held fixed in order to reflect the fact that governments in the region will continue to impose high excises on these products for revenue and health purposes.

27. This differs from the more optimistic assumption of an 8 percent export price gain in EU's agriculture and textile sectors used in Konan and Maskus (1997a).

28. Data for Jordan's and Lebanon's tariffs were compiled from Hoekman and Djankov (1997a); Morocco's and Tunisia's tariffs were obtained from Rutherford et al. (1993, 1995). A concordance consistent with the Egyptian IO table was developed for mapping tariffs into the 38 sectors of the model. Tariffs were weighted by 1996 import shares, using the UN COMTRADE database.

29. That government revenues may increase in response to a piecemeal tariff reform is discussed in Konan and Maskus (1997b).

PART THREE

Policy Challenges

CHAPTER 7

Enhancing Egypt's Exports

James H. Cassing, Samiha Fawzy, Denis Gallagher, and Hanaa Kheir-El-Din

The Government of Egypt (GOE) has set a target for GDP growth at an annual rate of 7 to 8 percent by the year 2000. An important part of the strategy for achieving this goal is policy reform aimed at enhancing export performance and attracting increased investment. Egypt currently has a unique opportunity to achieve its growth target by relying increasingly on the rapidly growing world economy and large amounts of international capital seeking productive investments.

However, there are serious obstacles to the globalization strategy. These threaten to undermine export growth and investment as well as to entice new job entrants into less productive jobs and new investment into artificially protected, less productive industries. As it stands, Egypt has been marginalized in international trade with a mere $3.5 billion of merchandise exports concentrated in a handful of traditional exports and petroleum. (Nonfactor service receipts such as those from tourism and the Suez Canal are $10.6 billion.) Manufactured exports amount to only $ 1.3 billion, of which half are textiles (World Bank 1997a). Had Egyptian exports simply grown at the world average since 1983, exports would be about twice what they are now. Despite low labor costs, rich natural resources, and an advantageous location, Egypt's share of world exports and imports has declined, as has the openness of the economy (Subramanian 1997). Thus, there is cause for concern regarding the fragility of the necessary preconditions for an export boom and the direction and pace of Egypt's current economic reforms. Although it is clearly the

GOE's intention to create an exporter friendly business climate, good intentions are insufficient to deal with the taxes and stifling bureaucracy that block initiatives and lower efficiency and productivity.

This chapter identifies and assesses the impact of several impediments to the globalization strategy. In particular, we focus on the structure of economic incentives resulting from the tariff/tax system, remaining NTBs to trade and investment, and problems with moving products through the ports and customs. These have an antitrade bias and discourage investment in the most productive sectors. Issues are illustrated by focusing on the impact of prevailing policies on five industries that have become the focus of some attention in Egypt.

The Structure of Tariffs

Egypt taxes corporations, individuals, commodities, and a number of other activities.[1] As far as international trade flows and investment are concerned, import duties and surcharges are of primary concern. There are no export taxes or quotas. The average nominal rate of protection (NRP) in 1997 was 24.6 percent. The ERP, which is a measure of the extent to which value added is protected, was 30.5 percent (table 7.1).[2]

ERPs are highly correlated with the NRP; the estimated rank correlation coefficient is 0.98. For agriculture, the ERP is somewhat higher than NRP on average, but both measures of protection are lower than 10 percent. Manufacturing also enjoyed an ERP higher than the NRP, and both are significantly higher than for agriculture, 34 percent and 27 percent, respectively. The implicit NRP on material inputs (INRP)—a measure of the tax paid explicitly for imports or implicitly for import substitutes on inputs for various activities—is much lower at 7 percent. The tariff structure tends to favor consumer goods activities and transport equipment.

Both nominal tariffs (NRPs) and ERPs are highly dispersed. The standard deviation of nominal tariffs is 19.5 overall and 24.6 for manufacturing, with a range of 5 percent to 50 percent. ERPs are significantly more dispersed with a standard deviation of 34.2 in manufacturing and 26.9 overall. This indicates that some sectors are much more favored by the tariff structure than others and so are likely to attract resources away from sectors which are in fact more productive. Ironically, to the extent that capital and skilled labor are diverted to uses in less labor-intensive sectors, employment opportunities are suppressed and real wages, already lower due to high tariffs on consumer goods, are further reduced.

Sectors that are particularly favored by the tariff structure at the expense of other sectors, and of exports generally, include final wear, footwear, furniture, rubber and plastic products, porcelain, china, and ceramics, and means of transport. As an extreme example of the perversity of this tariff structure, furniture receives an 83.8 percent "subsidy" to its value added due to tariffs alone (it is also protected by international transport costs and port clearance costs), while cotton ginning exports has its value added essentially "taxed" at 10.9 percent.

Implications of the Tariff Structure for Exports

The current structure of Egypt's trade taxes gives rise to several concerns because the import duties are both very high and very dispersed, giving more protection to finished goods than to raw materials, capital goods, and other inputs. While this "cascading" tariff structure aims to foster manufacturing through import-substitution, in fact it creates an anti-export bias that is inconsistent with the GOE's current globalization strategy. A consequence of

TABLE 7.1 Nominal and Effective Protection Rates in 1997 (percent)

Activity	*NRPj*	*INRPi*	*ERPj*
Agriculture	7.14	4.81	8.20
1. Agricultural food products	6.82	5.04	6.62
2. Agricultural nonfood products	9.49	6.08	9.63
3. Livestock products	5.11	3.31	4.17
Manufacturing	27.37	7.62	34.22
4. Food processing	6.87	2.23	6.39
5. Beverages	271.64	11.34	-1781.7
6. Tobacco processing	85.00	-1.92	88.47
7. Cotton ginning	5.01	7.96	-10.89
8. Spinning and weaving	27.95	7.67	47.55
9. Final wear	46.64	14.56	55.86
10. Leather and leather products (excl. footwear)	31.13	17.43	47.57
11. Footwear	39.10	15.54	50.81
12. Wood and wood products (excl. furniture)	8.64	10.41	6.10
13. Furniture	49.90	8.19	83.80
14. Paper and printing	17.05	5.47	17.84
15. Chemicals (excl. petroleum refining)	10.01	2.65	9.20
16. Petroleum refining	11.81	-1.56	14.76
17. Rubber and plastic products	28.47	6.21	43.07
18. Porcelain, china, and ceramics	35.04	6.19	55.95
19. Glass products	20.65	9.91	23.20
20. Nonmetallic products	15.18	6.23	18.52
21. Steel, iron, and metallic products	16.06	7.68	18.06
22. Machinery and equipment	15.30	6.57	14.49
23. Means of transport	43.97	2.83	55.62
24. Other manufacturing	18.14	8.92	18.52
Average (excl. beverages and petroleum refining)	24.62	7.23	30.48
Standard Deviation	19.51	4.50	26.93

Note: *NRPj* = nominal rate of protection on output of activity *j*; *INRPi* = implicit nominal rate of protection on material inputs *i* in activity *j*; *ERPj* = effective rate of protection for activity *j*.

the prevailing tariff structure is that Egypt may well be taxing its nontraditional export sector out of existence. High import tariffs divert production and investment away from exporting and into the other sectors of the economy. The implicit export tax falls hardest on those industries that are least able to see their profit margins squeezed. Traditional exports such as petroleum, mineral resources, the Suez Canal, tourism, and to some extent agriculture, rely extensively on fairly industry-specific inputs whose values can simply absorb the tax and remain economically viable, although their level of profitability will be affected negatively. Nontraditional manufacturing industries have no such luxury—they must compete in the global marketplace with other high quality, highly competitively priced commodities. Profit

TABLE 7.2 Effective Rates of Protection to Exports in 1997 (percent)

Activity	*ERPj* Experiment 1*	*ERPj* Experiment 2**
Agriculture	-2.00	-1.52
1. Agricultural food products	-1.22	-0.87
2. Agricultural nonfood products	-1.42	-1.17
3. Livestock products	-3.35	-2.52
Manufacturing	-16.60	-7.77
4. Food processing	-7.78	-3.01
5. Beverages	94.99	60.20
6. Tobacco processing	-30.54	-5.52
7. Cotton ginning	-32.82	-32.79
8. Spinning and weaving	-17.34	-10.58
9. Final wear	13.69	-10.33
10. Leather and leather products (excl. footwear)	-17.61	-11.82
11. Footwear	-28.04	-24.68
12. Wood and wood products (excl. furniture)	-12.66	-3.38
13. Furniture	-10.80	-4.28
14. Paper and printing	-21.12	-0.99
15. Chemicals (excl. petroleum refining)	-13.94	-2.35
16. Petroleum refining	-2.61	-0.59
17. Rubber and plastic products	-18.27	-9.37
18. Porcelain, china, and ceramics	-5.92	-4.87
19. Glass products	-6.29	-1.57
20. Nonmetallic products	-5.20	-4.82
21. Steel, iron, and metallic products	-9.48	-7.58
22. Machinery and equipment	17.92	-2.29
23. Means of transport	-31.29	-3.25
24. Other manufacturing	-14.66	-4.06
Average	-14.61	-6.91
Standard Deviation	9.59	7.87

* Experiment 1 represents the effect on ERP of selling exports at the international price while producers of export goods pay the domestic price for their domestic and imported inputs.

** Experiment 2 represents the effect on ERP of selling exports at world price, and receiving duty drawback on imported inputs.

margins of nontraditional exports are already squeezed by transport and other non-tax costs and delays. Even a small export tax may be enough incentive to discourage exports and so the nontraditional export industries simply never appear. Matters are compounded by an additional tariff equivalent effect raising import-competing goods prices owing to NTBs working through high "red tape" costs at the ports (see below).

The direct burden of import taxes on exporters can be estimated through calculation of the ERP for firms that decide to export some of their product. Such firms must pay the tariff protected prices for inputs, whether imported or domestically produced under protection, but receive no such protection for their output prices since they are selling into the world market. Tariffs provide *negative* effective protection for exporters: value added per unit for firms that decide to export is on average between 6.9 percent and 14.6 percent lower than it would be in the absence of tariffs on inputs, depending on how well duty drawback works (table 7.2). For nontraditional exports trying to compete with high quality products on world markets, even the lower of these two numbers can erode any profit margin and be a substantial disincentive to export. Effective drawback clearly makes a large difference for most sectors, but not all (e.g., footwear and cotton ginning).

The extent of tariff induced bias against exports (B_x) can be estimated as:

$$B_{xj} = \left[\frac{1 + tj}{1 + sj} - 1 \right] \times 100 \qquad (1)$$

where t_j is the tariff rate on product $j - NRP_j$ and s_j is the export subsidy rate which represents the *potential* duty drawback per £E of export and has been calculated as $NRP_i \times m_{ij}$, where m_{ij} is the technical coefficient of imported commodity i per £E worth of product j. These coefficients have been obtained from the import technical coefficient matrix annexed to the 1991-92 IO table. The extent of the economy-wide average bias against exports decreased from 26.6 percent in 1994 to 19.7 percent in 1997 (table 7.3). This average, however, conceals large variations among various manufacturing activities. In particular, the incentives against exporting remain especially high in tobacco, final wear, leather and leather products, footwear, furniture, and porcelain, china, and ceramics.

Summarizing, tariffs amount to a 19.7 percent export tax economy-wide. Such a tax falls especially hard on nontraditional exports, which cannot absorb much of a tax on profits and still be price competitive on world markets. The effective rate of protection for exporters in every sector of the economy is negative and often large. Even with duty drawback, the tariffs burden exporters.

TABLE 7.3 The Extent of Tariff Induced Bias against Exports 1994 and 1997

	1994			1997		
Activity	*1+tj*	*1+sj*	B_{xj}%	*1+tj*	*1+sj*	B_{xj}%
Agriculture			9.385			6.745
1. Agricultural food products	1.089	1.004	8.495	1.068	1.003	6.480
2. Agricultural nonfood products	1.157	1.003	15.397	1.095	1.002	9.250
3. Livestock products	1.050	1.007	4.263	1.051	1.006	4.505
Manufacturing			29.354			21.711
4. Food processing	1.084	1.030	5.259	1.069	1.023	4.451
5. Beverages	13.705	1.038	1220.434	3.716	1.018	265.061
6. Tobacco processing	1.850	1.177	57.126	1.850	1.177	57.156
7. Cotton ginning	1.050	1.000	4.990	1.050	1.000	5.001
8. Spinning and weaving	1.376	1.037	32.692	1.280	1.028	24.439
9. Final wear	1.696	1.026	65.246	1.466	1.020	43.824
10. Leather and leather products (excl. footwear)	1.466	1.027	42.718	1.311	1.024	28.118
11. Footwear	1.639	1.018	60.951	1.391	1.015	36.983
12. Wood and wood products (excl. furniture)	1.120	1.056	5.064	1.086	1.043	4.146
13. Furniture	1.698	1.032	64.52	1.499	1.025	46.240
14. Paper and printing	1.171	1.089	7.539	1.171	1.088	7.592
15. Chemicals (excl. petroleum refining)	1.111	1.060	4.850	1.100	1.051	4.684
16. Petroleum refining	1.096	1.015	7.981	1.118	1.013	10.378
17. Rubber and plastic products	1.330	1.048	26.838	1.285	1.041	23.452
18. Porcelain, china, and ceramics	1.525	1.005	51.674	1.350	1.005	34.384
19. Glass products	1.332	1.047	27.285	1.207	1.032	16.906
20. Nonmetallic products	1.231	1.003	22.660	1.152	1.002	14.906
21. Steel, iron, and metallic products	1.230	1.016	21.119	1.161	1.011	14.818
22. Machinery and equipment	1.225	1.106	10.712	1.153	1.075	7.249
23. Means of transport	1.527	1.170	30.569	1.440	1.137	26.616
24. Other manufacturing	1.253	1.081	15.919	1.181	1.059	11.548
Average			26.631			19.670
Standard Deviation			21.350			15.755

Source: Balassa (1971), 331-332.

Nontariff Barriers

The main NTBs prevailing in Egypt are associated with delays in port operations, customs clearance, and certification of compliance with Egyptian standards. Remaining quotas on textiles imports are to be phased out as agreed under the Uruguay Round Agreement on Textiles and Clothing.

Egypt's Approach to Product Standards

The current system in Egypt of standards setting, quality control, and inspection has been the subject of exhaustive review over the last five years. A synopsis of findings and recommendations from several major USAID funded studies is reported in table 7.4. The general conclusion emerging from these studies is that the existing system of standardization and conformity assessment applied in Egypt imposes substantial additional costs on traders and is often inconsistent with international best practice.

Maritime Port Services

The costs of Egyptian port services act as a significant NTB to trade and a potential serious impediment to investment. An extensive and detailed analysis of the structure, competitiveness, and projected investment demands of Egypt's maritime port services was undertaken in mid-1996 by DEPRA.[3] The key issues identified in the 1996 report included:

- all port services including but not limited to pilotage, tugs boat services, stevedoring, shipping/clearance, safety/inspection, warehousing, and terminal operations/maintenance are essentially reserved for state entities and state owned operating companies;

- all tariffs, fees, and commissions charged by these state entities are either set by the responsible ministries or approved by them; and

- interlocking directorships and share ownership between the state operating companies and the port authorities who are responsible to the Ministry of Transport and Communications inhibit competition and reduce incentives to maintain and improve port facilities.

Freight plus port costs are as much as 40 percent of the value of some perishable goods requiring refrigerated containers. Port costs for containerized cargo average 9 to 14 percent of the CIF price (World Bank 1998). Seaport service charges are triple those of competitor ports; container freight rates are 15 to 20 percent higher than other Mediterranean ports; container handling

TABLE 7.4 Results of Studies of the Egyptian Standardization System

Findings	Recommendations
Research Study of the Quality Control System in Egypt (July 1996)	
• Quality standards are confused with safety standards. • Multiple centers of overlapping authority exist. • There is a lack of transparency and due process. • Compliance costs are high: additional costs to affected producers and traders range from 5% to 90%. • Exports lower by an estimated 9% to 12%. • Welfare loss equivalent to 1% of GDP. • Government resources expended on duplicative and unnecessary activities.	• Establish a single authority for the inspection and testing of an imported product. • Recognize international standards certification for nonfood imports and reduce inspection levels to minimum. • Establish due process and transparency in the quality control regulations. • Establish the Egyptian Organization for Standardization and Quality Control (EOS) as a voluntary standards institute. • Restructure the GOIEC.
Comparison of Egyptian Food and International Norms (March 1998)	
• EOS Standards appear to be used: - to carry out national health policy; - to help ensure consumer protection rather than relying on consumer education comprehensive fraud and product labeling laws; and - to assist in ensuring product safety rather than addressing certain infra-structure issues that should be in place to prevent unsafe or spoiled product.	• Clarify policy issues at ministerial level before carrying out further review of EOS standards. • Consider the development of guiding principles for the operation of EOS technical committees. • Reduce the prescriptiveness of standards. • Develop standards that are easier to understand and amend.

TABLE 7.4 (continued)

Findings	Recommendations
Comparison of Egyptian Food and International Norms (continued)	
• There appears to be a strong need within the Egyptian regulatory system to have and maintain a standard for each and every product. • Maintenance by Egypt of multiple regulatory inspection and control systems. • Differential application of standards to import vs. domestic product. • Tendency to establish provisions within standards based on weak or incomplete scientific information.	• Replace standards that regulate individual foods with standards that apply across all foods or a range of foods. • Consider the possibility of industry codes of practice as an alternative to regulation. • For controversial standards obtain outside peer review from governments and other organizations on re-drafted standards • Consider requesting the Codex Alimentarius secretariat to develop new standards where such standards would be helpful to assist Egypt in arriving at standards where consensus domestically has been difficult.
Pilot Study for Pre-Certification of Imported Products (March 1998)	
• Pre-inspection and pre-certification are viable alternatives for nonfood products to the presently existing system. • Many Egyptian standards and their application are incompatible with internationally accepted norms and WTO disciplines. • The GOE must agree on a clear definition of standards and technical regulations and ensure that they are used properly and consistently by all ministries and organizations. • Many categories or groups of products subject to testing do not appear to have any safety, public health or environmental implications.	• Reduce the number of imported products requiring inspection on entry. • Establish a register of repeatedly imported products. • Adopt a system of pre-shipment inspection and establish a system and procedures for the choice, recognition, registration, and continual assessment of competent inspection companies. • Speed up the process of harmonization with international standards. • Establish a National Product Conformity and Consumer Protection Board. • Establish a quality assurance department in to assure compliance with ISO 9000, laboratory accreditation and international standards and technical regulations.

Note: These studies can be downloaded from http://www.economy.gov.eg/depra.

cost are 2 to 3 times that of nearby ports; terminal handling charges double those of nearby ports; maintenance and housekeeping services are poor; vessel time lost is significant (nearly 10 percent of total chargeable time due to delay in testing for radiation and in time between unloading cargo and departure); and air-freight rates are twice as high as in other Middle East countries ($1 to $1.4 per kilogram). Overall, it was estimated that the seaport charges raise CIF cost for imports to Egypt by over 10 percent.

Prospects and Problems in Five Industries

Egypt's share in world exports and imports declined from 0.2 and 0.5 in the 1980s to 0.07 and 0.2 respectively, in 1995. The share of exports and imports of goods and nonfactor services to GDP dropped from 88 percent in 1985 to 47 percent in 1996-97 (Subramanian 1997). This section examines five industries (food, textiles and clothing, leather footwear, wooden furniture, and software) which have become the focus of some attention in Egypt and which are believed to have potential for export growth.

RCA indices suggest that Egypt has a strong comparative advantage in producing and exporting food and textile products and a disadvantage in furniture and footwear (Nathan Associates 1998b). Data are not available for software, but interviews with business people indicate that Egypt has a comparative advantage in this field. The spinning and weaving industry and the foodstuffs industry have experienced above average annual growth rates of

TABLE 7.5 Unit Labor Cost of Production in Manufacturing ($) 1992

Industry	Egypt	Jordan	Morocco	Tunisia	Turkey
Total manufacturing	9	11	12	N/A	11
Food products	6	11	7	6	9
Beverages	11	18	8	13	8
Tobacco	8	36	-	4	10
Textiles	12	13	-	12	15
Wearing apparel, excl. footwear	11	38	24	23	8
Leather products	15	12	21	N/A	8
Leather footwear	9	30	-	N/A	16
Wood products, excl. furniture	16	23	14	N/A	14
Furniture, excl. metal	13	31	-	N/A	11
Machinery electrical	8	13	14	11	10
Transport equipment	18	18	10	N/A	12
Professional/scientific equipment	23	35	12	N/A	17

Note: Unit Labor cost of Production = wages per worker/gross output per worker.
Source: The Economic Research Forum (1996).

exports since 1990 (4.6 and 6.0 per year, respectively); furniture in contrast has experienced a serious decline in exports (-28 percent per year since 1990).

Each of the five industries is more labor intensive than manufacturing as a whole. Capital/labor ratios are half or less than the average for the manufacturing sector. Other things equal, expanding exports in these industries would help achieve the GOE's primary goal of increasing employment. High labor intensity combined with relatively low unit labor costs increases the likelihood of expanding manufacturing exports (table 7.5).

Despite the potential, export and efficiency indicators reveal that these industries are under performing. Manufacturing exports grew by only one percent per year between 1985 and 1994, well below the average of 25 percent attained by dynamic developing countries. The five industries' share in Egypt's merchandise exports is negligible with the exception of textiles and clothing. Exports as a share of total output is also very limited: 1.2 percent in furniture, 1.6 percent in spinning and weaving, 2 percent in food, 4.3 percent in footwear, and 4.7 percent in cotton ginning. The exception is ready-made garments, where 40 percent of output is exported. This under performance in exports is certainly associated in part with the trade policy stance (implicit taxes on exports). But production inefficiency is also important. Most of the industries under study manifest lower levels of capital and labor productivity compared with the average of the manufacturing sector (table 7.6).

Low levels of efficiency are due to many reasons, of which the most important is the height of the current structure of tariffs. With the exception of the food industry (6 percent), the four other industries under study have high and above average effective rates of protection, exceeding 50 percent for fur-

TABLE 7.6 Efficiency Indicators 1994/95

	Labor productivity	Capital productivity
Food, beverages, and tobacco	16.57	0.93
Textile, clothing, and footwear excl. leather wear	7.69	0.46
Leather footwear	2.17	0.27
Wood products excl. furniture	17.88	1.32
Wood furniture	7.26	0.38
Paper products and printing	21.05	0.81
Chemicals	39.49	0.63
Nonmetallic products	30.20	0.33
Basic metallic	11.79	0.30
Machinery electric equipment and transport means	19.81	1.14
Electronics	8.19	1.56
Manufacturing total	18.34	0.60

Source: Calculated from CAPMAS (1997).

niture (83.8 percent), footwear (50.8 percent), final wear (55.9 percent), while spinning and weaving is nearly there (47.6 percent). This compares with the average ERP in manufacturing of 30.5 percent. In addition, low rates of capacity utilization coupled with high rates of inventories in most manufacturing are also responsible for poor levels of efficiency (Fawzy and Galal 1998).

A number of NTBs were discussed previously in this chapter. To identify which institutions constrain exports the most from a business perspective, a survey of a one hundred private firms in manufacturing was undertaken (for details on the sample, see Nathan Associates 1998b). Questionnaire returns suggest two broad findings. First, the severity of direct constraints to export (fig. 7.1) is not considered very high, compared with other institutional constraints to doing business in Egypt (fig. 7.2). This may be explained by the fact that most firms in Egypt produce for the domestic market rather than for export and therefore are not seriously affected by export problems.

FIGURE 7.1 Overall Ranking of Institutional Constraints

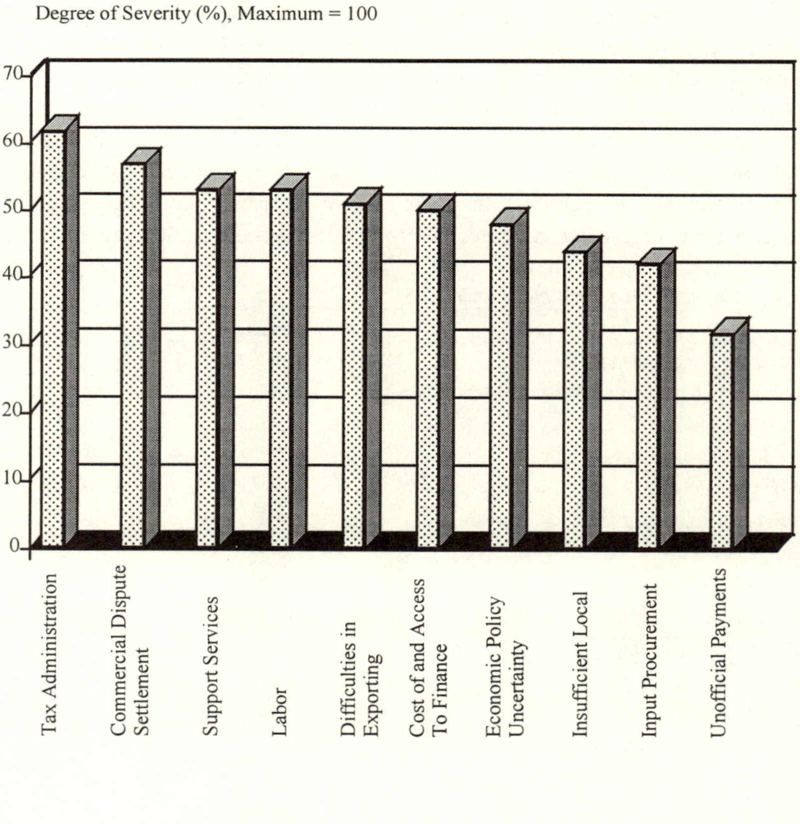

Second, with regard to the ranking of specific direct export constraints, firms rank the most binding constraints related to exporting to be high tariff rates on imported inputs, lack of marketing and distributing companies, inefficiency of drawback and temporary admission schemes, cumbersome export procedures, and, finally, the absence of export credit and insurance services, in that order (fig. 7.2).

The fact that tariffs on imported inputs (intermediate inputs and capital goods) are perceived to be the most binding constraint is not consistent with the previous analysis. Input tariffs are actually quite low and ERPs are consequently higher than NRPs overall. It is the domestic price of products which is inflated relative to export prices, thus inhibiting the growth of exports. High final product tariffs, plus other taxes and surcharges, increase the cost of both imports and exports, thereby impeding export expansion. Complaints about tariffs on imported inputs can also be attributed to the high share of imports in intermediate consumption (nearly 45 percent).

The severity of institutional constraints varies by industry. It is highest in the textile industry (60 percent), followed by the food and furniture industries (41 percent each), and lowest in the electronics sector (37 percent)

FIGURE 7.2 Export Constraints: Industrial Sector

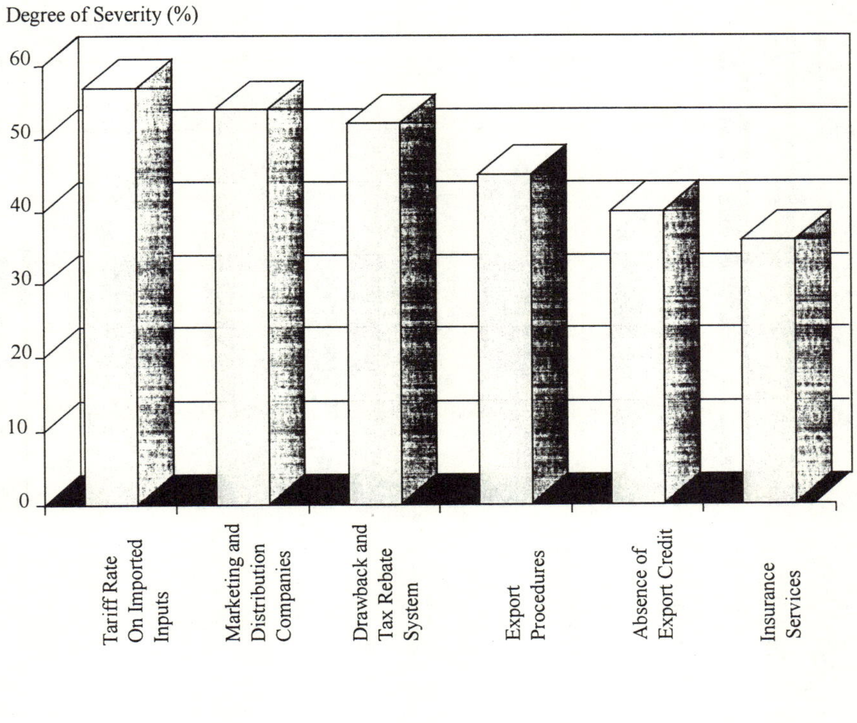

(fig. 7.3). Businessmen's perception of the degree of severity reflect, to a certain extent, the propensity to export in each industry, as measured by the percentage of exports to total production.

The survey results generally suggest that tariff levels on inputs and malfunctioning of the duty drawback system are the most critical elements that should be considered in promoting exports. The fact that tariffs on final products are not mentioned as a major problem may simply mean that businessmen in general are not aware of the direct link between import tariffs on final products and the "implicit" tax on exports. Representatives of each of the five industries universally remarked that domestic markets were much more profitable than export markets. This is consistent with the conclusion of this study that there is an implicit tax on exports of almost 40 percent.

Several other comments indicated a high degree of inefficiency in the five industries vis-à-vis competition in global markets. Companies tend not to be managed with a view to exporting, with the exception of ready-made garments, as witnessed by a lack of marketing staff with international experience. Moreover, unit costs tend to be high because plants almost universally operate

FIGURE 7.3 Export Constraints: Cross-Industries

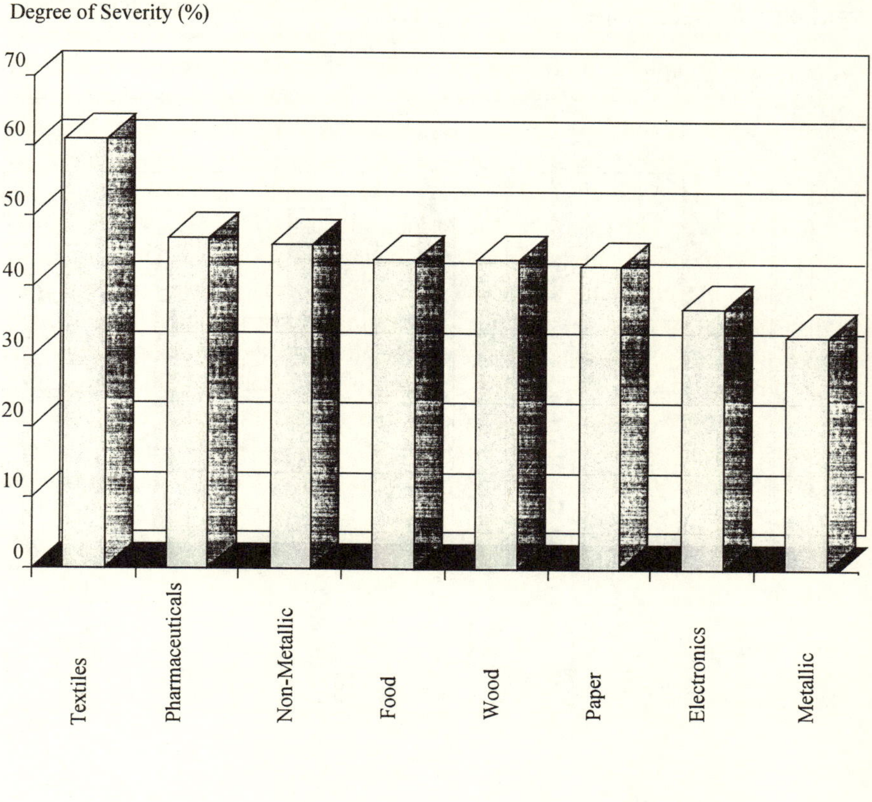

at less than 60 to 70 percent of rated capacity. Egyptian firms apparently lack international market promotion as part of their business strategy, face high domestic prices but low domestic demand, and must overcome a high implicit export tax to enter world markets. This appears to be a vicious circle of high domestic prices, low domestic demand, low utilization of plant capacity, and lack of incentives to expand output for world markets. Redundant labor was also mentioned as a negative factor affecting competitiveness, primarily by public-sector firms.

Comparative Advantage

A "pure" measure of comparative advantage is the domestic resource cost (DRC)—the cost in domestic resources of gaining or saving one dollar of foreign exchange (valued at world prices). Table 7.7 ranks four of the five industries for which data are available according to the DRC and compares this to the prevailing ERP, the importance of exports and a measure of RCA.[4]

The wood industry stands out as the most protected, costs more in domestic resources than the value of its product on the world market, has a low RCA, and is the poorest performer with respect to exports. Most efficiency measures were also low for this industry. Thus, this highly protected industry apparently needs protection to survive and is primarily domestically oriented. Clearly, lowering tariff protection precipitously could cause severe adjustment pressure, although it would be beneficial to the economy as a whole in the medium term as the wood furniture industry is currently wasting domestic resources per dollar of foreign exchange saved or earned. A gradual liberalization strategy is therefore called for to avoid large employment shocks.

The appropriate policy for the furniture industry is likely to differ qualitatively from other industries such as food processing. The latter is fairly efficient, is not highly protected, and has an RCA greater than one. Stimulating growth in exports for the food processing industry should have a high payoff and no major policy impediments to attaining such growth are evident. Vigorous negotiation with the EU to reduce tariff barriers would stimulate increased exports of processed food. Textiles is another special case, and the solution to its growth and export problems will have to be tailor-made. Current high export performance is owed largely to extensive use of a duty-drawback

TABLE 7.7 Performance Indicators of Selected Industries

Industry	DRC	ERP	Exports as % of Production	RCA
Food Processing	0.8	6.4	2.0	3.0
Textiles (Garments)	0.8	55.9	40.0	1.4
Shoes	0.9	50.8	4.3	0.25
Wood Furniture	1.7	83.8	1.2	0.41

mechanism and specialized production for export only. The bulk of the textile industry has very different characteristics. Duty drawback itself is an artificial policy, made necessary by the high tariff structure, and the focus of policy efforts should center on reducing these tariffs, in the process reducing the rents associated with access to the drawback privilege.

Policy should be designed to fit the various industry situations. If an industry is currently inefficient, removing protective tariffs suddenly could serve to create an employment crisis or unnecessarily penalize investors who have grown up under the protective umbrella. Those industries that are efficient and have a comparative advantage would benefit from rapid removal of tariffs. Domestic demand would increase, export prices would become relatively more attractive, and both domestic and export markets will expand, allowing more efficient use of plant equipment and labor.

For policy planning purposes, one can identify three categories of industrial situations that call for different policy interventions: (i) inefficient and highly protected; (ii) efficient and highly protected; and (iii) efficient and not protected. For the first category a gradual reduction in tariffs accompanied by government assistance during the transitional phase may be the most socially desirable policy. For the second category, rapid reduction of tariffs is advisable, with a small amount of targeted assistance to assist firms enter global markets. The third category may require promotional assistance from the government to expand exports.

Recommendations

While Egypt has delayed economic reform relative to much of the world, this has a certain advantage in that there is by now considerable documentation of liberalization experiences from around the world. Also, while structural reform has moved forward gradually, macroeconomic adjustment has moved more expeditiously, and the GOE now finds itself in a favorable macroeconomic environment conducive to more rapid structural reform.

Tariff and Tax Reform

The current structure of trade taxes in Egypt continues to be characterized by high, non-uniform tariffs that are rendered even more dispersed by the GST being applied to imports on a duty-inclusive basis. The strategy has been one of gradually reducing the highest tariffs and unifying the tariff structure into fewer, broader based rate bands. (As of July 1, 1998, there are six bands, with some exceptions, with a top rate of 40 percent).

A strong case can be made to move towards a lower, more uniform tariff schedule. In the extreme, suppose that there was only one tariff rate applied to all imports. In Egypt, according to data from the Ministry of Finance, that rate would be revenue neutral at somewhere between 10 percent and 15 percent. The advantages are many:

- There would be no dispersion in the tariff schedule. Therefore, while domestic production and sales are still protected to the detriment of exporting, within the group of protected activities the ERPs are a uniform 15 percent, thus giving no artificial advantage to one sector over another and thereby increasing the productivity of investment. This real income gain may itself lead to higher rates of investment and growth.

- Customs classification becomes a non-issue; product can move through the ports faster.

- The system is easy to administer.

- The flat rate eliminates the adverse interaction with the GST caused by its duty-inclusive application.

- The lower, uniform tariff is less likely to cause trade diversion, which erodes the gains from general trade agreements (see chaps. 5 and 6).

- Smuggling and so disrespect for the law would be less encouraged.

- Since the tariffs show no favoritism, lobbying for tariff protection would be reduced.

As a practical matter, the uniform tariff could be approximated to address political reality. As a general rule of thumb, the system should try to tax similar goods at similar rates (i.e., "grouping") in order to minimize tax distortions among products. Suppose that we divide the groups into final goods and essential food and inputs. Then, for example, there might be two rates: 10 percent for essential foods and (already subject to low tariffs) inputs and 20 percent for final goods. This would be approximately revenue neutral but considerably more efficient and easier to collect than prevailing tariffs.

The current GOE strategy concerning tariff reform entails cutting the highest tariffs and bringing these product groups into the next lowest rate band for tariffs over 30 percent. This approach makes sense economically and seems to be moving the tariff structure rationally. But tariffs are still quite high and dispersed. Assuming that the political will to reform can be maintained, a natural next step would be to set the next maximum tariff at 30 percent, leave the 20 percent rate intact, and consider unifying the other two rates at 10 percent. As the GST base is broadened, the unified 15 percent tariff rate could become reality, followed by uniform cuts. Duty drawback should be augmented by total rebate of the GST on exported items.

Given the current rates, the above approach would probably be nearly revenue neutral, as some lower rates might be raised. Reducing the top rates affects a small base and might even raise revenue, to the extent that at such high rates import demand is elastic. With the possible exception of tobacco and alcoholic beverages (for revenue, cultural, and religious reasons), exceptions to the maximum tariffs should probably be eliminated on efficiency grounds. Also, as tariffs come down, some exceptions to the tariffs might be phased out. One problem with exceptions to the tariff structure is that they are just ways of trying to avoid the negative consequences of tariffs and to distract attention from the actual source of the problems, namely, the tariffs themselves.

Addressing Remaining Nontariff Barriers

The leadership of the GOE has clearly signaled a direction of change that will result in reform and removal of remaining NTBs. The main challenge appears to be the resistance from within the public service to the pace and methods of this reform. Worldwide this type of structural reform is administratively and politically difficult to achieve as it *may* eliminate jobs but will *certainly* eliminate positions of discretion, influence, and therefore power within the public service. Nevertheless, achieving real sustainable economic growth in Egypt for the benefit of the mass of Egyptians will require sacrifice of position and power from both individuals and organizations in the public and private sectors.

Openness and transparency is a requirement of modern global economic relations as investors place a premium on reducing risk. The necessity for Egypt to develop commercial, legal, and financial transparency lies in the competitive fight for investment capital with other emerging economies of Central Europe and the MENA region.

Immediate adoption of harmonized international standards will place current producers on an equal footing with international competitors in the global market. The unfettered right of the international business community to establish investment in manufacturing and business services under FTAs with Europe and North America as well as with neighbors in the MENA region is critical to support Egypt's integration into the global economy. This is fundamentally an issue of convergence by Egypt to the evolving international norms and practices that improve the efficiency of firms and individuals to create and distribute wealth both globally and within individual countries. This process of convergence is often aided, and at times seemingly driven, by technological change that is readily understood and accepted. As the focus turns to convergence of property rights and the rule of law among independent countries, major players in the global market seek certainty and predictability. It is the credibility of the latter convergence that will determine Egypt's place at the core or the margins of global integration.

The road signs on this path might begin with joining the integration process of Europe within the EMA, supplemented by FTAs with Egypt's MENA neighbors. Other countries on the geographical or historical periphery of Europe such as Ireland and Poland have vigorously embraced harmonization and convergence of their business environments, resulting in growth rates that are treble those of comparator economies. GOE policy makers are well placed to direct the pace of Egypt's integration with the global economy which can best build domestic consensus for economic reform. However they are ill placed to slow down or otherwise affect the pace of global economic integration beyond Egypt's borders.

NOTES

The authors' names are listed in alphabetical order. This chapter is a substantially abridged version of a study by Nathan Associates, conducted by the Development Economic Policy Reform Analysis (DEPRA) Project, under contract to the United States Agency for International Development, Cairo, Egypt (USAID/Egypt) (Contract No. 263-C-00-96-00001-00). The full report can be downloaded from the website at <http://www.economy.gov.eg/depra>. The authors thank the DEPRA coordinator, Dr. Rollo Ehrich, and all entities, both public and private, who gave of their time to help this study achieve its purposes. We also particularly thank Mona El-Garf and Omnia Helmy, both from the Faculty of Economics and Political Science, Cairo University and Ahmed Moharram from Quality Management Systems for their contributions in providing background work and in helping with data and information collection.

1. See Nathan Associates 1998b, Appendix 1 for details.
2. By subtracting inputs from outputs estimated at world prices, one obtains a figure for value added at world prices. Using this information together with value added at domestic prices taken from the 1991-92 IO table, the ERP granted to each activity has been calculated. World prices have been compiled by deflating domestic prices by the nominal 1997 tariff on the respective outputs and inputs.
3. Development Economic Policy Reform Analysis Project, a USAID funded project.
4. The RCA of country i for product j is measured by the item's share in the country's total exports relative to its share in total world trade:

$$RCA = (Xji/Xti)/Xjw/Xtw)$$

where X denotes exports, t denotes total country trade, and w denotes world variables.

CHAPTER 8

Regulatory Regimes and Trade Costs

Jamel Zarrouk

The interface between regulatory policy and trade has received increased attention in recent years. As countries reduce traditional trade barriers such as tariffs and QRs, business and consumers become more aware of the impact of domestic regulatory regimes on trade. These often take the form of mandatory requirements that legislators or officials in the executive branch impose on imports of goods and services.

Domestic regulatory regimes are generally intended to protect public interests. However, enforcement of health, safety, and environmental protection norms requires testing and certification systems to assure that products satisfy technical requirements. Not only may the technical regulations and standards imposed by governments in exporting and importing countries differ, but testing and compliance procedures are often duplicative and discriminatory, giving rise to additional costs for traders. Such costs may be needless, in that the procedures that are applied do not necessarily benefit consumers or ensure better public health or environmental protection.

In the case of international service transactions, countries frequently restrict the mode of supply through which markets can be contested by foreign providers, or simply prohibit access altogether. This is often the case for activities such as insurance and banking, domestic transportation, basic telecommunications, or even distribution services. There is substantial evidence that such policies inhibit competition in service industries, impose costs on producers and consumers, and reduce export performance.

Since the conclusion of the Uruguay Round, trade-related regulations have risen in importance and have caused concern in both developed and developing countries. For instance, developing countries argue that industrial countries have expanded technical regulations that are beyond developing countries' competence to implement or do not take into account their special development needs, fundamental climatic or geographic factors, or techno-logical problems (UNCTAD 1999). Conversely, the business sector in industrial countries has complained about excessive control and inefficiencies in customs procedures for inspection and clearance in developing countries, arguing that customs-related barriers to trade have deterred numerous international firms from penetrating developing markets.

This chapter discusses the trade impact of certain regulatory regimes that are prevalent in the MENA region and options that can be considered to remove regulatory barriers to trade. Emphasis is put on the link between national efforts to facilitate trade and regional and multilateral cooperative approaches in designing and applying domestic regulations that reduce trade costs. A major obstacle in quantifying the impact of regulatory regimes on trade costs is the absence of information on domestic policies and their impact in the MENA region. This chapter relies in part on the limited literature that is available and on data collected through surveys of and interviews with traders and officials from selected countries in the region.

Conceptual Issues

Government intervention generally aims at overcoming domestic market failures. Examples are regulations that control the behavior of monopolies and state-owned or controlled industries/firms, offset information asymmetries, or ensure that missing markets do not lead to overexploitation of environmental resources. Regulatory regimes that aim to overcome either negative externalities or market failures may generate additional costs to cross-border trade in a way similar to NTBs to trade, although the intent of such regulatory regimes may not be to discriminate against foreign firms. The effect may be to raise the price of imports in a way equivalent to tariffs. Estimates of the impact of certain types of policies suggest they may exceed the level of import duties that apply on the imported products concerned. However, the difference between tariffs and regulatory policy effects is that customs duties are part of government revenues, while the enforcement cost of regulatory regimes at the border may constitute deadweight losses from which no one benefits. Attempts to quantify the impact of duplicative testing requirements and customs controls in the European Community before the EC-1992 program indicated that these could be equivalent to a tax of up to 2 percent of the average value of a shipment (Hoekman 1998a). Other estimates have placed transaction costs of inefficient customs clearance procedures at between 7 and 10 percent of the value of world trade in 1994 (Staples 1998).

Regulations for service industries may be motivated by market failure. However, exclusive rights for domestic suppliers of transportation and telecommunication services can significantly raise the costs of exporting activities and reduce the international competitiveness of domestic firms. Technical standards, prudential regulations, and qualification requirements in professional services can have serious trade-impeding effects (Mattoo 1999). Many countries require that activities such as legal, insurance, educational, and investment advisory services be provided by residents (who could be foreign nationals) or citizens. Providers of such services often must obtain national certification or licenses. A key problem here is that differences in standards and disparities in domestic educational systems can become a major constraint on contesting a foreign market.

National and International Responses to Trade-Related Regulatory Regimes

Countries have sought to reduce trade costs created by domestic regulatory regimes in a number of ways. In the area of technical regulations and standards, a country may adopt unilaterally international standards and best practices and accept or recognize the regulatory regimes applied by its main trading partners (Hoekman 1998a). A cooperative mechanism that is beginning to be used by developed countries is to conclude MRAs for product standards and testing and professional qualifications. The main objective of such arrangements is to ensure that goods that have been assessed in the exporting country do not have to be reassessed in the importing country without compromising product safety. Recent experience with MRAs has shown that these can involve long negotiations and are limited to sectoral product standards. To date, developing countries have not been included in any of the twenty-six MRAs concluded so far (according to WTO sources). Even in instances where mutual recognition has been used widely (such as in the EU), the impact has been constrained by the unwillingness of regulators to relinquish control over "home country supervision" (Messerlin and Zarrouk 1999).

MRAs in educational degrees and professional qualifications are useful instruments to facilitate the movement of professionals across borders and to avoid the emergence of new differences between recognition regimes around the world. Many countries concluded such agreements. For instance, the Latin American countries have agreements on the recognition of educational degrees and professionals obtained in each other countries. The United States has signed MRAs with Australia and Canada covering certain types of professionals such as chartered accountants and architects.

At the multilateral level, the Uruguay Round yielded important agreements to harmonize domestic regulations in the areas of technical regulations, sanitary and phytosanitary standards, and IPRs. The Agreement on Technical Barriers to Trade (TBT) provides rules and guidance for the preparation, adoption, and application of national standards and conformity assessment procedures. The Agreement on Sanitary and Phytosanitary Measures (SPS) sets out rules for the preparation, adoption, and application of standards related to animals, plant material, and human health. Both agreements require countries to follow the same procedures related to advance notification of proposed measures and the creation of information offices (enquiry points). While both agreements encourage member countries to use existing international standards, the SPS Agreement allows a member country to part with such standards for food safety and animal/plant health when this can be justified by scientific reasoning based on an assessment of the potential health risk. In contrast, under the TBT Agreement, a government may decide not to adopt international standards if they can argue that fundamental technological problems or geographic or climatic conditions make the standard inappropriate.

The WTO does not set product standards; international norms are developed by other bodies such as the International Organization for Standardization (ISO) or the UN Food and Agricultural Agency. As discussed at greater length by Hoekman (1998a), a large number of international entities have been created over time whose primary purpose is to develop standards. This also extends to services. An example is the Basle Committee on Banking Supervision. The Basle principles are voluntary minimum standards for banking supervision, prudential rules, and requirements. They also suggest standards for licensing, ownership transfer, and liquidation. All of these standards aim at encouraging "good" banking.

Thus, a mix of harmonization and (mutual) recognition efforts is being pursued with respect to domestic regulations in both regional fora and the WTO. International pressures can be expected for further harmonization of domestic regulations to ensure that these do not become trade barriers by creating real trade costs for firms.

Trade-Related Regulatory Regimes in the MENA Region

Many of the countries in the MENA region have undertaken major steps to implement tariff and fiscal reforms and to dismantle the QRs such as import prohibitions and licensing. Privatization programs have also been set up, although implementation has been slow in most countries in the region. Despite these efforts, substantial reforms are required to eliminate transaction costs that are created by trade-related regulatory regimes.

Comprehensive estimates of the total cost and incidence of the various regulatory barriers that confront producers and traders in the MENA countries do not exist. Virtually all of the studies that have tried to quantify the impact of trade-related regulatory regimes have focused on Egypt (see chap. 7 for a summary). There is an urgent need to undertake similar research and comparable data on regulatory costs and administrative inefficiencies in other MENA countries, especially as they relate to export performance. In what follows, the main trade-related regulatory instruments that raise real trade costs in MENA countries are discussed, using information and data collected from surveys and interviews with the private sector in selected countries.

Product Standards, Testing, and Certification Procedures

Most of the countries in the MENA region apply standards that are formulated and enforced by national bodies. Technical standards are predominantly related to food products, engineering goods, and consumer products. However, most of these national standards have no equivalence to or are below international standards. For instance, there are around 1,000 standards in Egypt, of which only 25 to 30 percent are in conformity with international standards (WTO 1999). Saudi Arabia has around 1,600 standards of which one-third is estimated to conform to international standards. INORPI, the Tunisian competent authority on standards, reports that 80 percent of the 940 mandatory standards are in compliance with international standards.

While standards are extremely useful for producers and consumers, they may be a potential NTB to trade when they are applied in discriminatory fashion to favor domestic production against foreign competition. Conformity assessment is the process through which a particular imported good is judged on whether or not it meets a standard and/or complies with a regulation. This process includes laboratory testing. An importing country needs to be certain that imported goods will not impose a risk to its consumers. Thus, since there is a need for the test data or inspection from exporting country to be reliable and for any decisions on safety made in another country to be trusted, conformity assessment may involve complex national rules and bear relatively high costs to exporters and importers. Still, the majority of developing countries allow only national testing entities to perform and produce test data for conformity. Limiting testing services to government test laboratories produce a system that is less transparent and more burdensome for business than one that allows for self-certification and use of private laboratories. In addition, most developing countries have limited qualified, government-owned or government-operated laboratories to test for conformity to national standards. In light of the increasing shipments flowing into developing countries, it is very difficult for developing countries to rely on such exclusive certification procedures. Indeed, there is an increasing drive to rely on foreign private or government-sponsored laboratories to perform these tests subject to accreditation rules.

MENA countries generally do not accept test data or product certifications issued by foreign laboratories or firms. In part this may reflect a belief that foreign laboratories are not competent to test against domestic safety standards. An interesting exception is a recent experiment by Saudi Arabia that relies on third-party testing of imports. The Saudi Arabian Standards Organization (SASO) has developed an International Conformity Certification Program (ICCP), a combined conformity procedure, preshipment inspection, and certification scheme that aims to facilitate shipments of selected categories of products by having them inspected prior to shipment to Saudi Arabia. The objective is to reduce rejection risks and the time needed for customs clearance at the Saudi port of entry, which benefits both exporters and importers (see box 8.1).

In contrast, both the refusal by standards authorities in many of the MENA countries to accept test data or product certifications issued through foreign laboratories and firms and inadequate availability of national laboratories with usually limited testing capabilities have led to direct and indirect additional costs to producers and consumers. A study on the Egyptian standards system gives an account of the resource costs imposed on firms and consumers as a result of sampling and testing inefficiencies and numerous fees paid for duplicative testing brought about by the enforcement of standards by different agencies affiliated to different ministries (Kheir-El-Din 1999). The estimated economic impact is a substantial increase in trade costs, ranging from 5 to 90 percent of the value of goods and a reduction of exports by 9 to 12 percent (see chap. 7). The welfare loss due to the current mandatory standards system has been estimated to be more than 1 percent of the GDP.

Quality Regulation Confused with Health and Safety Protection

Regulatory agencies in a number of MENA countries require suppliers to demonstrate compliance with quality requirements for human health and safety protection. For instance, food regulation that addresses food labeling, packaging, and nutrition concerns are quality measures that are required for human health. This contrasts with regulations that address microbiological contamination of food or identifying permitted food additives, which are considered SPS measures. Quality requirements on imports have become a cause for concern for WTO trading partners since the TBT and SPS Agreements came into effect. One major concern is that quality standards on food imports can effectively be an import barrier, especially when certain standards (e.g., labeling, lettering, or nutrient content) are used interchangeably for some measures that

BOX 8.1 The SASO International Conformity Certification Program

The Saudi Arabian Standards Organization is the sole agency responsible for the preparation, adoption, and application of standards in Saudi Arabia. Mandatory standards are applied equally to both imported and domestically made products to enforce health, safety, and environmental protection, national security, and public morals. SASO has set up the International Conformity Certification Program (ICCP), a pilot conformity assessment procedure that relies on the private sector to inspect shipments for compliance with Saudi standards. The ICCP is a *combined* conformity assessment, preshipment inspection, and certification scheme to regulate and monitor shipments of selected product categories prior to being shipped to Saudi Arabia. The program currently applies to 66 products categories divided into five groups: food and agriculture, electronics and electrical products, automobile and related products, chemical products, and others. The key element of the program is that each shipment must be determined to be in conformity with SASO standards (or their approved equivalents) before the certificate of conformity (required for every consignment) can be issued. This ensures both exporters and importers of a streamlined customs process that allows goods to clear faster and to face minimal rejection risk at the Saudi port of entry. So far, the SASO program has not been a complete success. It is considered costly by traders in Saudi Arabia's major trading partners. Complaints have been raised that the ICCP fees paid for preshipment compliance verification, which amount to 0.5 percent of the FOB value of the shipment, plus other fees for test certificates, are too high.

However, the interesting aspect of the SASO Program is that test data can be produced by nationally or internationally accredited laboratories approved by SASO. At the conclusion of the SASO-approved laboratory testing, a Conformity Test and Evaluation Report is issued and submitted to the Regional Licensing Center for verification of conformity to SASO requirements. The program closely follows ISO/IEC Guide 28 (General Rules for a Model Third Party Certification System for products), particularly with regard to products that have achieved full compliance with Saudi standards. These products qualify for a Type Approval License that allows their imports with the minimum of intervention.

A key aspect of the SASO Program is that SASO has contracted a specialized private firm to carry out these activities. This company is in turn assisted by a network of accredited testing laboratories and inspection bodies around the round. The SASO experience shows that compliance verification of national standards might be better and cost-effectively served through private testing firms and accredited labs.

Source: Messerlin and Zarrouk 1999.

are directly related to the safety of the food (e.g., materials that can be used safely for human health). Under the SPS Agreement, standards for food safety and health protection must be based on science and be based on an assessment of potential health risks. In contrast, food standards that deal with quality and packaging may be imposed for other reasons such as geographic or climatic factors, and thus are measures that come under the TBT Agreement.

As an illustrative example, the WTO report on Egypt stated that following liberalization of imports in Egypt, a number of previously banned products including poultry, eggs, coffee, iron tubes, ceramic sanitary ware, stoves, heaters, and washing machines were moved to the quality control list (WTO 1999). Egypt raised the number of imported products subject to quality control measures from 69 in 1992 to 182 in 1998. While such quality requirements may be imposed only to the extent necessary to protect human, animal, or plant protection, the scientific arguments regarding potential health risks are not always obvious in imposing such measures. Other product standards are confused with health and safety protection measures. Reported examples include excessive the amount of ink in a ball point pen or the length of matches. These are issues of consumer protection at best, not health or safety, and should not be subject to mandatory standards. Such specifications are more closely related to product characteristics (e.g., shape, size, and nutrient content) and are better left to be determined by the supplier and the importer. The government should concentrate on monitoring and enforcing standards for safety and health protection.

A major challenge has concerned shelf life requirements (i.e., "use by" dates). Both Egypt and Saudi Arabia require that at least half of the shelf life remain on the product when it is imported; otherwise, it may be denied entry to the domestic market. While the shelf life determination can be classified as an SPS measure for perishable products (i.e., date marking is important for the maintenance of food safety), the shelf life determination can be a TBT measure for shelf stable food products (i.e., date marking as it contributes mainly to maintenance of food quality). On the one hand, shelf life determination as a SPS measure must be justified on a scientific basis or the manufacturer's date when it can be scientifically proven. On the other hand, shelf life determination is considered a TBT measure when it can be based on arguments related to climatic and infrastructure conditions; thus it is less strict than the SPS measure.

Certain trading partners to Saudi Arabia argued that the half shelf-life requirement violates both the relevant Codex Alimentarius food standard (that Saudi Arabia has already adopted) and the SPS Agreement (which is not an obligation since Saudi Arabia is not yet a WTO member). Both the Codex and the SPS Agreement call for the acceptance of the manufacturer-determined shelf life when it is based on scientific studies and internationally recognized bodies. In the case of Egypt, the half shelf-life measure has been termed trade-restrictive by Egyptian importers. They argue that the shelf life of imported products is usually shortened by the cumbersome and slow inspection, testing, and other import clearance procedures, leaving very little time for the importer to move the product to the domestic market. To that extent, it is more effective that government agencies improve inspection and clearance procedures rather than enforce shelf life dates that play an important role mainly for perishable products.

Customs and Port Regulations

Excessive control and inefficiency of customs procedures combined with monopoly port services are widely reported to substantially increase the cost of import, in addition to creating an overall negative trading environment. Anecdotal evidence of administrative customs inefficiencies and its impact in several MENA countries is abundant. The average customs clearance transaction in MENA countries (e.g., Egypt, Lebanon) requires 25 to 30 stages and takes from one day to several weeks (Roy 1998). Valuation procedures are a major source of uncertainty for importers, as customs generally expects under-invoicing. In Jordan, the law rewards customs officers who uncover invoice falsification and charge penalties to the importers. It is the practice in some MENA countries that customs valuation officers question every invoice in order to charge penalties or collect "rewards." However, a number of Arab WTO members (Egypt, Morocco, and Tunisia) have stepped up efforts to improve inspection and clearance activities in anticipation of the full implementation of the GATT Customs Valuation Agreement which is to take effect by the year 2000.

A government monopoly of port services in virtually all of the MENA countries coupled with poor infrastructure for loading and shipping services imposes an implicit tax on importers and exporters. The cost per container discharged at the port of Alexandria, Egypt is reported to be double those of ports in Cyprus and three times as high as in Lebanon (WTO 1999). As noted in chapter 7, estimates of port service charges equal around 10 percent of the total cost of inputs of Egyptian industry, which weakens its international competitiveness.

Transport Regulations

Regulatory measures pertaining to maritime and road transportation may also restrict trade and raise costs. National maritime transport activities in MENA countries are dominated by state-owned shipping companies. Government port authorities own harbor infrastructure, and port facilities are run by government-owned agencies in most countries. However, there is a slow move in some MENA countries (Port of Aden in Yemen and Port Raysud in Oman) towards restructuring and reform through privatization and liberalization of port services with the aim of modernizing infrastructure and increasing efficiency. Interviews conducted with shipping companies in selected countries (Egypt, Jordan, Lebanon, Morocco, Saudi Arabia, and Tunisia) reveal that regulations that raise shipping costs most are (i) those favoring national carriers; (ii) restricting access to port services for privately-owned shipping companies (difficulties in obtaining shipping licenses from the port authority, maximum age requirements, specific design and safety conditions for the vessel); and (iii) cumbersome administrative procedures of port authorities.

Road transportation is a very important intraregional mode of transport for passengers and freight in many of the MENA countries. Countries with limited access to the sea, such as Jordan and Iraq, rely mainly on road transport for merchandise trade. MENA countries are known for imposing restrictive cross-border movement and transit regulations. The International Road Transport Union has reported that the most restrictive cross-border transportation can be found in some parts of Europe and the MENA region (WTO 1998c). Complaints from the interviewed transport professionals in the MENA region include excessive charges and unnecessary formalities that give rise to additional trade costs and impair the freedom of transit spelled out in Article V of the GATT.

To identify the most common regulatory barriers to cross-border movement of trucks in MENA countries the author sent a questionnaire to the relevant official authorities in Egypt, Jordan, Lebanon, Saudi Arabia, Tunisia, and Yemen. The compiled results reveal the following:

- Foreign trucks may not drive on weekends and public holidays (all of the surveyed countries);
- Visas may be denied to professional drivers of certain nationalities (Saudi Arabia and other GCC countries);
- Paperwork requirements may be changed without prior notification (all of the surveyed countries);
- Foreign trucks unloading in a country must return to their country of origin without cargo, i.e., empty (all of the surveyed countries);

- There are fiscal charges and other surcharges on road transport, e.g., excise duties on foreign diesel trucks, road usage fee, safety passage fees, etc. (Egypt, Jordan, Lebanon, Tunisia, and Yemen);
- Enforcement of technical regulations for weights and dimensions applied to foreign trucks (all of the surveyed countries); and
- Special permit requirements apply for foreign refrigerated trucks (Jordan, Lebanon).

Ranking Trade-Related Regulatory Regimes: Survey Results

In an attempt to gather further evidence on trade-related regulatory constraints on private firms in MENA countries, a survey of fifty randomly selected firms in five countries (Egypt, Jordan, Lebanon, Morocco, Saudi Arabia, and Tunisia) was conducted.[1] Two types of questionnaire supported by interviews were developed and sent to importers and/or exporters in the sample. The surveyed firms are representative of five main economic sectors: food processing, textiles and clothing, machinery and appliances, chemicals, and other manufactures (paper and printing, furniture, metallic products, and cement and ceramics). The compiled results from questionnaire returns are reported in table 8.1 by sampled import and export activities. The most binding regulatory

TABLE 8.1 MENA Traders' Ranking of Regulatory Constraints

Binding Constraints for Importing Firms	Score	Ranking
Customs procedures (inspection, valuation and quality control)	0.85	1
Port services (formalities, discharging, handling, storage, high fees)	0.75	2
Freight transportation regulation (road and maritime)	0.59	3
Import policy uncertainty	0.54	4
Binding Constraints for Exporting Firms	**Score**	**Ranking**
Competition rules in importing countries (anti-dumping actions)	0.95	1
Standards and quality control requirements (in importing countries)	0.72	2
Freight, insurance, export financing services	0.64	3
Customs procedures (in importing countries)	0.52	4

Note: Traders were asked in the questionnaire to rank the severity of a set of obstacles on a scale of 1 to 5. The score results were normalized to a scale of zero to 1 where zero means that the constraint is not binding at all and 1 means that the constraint is prohibitive. Regulatory constraints with a score equal or greater than 0.5 were retained in the final results.
Source: Survey.

constraints for MENA firms when they import are found to be customs procedures, port services, freight transportation, and high insurance premiums.

The fact that customs procedures comprising customs valuation, clearance, and quality control inspection are the most binding import regulations is consistent with the previous analysis. Inadequate or poor port services (discharging, handling, storage, formalities) ranked second confirms the previous discussion on the high cost of the government monopoly of port services. Freight transportation (maritime and road) ranks the third most binding regulation. Uncertainty about country's import regulations, which captures the firm's perception of openness of the trade regime and the credibility of the policy reforms, were ranked least binding.

As for regulatory constraints that exporting firms face in importing countries, anti-dumping measures or threats in the importing countries, notably the EU and the United States, are considered the most binding obstacle. Interviewed firms voiced concerns that increasingly protectionist use of anti-dumping procedures by major trading partners most frequently targets exports of the GCC petrochemicals and Egyptian cotton. Standards and quality control measures are ranked the second most binding constraint for exports. Surveyed food exporters believe that SPS measures pose a serious barrier to Egyptian and North African exports of agricultural products to the EU. Freight transportation, high insurance premiums and export finance rank third. Finally, customs procedures in importing countries and notably in major importing markets such as the EU are the least binding constraint.

Regulation of Service Industries

Regulatory policies that reduce competition in service industries can be very costly. The focus here is on four areas of regulation that are considered to have trade-restrictive effects and increase trade costs: exclusive distribution and agency laws, basic telecommunications, financial services, and qualification requirements in professional services.

Exclusive Commercial Agency Laws in Distribution Services

Distribution arrangements can effectively bar market access for name-brand products. Exclusive-distributor laws that have been applied in the MENA countries, most notably in the Gulf countries (Kuwait, Oman, Qatar, Saudi Arabia, and UAE), require that foreign suppliers appoint only citizens of the respective countries as local agents. Moreover, the Commercial Agency Law protects distributorship monopoly by preventing parallel imports.[2] In some countries (e.g., UAE), the law seems to grant an indefinite distribution monopoly to the appointed local agent. Even in the case of disputes between manufacturer and agent, the courts invariably find in favor of the local sole distributor.

The protection of exclusive commercial agents in the MENA countries through the restriction of parallel imports of legitimate goods, that may or may not carry the original manufacturer's warranty, can be regarded as an anti-competitive regulation. In this view, the consequence of such vertical relations that may arise between the manufacturer and the sole distributor means charging consumers higher prices. Another view is that a ban on parallel imports to protect exclusive distributors would allow for a segmentation of markets and the setting of one price per market. For instance, in a developing country with limited market size, local demand may be insufficient to support parallel imports and intrabrand competition. Therefore, limited demand will support higher prices and lower the economic welfare of developing countries with small markets.

Arguments favoring a ban on parallel imports to protect exclusive territorial distributor state that such a restriction is a primary motivation for the authorized distributors to invest in marketing and after sales services supplied to consumers. In addition, private contracts between the manufacturer or trademark holder and the exclusive distributor may lower the manufacturer's costs of monitoring product quality control and ensuring compliance with supply conditions (Maskus and Lahouel 1999).

Governments in the GCC countries have enforced the sole agent laws giving territorial distributors monopoly power over imports and sales of numerous brand-name products ranging from transportation equipment to electronics to cosmetics to food. It is notorious in the GCC countries that most international brands have been exclusively distributed by a small number of family-owned businesses that have enjoyed excessive rents from the oil boom era to modern times. The most direct way to measure these rents is to conduct price comparisons in the GCC markets with prices of similar goods in markets in which parallel imports are allowed, keeping other variables (tariff rates, internal taxes, market requirements, or others) constant. There may be, however, a great deal of complexity in precise determinations of rents, as cost structures differ across countries. Calculations by Will Martin using ICP data reveal large differences in Lebanon (see chap. 4). Similar studies should be undertaken for other MENA countries.

The coming WTO negotiations on services may well increase pressures for some general reforms of the GCC sole agency law to accommodate liberalization of international trade in services, including granting national treatment and the right of establishment to foreign firms.

TABLE 8.2 Main Indicators on Telecommunications Services in MENA Countries, 1999 data

	Telephone Services				Internet Services			
Country	Waiting time for installation of a direct line	Charge to call UAE ($/minute)	Cheap call tariffs ($/min.) and Time of the Day	Local Business Evaluation of Telephone Services	Internet Available	Annual subscription fees ($)	User's fees ($)	Party offering Internet Services
Algeria	One year +	2.20	(9PM-5AM)	fair	yes	-	172/month	Govt. entity
Bahrain	One week	0.77	0.45 (7PM-AM)	very good	yes	489	1.60/hour	Govt. entity
Egypt	One year +	1.20	(9PM-6AM)	good	yes	260	open	Private
Jordan	One month	1.00	(10PM-7AM)	good	yes	-	20/month	Private
Kuwait	One month	1.00	0.69 (7PM-7AM)	good	yes	-	312/month	Govt. entity
Lebanon	One month	1.75	No	good	yes	1000	45/month	Private
Libya	Six months +	4.00	No	good	no	-	-	-
Oman	One month	0.78	0.45 (8PM-6AM)	good	yes	-	130/month	Govt. entity
Mauritania	One month +	15.00	No	good	yes	500	41/month+4H	Govt. entity
Morocco	One month +	1.60	(8PM-7AM)	fair	yes	750	open	Private
Qatar	One week	0.55	0.28 (8PM-7AM)	good	yes	55*	17/month +1.7H	Govt. entity
Saudi Arabia	Six months +	0.80	0.5 (8PM-10AM)	good	yes	-	386/120 hours 630/unlimited	Govt. entity
Sudan	Six months +	2.00	No	good	yes	495	50/month	Govt. entity
Syria	Two year +	1.30	(10PM-3AM)	fair	no	-	-	-
Tunisia	One month +	2.00	1.6 (8PM-6AM)	fair	yes	600	open	Private
UAE	One week	0	(9PM-7AM)	very good	yes	81*	45/month	Govt. entity
Yemen	One year +	1.50	No	fair	yes	335	0.10/minute	Govt. entity

* Registration charge.

Source: Grateful acknowledgement goes to Mr. Nemat Al-Ayyach, Head of Trade Information Section at The Arab Trade Finance Program (ATFP) for collecting the above data without implicating his responsibility or that of the institution for which he works.

Basic Telecommunications

Communication networks have become extremely important in facilitating international trade and expanding it to cover a broad range of services. Examples are long distance services or "back office" type activities, in which a company assigns certain operations to foreign affiliates, such as data entry or transactions processing for insurance claims (World Bank 1995). Cheaper basic communications can reduce the costs of export activities and contribute to enhancing competitiveness of firms.

Basic telecommunications are among the most regulated services sector in virtually all MENA countries. The telecommunications market in the region is characterized by state monopolies supplying basic telecommunications in their respective territories and inadequate telecommunications services. The estimated waiting time to install a direct line ranges between one week, in most of the GCC countries, to over one year in countries such as Algeria and Egypt and as long as four years in Syria (see table 8.2). The average cost of international calls has been falling worldwide as a result of new technologies, the advent of cellular networks, Internet access, and enhanced bilateral cooperation. In contrast, the average cost of an international call in MENA countries still remains high. Internet services, although available in all of the countries except for Syria, are still expensive relative to those provided by international competitors. High prices reflect in part the fact that basic telecommunications are a significant source of government revenues and jobs in many countries in MENA.

In light of the changing technologies that bring about development of new services, inadequate domestic telecommunications networks and services are impediments toward achieving a country's full economic potential. A national telecommunications monopoly is not conducive to attracting the investment or the innovations needed to ensure that firms can exploit the potential offered by electronic commerce. Many countries in the region (Egypt, Morocco, Saudi Arabia) are in the process of privatizing telecommunication services to improve national infrastructure and services. Moreover, opening telecommunications to foreign participation or ownership would introduce new technologies at a faster pace, such as foreign cellular network operators and Internet services providers. Improvement in telecommunications services would thus improve the business environment and will have a significant payoff.

Financial Services

Regulatory regimes pertaining to financial services that affect trade costs are large associated with impediments to the establishment of contestable markets. They can be separated into domestic financial regulation and barriers to the free flow of international financial services. Illustrative examples of domestic regulation include the existence of dominant state ownership of the banking system, restrictions on the licensing of domestic banks or branches on the basis of geographic location, or allowing only some banks to provide services to specific sectors of the economy. All such measures limit competition in the financial sector and cause both the cost of financial services and the risk margin that is usually added to the basic cost of funds to be high.

Many of the MENA countries' financial sectors have been subject to reforms to stimulate competition and diversify the number and origin of financial services suppliers. Liberalization of financial services in MENA countries has been slow and large public sector banks and insurance companies continue to dominate the economy despite the implementation of privatization programs. However, there have been efforts to eliminate or reduce discrimination in the treatment of public and private banks and insurance companies at many levels. For instance, in Egypt the government has cut the stakes of the large banks in joint venture banks with foreign participation. These joint ventures were initially created to serve the international financing needs of Egyptian companies, especially import finance and U.S. dollar-based funding (Financial Times 1998).

Another vital aspect of financial sector reforms in MENA countries has been strengthening the regulatory and supervisory framework in order to be broadly in line with international practice. However, there is still need for improvement in transparency, both in the reported quality and quantity of financial data by banks and insurance companies as well as compliance with standards for the governance of financial institutions (e.g., international accounting standards and standards for licensing requirements according to the Basle principles) (IMF 1998).

Restrictions on international contestability of the domestic financial sector can take the form of barriers to entry (market access) and absence of national treatment. Absent entry by international financial services firms into the domestic financial system, inefficiencies and poor quality of domestic financial services may remain. Competition among domestic financial service providers may be insufficient to change the highly concentrated market structure and monopolistic practices. For instance, the new banks may collude with existing banks, or they may simply be squeezed out of the market by natural monopoly. In such cases, foreign banks, if allowed to enter the market, would strengthen competitive forces in the sector. With superior technology and relatively lower costs of operation, the entry of foreign banks would tend to stimulate competition among domestic financial service providers. In the MENA region, there is great diversity in current entry barriers across the countries and sectors within the countries, varying from the most liberal (Egypt, Lebanon, and Morocco) to the virtually closed (Algeria, Syria). Entry conditions tend to be slightly more liberal in international banking services than for insurance or securities markets, although there are very different regulations from country to country in this regard.

As far as national treatment is concerned, foreign financial service providers may face discrimination in favor of domestic providers (banks, insurance companies, and stockbrokers). For instance, the GCC countries do not permit foreign control of domestic financial institutions. Moreover, the ability of foreign banks to establish branches is much more limited than for the domestic banks in most of the MENA countries. In many of GCC countries, foreign banks (even though under majority local ownership) are subject to profit taxes while the other local banks are exempted.

Qualification Requirements in Professional Services

Trade in labor services in the MENA region is relatively large. Arab countries are among the largest exporters and importers of labor services to the region and to developed countries. Intraregional flows of trade in labor flows have been a more important channel for trade than the intraregional flow of goods (Fischer 1996).

The movement of labor within the MENA region has been facilitated by the liberal regulatory regimes that the GCC countries have applied in the recognition of foreign diplomas or professional certificates. Generally speaking, government sets up policy regulations requiring that activities such as legal, insurance, educational, and services be provided by residents (who could be foreign nationals) or citizens. Often these service providers must certification or licensing in fields such as law, accountancy, and medicine through national institutions (domestically) or through the mutual recognition principle. In the case of the GCC countries, the standards are often set through unilateral recognition of foreign diplomas and certificates. For instance, the Ministry of Health in most of the GCC countries decides that the professional qualifications of doctors trained and certified in certain countries are sufficient for them to practice. More recently, in an attempt to raise standards, GCC governments have allowed the establishment of professional bodies (in the field of medicine and accountancy) that are in charge of establishing equivalency of foreign diplomas or training programs, thus ensuring that international standards are met by domestic as well as foreign service suppliers. Moreover, the government has also set up tests of competence in addition to the equivalency requirement for foreign doctors applying to practice in a GCC country.

In other MENA countries, there have been some regional efforts under the auspices of the Arab League to achieve mutual recognition of educational degrees and certain professional qualifications obtained abroad. However, no formal agreements in the form of MRAs have yet been reached.

TABLE 8.3 Dealing with Regulatory Regimes at the Multilateral, Regional, and National Levels

Regimes	Multilateral Approach	Regional Approach	Action Required at National Level
Standards and CAP			
Standards, Testing, Certification, Marking, Shelf-life Measures	Implementation of: - TBT–SPS Provisions (WTO). - Adoption of ISO, ISO/IEC, CODEX.		- Notification obligation. - Adoption of international systems for conformity assessment. - Single contact point for information (enquiry point). - Accept private labs for testing.
Market Surveillance at the Borders			
Customs Procedures	Implementation of Article VII, GATT (Customs Valuation). Adoption of Revised Kyoto Convention.		- Reduce red tape. - Streamline inspection, customs procedures. - Apply risk assessment procedures, audit-based systems of control.
Port Services			- Liberalization. - Privatization scheme of port facilities; start with leases of port services and contractual management.
Physical Movement of Consignments			
Transport and Transit		Implementation of the Arab League Agreement on Transit by Road; Harmonize: - Fiscal charges (excise duties on fuel, road use charges, and tolls).	- Reduce red tape at the border.

TABLE 8.3 (continued)

Regimes	Multilateral Approach	Regional Approach	Action Required at National Level
Transport and Transit (continued)		- Technical regulations (weights, dimension of specific trucks). - Allow for cabotage (foreign trucks return loaded to original destination).	
Domestic Monitoring			
Exclusive Commercial Agency Law			- Adoption of procompetitive approach in which government allows termination of contracts by manufacturers while allowing parallel imports.
Qualification Requirements in Professional Services		- Mutual Recognition Agreement (MRAs) for educational degrees and professional qualifications.	- National law amendment; manpower training.
Intellectual Property Rights	TRIPS		- Open branches in main cities for copy right/trademark registration.

Note: TBT: The Agreement on Technical Barriers to Trade; SPS: The Agreement on Sanitary and Phytosanitary Measures; ISO: International Organization for Standardization, ISO/ISO/IEC: ISO/International Electro-technical Commission; CODEX: Codex Alimentarius of The World Health Organization (WHO) and Food and Agriculture Organization of The UN (FAO); TRIPS: The Agreement on Trade-Related Intellectual Property Rights.

Dealing With Regulatory Regimes: Policy Options

There are a number of key reform measures that MENA countries need to consider in their efforts to reduce regulatory barriers to trade. Certain trade-related regulations must be addressed at the national level, while others are best pursued through a multilateral approach or even regional cooperation. Note that regulatory challenges that should be addressed at the national level aim to increase economic efficiency and thereby the country's welfare. In contrast, multilateral and regional harmonization of domestic regulations aims to ensure market access and the ability of countries to operate in each other's markets. A summary of key regulatory policies that need to be addressed at the national, regional and multilateral levels is presented in table 8.3.

Harmonization of Standards and Conformity Assessment Procedures

First, in the areas of standards and certification for conformity assessment, MENA countries need to speed up adoption of and compliance with international standards. This can be pursued unilaterally or cooperatively. Many countries in the MENA region already use product standards developed in Europe or the United States. A complement of such unilateral harmonization to the standards of a major trading partner is unilateral recognition of foreign standards, mainly international standards.

MRAs have not been used by any of the MENA countries. Such agreements require lengthy negotiations to be concluded. However, the European Mediterranean FTAs signed with Jordan, Morocco, and Tunisia call these countries to adopt compatible conformity assessment procedures with those in the EU. As far as certification for conformity assessment is concerned, MENA countries should allow for third-party execution of compliance verification of national mandatory standards. To this end, countries need to develop a recognition program that would lay out the conditions for laboratory qualifications. The accredited laboratories, in turn, would test for conformity to regulatory standards. Opening testing services to private firms would help streamline the customs process to allow goods to clear faster and to face minimal rejection risks. Moreover, involving private firms in testing would enhance transparency of the certification system and ensure national treatment of foreign producers.

Market Surveillance at the Borders

Second, in the area of market surveillance at the border, MENA countries need to improve customs procedures and undertake port services reforms. At the national level, many of the countries have initiated reforms to streamline the administrative procedures imposed by other agencies on cross-border trade and have started implementing improvements in the valuation process (i.e., valuation on the basis of transaction value of the imported good) required under GATT. The same trends of restructuring and reform have also been taking place for port services through liberalization and privatization (e.g., lease and management of port facilities by the private sector).

Cooperation at the multilateral level should be considered as a way to consolidate the benefits from unilateral reforms. This could involve greater scheduling of commitments under the GATS and adoption of good customs practices as specified by the revised Kyoto Convention. This would help harmonize national customs procedures to international standards and facilitate trade, in the process substantially reducing transaction costs (see box 8.2).

Deregulate Physical Movement of Consignments

Third, reducing regulatory barriers to freight (maritime and road) transportation may be obtained through regional cooperation, as MENA countries share very long borders with each other. Members of the Arab League should negotiate an agreement on maritime transportation to commit to reduce restrictive measures for access to neighboring ports, facilitate transshipment, and simplify port procedures. Such an agreement would reduce the high transportation costs that have been considered a main binding constraint, according to the survey results reported in table 8.1. Regional cooperation to reduce regulatory barriers on cross-border road transportation service (such as allowing for cross-border cabotage services for freight) is also highly desirable to increase domestic competition in transport services and enhance quality.

Pro-Competitive Domestic Monitoring

Fourth, pro-competitive reform initiatives by the government in the MENA countries are required in a number of areas, including exclusive commercial agent laws, qualification requirements in the professional services, and intellectual property rights. In addressing exclusive distribution and sole agency laws, the adoption of a pro-competitive regulatory principle that relies on private enforcement of distribution contracts and effective regulation of parallel trade (i.e., favorably treating parallel imports) can prove a superior device against price collusion that results in higher consumer prices. Many Arab countries have initiated reforms of their IPRs systems to conform to the TRIPS Agreement. As argued by Keith Maskus, stronger regulation of IPRs must be accompanied with an effective competition policy to distinguish various forms of market behavior related to licensing and sales agreements (distribution

BOX 8.2 International Convention on the Simplification and Harmonization of Customs Procedures in the MENA Region: The Revised Kyoto Convention

Reform of customs procedures can be achieved through internationally based standards such as the World Customs Organization (WCO) International Convention on the Simplification and Harmonization of Customs Procedures, known as the Kyoto Convention. It comprises a set of principles and thirty-one annexes that lay out standards and recommended best practices for customs procedures or arrangements. Drawn up in 1973, the Kyoto Convention has not been a successful multilateral instrument because of its non-binding nature and the many outdated annexes that do not reflect current techniques and new developments such as risk assessment, audit-based systems of control, or automated systems. Efforts are ongoing to revise the Kyoto Convention to reflect these developments and to become a comprehensive set of "good administrative practice" as far as imports and exports, transit, and warehousing is concerned. Expected major changes to the Convention include a set of guidelines drawn from best practices with specific examples from particular countries and customs administrations to assist other countries with documented successful experiences. Implementing the revised Kyoto Convention will require a significant amount of effort (and funds), particularly for valuation and enforcement training and building relationships between Customs and the business communities in developing countries (both traders and Customs officials will have to learn and understand the new requirements and procedures).

A key issue is whether the provisions of revised Kyoto Convention will be binding or not. The WCO, the body that has developed the convention, does not have an enforcement mechanism of its own. This suggests another institution with an effective "dispute settlement" mechanism will need to be brought in to enforce the convention if this is desired by signatories. One natural candidate in this connection is the WTO. Some WTO members have argued that the WTO should not be used to ensure enforcement of an instrument that has been developed by another organization. A counter-argument to this view is that the WTO has a mandate to achieve greater coherence in global economic policymaking by cooperating with other international organizations. The WTO members have already given the WCO the responsibility for developing the rules of origin for non-preferential trade, in addition to the responsibility for promoting the WTO Agreement on Customs Valuations (including technical assistance to those countries in transition from the old GATT valuation system). WCO/WTO cooperation in enforcing a new Kyoto Convention would mean that customs administrations in all the WTO members operate under the same rules. This can be regarded as yet another trade facilitation measure that would benefit the international business community.

Source: Drawn from Messerlin and Zarrouk 1999.

contracts) (see chap. 9). Countries in the MENA region need to develop competition authorities that have the capacity to recognize anti-competitive behavior (including protected monopolies and exclusive-distributor laws).

Since many countries in the MENA region are net exporters of professionals (e.g., Egypt and Jordan), an effective regulatory policy would be to upgrade national standards and seek recognition—through the conclusion of MRAs—of educational degrees and professional qualifications in other countries. This applies especially to those countries that are potential importers of professional services, particularly the GCC countries.

Conclusion

Regulatory regimes may have undesirable economic effects on competition, especially competition from imports, and can reduce the competitiveness of domestic firms engaged in export activities. Inefficiencies in customs clearance procedures, port and ancillary services, and transportation and telecommunications services all impose real resource costs on firms and businesses. In recent years, many countries in the MENA region have made efforts to harmonize national standards with international standards. Despite these efforts, the majority of standards in the MENA countries are not equivalent to international standards. Some innovative efforts to outsource conformity assessment to the private sector have emerged in the region. But, distortionary regulatory regimes cannot be eliminated on a unilateral basis only. International cooperation is required to achieve mutual recognition of testing and certification procedures.

The ability of foreign firms to enter service markets remains highly restrictive in MENA countries. Market access restrictions for services usually involve not only barriers to foreign services transactions but also policies affecting the physical entry of services providers into markets. Such policies reduce competition in service industries and raise the trade costs of doing business abroad.

Dealing effectively with regulatory reforms to reduce restrictive measures to cross-border transportation and mutual recognition of qualification requirements in professional services in a regional context can provide a positive economic outcome. Other regulatory reforms in services are more effectively dealt within the GATS context. The advent of the WTO 2000 negotiations in services is an opportunity for the MENA countries to consider reforms and give a great deal more thought to the design of far-reaching regulatory reform programs, sector by sector, in order to evaluate the consequences and tradeoffs involved.

Overall, there is a general need in MENA countries to collect data and information in order to conduct accurate cost-benefit analyses of existing regulatory policies and assess possible improvements and alternatives. It is also important to design programs for decision-makers to effectively manage the transition to a deregulated environment.

NOTES

1. The survey was undertaken by author in the course of an internal broad study for the Arab Trade Financing Program (ATFP), a regional financial institution specialized in refinancing intra-Arab trade. Sample survey questionnaire and interviews were conducted in 1996.

2. Parallel imports are goods shipped into a country without the authorization of the manufacturer or the patent or the trademark holder after those goods was distributed legitimately elsewhere.

CHAPTER 9

Strengthening Intellectual Property Rights in Lebanon

Keith E. Maskus

An issue of great concern to decision makers in many developing countries is the impact of strengthening protection of intellectual property rights (IPRs). In this chapter, simple partial equilibrium models are used to analyze and discuss the likely economic impacts of introducing stronger IPR protection in Lebanon. Such strengthening will be required by the WTO agreement on Trade-Related Intellectual Property Rights (TRIPs).

The chapter begins with a brief description of the IPR system in Lebanon as of 1996 and a summary of a survey of Lebanese manufacturing and service firms in key sectors that provided information on industrial structure and use of IPRs, along with anticipated impacts of a new intellectual property regime. Most of the chapter focuses on the economic effects that could emerge in a small economy such as Lebanon in response to strengthened IPRs. Illustrative calculations are undertaken of the possible static impacts of stronger IPRs on key sectors, using partial equilibrium techniques.

The IPRs System in Lebanon, 1996

Legislation in Lebanon covers patents, industrial designs, trademarks, copyrights, unfair competition, and penalties for infringement. The provisions of the law stem directly from related French intellectual property law developed in the nineteenth century. The law rests on two foundations. First, Lebanese IPRs officials undertake no substantive examinations of applications for industrial property protection (patents, designs, trademarks) for novelty, but rather inspect applications solely for their satisfaction of formal requirements.

Opportunities are provided for private opposition of grants. Second, enforcement of IPRs is left largely to private actions, in which firms assemble evidence of infringement and use the police and courts to achieve its elimination or deterrence. These principles are commonly followed in developing countries. Lebanon is unusual primarily in having an enforcement system that provides effective disciplinary action against infringement in some circumstances. As in many developing countries, existing IPR protection is inconsistent with requirements under the WTO TRIPs agreement in a variety of respects. While Lebanon is not a WTO member, these inconsistencies will have to be removed if the government decides to seek accession.

Patents are awarded in Lebanon without substantive examination for novelty relative to prior art in the field; the applicant need only fulfill certain formalities in the application. Any interested party can file an opposition claim in the courts (not with the Intellectual Property Office [IPO]), claiming that the invention is not sufficiently novel, that the claim is misleading, or that the technical specifications in the application are inadequate to reveal the nature of the invention to skilled practitioners. Patents are awarded for fifteen years from the filing date. Patents are not awarded for pharmaceutical compositions (drug products), an exclusion that is standard in developing countries but would have to be removed under the TRIPs agreement. Approximately 10 to 15 percent of patent applications are denied by patent officials during initial review, largely because the technical specifications are inadequate. Patentees have exclusive rights to exploit their inventions through production, importation, and licensing, subject to revocation for non-working.

Industrial designs and models are protected upon filing, subject to a requirement of novelty and originality, again enforced by potential opposition claims in the courts. Protection implies the exclusive right to sell or otherwise work the design or model. The initial period of protection is 25 years, with an automatic renewal upon application of a further 25 years. This duration far exceeds standard international practice. Protection lapses if the applicant does not publicize the design or actively request maintenance of its secrecy within five years.

Trademarks are protected upon filing subject to certain formalities and basic exclusions relating to government symbols and public morality. There is no protection for geographical indications and no explicit protection of well-known marks that are not registered in Lebanon. Filings are subject to opposition within five years in the courts if other firms have written proof of first use. Trademarks provide exclusive rights to market products using the names and marks and to prevent use of confusingly similar names and marks. Protection of registered marks lasts 15 years and is indefinitely renewable. Approximately 20 percent of trademark applications are denied on the basis of inadequate satisfaction of formalities or prior registry of marks.

The Lebanese copyright law protects all types of literary, artistic, and musical creation without explicit exclusions. Copyrights are provided for life of the author plus 50 years and for 50 years in the case of corporate copyrights. These periods are fully consistent with international norms. Copyrights provide exclusive rights to produce and sell copies of literary and artistic creation and are fully transferable by creators.

Like those of most developing economies, Lebanon's IPO is woefully understaffed, while the officials are not specifically trained in IP issues. A small reorganization is contemplated currently, with a slight increase in staff and a split of the office into branches for industrial property and literary and artistic property. This change will help the technical situation only marginally. The limited resources and expertise of the intellectual property officials will continue to act as a drag on exploitation of IPRs in Lebanon for the foreseeable future.

The Relevance of IPRs for Industries

The simulation analysis that follows is based on a survey of 117 Lebanese manufacturing and service firms that have some potentially important relation to IPRs, using a questionnaire developed by the author and administered by a consulting firm in Beirut in July 1996. The industries are basic chemicals and metals, clothing and textiles, cosmetics, food products, furniture, leather products, films, publishing, and broadcasting, pharmaceuticals, plastics, paper, and glass, and software. Selected firms in each category provided information on sales, employment, trade patterns, and cost structures.

The use of IPRs in Lebanese business is limited. In several industries (basic metals, clothing, furniture, leather products, and plastics, paper, and glass), IPRs were seen as relatively unimportant in setting business strategies. Patents are infrequently applied for (and the number is falling according to private IP experts), are typically on minor improvement inventions, and the disclosure requirements provide little effective technology transfer. Firms rarely try to enforce their patents or designs against infringement, both because of the limited penalties available (suggesting a small deterrent effect) and because court procedures in patent cases can be quite lengthy and costly. Indeed, deficiencies in technical expertise relating to patents within the administrative and judicial systems is likely a strong contributing factor to the limited use of patents. In turn, Lebanon suffers from limited indigenous technological development and technology transfer in the absence of effective patent protection.

Trademarks are more heavily registered and used than patents and designs. Several consumer-goods firms have developed distinctive trademarks or work to protect their rights vis-à-vis foreign trademarks for which they have a licensing agreement and that they register in Lebanon. In part, this greater use of trademarks may be attributed to Lebanon's reasonably effective (according to trademark lawyers) private enforcement mechanism that is backed up by powers of police seizure, customs measures at the border, and judicial relief. These procedures are already largely consistent with international standards. However, numerous industrialists complain about trademark piracy in nearby countries. Complaints also exist about the high cost of legal enforcement of trademarks in Lebanon and neighboring countries, which is viewed as a disincentive to product development.

Counterfeiting should be of special concern to a country like Lebanon, in which consumer-products firms, service firms, and others bear great potential to build recognizable brand loyalty in the region and even in European markets. To date, such firms have had limited incentives to invest in such market-building in the Middle East, which points to the need for pursuing effective trademark protection in the region as well.

Firms tend to focus their R&D functions on local market research. The larger firms tend to believe that they will benefit from stronger IPRs as the smaller firms, which are more prone to undertake infringing activity, come under greater pressure to reduce trademark piracy. Enhanced trademark protection could well generate additional product and design development by these firms for sale in Lebanon and the region.

Lebanese pharmaceutical firms primarily produce drug formulations for sale under their own brand names. Pharmaceutical products are not currently patentable in most developing countries, so that chemical active ingredients, which might be patentable in some regions, are widely available. Generic substitutes are also commonly available. Thus, Lebanese firms do not use pirated copies of patented drugs as inputs, and their formulations are safe and effective. Competition is based primarily on price and reputation, protected by trademarks. Several Lebanese brands are well known in the Middle East and Africa.

Despite the existence of some production in Lebanon of foreign-patented products under license (drugs which have a market in Lebanon and neighboring countries due to brand appeal), the core of the production market lies in wide access to competitive ingredients on the global marketplace. The core business of Lebanese drug firms (as in most developing countries) is product differentiation in drugs and cosmetics based on slight variations of chemical formulations. This is perfectly legal. However, the extension of patents to drug products in Lebanon, if used by foreign firms and their local agents, would remove access to unpatented ingredients and markedly raise input costs. Process patents would also become harder to invent around if Lebanon accepts the international standard of reversal of the burden of proof in such cases. Many Lebanese drug firms would need to pursue technology-licensing agreements with the major international pharmaceutical firms in order to convince them to place production facilities in the country. It is unlikely that Lebanese drug firms, on their own, could afford to engage in the massive R&D programs required to develop patentable active ingredients in order to support their own products.

The cosmetics and food products industries are sensitive to patents and trademarks. Both sectors rely to some extent on inputs that could be patented under the new law and are, therefore, vulnerable to associated increases in cost or reductions in availability. At the same time, both sectors have a noteworthy history of product and brand-name development, with the larger food-products makers owning recognizable names in Lebanon and regional markets. Both groups currently suffer from significant trademark infringement and will benefit from stronger enforcement of their rights.

In the entertainment and media sectors (films, music, publishing, and broadcasting), copyright protection is a key component of incentives for creation. Despite limited copyright enforcement, Lebanon has established a clear competitive advantage within the Middle East as a producer and distributor of literary and creative works, including films, television, advertising, music, and books and periodicals. The ultimate source of this advantage is the relatively large pool of creative talent in Lebanon.

Unauthorized copying of video tapes and music recordings is common, and book publishers complain that their texts are frequently copied and sold, both in Lebanon and in neighboring nations. The firms interviewed already pay full charges to foreign copyright owners for their sales rights and do not anticipate a rise in these fees with stronger Lebanese copyrights. Rather, they expect sharply rising sales and prices as local copiers are closed down. Interestingly, even though Lebanese film and television program producers do not claim to suffer pirated copying of their products, they intend to produce more films for regional distribution in the event of stronger copyrights.

The software industry is heavily dependent on copyright protection. Unauthorized copying is widespread in Lebanon with as much as 95 percent of the programs in use being obtained this way. Such copying largely is confined to well-known international programs such as Windows, AutoCAD, Lotus, Excel, and FoxPro. The Lebanese industry is characterized by considerable inventiveness and fluidity on the part of local programmers, who develop applications programs for particular uses such as banking, finance, and transportation. They also perform custom installation of software systems, service, and networking. Several firms are affiliated with foreign software companies and either pay license fees or buy platform software at full price, including charges for use rights. Other firms routinely load pirated software into the hardware packages they sell. If Lebanon strongly enforced copyrights, hundreds of small software-copying houses would close down, while software firms would be unable to incorporate unlicensed copies into systems installations. Software would be more expensive in Lebanon, although of higher quality. Applications designers would likely benefit from the changes due to business expansion and improvement in Lebanon's reputation for software development.

The Economics of IPRs in a Small Developing Economy

For purposes of discussion, the effects of strengthening intellectual property protection in a small developing economy can be organized into short-run (static) impacts through pricing, output, and trade for a given market structure, and long-run (dynamic) impacts through FDI, technology transfers, and innovation within and for the Lebanese market.

Short-Run (Static) Economic Effects

Lebanon is largely a net importer of technological information and innovative products and services. At present, there is relatively little basis for technology and product development. As an importer, one anticipated outcome of stronger protection would be a rise in royalty payments to foreign rights-holders. Firms (including domestic exclusive agents) that are in an exclusive position to sell their goods protected by IPRs might be expected to raise the prices paid by consumers and industrial users. Particularly sensitive areas such as pharmaceuticals, software, and agricultural chemicals raise the greatest fears in terms of price increases. However, if stronger IPRs expand the use of and access to leading foreign technologies, the result could be a reduction in production costs and transaction costs on the input side. Also, IPRs do not necessarily create strong monopoly positions that generate high prices and limited access. Instead, like a right to tangible property, they define the conditions under which a right-owner competes with potential rivals. A right-holder is rarely placed in a strong monopoly position by a patent, trademark, or copyright. Rather, there is typically competition from other products and technologies.

The likelihood and extent of such monopolization depends on how competitive markets are otherwise. To some degree, this is a function of the scope of the protected claim (subject matter in patents, reverse engineering possibilities in software, fair use in textbooks, and so on). For example, a patent grant carries a disclosure requirement in which the technical aspects of patented materials are made available for inspection and others may use the information to develop follow-on inventions. The narrower the claim, the easier it is to invent around a patent. Thus, IPRs may help spur dynamic competition even if, at times, they may limit competition among existing products and technologies. This incremental nature of innovation is a crucial characteristic of most technical progress, especially in developing economies.

Stronger IPRs will, *ceteris paribus*, encourage right-owners to engage in additional price discrimination across markets, with prices dependent on demand elasticities. The more inelastic the demand in a particular country, the higher the price, although again the precise impact depends on the scope of the property right including enforcement and alternative regulatory mechanisms. Thus, it is important to understand the basic determinants of demand elasticity.

One determinant is the extent of product and technology differentiation available. Countries with stronger incentives for such differentiation may experience lower mark-ups on IPRs-protected goods. Product differentiation is most in evidence in wealthy countries and in middle-income economies with growing consumption possibilities and expanding technical sophistication in production. Countries that erect limits on domestic competition tend to experience stronger price impacts of IPRs.

A second determinant is the degree of market segmentation across countries, because segmented markets are key for supporting differential pricing strategies. Stronger IPRs themselves are means of expanding such segmentation, particularly if patents, trademarks, and copyrights are protected in conjunction with rigorous controls on parallel imports. A similar conclusion holds for trade barriers and investment restrictions. Thus, the potential impact of stronger IPRs on a small developing economy, such as Lebanon, depends greatly on the country's approach to international competition, including the treatment of parallel imports and exhaustion in the definition of exclusive rights.

A third determinant of demand elasticity is the set of regulations on prices or quantities in key areas such as drugs. Such regulations need to be firmly grounded in economic and social objectives and designed to minimize interference with effective competition.

Finally, and quite importantly, demand elasticity for each firm's product depends critically on the structure of market competition, even if products are not much differentiated. Market structure is a function of market size (the number of firms a market can support), regulations covering entry and exit (for example, exclusive-agent contracts or trade restrictions and limits on establishment rights), the number of potential external supply sources (exporting nations), and the scope of intellectual property protection, among many other things.

Thus, for understanding the static price impacts of stronger IPRs, it is convenient to think of domestic and foreign firms as contesting the local market before and after the change in policy.[1] Such a framework illustrates the crucial importance of information of the prevailing market structure and changes therein. If it is believed that the effect of introducing pharmaceutical product patents is to convert a perfectly competitive market into a monopolized market, the resulting price increase could be very high (Maskus and Konan 1994). Much more likely, however, is a situation where domestic firms produce and sell both pirated drugs and legitimate competing drugs (generics or similar products). In this case, the effect will be limited, especially if it is recognized that the aggregate price impact of drug patents will be attenuated by foreign competition.

In assessing such impacts, it must be remembered that Lebanon is a small open economy and therefore intimately linked to prices established in international markets. In most cases, one would not expect the introduction of stronger IPRs in Lebanon to perceptibly alter the pricing strategies of foreign firms in Lebanon because the market is so small (although this conclusion needs qualification to the extent that such firms might view Lebanon as an entree into the larger Middle East market). Rather, the more tangible impact of strengthened IPRs will be to reduce competition from infringement of patented and trademarked goods and from unauthorized copying of copyrighted goods. In this context, *domestic* prices may be expected to rise for key products, services, and technologies, although the degree of such price increases will depend on the remaining extent of legitimate competition. There could be an important welfare gain from higher product quality for consumers and industrial users as protected goods supplant infringing goods, which could have an important dynamic spillover dimension in terms of feeding better technologies into Lebanese production.

On the supply side, one of the initial impacts from enforcing stronger IPRs is reduction in output and employment of firms that had been producing counterfeit copyrighted and trademarked products or using patented inputs. Whether this promises net economic costs or benefits depends on particular circumstances. Direct losses in employment, wages, and output themselves depend on market structure, including the extent of copying. However, as indicated above, such output could be replaced by higher quality goods and technologies, albeit at (perhaps) higher prices. Furthermore, the resources displaced should find their way into other forms of economic activity. Many of the sectors that would be negatively affected by stronger IPRs (software copying, book, music, and video copying, clothing and perfume knockoffs, and the like) are highly fluid in terms of resource use and have low entry and exit barriers. Moreover, with stronger copyrights and trademarks, foreign right-holders could choose to license such production to new or existing domestic firms. There is evidence from some nations that have reformed their IPRs policies that counterfeiting firms can readily shift to legitimate production under the new regime. It is even conceivable that net impacts on wages and employment could be positive, with a lag, although again much depends on where the output is to be sold and relevant demand characteristics.

If labor must be transferred out of such activities, the country's ability to do so is a positive function of its growth rate, its skill basis, and the depth of the economy's industrial structure.

Long-Run (Dynamic) Economic Effects

Dynamic impacts of stronger IPRs include effects on FDI and technology transfers. Firms become multinational enterprises (MNEs) because FDI helps them exploit some combination of ownership, location, or internalization advantages (Dunning 1980; Markusen 1995). Ownership advantages refer to some characteristic of products or technologies that are proprietary to the firm and provide marketing or cost advantages. Obvious examples include new products, processes, computer programs, and trade names. Thus, a direct role for IPRs, especially patents and trademarks, arises in raising the returns to such advantages through FDI. IPRs can also be relevant in protecting internalization advantages, which pertain to the ability of firms to save on transactions, contracting, and monitoring costs by undertaking certain activities within the firm. For example, if firms license their technology or product to an unrelated foreign firm, it may be hard to prevent that firm from revealing the technology or diminishing the product quality (thereby damaging the original owner's reputation). To the extent that stronger IPRs in a country improve confidentiality, contract maintenance, and monitoring capabilities, one would anticipate additional inward technology flows. FDI could fall, however, since arm's-length contracting costs would also fall. It seems likely that the balance of the positive ownership effects and the negative internalization effects would be a net increase in incentives to invest as IPRs are strengthened.

The empirical evidence favors the notion that stronger IPRs attract investment (Mansfield 1994). In a simultaneous econometric framework in which U.S. firms can choose four ways to exploit their proprietary goods or technologies (exports, taking out patents, selling from subsidiaries, and new FDI), it was found that the strength of patent laws in developing countries has a strongly positive effect on both local sales and FDI. *Ceteris paribus*, nations with stronger IPRs attract more investment interest from U.S. multinationals (Maskus 1998).

Estimates of Static Output and Employment Effects of Stronger IPRs

For several reasons, is impossible to provide accurate predictions about the expected impacts of stronger IPRs on sales, employment, prices, and trade in domestic industries. The ultimate impacts depend critically on changes in the market structure that will emerge after the policy change, including various elasticities of demand and supply, competition among firms, trade flows, the number of foreign trading partners, and FDI. Many of these variables are difficult to predict. Attempts at quantifying some of the potential impacts of stronger IPRs can therefore only be illustrative and should be interpreted with great caution. Nonetheless, it is useful to undertake simulations such as the ones presented in this chapter because they help to identify the likely gainers and losers of reform.

It is useful to organize industries into groups that rely on different forms of IPRs—copyrights, patents, and trademarks. Copyright industries include software and publishing and entertainment. Industries that rely on patents and trademarks include chemicals and pharmaceuticals, cosmetics, and food products. In what follows, results of numerical simulations made using partial-equilibrium models of the pharmaceuticals, software, and publishing and entertainment industries are reported. The models are linked across segments of each sector, including a domestic set of small manufacturing firms, large manufacturing firms, import-distribution firms, and importing firms that infringe IPRs, as appropriate.

The framework of the partial equilibrium models used is laid out in the appendix, including key equations. Important parameters include demand and supply elasticities, substitution elasticities in demand among market segments (which produce differentiated goods), the share of input costs spent on goods subject to royalty charges for use of IPRs, markups over marginal cost of importer-distributors, the extent of piracy, and market shares of producing segments. The models are capable of calculating relative changes in prices, quantities, revenues, value added, and employment subject to data or assumptions on key parameters. They are static models only, however, and do not account for endogenous dynamic effects of IPRs.

Patent and Trademark Sectors: Pharmaceuticals

One of the industries most affected by IPRs is pharmaceuticals. There are three types of firms in Lebanon. First, there are approximately eight medium-sized to large-sized manufacturing firms, producing mainly generic drugs, suppositories, and unpatented treatments. Average sales in these firms are around $1 million and average employment is 55 workers. According to the *Industrial Census*, the ratio of value added to output in chemicals is 0.47, which is taken as the initial ratio for the simulations. The same source provides data on employment and salaries of full-time and part-time workers. Combining these figures with employment reports in our survey, the average wage in these firms is some $4,100. This compares to the implicit ratio of value added to labor of $8,545. Some 10 percent of revenues are spent on patented intermediate inputs, such as active ingredients for particular formulations, while another 5 percent might be spent on implicit trademark charges. These figures are summarized in the first panel of table 9.1.

Survey respondents also indicate that there are three sizable import distributor firms in pharmaceuticals; for one of these firms, drugs is one of many distributor lines. Average sales revenues are $16 million on their pharmaceuticals operations, with employment of 200 per firm. The average wage of $3,700 is lower due to the higher use of part-time workers. Using the value added ratio for manufacturers would be inappropriate here because value added basically consists of the markup over import costs, used to pay for local distribution costs. Assuming a 50 percent markup (mentioned as reasonable in the survey), the revenue figure is calibrated to be consistent with distributors having 75 percent of the market initially, which accords with interview responses. This procedure generates per-firm revenues of $16 million and per-firm value added of $5.3 million. Value added per worker then becomes $26,500, reflecting the large markup in distribution. It is assumed that IPRs cost shares are double those of the large manufacturers because distributors deal directly with foreign firms owning intellectual property.

Some 30 small manufacturing firms also exist, with average revenue of perhaps $50,000 and employment of five workers. The .47 ratio is applied to generate value added per firm and then value added per worker of $4,700, in comparison to an average wage of $3,800. It can be assumed that these manufacturers have the same IPRs cost shares as the larger ones but that a small share (10 percent) of revenues in the small fringe firms is garnered by falsifying trademarks.

There are frequent complaints about the prevalence of pirated imported drugs coming from neighboring nations. Speculative evidence on the extent of this activity suggests it is around 10 percent of the market. Imports are calibrated at this level, assuming all of them violate trademarks. An assumed 200 such small firms with four workers on average and a similar value-added-to-sales ratio generates the remaining data. Assuming that these firms make no attempt to pay for authorized trademarks and patents, IPR cost shares are zero.

The static effects of stronger patents and trademarks are calculated using the model in the appendix. To determine changes in employment and the number of firms (assuming free entry and exit, which may be inappropriate in the distribution sector), a fixed ratio of value added per firm and of value added per worker is maintained, as given in the top panel of the table. Import distributors are assumed to maintain a fixed 50 percent markup throughout the policy changes, which implies a demand elasticity for their goods of -3.0. Next, stronger patents are captured by assuming a 50 percent rise in explicit and implicit charges for their use on the existing volume of patented inputs, in addition to a reduction in infringing imports. Finally, stronger trademarks are captured by assuming both that the volume of trademark piracy is reduced by 50 percent and that there is a 20 percent rise in charges for legitimate trademark use.

Because foreign and domestic firms would take some advantage of a stronger patent law, they would be expected both to register more patents and to charge higher fees for use of patented chemicals that are inputs into pharmaceuticals production. Recent experiences from Italy and Brazil suggest as much as a doubling of prices of key patented ingredients could occur. Because Lebanon is a small and competitive market, it seems unlikely that such strong increases could emerge; thus, I simulate the impacts of a 50 percent rise in fees for patent use and prices of patented chemicals. Second, some unknown percentage of imported pharmaceuticals from countries without stronger patent regimes will be judged illegal in the future as Lebanon

TABLE 9.1 Static Effects of Stronger Patent and Trademark Protection on Pharmaceuticals

1. Basic Data (Segment Number)				
	Small (1)	Large (2)	Distributors (3)	Infringing Imports (4)
Number of Firms	30	8	3	200
Avg. Revenue	$50,000	$1.000m	$16.000m	$32,000
Avg. Value Added	$23,500	$470,000	$5.300m	$15,000
Avg. Employment	5	55	200	4
VA/Employment	$4,700	$8,545	$26,500	$3,750
Avg. Wage	$3,800	$4,100	$3,700	$2,800
Total Revenue	$1.500m	$8.000m	$48.000m	$6.400m
TM Piracy	$150,000	-	-	$5.440m
Patent Piracy	-	-	-	$960,000
Total Value Added	$705,000	$3.760m	$16.000m	$3.008m
Cost Share Patents	0.1	0.1	0.2	0
Cost Share Trademarks	0.05	0.05	0.1	0
2. Patent Cost Effects (50% Rise in Patent Charges and Removal of Infringing Imports)				
Parameters: $e_{D1}= e_{D2} =e_{D3}=e_{D4} = -3.0$; $e_{S1}=e_{S2}=2.0$				
	Small	Large	Distributors	Infringing Imports
Number of Firms	26	7	21	92
Avg. Revenue	$55,452	$1.099m	$20.00m	$30,000
Avg. Value Added	$23,772	$470,901	$5.600m	$14,983
Avg. Employment	5.1	55.1	211.3	4.0
Total Revenue	$1.442m	$7.689m	$40.000m	$5.760m
TM Piracy	$144,175	-	-	$5.760m
Patent Piracy	-	-	-	$0
Total Value Added	$618,058	$3.296m	$11.200m	$2.877m
Cost Share Patents	0.15	0.15	0.3	0
Changes:	Small	Large	Distributors	Infringing Imports
Number of Firms	-4	-1	-1	-8
Employment	-18	-54	-177	-33

TABLE 9.1 (continued)

Total Revenue	-$58,253	-$310,680	-$8.000m	-$640,000
Total Value Added	-$86,942	-$463,689	-$4.800m	-$131,200
Price(%)	+1.9	+1.9	+8.3	+5.0

3. Trademark Cost Effects (50% Reduction in Piracy; 20% Rise in TM Charges)

Parameters: $e_{D1}= e_{D2} = e_{D3}=e_{D4} = -3.0$; $e_{S1}=e_{S2}=2.0$

	Small	Large	Distributors	Infringing Imports
Number of Firms	25	7	2	160
Avg. Revenue	$55,289	$1.090m	$19.273m	$24,000
Avg. Value Added	$23,805	$458,667	$5.258m	$14,990
Avg. Employment	5.1	53.7	198.4	4.0
Total Revenue	$1.382m	$7.628m	$38.545m	$3.840m
TM Piracy	$138,200	-	-	$3.840m
Total Value Added	$595,127	$3.211m	$10.516m	$2.398m
Cost Share Trademarks	0.06	0.06	0.12	0.0

Changes:	Small	Large	Distributors	Infringing Imports
Number of Firms	-1	0	0	-32
Employment	-5	-10	-26	-128
Total Revenue	-$59,523	-$61,148	-$1.455m	-$1.920m
Total Value Added	-$22,931	-$85,639	-$683,636	-$478,401
Price(%)	+2.1	+0.4	+1.8	+16.7

4. Demand Substitution Effects

Parameters: $e_D=-0.5$; $e_{D1}= e_{D2} = e_{D3}=e_{D4} = -3.0$; $e_{S1}=e_{S2}=2.0$; $e_{S4}=3.0$; $e_{C1}=e_{C2}=2.0$; $e_{C3}=1.0$; $e_{C4}=2.45$

	Small	Large	Distributors	Infringing Imports
Number of Firms	27	7	2	125
Avg. Revenue	$54,726	$1.183m	$19.279m	$24,025
Avg. Value Added	$23,563	$498,123	$5.260m	$15,006
Avg. Employment	5.0	58.3	198.5	4.0
Total Revenue	$1.478m	$8.284m	$38.557m	$3.003m
TM Piracy	$147,800	-	-	$3.003m
Total Value Added	$636,193	$3.487m	$10.520m	$1.876m

Changes:	Small	Large	Distributors	Infringing Imports
Number of Firms	+2	0	0	-35
Employment	+9	+32	0	-139
Total Revenue	+$95,378	+$656,189	+$11,954	-$836,859
Total Value Added	+$41,066	+$276,188	+$3,261	-$522,688
Price(%)	+2.3	+2.9	0	-5.4

5. Joint Changes of all Policies and Responses

	Small	Large	Distributors	Infringing Imports	Net
Number of Firms	-3	-1	-1	-75	-80
Employment	-15	-32	-203	-300	-550
Total Revenue	-$22,397	+$284,362	-$9.443m	-$3.4m	-$12.6m
Total Value Added	-$68,807	-$273,141	-$5.48m -	$1.13m	-$6.96m
Price (%)	+6.3	+5.2	+10.2	+16.2	+10.0

enforces the patent law. I capture this possibility by assuming that 15 percent of current pharmaceutical imports from infringing firms would violate potential patents and are, therefore, removed from commerce. I assume that domestic firms do not produce such infringing goods in appreciable quantities. The changes envisioned here would emerge only after a phase-in period of Lebanon's choosing, such as ten years under terms of the TRIPs agreement.

The second panel of table 9.1 provides results of the simulations, which depend on assumed elasticities. Notice first that enforcement against import infringement is assumed to eliminate patent violations. The removal of the infringing 15 percent of imports raises price in that segment by 5.0 percent, given the demand elasticity of -3.0, and reduces revenues by $640,000. Value added falls by $131,200, causing eight firms to leave the sector and employment to fall by 33 workers.

Both the small manufacturers and the large manufacturers are directly affected by the higher patent fees, raising their patent cost shares from 0.1 to 0.15. This cost increase translates into a price rise of 1.9 percent, which is calculated from the original cost shares and the elasticities of demand and supply. That is, the 50 percent rise in patent fees generates a 5 percent rise in costs, given the patent cost share, of which 1.9 percent is passed on in higher prices. It may be that this "pass-through elasticity" is unreasonably low, though it could also be argued that Lebanon's product prices are largely fixed through both import-competition effects and government regulation. In any case, it points out that even large increases in patent charges on the Lebanese market need not translate into significant price hikes. Because demand is assumed to be elastic in each segment, revenues fall for both groups of firms. Further, value added is squeezed on the cost side by more than the price increases, causing value added to fall by around $87,000 across the small firms and by around $464,000 among the large firms. This effect results in four small firms and one large firm leaving production, with joint employment falling by 72 workers.

I assume that the importer-distributors maintain a markup of 50 percent over import costs, which is equivalent to assuming a fixed demand elasticity of -3.0. I also assume that these distributors are capable of purchasing as much pharmaceuticals as they wish at the prices set by foreign patent-owning firms. Suppose that initially such firms charge a 20 percent patent markup and that stronger Lebanese patents induce a 50 percent increase in this markup, to 30 percent. Then the implicit rise in import price to distributors is 8.3 percent [(1.3/1.2)-1 = 0.083]. Distributors pass this directly on to users, which induces a reduction in quantity demanded of 25 percent along a fixed demand curve. Under these circumstances, distributors experience a decline in revenues of $8 million and in value added of $4.8 million. In response, one such firm leaves the market and employment falls by 177 workers. Of course, these results may be too strong. If, for example, distributors had a fixed markup of 100 percent (assuming a demand elasticity of -2.0), then employment would fall by only 128 workers. Similarly, the effects would be weaker if the underlying cost share accorded to patents or the increase in patent charges were lower.

Overall, stronger patents and their enforcement are simulated to reduce static employment over the phase-in period by 282 workers, or 14 percent of the initial employment industry-wide. Revenue and value added decline sharply in the import-distribution sector.

I attempt to capture the impacts of a stronger and better-enforced trademark law by assuming that it generates both a 50 percent reduction in trademark piracy in the pharmaceuticals sector and a 20 percent increase in trademark licenses and embodied prices. The former change is consistent with recent experiences in other developing countries in attempting to clean up trademark counterfeiting. It is possible to remove a significant portion of counterfeiting but nearly impossible to eliminate it entirely. The assumption that the trademark-induced price increase of 20 percent is lower than its counterpart for patents comes both from the fact that pharmaceutical firms in Lebanon largely operate under their own trademarks and would face little increase in such costs from abroad and that trademarks tend to embody lower license fees and implicit prices than patents.

Stronger trademarks hit the infringing import sector hardest. By assumption, all its revenue after the patent change stems from piracy. The cut of 50 percent (by volume) enforced by the Lebanese customs authorities generates a price increase of 16.7 percent on remaining pirated goods, given the demand elasticity of -3.0. Accordingly, revenues fall by a third, while value added falls somewhat less because the loss in import volume is offset by the price gain. The number of firms is simulated to fall by 32, with an employment loss of 128 workers.

In this case, there is a difference between small and large manufacturers because the former are assumed to include some trademark infringers in Lebanon. In particular, assume that 10 percent of revenues of small firms derive from counterfeiting pharmaceutical trademarks, which may well be an underestimate. Such piracy is assumed also to be cut by 50 percent in volume, generating a -1.67 percent price hike. However, this industry segment also pays trademark fees, which are assumed to rise from 5 percent of costs to 6 percent (a 20 percent increase). This cost increase generates an additional partially passed-through price increase, so that the full price increase is 2.1 percent. One more small firm closes down, causing an additional loss of five jobs, though net impacts on revenues and value added are small in relation to industry size. On the other hand, large manufacturing firms are assumed not to be engaged in trademark piracy. They are affected only by the relatively minor cost increase from stronger trademarks. While no additional firms shut down, there are another 10 workers laid off because of marginally lower value added in the segment.

Distributors find their trademark cost shares rising from 0.1 to 0.12. The implicit price increase from foreign trademark owners is 1.8 percent, which distributors pass on fully at a fixed markup. Revenues again fall because of elastic demand, generating a follow-on loss in value added of around $685,000 and in employment of 26 jobs. Overall, trademark-cost effects would reduce employment by 169 jobs beyond the patent-cost effects, or 8.5 percent of industry employment. In this case, however, job losses are concentrated among the counterfeiting import firms.

Finally, it must be recognized that, because the products marketed by various market segments are imperfect substitutes, as prices change there will be demand shifts among the industry groups. The appendix provides a methodology for sorting out these shifts relative to aggregate price and quantity indexes. In brief, segments with price increases that are higher (lower) than the industry weighted average price hike will find demand for their products declining (expanding). Weights are given by segment shares in initial industry revenues. In the third panel, I maintain the same own-demand and supply elasticities (adding a high supply elasticity for segment four, given its role as a residual importer), but incorporate values for cross elasticities of demand. I assume that the cross elasticities are fairly high (2.0) for the manufacturing groups but lower for the import distributors, which reflects the idea that consumers may have fairly low substitution between recognized imported drugs and locally produced substitutes. The cross elasticity for the infringing import sector is calibrated to balance the market with the change in the aggregate quantity index. Thus, I assume separability in demand between pharmaceuticals and other goods, which may be too strong an assumption but avoids the need for a general-equilibrium specification of demand. This calibration results in a cross elasticity of 2.45.

With these parameters, the model simulates that demand will rise noticeably in the two manufacturing groups but not appreciably in the distribution sector.[2] As a result, price rises by 2.3 percent and 2.9 percent in the manufacturing groups, with the large firms enjoying an estimated revenue gain of $656,000 and a gain in employment of 32 workers. However, a point that should be carefully noted is that demand shifts sharply away from the infringing import segment. In particular, as an economy clamps down on counterfeit activity, the price of the remaining pirated goods tends to rise, causing demand to be diverted into other sources of supply, a phenomenon that has been noted in other developing countries. This fall in demand reduces price by 5.4 percent and value added by nearly $523,000, with a fall in employment of another 139 workers.

The fifth panel of the table calculates the joint effects of these changes, though no allowance is made for interaction effects among them. Overall, in static terms the economy is simulated to lose 80 firms, most of them in the infringing import sector. Employment is simulated to fall by 550 workers, or 27.6 percent of initial industry employment.[3] These job losses are concentrated in import distribution and in the pirating import firms. Overall revenues are predicted to decline by around $12.6 million, and it is interesting to note that the large manufacturing firms actually register a revenue expansion, though a decline in value added. The weighted-average price increase is 10.0 percent.[4] Again, keep in mind that these static impacts would be experienced over a period of years as the new industrial property law is implemented and enforced or as Lebanon joins the TRIPs agreement.

Caveats

These calculations rely exclusively on comparative-static, partial-equilibrium models of the pharmaceuticals sector. Readers should not infer any welfare implications from these results because they cannot be used to compute changes in consumer well-being or social utility. Rather, they are presented solely as illustrative calculations of important potential market responses to changes in IPRs regulations. In that sense, they provide a useful characterization of prospective price and output effects within the pharmaceutical sector alone. Policy makers may wish to consider such impacts in assessing wider regulatory positions. For example, while a 10 percent price increase for drugs over some transition period may not seem significant, the possibility of higher prices for medicines should alert the Ministry of Health to budgetary costs and issues of consumer access to treatments. The Ministry already has an extensive system of price controls in place for pharmaceutical formulations, covering both imports and domestic production and sales. Such regulation is acceptable under terms of the TRIPs agreement, so long as it does not unduly prejudice the interests of patent holders through compulsory licensing and punitive price limits. Like other countries, Lebanon will need to establish a balance between assuring access at reasonable prices and discouraging imports and production through excessive regulation.

Because Lebanon is a net importer of pharmaceutical products and technologies and because currently it has relatively little inventive capability in the sector, static impacts of stronger patents are liable to be negative, as the calculations indicate. There is no evidence available to support calculations of dynamic impacts and I do not attempt to do so. However, some important dynamic effects could emerge over time that are worth mentioning here. First, demand for pharmaceuticals is income-elastic, meaning that as the Lebanese economy grows, there should be rising relative demands in the sector. Whether this demand is concentrated on imports or on domestic production depends heavily on competitive actions taken over the near term by Lebanese pharmaceutical firms. Second, while it is quite unlikely that any Lebanese drug firm would undertake the massive amounts of R&D required to develop new and patentable medicines and ingredients, stronger trademark protection should provide additional incentives for brand-name development, marketing, and product differentiation of legitimate medical formulations. Third, as Lebanon cleans up trademark counterfeiting and recognizes patentable formulations, it will become a relatively more attractive location for foreign firms to invest in local production and even minor R&D facilities, as opposed to distribution facilities alone. The Lebanese pharmaceutical industry is currently characterized by a remarkable absence of technology-sharing agreements and FDI compared to the country's income levels. Lebanese pharmaceutical firms will find it increasingly important to link up with major international firms in order to ensure access to technologies and production rights as patent coverage is tightened. Successful linkages of this sort should imply growing demand for Lebanese production that could easily outweigh the negative static effects noted above on output and employment. However, this process is likely to be more dependent on political stability and regional marketing prospects that on the provision of stronger patents.

Copyright Sectors: Software

A somewhat different modeling approach is adopted in this sector to account for the effects of important joint products: computer programs (software) and computers themselves (hardware). According to respondents to the survey, there are 70 to 100 "recognized" software development firms, seven of which are also manufacturers, and another 400 or so small firms. I take the latter group to be the fringe firms selling pirated software in two forms: direct copies and copies embodied in hardware purchases. In the survey, the minimum sales reported for a recognized firm were $70,000. I assume that average sales of the fringe firms are $50,000. Employment in the former group averages around ten workers per firm, although there is a wide range, while employment in the latter group might average five workers per firm. Assuming that three of these workers are full time, earning an annual salary of $4,000, and two are part-time, earning an annual salary of $1,000, salary costs per fringe firm amount to $14,000. Of the recognized firms, two are also distributors of software imports under license to companies such as Microsoft, Sun, and Novell. These firms are larger, averaging 50 employees.

The fringe firms sell two products: personal computers (PCs) and pirated software over the shelf. PCs are sold with pirated software loaded in.

Distributors sell legitimate copies of software, while applications firms sell both their own programs and PCs with licensed software loaded in. Approximately 15,000 PCs per year are sold in Lebanon, with average prices of perhaps $1,500 (fringe) or $2,000 (legitimate). Moreover, it is estimated that 95 percent of software sold by volume in Lebanon is pirated. Putting these data together, I construct the basic data in panel one of table 9.2; calibrating sales volumes to reported average revenues per firm and to firm sizes yields the figures indicated.

A simpler model for software is used than in the patent sector. The software industry is better captured by three segments (infringers, distributors, and developers) than by the four-segment breakdown. Moreover, in buying foreign software platforms and legitimate copies, Lebanese developers and distributors are already paying prices that embody international protection of copyrights. It is unlikely that stronger copyrights in Lebanon would induce higher costs for these inputs, so possibilities of higher copyright charges are ignored. Thus, the effect of stronger copyrights would only raise costs of avoiding detection on the part of infringing firms, causing a reduction in the supply of pirated software copies and a hike in their price. Accordingly, rather than calibrate demand-substitution effects to an average price increase in the segment, I simply employ cross-elasticities of demand between infringing software and legitimate software. Note that prices for legitimate copies and domestically produced programs will rise by virtue of removing much of the supply of illegitimate copies from the marketplace.

Suppose that Lebanon clarifies that software is copyrightable and undertakes an enforcement program that is 50 percent effective in reducing sales of pirated programs, both through PCs and over the shelf. In the partial-equilibrium model, I assume first that PCs are imperfect substitutes because the cost of software and the service contracts provided by legitimate firms differ from those offered by infringing firms. Second, software sold by fringe firms, distributors, and applications firms are imperfect substitutes. The cross elasticity with respect to applications programs is surely smaller than that with respect to the distributors' programs, which are legitimate versions of the pirated copies. Hence, the former elasticity is assumed to be 1.5 and the latter 2.5. Third, distributors maintain a fixed (50 percent) markup on software and their foreign suppliers do not raise their license fees with stronger copyrights. Demand elasticity for their distributed software is -3.0 and is held constant as the market adjusts. Fourth, for the developers, software supply elasticity is 2.0 and demand elasticity is -1.5, while both elasticities are held constant. Fifth, fringe firms buy single legitimate copies of several platforms and spread these fixed costs over copies for PCs and other sales. Sixth, revenues per firm are held the same after the introduction of copyrights and there is free entry into each segment of the market. Revenue per employee is held constant in each segment. The first five assumptions are designed to reflect responses indicated by managers interviewed in extensive meetings but may well be inaccurate.

Applying stronger copyrights to the infringing firms generates the results in the second panel, under "Copyright Enforcement Effects." Copyrights are assumed to cut in half pirated sales of software through PCs and over the counter. There is exit of firms out of pirating but by less than half the number of original firms because of price increases per unit of output. With the assumed demand elasticities, the cost of pirating software (and its unit price) rises by 33 percent because of additional efforts to avoid detection. PC prices also rise by 25 percent. Declining sales volumes cause employment to fall by 717 workers in the fringe segment, or 36 percent of that segment's initial workforce. Revenues fall by over $7 million. Clearly, there is substantial uncertainty about these figures.

Panel three contains results of the substitution in demand away from infringing PCs and software to products of developers and distributors, while assuming no subsequent demand shifts back toward fringe firms. Two firms are simulated to enter the distributor market (the change in per-firm revenue is required to achieve an integer figure for firms) and 34 firms to enter the applications-development market. More distributors emerge as foreign software providers find it advantageous to establish additional contacts with agents in Lebanon. Distributors sell more legitimate copies of foreign software at a constant price (reflecting my assumptions of a constant markup and no rise in foreign charges), generating $1.4 million more in revenues and expanding employment by 83 workers. The entry of firms into applications could reflect, in part, decisions by some fringe firms to shift into legitimate production. Applications firms sell more PCs at an 11.7 percent higher price and a

TABLE 9.2 Simulated Effects of Stronger Copyrights on Software

1. Basic Data (Segment Number)

	Fringe (1)	Distributors (2)	Developers (3)
Number of Firms	400	2	90
Avg. Revenue	$50,000	$850,000	$295,000
Avg. Employment	5	50	10
Rev./Employment	$10,000	$17,000	$29,500
Avg. Wage	$2,800	$3,800	$3,500
Total PCs Sold	8,000	0	7,000
PC Price	$1,500	-	$2,000
Total SW Sold (Units)	408,000	2,500	19,500
With PCs	8,000	-	7,000
Pirated Shelf	400,000	0	0
Price	$20	-	-
Legitimate Shelf	0	2,500	12,550
Price	-	$680	$1000
Revenues	$20.000m	$1.700m	$26.500m

TABLE 9.2 (continued)

2. Copyright Enforcement Effects (50% Reduction in Piracy) (Parameters: $e_{D1}^{PC} = -2.0$; $e_{D1}^{SW} = -1.5$)

	Fringe	Distributors	Developers
Number of Firms	257	2	90
Avg. Revenue	$49,935	$850,000	$295,000
Avg. Employment	5.0	50	10
Total PCs Sold	4,000	0	7,000
PC Price	$1,875	-	$2,000
Total SW Sold (Units)	204,000	2,500	19,500
With PCs	4,000	-	7,000
Pirated Shelf	200,000	0	0
Price	$26.67	-	-
Legitimate Shelf	0	2,500	12,500
Price	-	$680	$1,000
Revenues	$12.833m	$1.700m	$26.500m

Changes:	Fringe	Distributors	Developers
Number of Firms	-143	0	0
Employment	-717	0	0
Revenues	-$7.167m	0	0
Price PCs (%)	+25.0	NA	0
Price SW (%)	+33.0	0	0

3. Substitution Effects ($e_{D3}^{PC} = -1.5$; $e_{S3}^{PC} = 2.0$; $e_{C3}^{PC} = 2.0$; $e_{D3}^{SW} = -1.5$; $e_{S3}^{SW} = 2.0$; $e_{C2}^{SW} = 2.5$; $e_{C3}^{SW} = 1.5$)

	Fringe	Distributors	Developers
Number of Firms	257	4	124
Avg. Revenue	$49,935	$779,167	$295,809
Avg. Employment	5.0	45.8	10.0
Total PCs Sold	4,000	0	8,647
PC Price	$1,875	-	$2,235
Total SW Sold (Units) 2	04,000	4583	24,150
With PCs	4,000	-	8,647
Pirated Shelf	200,000	0	0
Price	$26.67	-	-
Legitimate Shelf	0	4,583	15,503
Price	-	$680	$1,117
Revenues	$12.833m	$3.117m	$36.656m

Changes:	Fringe	Distributors	Developers
Number of Firms	0	+2	+34
Employment	0	+83	+343
Revenues	0	+$1.417m	+$10.106m
Price PCs (%)	0	NA	+11.7
Price SW (%)	0	0	+11.7

4. Joint Changes

	Fringe	Distributors	Developers	Net
Number of Firms	-143.	+2	+34	-107
Employment	-717	+83	+343	-291
Revenues	-$7.167m	+$1.417m	+$10.106m	+$4.356m
Price PCs (%)	+25.0	NA	+11.7	+17.8
Price SW (%)	+33.0	0	+11.7	+18.5

markedly higher amount of own-developed programs. Revenue rises sharply for these firms overall by over $10 million, with employment expanding by 343 workers.

Overall, there is a net reduction in firms of 107, of employment in the software industry of 291 workers (9.7 percent of total initial employment), and a gain in revenues of $4.4 million. The weighted-average price increase in PCs is 17.8 percent and in software is 18.5 percent. Again, the essential reason that legitimate firms experience positive static effects in software, as opposed to those in pharmaceuticals, cosmetics, and food products, is that such firms already pay global market prices for basic software platforms, which prices embody returns to copyrights.[5] It is unlikely that the acquisition costs of these programs would rise in the event of stronger Lebanese copyrights, so there is no direct cost increase. At the same time, these firms currently find their sales prospects in Lebanon and the surrounding nations to be seriously curtailed because of endemic software piracy by the small fringe concerns. Accordingly, it is sensible to expect stronger demand shifts toward programs sold by local developers and distributor firms as copyrights take hold.

Again, these calculations must be treated with great caution because they reflect only a guess about the relevant elasticities, informed by limited market-based data. However, they do illustrate some useful points. First, output and employment declines in the fringe firms will be offset to a significant degree by increases in the legitimate firms. If this program were phased in over five years, the per-year change in employment would be quite small in relation to Lebanon's economy, although it is possible that the fringe firms would close down more rapidly than the expanding firms would take up the available workers, suggesting a temporary adjustment problem. Second, inter-segment price relationships can be fairly subtle, depending on cross-elasticities and cost-generated supply shifts. In most cases, the elasticities assumed here are understated since software products are probably highly substitutable in practice. Using higher estimates would tend to magnify the inter-segment shift of resources. Third, some of these changes would be significantly blunted if there were no entry possible into the distributor segment and if existing distributors reacted to the stronger copyrights by raising their markups. For example, an increase in the markup to 75 percent, associated with a reduction in demand elasticity from -3.0 to -2.33, could be expected to cut software sales through distributors to around 2,800 units and raise basic software prices by perhaps 38 percent. In turn, this would result in higher software costs for the applications firms. However, in interviews, distributors indicated a clear intention to expand sales in the event of stronger copyrights.

This rough analysis is strictly static in nature. There is no evidence available to support calculations of dynamic changes. Some potential qualitative effects are worth pointing out, however. First, it is likely that as the presence of pirated software diminishes in Lebanon, the demand for legal copies should rise in order to improve interoperability of computer systems and to raise quality of computing operations. This should also increase demand for the services of legitimate software firms for applications and service contracts. Indeed, several of these firms are quite enthusiastic about their business prospects under strong copyrights, predicting sales increases of anywhere from 100 percent to 1000 percent over five years. Second, whereas I have assumed fixed revenues per firm, it is likely that many applications firms will expand and use additional revenues to fund further program development, with potentially important technological benefits for using sectors such as banks, hotels, and insurance firms. Third, larger markets for software should increase the incentives for Lebanese firms to reverse-engineer platform programs and applications programs. This process is important for ensuring effective technology acquisition from software purchases and should be allowed under Lebanese law so long as it does not simply result in unauthorized copying. In this context, it is important to reiterate the need for Lebanon to update its copyright law to incorporate provisions for information technologies. Finally, it is evident that Lebanon has a strong and entrepreneurial set of programmers with businesses that are well positioned to export to Middle Eastern markets. This fact is likely to attract additional technology-sharing agreements and joint ventures with foreign software firms, particularly if there is additional regional integration and harmonization of copyright law and enforcement.

Printing and Publishing, Music, and Film

Printing, editing and publishing, music recording, video distribution, and the creation of theatrical film and television programs are all significant in Lebanon. Some areas are considerably more subject to piracy than others. Film videos and recorded music are widely copied in Lebanon and surrounding countries. Unauthorized copies of textbooks are also frequently marketed and appear to be easily available at university bookstores. Arabic literature, which represents the main business activity of several publishers, induces some illegitimate copying but in smaller volumes because literary books and poetry encounter smaller niche markets. Lebanon has a new and vibrant industry making Arabic-language films and television programs, which experience virtually no copying. A similar analysis to that of software can be applied to these sectors. Assume that stronger copyrights in the publishing sector result in a 50 percent cut in sales volume of unauthorized books and a 50 percent rise in the cost share for publishers of copyright charges, reflecting higher royalty payments. Assume further that the initial cost share is ten

TABLE 9.3 Effects of Stronger Copyrights on Printing and Publishing

1. Basic Data (Segment Number)

	Printers			Publishers		
	Fringe	Small	Large	Fringe	Small	Large
Number of Firms	300	100	20	250	75	15
Avg. Revenue	$20,000	$42,000	$1.200m	$30,000	$40,000	$2.000m
Avg. Employment	4	6	30	4	5	40
Rev./Employment	$5,000	$7,000	$40,000	$7,500	$8,000	$50,000
Avg. Wage	$2,800	$3,200	$3,800	$3,800	$2,800	$3,800
Revenues	$6.000m	$4.200m	$24.000m	$7.500m	$3.000m	$30.000m
Pirated	$6.000m	-	-	$7.500m	-	-
Copyright Cost Share	-	-	-	0	0.1	0.1

2. Copyright and Demand Substitution Effects (50% decline in piracy and 50% Rise in CR Fees)

Parameters: $e_{D1} = e_{D2} = e_{D4} = e_{D5} = -2.0$; $e_{D3} = e_{D6} = -1.5$; $e_{S2} = e_{S3} = e_{S5} = e_{S6} = 2.0$; $e_{C2} = 2.0$; $e_{C3} = 1.0$; $e_{C4} = 2.18$; $e_{C5} = 2.5$; $e_{C6} = 1.5$

	Printers			Publishers		
	Fringe	Small	Large	Fringe	Small	Large
Number of Firms	225	130	24	164	75	15
Avg. Revenue	$20,000	$42,000	$1.194m	$30,073	$40,059	$1.972m
Avg. Employment	4.0	6.0	29.8	4.0	5.0	39.9
Revenues	$4.500m	$5.460m	$28.645m	$4.932m	$3.004m	$29.9m
Pirated	$4.500m	-	-	$4.932m	-	-
Copyright Cost Share	-	-	-	0	0.15	0.15

3. Changes by Segment

	Printers				Publishers			
	Fringe	Small	Large	Net	Fringe	Small	Large	Net
Number of Firms	-75	+30	+4	-41	-86	0	0	-86
Employment	-300	+180	+116	-4	-342	+1	-2	-343
Revenues(m)	-$1.500	+$1.260	+$4.645	+$4.405	-$2.568	+$.004	-$.083	-$2.647
Price (%)	+25.0	+10.0	+6.5	+13.2	+37.3	-0.3	+0.5	+7.3

4. Net Changes Industry-Wide

Number of Firms	-127
Employment	-347
Revenues	+$1.758m

percent, while printers do not directly pay these charges.[6] Any price increases in the printing sector affect costs in the publishing sector as well, so the model in the appendix is used for calculating demand-substitution effects.

Combining these circumstances, revenues for the legitimate firms in the fringe printing segment fall, as does the share of pirated printing. Revenues of small and large legitimate printers rise. Applying the fixed coefficients for revenues per firm and per employee to these changes, the number of pirating firms would fall by 25 percent. Entry by new firms would take up production and virtually offset the employment loss (table 9.3).

In the publishing sector, there is a decline of pirating firms, with an associated job loss, reflecting copyright enforcement and demand shifts away from higher-priced illegitimate books. For legitimate publishers, the cost increase from higher copyright charges essentially balances the demand increases from the substitution effect, causing virtually no impact on net production or employment.

In the case of music and video, stronger copyright enforcement would increase prices significantly and reduce employment in fringe firms engaged in pirating activities. Net revenues increase as the turnover of large domestic producers exceeds the losses incurred by pirating firms.

In films, TV and broadcasting, the industry gains unambiguously. In contrast to video copying, production of cinematic films, television programs, recorded advertising, and broadcasting is costly. Accordingly, the industry is not directly affected by piracy. Lebanese films and programs are not copied, both for technical reasons and because there is little economic gain to be had in doing so. Moreover, the sector pays little in copyright fees because it develops its own creative programming. Lebanon has a young and strong film, advertising, and television sector. Stronger copyright enforcement could have a small indirect impact on this industry segment by shifting demand from pirated videos to Lebanese-produced filmed entertainment. Thus, assuming a cross-elasticity of demand between video piracy and Lebanese films of 0.5, demand for the latter would rise by 8.4 percent. Revenues would rise, perhaps inducing entry of an additional firm and more employment.

The net reduction in firms and employment in table 9.4 reflects closure of small firms that currently infringe on protectable copyrights that would be better enforced. Such firms tend to be small and to have assets that could be relatively easily transferred to other activities. Displaced workers are likely to be relatively unskilled. Some will find their way into employment in the expanding firms, probably at a higher average wage.

As piracy in Lebanon is aimed primarily at copying foreign textbooks, movies, and music, stronger copyright enforcement is unlikely to induce a creative response by Lebanese firms in terms of literature, music, and films because they do not face much direct copying..However, some dynamic gains could be induced by stronger and more harmonized copyright protection in the Middle East. Lebanon is well positioned as a regional net exporter of television programming and broadcasts, cinematic films, and music.

Conclusion

The calculations performed in the foregoing subsections should be approached with great caution. They are based on highly simplified, partial-equilibrium models within each industry and calibrated to data that provide only rough approximations to true economic activity. The simulations performed are sensitive to the elasticities assumed. They are strictly static, allowing only for impact effects of cost increases from stronger enforcement, foreign reactions in raising charges for intellectual property rights, and demand shifts across imperfectly substitutable product segments in demand. Indeed, it is likely that the computations are excessively static; in multiple-segment industries

TABLE 9.4 Stronger Copyrights on Music and Video, and Film Industries

1. Basic Data (Segment Number)

	Music and Video		Film
	Fringe (1)	Large (2)	Large (3)
Number of Firms	500	23	8
Avg. Revenue	$15,000	$1.000m	$4.000m
Avg. Employment	3	20	100
Rev./Employment	$5,000	$50,000	$40,000
Avg. Wage	$2,800	$3,800	$4,000
Revenues	$7.500m	$23.000m	$32.000m
Pirated	$7.500m	-	-
CR Cost Share	0	0.1	0

2. Copyright Enforcement and Demand-Substitution Effects (50% Reduction in Piracy and 50% Rise in CR Fees) Parameters: $e_{D1} = -3.0$, $e_{D2} = -2.0$, $e_{D3} = -1.5$; $e_{S2} = e_{S3} = 3.0$; $e_{C2} = 1.5$, $e_{C3} = 0.5$

	Music and Video		Film
	Fringe (1)	Large (2)	Large (3)
Number of Firms	333	26	9
Avg. Revenue	$15,015	$1.007m	$3.801m
Avg. Employment	3.0	20.1	95.0
Revenues	$5.000m	$26.200m	$34.200m
Pirated	$5.000m	-	-
CR Cost Share	0	0.15	0

3. Changes by Segment

	Music and Video			Film
	Fringe (1)	Large (2)	Net	Large (3)
Number of Firms	-167	+3	-164	+1
Employment	-500	+64	-436	+55
Revenues	-$2.500m	$3.179m	+$679,000	+$2.207m
Price	+16.7	+8.0	+10.1	+2.3

(pharmaceuticals, cosmetics, food products, and publishing), potential demand expansion effects are constrained by calculating demand shifts relative to an aggregate price increase. On the other hand, the computations do not allow for the possibility that stronger IPRs would enhance the market power of local agents. It is uncertain how important this effect would be in practice; much depends on the particular industry, its market structure, and demand characteristics.

The most important limitation of static calculations is that they necessarily imply a reduction in activity in those firms that had been engaging in unauthorized use of intellectual property and now must pay for it or lose access to it altogether, without recognizing potential dynamic gains that could emerge over the long term. It is worth briefly reiterating them.[7]

First, Lebanon may reasonably expect some increase in FDI after phasing in stronger IPRs. The new regulatory environment, if well enforced, would raise the returns to FDI, particularly in sensitive sectors such as pharmaceuticals and local biological research, though there could be additional interest also in trademark-sensitive consumer products. The responsiveness of FDI to improved IPRs is not well understood, although evidence suggests it is positive in large developing countries (Mansfield 1994). However, IPRs are only one of a set of factors that influence FDI, including local treatment of investment, market size and dynamism, human capital availability, and macroeconomic stability. For example, FDI will be little changed in Lebanon if stronger IPRs are not accompanied by appropriate deregulation of restrictions on foreign investment. Similarly, FDI is likely to be more sensitive to regional economic integration and policy harmonization that could expand market size and enhance business certainty.

Second, Lebanon could experience increases in product development by local firms, which are currently suffering the largest injuries from inadequate IPRs. While it is unlikely that Lebanese firms would generate significant technical advances that could be protected and marketed globally, numerous opportunities exist for developing additional consumer products and business services for the Lebanese and regional markets. Lebanese sectors that seem particularly well positioned for this purpose include cosmetics, food products, software applications, publishing, and film production and advertising. It is likely that this will be the strongest dynamic gain forthcoming from the new policy regime.

Third, Lebanese firms should find it easier to enter into joint ventures and technology-sharing or product-licensing agreements with foreign firms as a result of stronger IPRs. Thus, while stronger intellectual property rights will make it harder for local firms to imitate foreign technologies, products, and designs, they should assist legitimate firms in providing greater access to authorized information. Provided this enhanced technology transfer is employed in a competitive fashion in Lebanon, the economy should reap some dynamic benefits.

Fourth, to the extent that there is additional technology transfer to Lebanon and further local product development, the average quality of products and services on the market should rise. While the associated price impacts would be problematic for low-income consumers, there should be dynamic gains from greater efficiency of inputs over time, while consumers will benefit from additional certainty about the signaling value of trademarks.

Appendix 9.1 General Equations for Partial-Equilibrium Models

Effects of Cost Increases Caused by Higher Fees for IPRs or Input Prices

Firms that use inputs for which royalties are charged or whose prices incorporate charges for using patents, trademarks, or copyrights would expect to see a rise in those costs with stronger IPRs. The rise in costs would reduce value added unless the firm can pass the costs onto consumers in higher prices. Assume that a final good j uses n intermediate inputs but only the first input is subject to IPR-related price changes. Other input prices are invariant to IPRs. Also, assume that physical input coefficients (a_{ij}) are fixed. Then value added is:

$$VA_j = Q_j(P_j - P_1 a_{1j} - \Sigma P_i a_{ij}) \quad (1)$$

where the summation covers non-IPRs inputs. The term in parentheses is called a "value-added price" in the trade literature. Taking the total derivative of this expression yields:

$$dVA_j = Q_j(dP_j - a_{1j}dP_1) + (P_j - P_1 a_{1j} - \Sigma P_i a_{ij})dQ_j \quad (2)$$

With further manipulation this expression may be converted to:

$$dVA_j = Q_j P_j(dP_j/P_j) - Q_j a_{1j} P_1(dP_1/P_1) + VA_j(dQ_j/Q_j) \quad (3)$$

We can write this expression in discrete terms as: (4)

$$VA_j^1 - VA_j^0 = Q_j^0 P_j^0\{(P_j^1/P_j^0) - 1\} - Q_j^0 a_{ij} P_1^0\{(P_1^1/P_1^0)-1\} + VA_j^0\{(Q_j^1/Q_j^0 - 1\}$$

These components are observable. Initial value added is computed as a share of gross output, with data taken from the Industrial Census. $Q_j^0 P_j^0$ is initial sales revenue. The term $Q_j^0 a_{ij} P_1^0$ indicates costs of IPR goods, which may be calculated if we know the IPR cost share of total revenues. The survey results provided some information on those shares. The terms in parentheses are percentage changes in prices and quantities, which may be computed from assumed elasticities. Notice that value added can rise or fall as a result of stronger IPRs on inputs, while the effect of this cost increase is proportional to the share of IPRs in costs. A rise in the cost of input 1 proportionally shifts up the supply curve. It is straightforward to show that this shift is captured by:

$$P_j^2/P_j^0 = 1 + (1/P_j^0Q_j^0)\{Q_j^0a_{1j}P_1^0[(P_1^1/P_1^0)-1]\} \tag{5}$$

Again, each of these terms is observable if we know the proportional increase in per-unit charges for use of IPRs. While this is the upward shift in the supply curve, the actual impact on market price depends on market demand and supply elasticities:

$$P_j^1/P_j^0 = \{1 - (e_{Dj}/e_{Sj})\}/\{(P_j^0/Pj^2) - (e_{Dj}/e_{Sj})\} \tag{6}$$

where the demand elasticity is negative and the supply elasticity is positive. Having calculated the proportional price change, the quantity change is:

$$Q_j^1/Q_j^0 = 1 + e_{Dj}\{(P_j^1/P_j^0) - 1\} \tag{7}$$

An Importer-Distributor with a Fixed Markup

Some of the equations above would not hold for imperfectly competitive firms. I assume that all firms are competitive except importers that have an exclusive agency relationship with one or more foreign exporters. There may be several such distributors, but the agency relationship constitutes an effective entry barrier. In general, markups are endogenous and depend on demand elasticity. However, to simplify the analysis, I assume that each distributor charges a fixed markup θ. Thus, $P = MC(1+\theta)$. For this firm, marginal cost is the price charged by its foreign supplier(s), including any implicit or explicit royalty charges. Assume that Lebanon is a small country in the sense that the basic foreign price is fixed but that foreign suppliers could react to observing stronger IPRs by changing their royalty charges. Then $P_f^0 = P_N(1+\tau^0)$ and $P_f^1 = P_N(1+\tau^1)$ give marginal costs to the importer, where the τ indicates exogenous royalty charges. Ignoring sectoral subscripts, with a fixed markup the ratio of home market prices charged by the distributors in Lebanon before and after the increase in IPRs price is simply:

$$P^1/P^0 = (1+\tau^1)/(1+\tau^0) \tag{8}$$

and the distributor's import sales change according to demand elasticity:

$$M^1/M^0 = 1 + e_D(P^1/P^0 - 1) \tag{9}$$

The formulas developed earlier for changes in value added hold in this case as well.

Substitution Effects among Market Segments

As prices change within each market segment, demand will shift among the segments under the assumption that they produce differentiated goods. This issue is quite difficult to handle in a partial-equilibrium framework and requires some simplifying assumptions. Assume first that price and expenditure changes in an industry group are separable from other products and services. Second, because the existence of multiple market segments makes it complicated to handle all possible relative price shifts, define an aggregate price index which is a weighted average of segment price indexes:

$$dP/P = \Sigma\omega_i^0(dP_j/P_j) \tag{10}$$

where the weights are each segment's share of initial industry total revenues. The price changes calculated here are those after accounting for the cost effects of stronger IPRs. Assume that an industry-group "demand function" exists with price elasticity e_D. It captures the economy's overall demand for a product within which consumers allocate expenditures according to price and quality. I choose initial market shares as weights and hold them fixed here (a "Laspeyre index") for convenience because of lack of data. A better approach would be to construct weights based explicitly on specified preferences in some aggregate utility function.

Having calculated the aggregate price change and knowing the aggregate elasticity, we may calculate the aggregate quantity change in demand, dQ/Q. The key issue is how to allocate this shift among segment quantity changes. For this purpose, consider the following system of equations:

$$dQ_j/Q_j = e_{Cj}(dP/P - dP_j/P_j) \tag{11}$$

$$\Sigma\, \omega_j dQ_j/Q_j = dQ/Q \tag{12}$$

$$e_{Cj} > 0 \tag{13}$$

Here, the e_{Cj} terms are cross-demand elasticities for each segment with respect to the average price increase within the group. I assume that all goods are substitutes, so the elasticities are positive. I impose the constraint that the weighted average of resulting demand changes must exhaust the aggregate demand change. The first two equations really are $(n+1)$ equations in 2n unknowns, the output changes and the elasticities. Thus, the analyst needs to find data on (or assume values for) *n-1* of the elasticities and use these to calibrate the final elasticity and calculate the output changes. This is the procedure adopted in this chapter.

The implied demand shifts are incomplete because they do not allow for iterative changes in demand that could be accomplished in a more complicated model. However, these second-order effects are usually small, and I ignore them here. Within each market segment, as demand rises (for those sectors with below-average price increases) or falls (for those with above-average price increases), there will be subsequent impacts on quantity and price. These demand shifts have effects analogous to those of the supply shifts above. Let Q_j^2/Q_j^0 indicate the relative demand shift calculated in the last set of equations. In competitive markets, the actual relative quantity and price changes would be:

$$Q_j^1/Q_j^0 = (Q_j^1/Q_j^2)(Q_j^2/Q_j^0) \tag{14}$$

where:

$$Q_j^1/Q_j^2 = \{1 - (e_{Sj}/e_{Dj})\}/\{(Q_j^2/Q_j^0) - (e_{Sj}/e_{Dj})\} \tag{15}$$

$$P_j^1/P_j^0 = 1 + (1/e_{Sj})\{(Q_j^1/Q_j^0) - 1\} \tag{16}$$

Finally, note that under the assumption that Lebanon is small, the higher IPRs-inclusive price charged to import distributors is unchanged as a result of these demand shifts. Accordingly, with a fixed markup, these firms experience only a relative quantity change.

NOTES

1. See, e.g., Maskus (1990), Maskus and Konan (1994), and Subramanian (1991).

2. The small impact in distribution reflects its large initial weight in industry revenues, so that the price increase here is nearly identical to the aggregate price increase.

3. Readers should not take literally the claim that initial employment is 1,990 workers. This is just an estimate based on the survey and likely misses a substantial portion of actual employment. However, the processes illustrated here would suggest a decline in employment of a similar percentage of whatever actual employment is.

4. The weights are based on each industry segment's share of initial industry revenues.

5. Results for cosmetics and food products may be found in Maskus (1997).

6. According to interviewees, copyright fees are currently 7 to 10 percent of publishing sales. A 50 percent rise in average license fees (likely an overestimate) would then increase costs by a maximum of 5 percent.

PART FOUR

Institutional Options

CHAPTER 10

The Greater Arab Free Trade Area: Limits and Possibilities

Jamel Zarrouk

The Greater Arab Free Trade Area (GAFTA), launched by the member states of the Arab League on January 1, 1998, is a recent example of renewed attempts at regional integration in the MENA region.[1] The objective of the GAFTA is the elimination of import duties and other barriers to trade on goods of Arab origin over a ten-year period. As a result, by 2008 intra-Arab imports will enter each country of the region—spanning Morocco in the west to Oman in the East—without encountering tariffs or tariff-like barriers.

Two factors have been advanced for the recent interest in creating a region-wide FTA. First, many of the countries in the region have implemented reforms to reduce the economic role of the public sector and shift away from import substitution. As a result, there is greater scope for the region to expand intratrade and to exploit investment opportunities. Second, the post-Uruguay Round tariff and nontariff reductions and the strengthening of the multilateral trading system (the advent of the WTO) have raised fears of marginalization of MENA economies that have relied on preferences for their exports to industrial markets.

Responses to this challenge have included increased interest in WTO membership and the conclusion of a series of "Association Agreements" between the EU and the Southern Mediterranean countries. Such agreements involve the complete liberalization of trade with the EU over a twelve-year period. The agreements are expected to foster trade and development and to attract FDI in the Southern Mediterranean region. However, there is a danger that the association agreements will give rise to trade diversion and discourage intraregional economic ties. If all the Arab Mediterranean countries do not have comparable FTAs with each other—that is, if they do not conclude a single free trade area—then the common denominator of the association agreements will be the EU. This may lead to a situation in which foreign investors choose to invest in the EU "hub" in order to service all the Arab "spokes." Minimizing this so-called "hub and spoke" effect (Wonnacott, 1996) by lowering intraregional trade barriers is a major incentive for creating a single free trade area among Arab countries in the MENA region.

The Past Legacy of Regional Integration Efforts

The history of RIAs in the MENA region is not encouraging for prospective intraregional trading blocs. Examples of unsuccessful regional initiatives include the 1953 treaty to organize transit trade among the states of the Arab League, the 1964 Agreement establishing an Arab Common Market (ACM),[2] and more recently, the 1981 Agreement for Facilitation and Promotion of Intra-Arab Trade, signed by eighteen member states of the Arab League. Broadly speaking, the impact of these agreements on regional trade has been extremely limited. Intraregional trade among Arab countries expanded little during the last two decades, and its share in total regional trade has remained small. The relative importance of intratrade in total Arab trade rose moderately during the ten-year period of 1986-97, reaching 9 percent of total trade as measured by imports and exports. This compares unfavorably with more successful trading blocs such as the EU, NAFTA, and the recent Customs Union (MERCOSUR) between four Latin American Countries, each of which enjoy much higher intraregional trade (table 10.1).[3]

An important shortcoming of regional integration efforts in the MENA region has been that virtually all RTAs have been declarations of intent on the part of the country signatories. They were not binding or comprehensive; coverage was determined through negotiations following a product-by-product approach. Countries could pick and choose manufactured products for tariff exemptions. None of the agreements laid out time schedules for the elimination of tariffs and trade barriers.

The failure of the first wave of Arab regionalism led some countries to devote their efforts to pursuing smaller-scale regional groupings in the 1980s. Three regional groupings were founded. The GCC, established in 1981 by Bahrain, Kuwait, Oman, Qatar, Saudi Arabia, and UAE, emerged as the only

TABLE 10.1 Intraregional Trade (Percent of Total Trade)

	1980	1984	1989	1994	1997
Intra-Arab	6.2	7.3	10.2	8.8	9.0
INTRA-EU	61.0	58.8	65.2	61.9	57.1
Intra-MERCOSUR	10.7	6.7	11.5	19.5	21.0

Source: *Direction of Trade Statistics*, IMF; Yeats (1997) for MERCOSUR data.

viable subregional free trade area in the MENA region. The other two were the short-lived Arab Cooperation Council between Egypt, Iraq, Jordan, and Yemen, and the Maghreb Arab Union established by Algeria, Libya, Mauritania, Morocco, and Tunisia. The empirical evidence indicates that although intratrade of these smaller scale groupings grew, this expansion was far less than that which occurred in external trade (Zarrouk 1992).[4]

The discouraging attempts at regional integration have been attributed to a variety of economic and political factors. To name a few, on the economic side, most Arab countries (with the exception of the GCC countries) have pursued industrial strategies founded on import-substitution and a large public sector. This has led to high protection across industries, nontransparent trade policies, huge investments in state-owned industrial enterprises, and human skills that are unsuited to a competitive market economy. Moreover, Arab governments ended up relying on import duties as an important source of revenue, lacking the administrative capacity to introduce broad-based domestic consumption taxes.[5] Bureaucratic red tape to protect rents that accrue to domestic producer interest groups, politicians, and government officials also contributed to the failure of Arab RTAs.

Political factors also worked against efficiency and mutual confidence. Arab countries did not seem to have sufficient incentives to integrate. This was translated into mistrust and an unwillingness to make binding commitments to a regional liberalization scheme covering substantially all trade. Finally, but not least, political differences among the Arab leaders have weighed heavily in the Arab economic relations.

Recent international experience from successful RTAs (e.g., the EU, NAFTA) suggests that unless such arrangements maintain open trade regimes relative to the rest of the world, they will fail to induce substantial regional trade increases. A number of Arab countries have been implementing trade liberalization since the 1980s: there have been moves in Morocco, Tunisia, Egypt, and Jordan to reform trade policy to spur improvements in efficiency and install more market- and export-oriented economies. Moreover, the traditionally open economies of the GCC and major oil exporting countries have diversified into petrochemicals and energy-intensive industries exporting products to both industrial and developing markets.

The change in the international trading environment is expected to have significant implications for the prospects of regional and intraregional trade. The implementation of the Uruguay Round Agreements is expected to create new trading opportunities for countries that are well integrated into the world economy. As mentioned, Arab countries, having relied for a long time on preferential access to the markets of their key trading partners such as the EU now face the challenge of less-advantageous access to these markets. The Arab League initiative establishing the GAFTA must be seen in the light of these developments. The GAFTA comprises a region with a population of approximately 255 million and a GDP of over $600 billion (see table 10.2).

Provisions of the Executive Program Establishing GAFTA

The Executive Program for the establishment of the GAFTA aims to revive the 1981 Agreement for Facilitation and Promotion of Trade among the member states of the Arab League. In contrast to previous attempts, this program came up with specific commitments in terms of across-the-board elimination of tariffs, tariff-like charges, nontariff measures, and rules of origin.

Coverage and Scope of Tariff Reductions

The GAFTA program consists of progressive, linear, and automatic tariff reductions over ten years at a rate of 10 percent per annum. Thus, tariffs will be totally abolished by the year 2007, and the member countries agree to bind the national tariff schedules, which were applied on December 31, 1997. In the case of countries that have not ratified the agreement, the bound tariffs are those apply at the time they notify the Arab League (which assumes the functions of the GAFTA Secretariat) of the ratification and endorsement of the program. Tariff-like charges and additional taxes are covered by the program and are treated like normal tariffs.

Regarding liberalization of industrial products, member countries are allowed to draw up a list of exceptions from tariff reductions during the first years of the implementation of the Executive Program. Exceptions are intended to enable local industry to carry out the restructuring needed to improve their competitiveness before having to face competition from other GAFTA countries' imports. However, member countries requesting such exceptions must provide a report showing in full the economic impact on the national economy and the duration for which exceptions are sought for each good (defined at the 6-digit HS level) for reductions in tariffs and tariff-like charges.

As far as liberalization of agricultural products is concerned, the program introduces safeguard measures to allow member countries to suspend applying tariff reductions on some produce during the peak harvest seasons. The committee supervising the implementation and the follow-up of the GAFTA Executive Program must approve any products benefiting from such measures. The duration of the seasonal exclusion from the tariff and other import taxes reductions for any eligible produce cannot last more than seven months. Moreover, each GAFTA country is allowed to submit a list of a maximum of ten produce items for suspension, with total duration for all the produce items subject to suspension from tariff and tariff-like reductions not to exceed forty-

TABLE 10.2 Basic Economic Indicators of GAFTA Member Countries 1997 *

	1997 GDP ($ Million)	1997 Population (Thousand)	Merchandise Exports ($ Million)	Share in Intra-GAFTA Exports (%)	Share in World Exports (%)	Merchandise Imports ($ Million)
Algeria	47,869	29,297	13,820	8.0	0.26	8,130
Bahrain	6,349	620	1,669	1.0	0.03	2,618
Egypt	75,484	59,758	3,921	2.3	0.07	14,059
Iraq	78,856	21,305	2,331	1.4	0.04	765
Jordan	6,976	4,600	1,505	0.9	0.03	4,102
Kuwait	30,206	2,209	14,280	8.3	0.27	7,747
Lebanon	14,865	3,290	642	0.4	0.01	7,457
Libya	33,994	5,044	9,285	5.4	0.17	8,086
Mauritania	1,044	2,374	525	0.3	0.01	601
Morocco	33,514	28,219	4,659	2.7	0.09	7,856
Oman	15,800	2,256	6,515	3.8	0.12	5,191
Qatar	9,193	696	4,652	2.7	0.09	4,010
Saudi Arabia	146,494	19,258	64,554	37.5	1.21	29,014
Syria	16,239	15,100	979	0.6	0.02	1,007
Sudan	10,109	31,661	594	0.3	0.01	1,580
Tunisia	18,934	9,240	5,569	3.2	0.10	7,966
UAE	49,334	2,624	34,013	19.8	0.64	26,614
Yemen	5,786	16,482	2,529	1.5	0.05	2,039
Total GAFTA	601,046	254,033	172,042	100.0	3.23	138,842

	Share in Intra-GAFTA Imports (%)	Share in World Imports (%)	Services Exports ($ million)	Share in Total Goods & Svcs. Exports (%)	Services Imports ($ million)	Share in Total Goods & Svcs. Imports (%)
Algeria	5.9	0.15	. . .	. . .	. . .	. . .
Bahrain	1.9	0.05	1,347	44.7	432	14.2
Egypt	10.1	0.26	9,651	71.1	7,154	33.7
Iraq	0.6	0.01	. . .	. . .	. . .	. . .
Jordan	3.0	0.08	1,830	54.9	1,348	24.7
Kuwait	5.6	0.14	1,513	9.6	4,302	35.7
Lebanon	5.4	0.14	. . .	. . .	. . .	. . .
Libya	5.8	0.15	. . .	. . .	. . .	. . .
Mauritania	0.4	0.01	17	3.1	162	21.2
Morocco	5.7	0.15	1,886	28.8	1,459	15.7
Oman	3.7	0.10	. . .	. . .	. . .	. . .
Qatar	2.9	0.07	. . .	. . .	. . .	. . .
Saudi Arabia	20.9	0.54	4,484	6.5	13,926	32.4
Syria	0.7	0.02	1,366	58.3	1,302	56.4
Sudan	1.1	0.03	37	5.9	169	9.7
Tunisia	5.7	0.15	2,552	31.4	1,056	11.7
UAE	19.2	0.50	. . .	. . .	. . .	. . .
Yemen	1.5	0.04	127	4.8	614	23.1
Total GAFTA	100.0	2.59				

* Data on Djibouti and the Comoros Islands are not available. Palestine has been excluded from the analysis as it is a member of a customs union with Israel and does not have free trade flows with the other GAFTA countries.

... Data not available.

Source: Arab Monetary Fund, *Arab Joint Economic Report, 1998*; WTO *Annual Report 1998*.

five months. So far, ten GAFTA countries have submitted a list of agricultural products subject to seasonal exception from tariff reductions, covering a total of thirty fresh vegetable and fruit produce items (at the 6-digit HS level).

The tariff reduction scheme adopted in GAFTA is an across-the-board tariff reduction approach. This offers the advantage of being transparent and ensures that high tariffs are reduced faster than lower tariffs in absolute terms. However, the extent to which this approach will boost intraregional trade flows is dependent on the magnitude of tariff dispersion as well as the effective rate of protection across industries in individual member countries. Tariff structures among the GAFTA member states are uneven, with some countries having high tariff protection and others very low. A summary of the status of tariffs and internal tax in the individual GAFTA countries is provided in table 10.3. GAFTA countries can be classified into low tariff countries—the Gulf countries (Bahrain, Kuwait, Qatar, Oman, Saudi Arabia, and UAE) with simple average tariffs ranging from 4 to 20 percent—and relatively high tariff countries, such Egypt, Jordan, Morocco, Syria, and Tunisia, with tariffs ranging between 25 and 100 percent (and attaining a maximum of 235 percent in Syria).

A notable characteristic of tariffs in the GAFTA countries is tariff escalation. Tariffs on raw materials are considerably lower than those on semi-processed and final products. Illustrative examples from Egypt, Morocco, and Tunisia are presented in table 10.4.[6] Tariff escalation is most pronounced in textiles, clothing, leather, and basic metal industries: average tariffs on finished products in these industries are multiples of (low) tariff levels on raw materials. Moreover, escalation is most marked in high tariff countries and least pronounced in the GCC countries.

The implementation of across-the-board approach to tariff reductions on liberalization of trade barriers among the GAFTA countries could have a significant trade creation effect since most member countries apply escalating import duties, which make the effective rate of protection (i.e., protection accorded to local value added production) higher than the nominal rates of protection (i.e., protection to local finished products). High rates of effective protection have a number of negative effects on intraregional trade in the processed products. Since GAFTA countries are mostly low- to middle-income countries, they exhibit high demand in simple consumer goods. The high effective protection raises the price of final products, tends to reduce consumption, and retards the development of efficient processing industries by limiting scale effects that would be attained in a larger (regional) market (Hoekman and Djankov 1997a). This view on the effects of high effective protection suggests that GAFTA countries, which levy relatively low import duties (such as the GCC countries), face small potential for increasing imports

TABLE 10.3 Status of Tariffs, Surcharges, and Internal Taxes on International Trade in Selected GAFTA Member Countries 1997

Tariffs (ad valorem rates)	Bahrain	Egypt	Jordan	Kuwait	Lebanon	Morocco
Maximum rate	100	54	40	100	100	45
Minimum rate (nonzero)	5	1	5	4	2	5
Number of tariff rates/ bands	5 (rates)	8 (bands)	6 (bands)	3 (rates)	12 (rates)	7 (rates)
Simple (unweighted) average tariff rate	20	26.8	22	4	17	23.5
Other tariff-like charges on imports	No	Yes	Yes	No	Yes	Yes
Duty free entry (% of total imports)	. . .	0.2	. . .	. . .	. . .	. . .
Average weighted tariff rate						
(by value of imports) %	3.6	16.7	12.3	3.5	44	14.9
Tariff revenue/ GDP, in % (1996)		3.5	7.7	1.0	6.8	4.3
Broad-based consumption tax	No	General	General	No	No	Value-
on imports and domestic goods		Sales Tax	Sales Tax			added Tax
Rates (in %):		(GST)	(GST)			(VAT)
Goods	. . .	5, 25	10, 20	. . .	. . .	(0, 7,10, 14, 20)
Services	. . .	5, 10	10	. . .	. . .	

Tariffs (ad valorem rates)	Oman	Qatar	Saudi Arabia	Syria	Tunisia	UAE
Maximum rate	100	100	100	235	45	80
Minimum rate (nonzero)	5	4	7	7	5	4
Number of tariff rates/ bands	6 (rates)	3 (rates)	5 (rates)	9 (rates)	26 (rates)	3 (rates)
	(0,5,20,25,	(4,20,100)	(0,7,12,			(4, 20, 80)
Simple (unweighted) average tariff rate	5	4	12	47	33	4
Other tariff-like charges on imports	No	No	No	Yes	Yes	No
				(numerous)	(few)	
Duty free entry (% of total imports)	. . .	. . .	18.4	. . .	. . .	. . .
Average weighted tariff rate						
(by value of imports) %	3.1	. . .	9.5	21.8	22.2	. . .
Tariff revenue/ GDP in % (1996)	1.0	. . .	. . .	2.5	8.1	. . .
Broad-based consumption tax						
on imports and domestic goods	No	No	No	No	(VAT)	No
Rates (in %):					(0,6,10,18,24)	
Goods						
Services						

Notes: Higher tariff ceiling is applied on alcoholic beverages passenger cars, tobacco and tobacco products; poultry (80% in Egypt), clothing (Tunisia). For the GCC countries (Bahrain, Kuwait, Oman, Qatar, Saudi Arabia, and UAE), higher tariff ceiling is applied on alcoholic beverages, tobacco, and tobacco products only. Also note that a tariff band may have more than one rate. Added GST is applied to passenger cars and other vehicles.

Source: IMF; World Bank; WTO "Trade Policy Review" on Egypt, Morocco, and Tunisia.

through GAFTA. However, many of the manufactured goods exported by the GCC countries face relatively high duties in other Arab country markets, so the potential for export expansion is high.

The most serious shortcomings of the GAFTA program pertain to loopholes in the safeguard measures that give members the right to exclude from immediate liberalization certain industrial and agricultural products. The list of exceptions that member countries (Jordan, Lebanon, Morocco, Syria, and Tunisia) have submitted to date includes semi-manufactures and consumer goods competing with domestic production (e.g., plastics, mechanical appliances, television sets, steel and iron sheets). Moreover, the transition period (to last for as long as four years) for the excluded industrial products allows for pressure from interest groups to resist market opening, thereby reducing the ability of GAFTA to realize its full potential for regional trade expansion. Similarly, the right to suspend from the liberalization scheme certain agricultural products during the crop/harvest seasons and for the full transitory period—ten years until the time for full elimination of tariffs—substantially limits the liberalization of intraregional agricultural trade.

Elimination of Nontariff Restrictions

The Executive Program calls for the development of a work schedule to eliminate or at least reduce NTBs. To reach this goal, the negotiating committee on NTBs agreed on a common list of goods whose imports are prohibited for religious, health, environment, and national security reasons. This list is to be reviewed on a yearly basis. The committee is also mandated to sort out all the other NTBs applied by each member country and to start negotiations for their elimination. GAFTA member countries will apply the reciprocity principle in the event that another member does not remove unjustified NTBs. To date, GAFTA members have not entered into negotiations to remove the types of NTBs that constrain intraregional trade flows the most.

Although the use of QRs has been declining in GAFTA countries partly as a result of unilateral trade reforms implemented by some member countries (Egypt, Jordan, Morocco, and Tunisia), NTBs in the form of import licensing for safety and health standards are still applied, mainly for processed foodstuffs and, to a lesser extent, semi-manufactures. In the GCC countries, NTBs are relatively low. However, Syria continues to impose import license requirements for virtually all imports.

Regarding subsidies, countervailing measures, safeguards, and anti-dumping measures, the program calls for the application of international rules. Although the program does not make explicit reference to the relevant WTO

TABLE 10.4 Tariff Structure in Selected GAFTA Member Countries 1997

	Egypt			Jordan			Morocco
	Intra-GAFTA			Intra-GAFTA			Intra-GAFTA
HS-Chapters*	Share of Imports	Simple Average 1998	Range	Share of Imports	Simple Average	Range	Share of Imports
1-5	1.0	19.2	3-40	0.9	7.0	3-7	0.1
6-14	4.0	19.3	1-40	9.3	15.0	3-15	1.2
15-24	1.8	21.8	1-3000	2.4	11.0	11-41	1.2
25-27	14.8	5.0	5-40	56.8	6.0	4-43	75.5
28-40	33.0	19.8	0-40	13.8	15.0	11-99	11.7
41-43, 64-67	0.0	37.4	30-40	0.2	47.0	...	0.0
44-48	0.7	22.1	5-40	1.2	18.0	...	0.3
49	0.7	22.0	0-40	0.3	12.0	...	0.7
50-63	3.2	39.3	5-54	3.7	41.0	29-41	4.2
68-71	0.4	27.0	10-40	1.1	35.0	16-17	0.1
72-83	26.9	14.5	1-30	8.4	16.0	16-43	3.6
84-85	5.7	11.2	0-40	1.6	16.0	31-200	1.2
86-89	5.0	23.6	0-135	0.1	31.0	...	0.1
90-92	0.7	14.7	5-40	0.0	25.0	...	0.1
93-97	2.2	26.3	0-40	0.2	16.0	16-51	0.2
Total	**100.0**	**26.8**	**0-3000**	**100.0**	**22.0**	**4-51**	**100.0**
Value of Intra-GAFTA Imports ($ million)	692.0			963.0			890.9

	Morocco		Saudi Arabia			Tunisia		
	Nominal Tariff		Intra-GAFTA	Nominal Tariff		Intra-GAFTA	Nominal Tariff	
HS-Chapters	Simple Average	Range	Share of Imports	Simple Average	Range	Share of Imports	Simple Average	Range
1-5	33.3	0-365	16.5	7.0	0-7	0.3	39.8	20-43
6-14	29.0	0-365	14.0	7.0	0-7	6.1	34.4	10-43
15-24	42.0	2.5-365	11.6	12.0	12-100	2.3	42.0	23-43
25-27	5.0	2.5-17.5	2.2	12.0	12-20	63.6	22.9	0-43
28-40	14.8	0-35	18.1	12.0	7-20	13.6	23.2	15-43
41-43, 64-67	34.0	30-35	1.1	12.0	12-20	1.0	36.8	20-43
44-48	24.4	2.5-35	4.7	12.0	12-12	1.1	36.2	10-43
49	22.5	0.0-35	0.5	12.0	7-12	0.9	29.3	0-43
50-63	31.6	0-35	4.3	12.0	12-12	2.5	39.1	17-43
68-71	22.0	0-35	5.3	20.0	12-20	0.4	38.4	20-43
72-83	11.6	0-35	15.5	12.0	12-20	5.9	25.4	0-43
84-85	18.4	0-35	2.4	12.0	12-12	1.0	19.3	0-43
86-89	22.5	12.5-35	1.5	12.0	7-12	1.1	26.5	0-43
90-92	13.7	0-35	0.6	12.0	7-12	0.1	26.3	0-43
93-97	25.0	5-35	1.7	12.0	12-20	0.1	37.3	10-43
Total	**23.5**	**0-365**	**100.0**	**12.0**	**0-100**	**100.0**	**33.2**	**10-43**
Value of Intra-GAFTA Imports ($ Million) 1997			1967.0			505.0		

* See endnote 6 for descriptions.

Source: WTO Trade policy reports on Egypt, Morocco, and Tunisia; Memorandum (Saudi Arabia, Oman, Jordan); Hoekman and Djankov (1997a).

agreements in these areas, since only eight GAFTA countries are WTO members and four others are seeking membership, it would appear that these are the rules that are referred to.[7]

As noted in other chapters in this volume, customs and administrative procedures associated with importing are still important trade barriers facing intraregional trade in MENA region. The program calls for some harmonization related to customs clearance procedures. However, the program does not contain provisions for harmonization of other major regulatory regimes relating to product standards, testing and certification procedures, and environmental standards. In the area of freight transport by road, which plays a very important role in intraregional trade exchanges, the member states of the Arab League signed an earlier agreement to simplify the transit of goods and persons.[8] However, there has been no legal enforcement for the implementation of this agreement, and there are periodic reports citing barriers to cross-border trade as described by the road transport profession. These range from closure of roads and motorways for political reasons (e.g., the closure of the Algerian-Moroccan borders and the closure of Iraqi borders with its neighboring countries), delays, and cumbersome cross-border regulations (such as no driving on weekends and public holidays or the refusal of visa issuance for professional drivers of certain nationalities; see chap. 8).

Rules of Origin

As is the case with any FTA, the GAFTA embodies rules of origin for duty-free treatment. The GAFTA value added requirement is set at 40 percent, and two methods for origin calculations were drawn. The first one is based on the local value added approach which adds up the value of parts and materials procured from domestic sources plus the value of domestic assembly, labor, overhead, and financing costs. The other approach is the "net cost" approach, which subtracts specified imported expenses from the transaction price to determine the base for calculating the ratio of foreign to domestic content. An important feature of GAFTA the elaboration of detailed preferential rules of origin for GAFTA-made products. Rules for cumulation of origin among the GAFTA countries have been adopted, thus allowing for materials obtained from one member country and incorporated into a product worked out or processed in another member country to be considered as obtained in the latter country. Finally, the program calls for the need for harmonization of preferential rules of origin drawn in the context of the Euro-Mediterranean FTAs between the Arab Mediterranean countries and the EU.

At first, the cumulation of rules of origin for products made in GAFTA countries may help create backward and forward linkages between the member countries and increase the potential for IIT. A further extension of cumulation of the EMAs and the GAFTA countries would be more beneficial to member countries in both groupings and would also help reduce the emerging "hub and spoke" nature of the EMAs (Hoekman and Djankov 1997a).[9]

Institutional Structure

Management of GAFTA is through the Council of Ministers of member states and through an executive and follow-up permanent body. So far, GAFTA has a functioning Secretariat that comes under the Economics Department of the Arab League Secretariat. This FTA Secretariat is in charge of handling the circulation of papers between the commissions and working subgroups.

An innovation in the Executive Program is the call for the private sector (chambers of industry and commerce in Arab countries) to monitor the implementation of the different stages of the program. Pursuant to this end, the Union of Arab Chambers of Commerce has been requested to submit to the Council of Ministers and its executive body a semi-annual report detailing the difficulties that traders encounter in dealing with the customs administration and any other regulatory agencies of individual member countries. The bolstering of the private sector's role in monitoring those problems that occur in the implementation of the Executive Program and raising them in the Arab Council of Ministers is expected to enhance the transparency of the member countries' trade practices.

Economic Implications of GAFTA

Quantification of the impact of GAFTA on the economies of member countries is not straightforward, partly due to many concurrent effects that are difficult to measure. An important factor that may overestimate the GAFTA effect is the existence of several bilateral preferential schemes between Arab countries. These agreements provide partial exemptions from tariffs to a list of products drawn by member countries. By allowing preferential treatment to some products and denying it to other goods of national content, these protocol agreements are likely to undermine the effects of regional liberalization under GAFTA scheme.

A qualitative assessment of the impact of GAFTA on the economies of member countries can be undertaken by drawing on standard customs union theory. Traditionally, a FTA among developing countries is assumed to be a substitute rather than a complement to trade between developing and developed countries. Accordingly, any preferences provided to intraregional trade would divert an equivalent amount of trade with industrial countries and reduce the region's dependence on these countries. Since trade creation and trade diversion are traditionally static in nature, the static impact of GAFTA is likely to be dominated by trade diversion. However, empirical evidence shows this is not always the case since products which are of primary importance to developing countries are normally capital-intensive goods in which they do not have a comparative advantage. In the case of GAFTA, Zarrouk (1999) finds that the majority of dynamic products in intraregional trade are not in sectors that are of primary importance in Arab countries' exports to the EU.

There are also potential dynamic effects from establishing a regional FTA that are associated with the flow of new investment, improved productivity, and lower transaction costs. The potential dynamic effect of GAFTA is expected to result from enlarging market size, to the extent that a larger market can attract industry. Such investment flows to GAFTA would be, in part, induced by the Euro-Mediterranean FTAs signed or scheduled to be signed between the EU and each of the Arab Mediterranean countries. Ultimately, GAFTA will minimize the so-called "hub and spoke" effect. If intra-GAFTA trade flows freely among the Arab countries, then foreign investors and firms from the EU have an incentive to invest in the Arab Mediterranean countries as "spokes" to attain access to all GAFTA countries, rather than to locate in the EU as the "hub" (Zarrouk 1999).

Another determinant of the welfare effect of GAFTA results from the creation of opportunity to develop comparative advantage, i.e., the opportunity to produce and sell in a regional market before venturing into more intense international competition. Infant industries in several GAFTA countries have been able to develop a comparative advantage in markets of neighboring countries, but only in the shelter of a protected market, generating social benefits along the way. For instance, the Arab GCC countries, endowed with capital resources, have acquired high-skill technologies that are adapted to produce suited exportables to both developing and developed countries (e.g., petrochemicals, plastics). Little change is expected in imports of labor-intensive light manufacturing, especially textiles and clothing, leather, footwear, and furniture. These are sectors where the relatively more diversified economies have comparative advantage but are so similar that there are limited opportunities for intratrade (see chap. 1).

However, the positive signs of rapidly increasing IIT levels in the Arab region as a result of their efforts to diversify economies might provide new channels for intra-industry cooperation even in those labor-intensive light manufacturing sectors (see chap. 3). For instance, Arab countries have not developed so-called outward processing in intratrade. This consists of shipping semi-finished products to another Arab country for further processing. The processed good is then exported back to the original Arab supplier/retailer or exported to developed countries (e.g., the EU). In this respect, the garment industry and the base metal industry can be a potential candidate to reduce production costs and risks associated with development of export markets.

As for consumer welfare, tariff reductions would expand intratrade (this benefit is subsumed in trade creation), assuming a price elastic demand for imports. In addition, Arab consumers might start to substitute imports (i.e., trade diversion) from producers from GAFTA countries for imports from outside

GAFTA countries (mainly developed countries). With full elimination of tariffs and other trade barriers, Arab importers would experience some efficiency gains from the shift to trade with other Arab countries that are lower-cost producers.

Finally, GAFTA will bring about tariff revenue losses, especially for countries with a relatively high intratrade share in their global trade (e.g., Jordan). However, these revenue losses might be offset by tariff revenue generated from increased imports resulting from tariff reductions and lower import prices, provided that other man-made trade barriers in many Arab countries are removed. The extent to which new revenues will offset customs revenue loss will depend primarily on internal tax reforms: the introduction of broad-based consumption taxes, such as the VAT in Tunisia and Morocco and the excise tax in Egypt and Jordan.

Deepening Integration among GAFTA Countries

So far, GAFTA has been limited to regional liberalization of merchandise trade. This effort at regional integration alone is not sufficient to ensure a more credible path for attainment of further domestic market efficiency gains allowing GAFTA member countries to face greater competition on world markets. There is a need to extend regional liberalization to the areas of trade in services and services-related movement of natural persons. Regional cooperation for harmonization and mutual recognition of technical regulations and product standards can also enhance the gains from GAFTA. Finally, ensuring coherence between the GAFTA and the Euro-Mediterranean FTAs through incorporation in GAFTA of the binding rules and various policy harmonization initiatives that are included in the EMAs would help GAFTA countries confront the rising competition from emerging world exporters in Asia and Eastern Europe.

Regional Options for Liberalizing Trade in Services

The absence of provisions for free movement of services and the right of establishment in GAFTA reduces the benefits of the agreement, given that services trade is generally complementary to merchandise trade. In fact, there is no single import or export transaction that does not involve one type of service or another (financial services, insurance, shipping, and so on). GAFTA countries that are WTO members have also done little to open their services markets through commitments within the GATS. Extending the agreement for regional liberalization to services trade is a critical option to attract investment, not only from within GAFTA countries but also from non-member countries.

Data on trade in commercial services in GAFTA countries show that they are not significant exporters or importers in world trade. Only Egypt ranks among the world's leading exporters—coming in at 29th (WTO 1998a). Among the leading importers, Saudi Arabia is ranked 29th, followed by Egypt at 35th. At the regional level, intraregional shares in total trade in commercial services have been relatively larger than for merchandise trade, reflecting the need for proximity in services delivery and preferential treatment for Arab services-related investment (table 10.5). Available data on the composition of intraregional trade in commercial services reveal that travel and tourism is the most important service exported by Egypt, Morocco, Syria, Tunisia, and UAE to GAFTA countries, followed by transportation and insurance. Business and financial services (excluding insurance) rank a distant third.

Barriers to trade in services in GAFTA countries are clearly important. Several country studies have showed that domestic distortions inhibiting export expansion in MENA countries reside in the inefficient regulation and lack of competition which generate costly and low quality services (World Bank 1995b; chap. 6 in this volume). This translates into higher insurance premiums and high port service costs as well as low-quality transport and lack of storage facilities. A regional agreement which allows free entry into services activities should help domestic services companies to expand to regional markets before venturing into the more competitive world markets.

Transportation Services

Trade in transportation services should lie at the heart of intraregional efforts to facilitate merchandise trade among GAFTA countries. Maritime transport remains by far the principal means of intraregional transport of goods, although the rate of growth of cargo transport both by air and by road has been faster

TABLE 10.5 Comparative Shares of Intraregional Trade in Merchandise and Services for Selected GAFTA Member Countries 1997

	Egypt		Morocco		Tunisia	
	Goods	Services*	Goods	Services*	Goods	Services*
World Exports/receipts ($ million)	3921.0	9651.0	4659.0	1886.0	5559.0	2552.0
Intra-GAFTA Exports/receipts ($ million)	496.0	1604.0	296.0	151.8	422.0	317.7
Share of Intra-GAFTA Exports (%)	12.6	16.6	6.4	8.0	7.6	12.5
World Imports/payments ($ million)	13020.0	7154.0	8262.0	1459.0	7750.0	1056.0
Intra-GAFTA Imports/payments ($ million)	692.0	846.0	891.0	95.0	505.0	96.0
Share of Intra-GAFTA imports (%)	5.3	11.8	10.8	6.5	6.5	9.1

* Commercial Services.

Source: For merchandise trade, International Monetary Fund, *Direction of Trade Statistics*; for commercial services statistics, Central Banks of Egypt, Morocco, and Tunisia.

during the recent years. A regional agreement on common shipping policy principles would foster competition and improve the quality of transport services to producers. Shipping companies surveyed in selected GAFTA countries (Morocco, Egypt, Lebanon) identify three crucial elements to be incorporated in a regional agreement: commitments to reduce measures either favoring the use of national carriers, or restricting/regulating access to port and port services; reduction of abusive tariffs for transshipment and unjustifiable liability claims by customs; and simplification of cumbersome administrative and port procedures.

Land transportation services are a very important cross-border mode of passenger and freight transport in the GAFTA countries. This is due to the number of borders in the MENA region and the increasing passenger transport across the frontiers as a result of the high movement of migrant labor. However, the regulatory regime for road transport is highly restrictive in the GAFTA countries. For instance, cross-border freight transport returning with cargo is not allowed by most of the GAFTA countries. Internal cabotage is also not allowed in virtually all the GAFTA countries. Hence, there is a need for a regional agreement that involves some harmonization of transit charges as well as elimination of excessive tariffs that increase the administrative cost of trade in GAFTA countries. In addition, fostering competition through allowing progressive cabotage services for passenger and freight transportation would increase the contestability of markets and improve service quality.

Financial Services

Another crucial area is financial services. There should be some harmonization of banking and insurance regulations and the provision for the right of establishment. There is relatively little integration among the financial institutions in the GAFTA countries, although it is more significant in banking activities. However, there are wide asymmetries in GAFTA financial services markets. This is reflected in the large gap between the unilateral liberalization of financial services that has been pursued in the context of structural adjustment programs and the commitments made by GAFTA countries under the GATS in financial services. For instance, Egypt, the most advanced country in liberalizing its financial sector, imposes the right to apply economic needs tests or other discretionary procedures before allowing new entry in this sector. The commitments of other GAFTA members are more restrictive, reflecting the half-hearted commitment by GAFTA countries to multilateral liberalization.

The right of establishment for national banks on a preferential basis in each others' markets could bring additional efficiency gains to GAFTA, especially by eliminating the highly concentrated market structure and oligopolistic practices. However, as domestic financial institutions in most of the GAFTA countries have comparable high operating costs, with comparable technology and innovations, the real efficiency gains would come from further integrating domestic financial markets into the world financial markets in order to facilitate capital and technological flows into the region.

Some harmonization efforts among the member states of the Arab Monetary Fund (a regional financial and development institution established by the states of the Arab League in 1977) have been undertaken in the banking regulation area. These have led to the establishment of the Arab Trade Financing Program (ATFP). This regional trade financing scheme refinances export and import credits for intra-Arab trade in goods excluding crude oil. More recently, a network of national commercial banks launched an intra-regional bank to find new operational mechanisms to promote intraregional trade. The Arab Monetary Fund has been hosting a regional group for banking supervision made up of heads of prudential supervision in the Arab Central Banks. The group is a regional advisory body for the GAFTA Central Banks to suggest prudential rules and requirements, and supervision methods for both national banks and cross-border activities, consistent with the core principles of the Basle Committee. It would be useful for coordination in financial services to be extended to certain basic management principles for financial intermediaries, including standards of accounting and auditing, compatibility of systems, network linkages, user rules and/or rate of commission. Little work has been done by GAFTA countries in this area.

Intraregional Mobility of Professional and Technical Labor

For many GAFTA countries, labor services are the mainstay of their service exports. The movement of labor is in fact inseparable from the content of services itself. Equally important are the temporary movements of persons that complement and facilitate both merchandise and services trade among GAFTA countries. Surveys of firms in MENA countries generally perceive direct personal contacts, business meetings, and participation in regional exhibitions as the main channels to cultivate business links in the MENA region. From the viewpoint of efficiency, free movement of skilled labor has become an efficiency-enhancing factor of production for many construction, restoration, and repair services. In the development of computer applications, movement of software consultants may be a precondition for the delivery of computer software (Devlin and Page 1999).

Cooperation among GAFTA countries to promote professional/technical labor mobility in the context of a FTA that removes restrictions on the temporary admission of this skilled labor is desirable. Such an agreement would allow growing sophisticated services in the GAFTA markets to develop their export capacity in regional markets. Some important measures for freer mobility of professional and skilled labor in the context of GAFTA include harmonization (recognition) of professional certification standards, e.g., that the professional qualifications of doctors trained and certified in member countries are sufficient for them to practice. Other measures are related to easing the process of granting visa and work permits for temporary movement of corporate personnel, engineers, architects, accountants, lawyers, and computer programmers.

Technical Regulations, Standards, and Customs Procedures

Technical regulations and mandatory standards intended to protect human health and the environment can become serious barriers to trade. The duplication of testing and certification requirements for imported products that may already be subject to equivalent controls in the exporting country imply additional compliance costs for exporting firms and thus higher prices to consumers in the importing market. Similarly, redundant customs procedures and red tape that may be imposed on both for exporters and importers impose additional costs on firms in the forms of wasted time and financial resources (see chap. 8).

A regional agreement on mutual recognition of national standards in areas involving mandatory standards or regulations, especially for foodstuffs, pharmaceuticals, and consumer products, is required. Elimination of the need to determine whether national standards have been met through testing and certification in importing countries would facilitate intraregional trade and arbitrage by allowing any purchaser to choose his supplier freely from within the free trade area. Another crucial area is to pursue harmonization among GAFTA countries of customs procedures and related documentary requirements, with a main objective being to accept self-declaration such as the EU's Single Administrative Document. If accompanied by simplification, harmonization can do much to reduce the very heavy administrative costs of trade in the GAFTA countries.

Ensuring Coherence between GAFTA and the Euro-Med FTAs

EU association agreements with Arab countries are expected to have important implications for the trading prospects of GAFTA. A key aspect of these agreements is that, on the one hand, they enable Arab signatory countries to commit themselves to a harmonization process of their domestic laws and standards with international (EU) norms, thereby making it easier for domestic producers to penetrate foreign markets. On the other hand, the EU is committed to the provision of financial assistance for the adjustment costs resulting from the FTAs. The expected payoffs of such FTAs with the EU include an improvement in productivity and greater specialization in the production of higher value-added industrial products. This is also a way to ensure that Arab Southern Mediterranean countries benefit from the growth and income generation effects of global liberalization. As far as GAFTA is concerned, it is expected that the EU Association Agreements would support the Arab FTA through cumulation for rules of origin purposes of products manufactured in any of the Arab FTA members as well as the EU. This may contribute to creating backward and forward linkages between Arab countries and usher in expansion of Arab IIT (Hoekman 1998b).

There have been counter-arguments, however. It has been noted that preferential trade liberalization is a second best option and that "locking in" policy commitments for domestic market access with the WTO and the adoption of international standards and norms rather than the EU ones is superior. Countries take more advantage from the world markets at large than from preferential trade liberalization. Nevertheless, if one examines the learning-by-doing of export-oriented industries in the Southeast Asian countries, it can be seen that these generally started by aligning their production standards to one major foreign market (Japan) for access before learning to adapt production to international norms.

An area in which the Euro-Med FTAs are particularly crucial is the harmonization of domestic economic policies, particularly the alignment of national production standards, customs procedures, and competition policy of Arab Mediterranean countries with those of the EU. The agreements commit the Arab Mediterranean countries to adopt EU competition laws at the end of a transition period. The EMAs could act as a binding mechanism for GAFTA members, inducing greater credibility in the implementation of a full-fledged GAFTA.

Summary and Conclusion

This chapter has examined the provisions of the Arab League Executive Program establishing the GAFTA and the possible effects of such a regional trading arrangement. In assessing the elements of the agreement, forces that are likely to stimulate the prospects for intraregional trade expansion are identified. First, the agreed Executive Program involves for the first time commitments by Arab countries to come forward with a complete preferential scheme covering most products to be liberalized from tariff and most NTBs within ten years. Such trade liberalization would enhance competitiveness of manufactured products by materials that are produced in the Arab region.

Similarities in industrial structure in Arab countries as a result of similar factor endowments (oil, oil products, and labor) suggest that the spread of manufacturing and growing intra-industry specialization would provide a stimulus to regional IIT expansion. As tariff levels and NTBs are still quite high for most Arab countries—with the exception of the GCC—liberalization of Arab trade could have a significant trade creation effect, even though trade diversion away from lower-cost, more-efficient sources outside the region may occur. However, overall, as the relatively more diversified Arab countries seek to take advantage of the new global trading opportunities provided through WTO membership (as Arab countries are increasingly becoming members), external tariff levels will also come down, leading to more trade creation.

However, GAFTA addresses regional liberalization of merchandise trade only. This is not sufficient to ensure that GAFTA member countries will be able to confront the competition on world markets. Deeper integration is required (see box 10.1). First, there is a need to extend liberalization to the areas of services (e.g., transport services, financial services), service-related movement of natural persons (temporary movement of skilled labor), and mutual recognition of regulatory regimes relating to mandatory standards—for product safety, professional certification, prudential regulation, and so on—if member countries are to maximize gains from GAFTA.

The MENA region as a whole has long been disengaged from integration with the world economy. Past isolation from broader trends in the world economy has resulted in the region falling behind in increasingly competitive world markets. The renewed interest in pursuing the regional option should help the Arab countries catch up with the competition. Overall, deeper integration built on the innovations in the Uruguay Round agreements (particularly in services) offers a more credible path toward attaining successful regional trade liberalization in the MENA region relative to previous regionalism.

Finally, efforts should be made to ensure coherence between GAFTA and the Euro-Mediterranean FTAs. The EMAs provide a binding mechanism for Arab Southern Mediterranean countries to commit to the harmonization of domestic economic policies—particularly the alignment of national competition policy, product standards, customs procedures, and subsidies—with those of the EU. If this occurs, thereby reducing the costs of trade, there will be spillover effects on GAFTA as the costs of intra-GAFTA trade fall as well. The EMAs should also support GAFTA through cumulation for rules of origin purposes, creating additional linkages between Arab countries and the EU.

BOX 10.1 A Scenario for Deep Integration under GAFTA

GAFTA STATUS QUO

Merchandise Trade Liberalization

- Industrial and Agricultural Products: 10 percent of tariff and para-tariff reduction per year (starting 1998).
- Preferential Rules of Origin: 40 percent of GAFTA value added requirement.
- Nontariff Measures Reduction.
  - List of prohibited products.
- Safeguards Measures include:
  - Seasonal calendar for agricultural products.
  - Exceptions for certain industrial products from tariff and para-tariff reduction scheme, for not more than four years.
- Private sector monitoring of GAFTA implementations (Union of Arab Chambers of Commerce).

Services Trade Liberalization

(No provisions in GAFTA).

DEEPER INTEGRATION SCENARIO

Merchandise Trade Liberalization

- Harmonization of national standards, MRAs for conformity assessment.
- Trade facilitation in harmonizing customs formalities, expeditions visas – multiple entry visas for professionals.

Services and Investment Liberalization

- Right of Establishment and free movement of professionals and skilled labor in crucial sectors.
  - Maritime Transportation.
  - Financial Services.
  - Business related services (Tourism, Computer, etc.).
- Incorporation of the 1982 Agreement on the free movement of capital under GAFTA.

Institutional Structure

- Creation of an Independent Secretariat with professionals and independent budget. Main function includes:
  - Designing, advising, and overseeing the elements of the GAFTA.
- Linking GAFTA to other regional FTAs (ensuring coherence in the level and magnitude of liberalization between GAFTA and the other regional and bilateral FTAs).
  - EMAs.
  - GCC.
  - UMA.
  - Bilateral Free Trade Areas between Arab countries.
- Greater coherence between GAFTA commitments and the members' commitments to the WTO.
  - More effective GAFTA dispute settlement mechanism that might be open to the private sector as well as government entities.

NOTES

1. The fourteen member states that signed the Greater Arab FTA are Bahrain, Egypt, Iraq, Jordan, Kuwait, Lebanon, Libya, Morocco, Oman, Qatar, Saudi Arabia, Syria, Tunisia, and UAE. The six remaining member states (Algeria, Djibouti, The Comoros Islands, Mauritania, Sudan, and Yemen) have not ratified the agreement yet. Palestine also signed the GAFTA, but is excluded from this analysis as it has a customs union with Israel and does not have free trade movement with the other GAFTA members.

2. The four initial member countries were Egypt, Iraq, Jordan, and Syria. Libya, Mauritania, and the People's Democratic Republic of Yemen joined later.

3. Argentina, Brazil, Paraguay, and Uruguay.

4. Zarrouk computed increases in intratrade as percent of GDP and compared them with increases in two other trade shares, external and total trade as a percent of GDP for two selected periods before and after the agreements were signed. These measures have been used as a test for the effects of trade policy on a country's trade pattern.

5. See Bernard Hoekman, "The WTO, the EU and the Arab World: Trade Policy Priorities and Pitfalls," in Nemat Shafik (ed.), *Prospects for Middle Eastern and North African Economies.* London: Macmillan Press, 1998.

6. Descriptions of the HS-Chapters used in table 10.4 are as follows:

HS-Chapter	Description	HS-Chapter	Description
1-5	Live animals, meat, fish	50-63	Textiles and clothing
6-14	Vegetables and fresh fruit	68-71	Articles of stone, cement, ceramic products
15-24	Prepared foodstuffs excluding alcoholic beverages	72-83	Articles of base metal
25-27	Mineral products	84-85	Machinery and mechanical appliances
28-40	Chemicals, plastics and articles thereof	86-89	Vehicles and transport equipment
41-63, 64-67	Leather, footwear, travel goods	90-92	Precision instruments and
44-48	Pulp and wood, paper products	93-97	Miscellaneous manufactures
49	Printed books, new papers		

7. The GAFTA countries that are WTO members are Bahrain, Egypt, Kuwait, Mauritania, Morocco, Qatar, Tunisia, and UAE. Those seeking membership are Jordan, Oman, Saudi Arabia, and Sudan.

8. The Agreement on the Facilitation of Transit and Transshipment among Arab Countries was concluded in 1978 by four states: Egypt, Iraq, Jordan, and Kuwait.

9. The rather narrow definition of GAFTA intraregional integration in the EMAs (such as the EU with Tunisia) comprises Maghreb countries only, not Mediterranean.

CHAPTER 11

Benefiting from WTO Accession and Membership

Bernard Hoekman and Jayanta Roy

Almost all countries in the MENA region have been reforming their foreign trade and domestic investment regimes to make the policy environment more conducive to fuller integration into the world economy. Despite these efforts, the extent of integration remains relatively low. One dimension of this lag is reflected in the limited extent to which MENA countries participate pro-actively in the multilateral trading system, particularly the WTO, the successor of the General Agreement on Tariffs and Trade (GATT). Although many countries in the MENA region are WTO members (Bahrain, Egypt, Israel, Kuwait, Morocco, Qatar, Tunisia, and UAE), many are not. Algeria, Jordan, Oman, and Saudi Arabia are in the process of acceding, while Iraq, Lebanon, Libya, Syria, and Yemen have yet to launch a bid for membership.

The creation of the WTO in 1994 with its three constituent elements—a new and expanded set of GATT disciplines, a General Agreement on Trade in Services, and an agreement on TRIPs—has major implications for both members and nonmembers. All countries in the MENA region will be affected by the liberalization of markets agreed to in the Uruguay Round and by the negotiations that are scheduled to be launched in 2000. In addition, members and countries that have yet to accede are confronted with numerous implementation requirements, many of which involve institutional reform and strengthening and many of which require significant financial resources if they are to be implemented in a manner that maximizes the positive development impact on the economy.

This chapter focuses primarily on the policy and institutional implications of WTO membership and accession for MENA economies. We discuss the mechanisms through which the benefits of membership can be maximized and the process of accession simplified.[1] Very much depends in this connection on the objectives of the governments concerned. The WTO is an instrument of international cooperation between (mostly) sovereign states. The objective is to limit the potential for governments to impose negative externalities upon other countries when implementing trade policies. The focus of attention of the WTO is therefore on the effect of national policies on other countries, not on the effect of a government's policies on its own economy. We argue that any assessment of WTO rules and disciplines from the perspective of a national government should focus on its internal implications. In order to fully benefit from membership (and accession), governments should use the WTO as a mechanism to support the implementation of a domestic policy mix that supports export-oriented production and attracts investment into activities in which the country has a comparative advantage. At the same time, domestic institutions must be created and supported that allow a government to be a player in the WTO club and defend its interests and market access rights.

After a brief summary of the main elements of the WTO, we relate the status quo in MENA countries to the WTO's requirements, providing an indication of how "far away" these countries are on average from multilateral standards of good practice. We then discuss the potential benefits of WTO membership and accession and what can be done to realize these benefits.

Basic WTO Rules and Disciplines

The implications of the WTO can be divided into four parts: the three multilateral agreements (GATT, GATS, and TRIPs), and their enforcement through consultation, transparency, and dispute settlement mechanisms. The three substantive agreements (treaties) have both institutional and policy implications.[2]

The GATT requires that trade policies and their implementation be nondiscriminatory. The use of QRs is in principle prohibited. WTO members may only use tariffs to restrict imports of agricultural products, and all such tariffs are bound.[3] Governments are subject to requirements relating to reduction of support granted to agricultural production and export subsidies, if any. Developing countries that have a per capita GNP above $1,000 become subject to GATT's prohibition on export subsidies. All trade-related investment measures (TRIMs) such as local content requirements that violate GATT's national treatment principle or its prohibition on QRs must be removed. The WTO's rules relating to product standards and SPS measures require that new regulations and conformity assessment procedures be based on international standards. The basis for customs valuation is to be the importer's invoice (transaction value).

Under the GATS, nondiscrimination principles also extend to measures affecting trade in services. While MFN is a general obligation, the sectoral coverage of national treatment and market access obligations is determined by country schedules. Six types of market access restrictions are in principle prohibited under GATS. These consist of limitations on (i) the number of service suppliers allowed, (ii) the value of transactions or assets; (iii) the total quantity of service output, (iv) the number of natural persons that may be employed, (v) the type of legal entity through which a service supplier is permitted to supply a service (e.g., branches vs. subsidiaries for banking), and (vi) participation of foreign capital in terms of a maximum percentage limit of foreign shareholding or the absolute value of foreign investment. National treatment is defined as treatment no less favorable than that accorded to like domestic services and service providers.[4] Each GATS member decides (negotiates) which service sectors will be subject to market access and national treatment disciplines, and what measures will be kept in place for that sector that violate market access and/or national treatment, respectively.

The TRIPs agreement requires WTO members to protect six types of intellectual property, including trademarks (to last at least 7 years; equal treatment to be given to service and trade marks; prohibition on compulsory licensing), geographical indications (prohibition on indications that mislead or constitute "unfair" competition), industrial designs (duration of protection of new and original designs to be at least 10 years; no protection required for designs dictated essentially by technical or functional considerations), and layout designs of integrated circuits (duration of protection at least ten years; protection to extend to products embodying layout design infringements; allowance of compulsory licensing). In the area of copyright, members are required to comply with most of the substantive provisions of the 1971 Berne Convention. Computer software is to be protected as a literary work under the Berne Convention. Copyright protection is to last for at least 50 years. Criminal procedures and penalties are to be applicable to copyright abuses (piracy) on a commercial scale. Last but not least, countries must comply with the substantive provisions of the 1967 Paris Convention on patents. Patent protection is to be provided for almost all inventions and is to be of at least 20 years duration after the date of filing.

Members must ensure that enforcement procedures are available under their national laws, permitting effective action against any act of infringement of IP rights. There are provisions on evidence supporting claims of violation of IP rights, injunctions, damages, right of information, indemnification of defendants, and existence of effective provisional measures to prevent an infringement of any IPR from occurring, as well as procedures to enable right holders suspecting the importation of counterfeit trademark or pirated copyright goods to lodge an application for the suspension of importation. Penalties in cases of willful trademark counterfeiting or copyright piracy on a commercial scale must include imprisonment and/or fines sufficiently large to constitute an effective deterrent.

In addition to substantive obligations, there are many notification and other transparency requirements, all of which require the existence of appropriate bodies or agencies that have the responsibility of satisfying them. All state trading enterprises must be notified to the Council for Trade in Goods, independent of whether or not imports or exports occurred. The introduction of or any changes in import restrictions justified for balance-of-payments purposes or any changes in the time schedules for the removal of such measures must be reported to the WTO. A consolidated notification, including all changes in laws, regulations, policy statements, or public notices, must be provided each year. All changes in sanitary or phytosanitary measures must be notified. Technical regulations (whether sanitary or product standards more generally) that diverge from international standards and have a potential significant effect on trade flows must be notified, with the added requirement of indicating the objective and rationale of the proposed regulation. The same applies to conformity assessment procedures that are not in accordance with relevant guides and recommendations issued by international standardizing bodies. Technical regulations of local governments on the level directly below that of the central government that diverge from international standards must also be notified. Members that maintain import-licensing procedures or change them must notify the relevant committee within sixty days of publication. All subsidy programs must be notified, with adequate information provided to allow other members to evaluate their trade effects and to understand their operation.

Enquiry points must be created with the responsibility for answering questions and providing relevant documents regarding SPS measures adopted or proposed, control and inspection procedures, production and quarantine treatment, pesticide tolerance, and food additive approval procedures. An enquiry point must also exist to deal with similar questions regarding technical regulations and product conformity assessment procedures that are carried out within the territory of a member by central or local government bodies. Yet another enquiry point must provide specific information to WTO members, upon request, on all relevant measures of general application which pertain to or affect the operation of the GATS.

There are many requirements concerning the procedures to be followed with respect to the imposition of contingent protection (safeguards, countervailing subsidized imports, and antidumping). Space constraints prohibit even a summary, but the implications for the institutions that implement such mechanisms are significant. Technically competent and trained personnel are required to administer the relevant laws. Methodics and manuals should be developed to ensure consistent application and interpretation of legal provisions and the various substantive criteria that must be satisfied. Measures relating to qualification requirements and procedures, technical standards, and licensing requirements may not unnecessarily restrict trade in services. Furthermore, they should be based on objective and transparent criteria, such as competence and the ability to supply the service, and not be more burdensome than necessary to ensure the quality of the service.

Implications for the Representative MENA Country

This brief and very incomplete survey of the WTO's rules and requirements is sufficient to illustrate that membership (or accession) will have major implications for the representative country in the region. In the past, many of the GATT disciplines were not applicable to developing countries as the rules were either voluntary or could be easily circumvented through invocation of loopholes such as the balance of payments provision (Art. XVIIIB). With the creation of the WTO, this has changed significantly. Almost all of the voluntary so-called Tokyo Round codes of conduct have been multilateralized: under the WTO, they apply to all members. There is also less of a willingness to tolerate excessive use (abuse) of the various loopholes in the WTO. Initially many of the "new" WTO disciplines did not apply in full force to developing countries because various transition periods were granted. Many of these transition periods will begin to expire in 2000. Among the WTO disciplines likely to have significant implications are a ban on local content programs and similar TRIMs, and requirements to enforce IPRs, use international standards, convert quotas to tariffs (e.g., in agriculture), and base customs valuation on transactions values (invoices).

As has been discussed at some length in many of the contributions to this volume (see, for example, chaps. 6, 7, and 8), trade costs created by regulatory regimes and barriers are quite high in many MENA countries. In some instances, existing trade policies and implementing procedures are not consistent with WTO requirements, implying that initiatives must be taken to converge towards what must be done under the WTO. Any lack of transparency in trade policy implementation (e.g., as reflected in the mix of tariffs, surcharges, and other fees; the way the import licensing regime operates; any apparent arbitrariness of customs valuation, etc.) can be expected to come under closer scrutiny, as will the conformity with substantive and procedural disciplines with respect to the application of product standards, the use of subsidies, and safeguard mechanisms.

Much will have to be done by MENA countries to make existing policies fully consistent with WTO rules. This is true for countries that were founding members of the WTO—most were not in compliance with many of the rules and disciplines because these were voluntary in the past—as well as nonmembers that are or will be seeking accession. There is less of a difference in terms of the burden of adjustment to the new WTO regime across members and nonmembers than might be expected.

Some examples are informative. Enforcement of mandatory product standards in MENA countries may require import licenses for products subject to standards. These are often only granted once products have been approved by the relevant ministry/agency. Such approval often requires inspection of the goods at customs, which raises costs to importers, delays customs clearance, and subjects importers to unnecessary uncertainty. The WTO encourages trade facilitation by the acceptance of certification by specialized foreign testing agencies and internationally recognized trademarks, as well as the adoption or recognition of international standards. Nonrecognition of internationally known certification bodies or international standards is not only contrary to the spirit of the WTO, it raises costs for importers and consumers. It also reduces the incentives for MENA enterprises to employ the services of certification entities and increase their awareness of the importance of quality standards in international trade. Current practices and procedures open a number of MENA countries up to claims that standards are being used as technical barriers to trade.[5]

Administrative procedures and requirements associated with importing are often burdensome, increasing the cost of imports substantially and thereby lowering the competitiveness of MENA firms on world markets. Many government bodies are involved in the import process, either collecting taxes or import duties or authorizing the release of imports. The numerous administrative controls can delay customs clearance by anything from a few days to several weeks. Valuation procedures in particular give rise to substantial uncertainty on the part of importers, who have an incentive to increase the value of goods for customs purposes. Customs officials in many MENA countries appear to be generally suspicious of invoice values, relying on price lists and declared values of "bona fide" importers of particular goods to determine the value of goods. The enforcement of import bans on products that are prohibited because of religious and moral reasons (pork, alcohol, and certain types of printed matter and video) also causes a significant burden on trade as it frequently entails the inspection of all consignments.

Clearly there is a lot to be done. What is required involves not just changes in policies but also changes in culture and strengthening of institutions. The costs associated with implementation of WTO requirements in several areas will be significant, as there will be a great need for comprehensive changes in business practices requiring large scale training, monitoring, and senior level management supervision. The magnitude of these costs must be determined on a case-by-case basis. Doing so is important in order to ensure that adequate resources are allocated to the required tasks. As noted by Finger and Schuler (1999), implementation of WTO commitments by developing countries has become a matter of concern for many WTO members because this can be very burdensome. They estimate that an entire year's development budget would be required in many of the least developed countries in order to implement WTO agreements on Customs Valuation and TRIPS in a manner that contributes to development. As noted by Finger and Schuler, the significant costs associated with attaining "WTO consistency" may imply that from a development perspective priority should not be given to implementation of WTO provisions. In many least developed countries, scarce resources may be better devoted to building infrastructure or improving public education. Most countries in the MENA region, however, have income levels that make it unlikely that financial resource constraints prohibit implementation of WTO agreements.

The Potential Benefits of WTO Membership

The net benefits of WTO membership are more difficult to quantify with any exactness than the costs of implementation. While on average the changes that are required by the WTO can be expected to have a high payoff, especially if they are designed to go beyond WTO consistency only to achieve development objectives, much depends in this connection on the "quality" of the investments that are made by each government to allow them to maximize the benefits of membership.

The WTO national treatment and MFN rules help ensure that resources will be allocated and used efficiently by requiring that foreign and national products are treated equally with respect to measures of indirect taxation and that all foreign products are subject to the same policies. The same outcome arises as a result of another key WTO principle: that the primary instrument of trade policy should be the tariff. This benefits a country because a tariff can be applied uniformly against all foreign firms, allowing the most efficient foreign producers to supply the market. Moreover, tariffs raise revenue for the government budget, while quotas do not. Ensuring that laws and regulations are consistent with WTO requirements may help governments in adopting good practices, policies, and institutions that are consistent with those found in countries that have successfully integrated into the world economy, thereby facilitating trade and helping to sustain economic growth.

As WTO members, countries are assured of receiving nondiscriminatory treatment in export markets. Although in general most countries receive MFN treatment with respect to tariffs, this is not guaranteed for nonmembers, introducing an element of uncertainty regarding market access conditions that may be detrimental to export development. WTO members can use multilateral dispute settlement mechanisms to enforce the nondiscrimination principle and other

WTO rules. This is a vital benefit of the WTO system as it gives small states with no power the ability to contest actions by large players. As the large countries have a strong stake in the functioning of the system, they generally abide by WTO rulings.

Indirect benefits may be as substantial than the direct benefits, if not more so. Investment, whether domestic or foreign, is stimulated by a stable and open policy environment under which the rules of the game are transparent and uncertainty regarding possible future policy changes is reduced as much as possible. To the extent that such investment involves production for export or relies upon access to international markets for imports of intermediate inputs and capital equipment, the WTO's rules and dispute settlement mechanisms can help assure investors that the policy regime in a country will remain open. Such assurances are particularly important for economies where the credibility of the policy regime is limited—even if governments pursue open trade and investment policies. This reduces the willingness of entrepreneurs to consider investments or, alternatively, increases the risk premiums that are imposed by international financial markets. The WTO as an institution can act as a "policy anchor" that can do much to both help attract investment and reduce the cost of capital (Francois 1997). The initial accession process and the periodic rounds of multilateral negotiations offer governments opportunities and additional arguments to pursue the domestic policy reforms that they wish to achieve in any event. This can be a substantial benefit if there are domestic interest groups that oppose reform or that support policies that are not optimal from a national welfare perspective. Multilateral surveillance of national policies for WTO consistency can also help move reforms forward and keep them on track.

A key determinant of the benefits of membership stem from the possibility that the WTO offers to governments to bind trade policies, i.e., to commit publicly to a certain trade regime. This takes the form of maximum tariff ceilings ("bindings") and specific commitments on market access and national treatment for service sectors. This credibility role of the WTO is of course a function of the depth of the commitments that are made. The greater the magnitude of the commitments (tariff bindings and the sectoral coverage of service commitments under the GATS), the greater the credibility effect. Indeed, without far-reaching bindings of policy, the WTO's impact will be limited. Transparency and credibility are also bolstered through the careful scrutiny countries undergo when acceding and periodically thereafter through what is called a Trade Policy Review. The cleaner a country's report card that emerges from a Trade Policy Review process, the more valuable the report as a potential marketing tool for the government in attracting FDI. And the more problems that are identified, the more useful the report may be to reform-minded interest groups in mobilizing support for changes in the status quo.

Realizing the Benefits: Implementation Challenges

Accession to and membership in the WTO offers a unique opportunity for governments to consolidate and carry forward trade liberalization policies and to sensitize domestic industries to the opportunities that exist for exporting to world markets. Of particular importance in this connection is the use of WTO membership to remove existing impediments to trade in order to ensure rapid clearance of imported goods, especially those that are inputs into the production of exportables, foster a stronger export mentality among domestic producers of "non-traditional" goods, and develop an export strategy. Without a diversified export industry, the practical relevance of the market access dimension of the WTO will be limited. A dynamic and fast growing economy requires a rapid increase in imports of the intermediate inputs that are essential for technological upgrading and diversification of the economy's industrial base. Such imports must be paid for by exports. Non-oil-related exports will have to bear the brunt of the marginal increase required, as oil-related exports are to a large extent subject to exogenous forces.

Development of a strong nontraditional export base is a major challenge. In many MENA countries, the development strategies that have been pursued in recent years have promoted a greater role for the private sector (including both domestic and foreign investors). The missing links are making the trade regime more efficient, more transparent, and more liberal; they create or strengthen existing institutions to promote and support trade and, for oil exporters, initiate a nation-wide campaign to step up growth in non-oil exports. WTO membership can help on all these dimensions. This in turn requires the establishment of an institutional capacity to enable governments to be well-informed regarding ongoing developments in major markets and on trade policy issues, to ensure that WTO obligations and rules are implemented in a way that helps achieve national economic development objectives, to actively defend national interests on issues that directly affect trade through WTO consultation and dispute settlement mechanisms, and to contribute substantively to debates on issues that have a more general impact on the functioning of the multilateral trading system.

A minimum necessary condition to achieve these objectives is the ability to participate in the meetings of the various Councils that administer the GATT, GATS, TRIPs, the Trade Policy Review Body, and the dispute settlement body (DSB). With the expansion of the multilateral trading system to services and TRIPs, the institutionalization of the multilateral surveillance of trade policies in the Trade Policy Review Body, and the further formalization of dispute settlement, there is a greater need for each member to have permanent representation in Geneva to monitor developments, present its views, and defend its rights. A number of developing countries do not maintain a mission in Geneva. Of those that do, many do not have anyone who focuses solely on GATT matters. Instead, the brief of the members of the mission is to deal with the myriad international organizations that are located in Geneva (e.g., the UN High Commissioner for Refugees, the World Health Organization, ISO, etc.).[6]

Membership in the WTO will have little effect unless countries are active participants. This requires the Ministry of Trade or Commerce to ensure that relevant information flows to and from the appropriate entities within the government and that the institutional capacity exists (is created) to be able to defend the nations interests (and those of the multilateral trading system more generally). In addition, there will be a need to cooperate with like-minded countries, collect information from—and interact with—the private sector, and to develop institutions that are responsible for monitoring and analyzing the economic effects of the governments trade-related policies.

A Central Government Apex Body: The Trade Policy Department

To play an effective and influential role in the WTO, positions should be clearly enunciated and well reasoned. This in turn requires a domestic process of policy formulation and preparation and submission of documentation that is streamlined with a clear demarcation of responsibilities between the Trade Ministry, the representative office in Geneva, and other competent ministries and affected bodies in the capital. In many countries in the region, arrangement for dealing with WTO matters are characterized by unclear lines of communication, inadequate systems for consultation of stakeholders, and a general lack of resources. If a country is to become an active user of the WTO, a strong secretariat function must be created in the Ministry of Trade or Commerce. For convenience, in what follows we shall use the term Trade Policy Department (TPD) to describe what is required. It should be emphasized that such a department is only one aspect of the institutions that should be developed and nurtured—it must be complemented by private sector consultative bodies and a "transparency institution." For purposes of discussion and clarity, the suggested organization of the TPD and its functions is developed in some detail. There are many variations possible on the template that is described.

The TPD should be headed by a Deputy Minister reporting directly to the Minister of Trade or Commerce (see fig. 11.1). The TPD should be responsible for operating the nation's representative office in Geneva, i.e., the nation's Permanent Representative to the WTO should report to the head of the TPD, not to the Foreign or other Ministry. The TPD should be entrusted with the task of interministerial coordination on all WTO-related issues, relying on the Permanent Representative for establishing and maintaining relationships with other WTO members and the WTO secretariat. The Geneva office requires clear instructions from the capital on the positions that should be taken in WTO meetings and must be able to channel information and briefings to the TPD, which in turn should transfer this to affected government bodies and other stakeholders.

The Geneva office should be large enough to allow participation in all major WTO committees and meetings. The office should present, promote, and defend national views on specific issues, seek the support of other major trading nations, and provide the TPD with regular information and reports on the positions taken by other WTO members. This broad mandate must be supplemented with a direct and constant interrelationship with TPD staff at headquarters. In this connection it is useful to develop a system through which officers are periodically rotated from the capital to Geneva and back. To ensure that the government has a strong and influential presence in Geneva, the office should have at least two professional TPD staff at the counselor or first secretary level in addition to the Ambassador.

An important function of the TPD is to act as the secretariat for an Interministerial Working Group (IMWG) to be created for all key topics where interministerial coordination is required. While the TPD should be responsible for the preparation of all papers that are to be submitted to WTO bodies, coordination and consultation with concerned ministries and agencies, as well as

FIGURE 11.1 Possible Structure of a Trade Policy Department

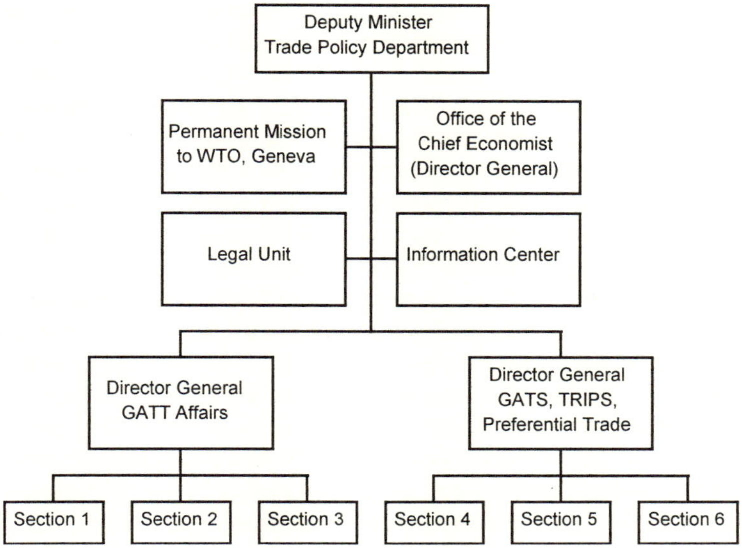

the private sector, is crucial. In many cases where the issue involves subjects of a technical nature that lie within the competence of other bodies, the TPD should request such entities to prepare position papers or factual reports, as required, providing the entities concerned with clear terms of reference prepared in consultation with the Geneva office. The TPD can also be made responsible for preparing economic analyses of policy issues as they arise, as well as the development of trade policy proposals more generally. In short, the TPD should be the primary locus of expertise on all subject matters relating to trade policy and the WTO.

The TPD will comprise a number of units. Some of these would have an advisory/support function and report to the Head of TPD, including an Economics Department, a Legal Advisory Unit, and an Information Center. Other units would have operational responsibilities and report to the Head of the TPD through two Director Generals. The Economics Department, led by a professional Chief Economist, should be responsible for preparing economic analyses of all key WTO issues as well as all trade policy initiatives. The Chief Economist and his staff would also provide economic input into the preparation of papers and reports relating to WTO issues where such input is appropriate. In order to help ensure that policy proposals take into account probable economic repercussions, the Chief Economist should be given a mandate to comment on all draft submissions to be made to the WTO, as well as trade policy initiatives more generally. This office would also be responsible for assisting and reacting to WTO Trade Policy Reviews, and be given responsibility for following "new" issues for which the WTO might establish rules in the future (e.g., competition or investment policy).

The Chief Economist and his staff should have access to commonly used tools for trade policy analysis such as the GTAP databases and general equilibrium simulation software, as well as the major on-line databases (such as the UN's COMTRADE). Given the paucity of well-qualified, analytical, policy-oriented economists in the civil service, a budget for retaining outside consultants to undertake specific research tasks and training on an ad hoc basis is necessary, especially when complex economic modeling is required. Such expertise is difficult to obtain in-house, and it is generally more cost-efficient to rely on out-sourcing of these tasks.

An Information Center can be given the task of streamlining information flows within the government on WTO-related issues, supporting the communications flow between the TPD and the Geneva Office, and providing access to the WTO, UN, and other global trade information networks. The information flows to be managed by the Center would comprise both text and statistical databases and include a link to the nation's statistical agencies to ensure that TPD staff have on-line access to national trade and national accounts statistics. A Legal Advisory unit is vital in assisting in the drafting of proposals to WTO committees and negotiating groups, preparing responses to queries and legal challenges from other members, and utilizing the WTO dispute settlement mechanism to prosecute cases.

A major function of the economic, legal, and information units is to support the operational departments in the TPD, as well as the Permanent Mission in Geneva. Each of these operational entities would be responsible for specific WTO subjects as well as the various non-WTO dossiers that have a trade-policy dimension (e.g., managing preferential trade relations). Each "section" or division would be charged with preparing background documentation for all IMWG meetings dealing with their respective subjects and ensuring that the required consultation with other concerned ministries/agencies and the private sector occurs. Section leaders should be assigned direct responsibility to prepare a consolidated government view on queries raised by WTO members on topics they cover. Operational units or sections must be managed by—and report to—senior officials, e.g., at the Director General level. Given the complexity of the subjects covered by the WTO, there is a need for division of responsibilities. One practical way of dividing these is to distinguish between GATT matters as opposed to issues arising under the GATS and TRIPs agreements. Each Director General must take a leadership role in the IMWG discussions, supported by staff that follows each of the specific topics on the agenda.

International Cooperation, Surveillance, and Domestic Consultation

The WTO is a complex organization that hosts hundreds of meetings on trade policy topics per year. Few countries will have the resources to be able to follow all topics and contribute to all meetings. One way of reducing the participation costs is to cooperate with other countries in attending meetings. This is a model that has been adopted by the Nordic countries, which not only share the burden of being represented at meetings by dividing the responsibility of attending meetings across member countries but also cooperate in developing common positions on substantive issues. A similar approach could be considered by Arab countries, given that many of these countries are active members of the Arab League and are engaged in a process of regional integration (GAFTA—see chap. 10).

A substantial burden on governments in terms of using and participating in the WTO process is collecting information on the trade policies of partner countries. To some extent, the Trade Policy Review Body provides a mechanism for keeping informed on what other WTO members are doing, but this is a very incomplete source of information as most countries are reviewed only every 4 to 6 years. It is important that governments rely on their private sector to act as part of surveillance mechanisms, encouraging firms to identify policies by trading partners that appear to violate WTO rules. For this to be effective, it is necessary that the private sector be well informed about what the rules are and that the government creates incentives for officials to listen and respond to complaints. This can be achieved through training and outreach programs and the creation of consultative mechanisms with the private sector and consumer organizations. The latter are vital if a nation is to be able to use the WTO dispute settlement mechanisms, as these groups must generate the information the government needs to defend national interests. Often, violations of the WTO are not contested by affected countries because individual firms lack the incentive to bring matters to the attention of their governments. Company staff involved in sales, forwarding, or intracompany trade may not have an interest in documenting and reporting trade restrictions or discriminatory policies. They may also find it difficult to determine whether a given measure constitutes a likely WTO violation—indeed, often they will be unaware of the rules of the WTO. Operational staff of trading enterprises may also have greater incentives to try to circumvent barriers by doing "whatever is necessary" than to "rock the boat" by complaining to their governments.

Another important factor restraining invocation of dispute settlement has been the cost to governments associated with bringing cases to the WTO. These costs, which are not only financial but also related to the scarcity of administrative resources, have constrained many developing countries in particular from using the system to their full advantage, which in turn is a factor that discourages enterprises from complaining.

The result of these various incentives is a collective action problem that leads to an inefficient outcome, both for individual firms and for the trading system as a whole. The problem is similar to that of the production of a public good where, without cooperation, under-provision is likely to result (Olson, 1965). Solutions to these information and enforcement problems should focus on increasing the incentive for firms to collect data and transfer this to the government to allow it to contest discriminatory policies. This could be done by reducing the costs of collecting such information by supporting the development of centralized information collection points (e.g., through chambers of commerce) and by increasing the incentive for government to pursue legitimate cases (e.g., by passing legislation that require governments to motivate decisions not to pursue cases).

Safeguard Instruments: Antidumping, Countervail, and Emergency Protection

The WTO makes allowance for a number of mechanisms through which members may impose tariffs in excess of tariff bindings (Finger 1998). These include actions to offset injurious dumping, to countervail the detrimental effects of foreign subsidy policies, to protect the balance of payments, and to protect domestic industries that have been injured by competition from imports more generally. In deciding whether to adopt any of these various mechanisms, it is important to fully understand the economic incentives confronting the various actors that are involved, as well as the administrative burdens that will be imposed on the government in satisfying the relevant WTO requirements in each area. Economic considerations and cross-country experience strongly suggests that some instruments are much more efficient and effective than others. In particular, antidumping is an instrument that can easily be captured by private business interests and has no economic rationale. Other instruments that are fully WTO-consistent exist that are less costly to the economy and ensure that the government retains control over its trade policy. The major example is safeguard protection to give an industry time to adjust to vigorous import competition. The advantage of such actions over antidumping is that they focus on the source of the problem (the fact that an industry cannot compete with imports), are applied on a nondiscriminatory basis, are subject to time limits, and must be phased out gradually over the set time period.[7]

Experience suggests that it is important that only one safeguard mechanism exists. If firms have the option of forum hopping and petitioning the government or the legislature directly for emergency protection, it will induce wasteful, rent-seeking lobbying. Many countries have antidumping legislation and often have not bound their tariffs in the WTO at applied levels. This gives domestic industries a choice between direct lobbying for an increase in a specific tariff, petitioning for antidumping relief, or the initiation a safeguard procedure. An important advantage of explicitly providing for only one safeguard mechanism is that it forces firms to use it, allowing the government to keep control of trade policy. The decision whether or not to protect should remain a political one, to be taken in full awareness of the economy-wide implications and after consideration of alternative instruments that are less distorting.

Designing WTO-Mandated Institutions to Support Exports

As mentioned previously, there are a large number of WTO requirements that have institutional design implications. Often the affected bodies will have responsibilities that go beyond the WTO. In the process of determining what needs to be changed in order to implement WTO provisions, governments should grasp the opportunity to take a broader view of the role and functioning of these various institutions. In this connection it is crucial to recall that the focus of WTO rules is on market access—ensuring that foreign firms can compete on domestic markets. While greater competition is generally beneficial to an economy, governments also need to ensure that the policies and mechanisms that are needed to support the functioning of the market are in place. For example, in the case of customs, trade facilitation requires much more than implementation of WTO valuation procedures. In the process of shifting to WTO valuation methods, governments should therefore assess more generally what can be done to move goods through ports more efficiently. In the case of standards, while in the process of setting up the WTO-mandated enquiry points, governments can seek to bolster the value added of such institutions by increasing their relevance to firms as sources of information on standards required in foreign markets. This is not required by the WTO but would ensure that the "return on investment" is magnified substantially. The need to consider strengthening competition policies when implementing the TRIPs agreement was discussed by Maskus in chapter 9. In all these instances the question to be asked is how to design reforms and go about implementing WTO obligations in a way that maximizes the potential for a positive impact on economic development. This is vital not just for policy design, but for creating and bolstering domestic constituencies that have a strong interest in the functioning of the WTO and perceive that national participation in the institution is beneficial to them.

Creating a Transparency Institution

Creation of an independent institution that that has the task of assessing and analyzing the impact of government policies on the efficiency of the economy can be a valuable complementary instrument to maximize the benefits of WTO membership. Establishment of institutions to enhance the domestic transparency of government decision-making on trade policy matters is encouraged by the WTO, but not required (Annex 3 WTO, paragraph B). Such a transparency body can help identify the costs and benefits for the economy as a whole of sectoral interventions and regulatory regimes more generally. Such a body can advise the government on the effects of specific trade policy on competition (market structure, concentration) and national welfare and can be required to prepare and publish a regular comprehensive report of the effects and incidence of the trade and investment policy stance that is maintained. Export and consumer interests should have the right to request investigations into the impact of the trade and regulatory regime that is maintained. In order to safeguard its independence, the mandate of the institution should be established by law and its funding be not only statutory, e.g., not at the discretion of the government but also adequate to attract qualified staff. A transparency body should have a purely advisory role vis-à-vis the government and not be a part of it; its task is to shed light by providing information and undertaking objective economic analyses.[8]

Conclusion

The WTO's policy disciplines and institutional obligations are to a large extent efficiency enhancing. Nondiscrimination and the many transparency provisions will reduce uncertainty in the market place as regards the applicable rules and procedures that must be satisfied in the import process. Perhaps the most important potential beneficial aspect of WTO membership is that it can be used as a precommitment device by governments that seek to enhance the credibility of a liberal trade policy stance and/or reform program. This will not be an automatic consequence of accession to—and membership of—the WTO, however, but requires unilateral decisions/measures and a significant investment in upgrading and strengthening institutions. Actions that could be taken in this connection include:

- Bind tariffs under the GATT at applied rates. If a country is in the process of trade liberalization, a decision to bind tariffs each time they are lowered will signal the importance that is attached to fundamentally changing the policy regime. Similarly, sectoral commitments under the GATS should be comprehensive, at a minimum locking in the status quo regulatory regime for all services.

- Ensure that safeguard instruments are designed in a way that minimizes the scope for easy re-imposition of protection. Ideally only one such instrument should be available to the domestic industry, and criteria should be such so as to ensure that all interests are considered before protection is imposed and that procedures reduce as much as possible the likelihood of protectionist bias.

- For each WTO agreement, determine how implementation can be pursued in a way that maximizes the relevance and usefulness of the bodies concerned to the development prospects of the economy. WTO consistency should be seen as a minimum requirement that will be far from first best from a development perspective.

- Create a transparency institution that has a statutory mandate to analyze the economic effects of existing and proposed trade policies. This should include a requirement to monitor the use of contingent protection, and evaluate its impact on the competitiveness of export industries and consumers more generally.

The WTO is not a panacea for governments as far as trade policy and institutions are concerned. Unilateral decisions concerning the policies, the trade laws, and the institutions that are maintained are a basic determinant of economic performance. Eliminating the regulatory barriers that constrain the ability of domestic industries to exploit the opportunities for specialization offered by full integration into the world economy requires more than WTO-consistency. Given a decision to liberalize trade and investment, the WTO can play a helpful role, especially as a credibility enhancing mechanism. But very much will continue to depend on the policies that are pursued independently by governments, and how governments go about implementing WTO agreements.

Notes

1. No attention is devoted to the likely economic impact of the agreements negotiated in the Uruguay Round, as this has been the subject of extensive research (e.g., Martin and Winters 1996). Important issues here relate to the reduction in preference margins, the eventual elimination of the Multifibre Accord (MFA), and the impact of agricultural liberalization in OECD countries on world prices for food and food products.

2. See Hoekman and Kostecki (1995) for a comprehensive survey of WTO rules and disciplines.

3. Quantitative import restrictions, variable import levies, minimum import prices, discretionary import licensing, nontariff measures maintained through state trading enterprises, voluntary export restraints, and similar border measures are explicitly prohibited (Agreement on Agriculture, Article 4).

4. However, such treatment may or may not be identical to that applying to domestic firms, in recognition of the fact that identical treatment may actually worsen the conditions of competition for foreign-based firms (e.g., a requirement for insurance firms that reserves be held locally).

5. Quality control (inspection) by the General Organization for Export and Import Control (GOEIC) in Egypt is illustrative. It is considered to be particularly intrusive and time consuming by importers. The GOEIC inspects a sample of every consignment of goods entering Egypt that is on a list of products subject to quality control. Testing of industrial products sometimes takes a long time, especially if the required equipment is not available. The GOEIC reportedly ignores internationally recommended methods of testing and certification and may not recognize internationally known and accepted quality and certification marks (such as that of the EU or the IOS).

6. See Michalopoulos (1998) on resource constraints and allocations of developing countries.

7. See Hoekman and Leidy (1990) and Finger (1998) for more comprehensive discussions.

8. For more on the task and role of such an institution, see Finger (1982), Tumlir (1985), and Laird and Messerlin (1989).

Contributors

James H. Cassing
University of Pittsburgh
Pittsburgh, PA

Dean A. DeRosa
ADR International
Falls Church, VA

Samiha Fawzy
Faculty of Economics and Political Science, Cairo University
Egyptian Center for Economic Studies, Cairo

Denis M. Gallagher
International Trade and Investment Consultant
Killarney, Ireland

Oleh Havrylyshyn
Policy Development and Review, International Monetary Fund
Washington, DC

Bernard Hoekman
Development Research Group, The World Bank
Washington, DC
Centre for Economic Policy Research, London

Hanaa Kheir-El-Din
Faculty of Economics and Political Science, Cairo University
Economic Research Forum for the Arab Countries, Iran and Turkey, Cairo

Denise Konan
Department of Economics, University of Hawaii
Honolulu, HI

Peter Kunzel
Middle East Department, International Monetary Fund
Washington, DC

Will Martin
Development Research Group, The World Bank
Washington, DC

Keith E. Maskus
Department of Economics, University of Colorado
Boulder, CO

Francis Ng
Development Research Group, The World Bank
Washington, DC

Jayanta Roy
Middle East and North Africa, The World Bank
Washington, DC

Elisabet E. Rutström
University of South Carolina
Columbia, South Carolina

Thomas F. Rutherford
University of Colorado
Boulder, CO

David Tarr
Development Research Group, The World Bank
Washington, DC

Alexander J. Yeats
Development Research Group, The World Bank
Washington, DC

Jamel Zarrouk
Economics and Technical Department, Arab Monetary Fund
Abu Dhabi, UAE
Economic Research Forum for the Arab Countries, Iran and Turkey, Cairo

References

Ahmed, R. and C. Donovan. 1992. *Issues in Infrastructural Development: A Synthesis of the Literature*. Washington, DC: International Food Policy Research Institute.

Anderson, K. and R. Blackhurst. 1993. *Regional Integration and the Global Trading System*. London: Harvester Wheatsheaf.

APEC (Asia-Pacific Economic Cooperation). 1994. *Achieving the APEC vision: Free and open trade in the Asia-Pacific*. Second report of the Eminent Persons Group. Singapore: Asia-Pacific Economic Forum.

Arab Monetary Fund. 1999. *Arab Joint Economic Report, 1999* (Arabic). Abu Dhabi.

Armington, P. 1969. "A theory of demand for products distinguished by place of production," *IMF Staff Papers* 16: 159-77.

Atiyas, Izak, Mark Dutz, and Claudio Frischtak, with Bita Hadjimichael. 1992. "Fundamental Issues and Policy Approaches in Industrial Restructuring," *Industry Series Paper No. 56.* Washington, DC: The World Bank.

Balassa, B. 1971. *The Structure of Protection in Developing Countries.* Baltimore, MD: International Bank for Reconstruction and Development.

———. 1979. "Intra-industry trade and the integration of developing countries in the world economy," in Herbert Giersch (ed.), *On the Economics of Intra-industry Trade*. Tübingen: J. C. B. Mohr.

Balassa, B. and L. Bauwens. 1987. "Intra-Industry Specialization in a Multi-Country and Multi-Industry Framework," *The Economic Journal* 97: 923-939.

———. 1988. *Changing Trade Patterns in Manufactured Goods.* Amsterdam: Elsevier Science Publishers.

Baldwin, Richard. 1995. *Towards an Integrated Europe*. London: Centre for Economic Policy Research.

Bautista, R. M. and A. Valdés. 1993. *The Bias against Agriculture: Trade and Macroeconomic Policies in Developing Countries*. San Francisco, CA: ICS Press.

Bautista, R. M., and D. A. DeRosa. 1996. "Agriculture and the new industrial revolution in Asia," *Discussion Paper No.13* (Trade and Macroeconomics Division). Washington, DC: International Food Policy Research Institute.

Bhagwati, Jagdish. 1982. "Directly unproductive profit-seeking (DUP) activities," *Journal of Political Economy* 90: 988-1002.

Bhagwati, Jagdish and Arvind Panagariya. 1996. "Preferential trading areas and multilateralism: strangers, friends, or foes?" in J. Bhagwati and A. Panagariya (eds.), *The Economics of Preferential Trade Agreements.* Washington D.C.: AEI Press.

Bhagwati, Jagdish and Donald R. Davis. 1994. "Intra-Industry Trade Issues and Theory," *Discussion Paper No. 1695,* Harvard Institute of Economic Research.

Blomstrom, M. and A. Koko. 1997. "Regional Integration and Foreign Direct Investment: A Conceptual Framework and Three Cases," *Policy Research Working Paper 1750*. Washington, DC: The World Bank.

Braga, Carlos, Raed Safadi, and Alexander Yeats. 1994. "Regional Integration in the Western Hemisphere: Déjà vu All Over Again," *The World Economy* (July).

Brooke, Anthony, David Kendrick, and Alexander Meeraus. 1988. *GAMS: A User's Guide*. Redwood City, CA: The Scientific Press.

Brown, Druscilla, Alan Deardorff, and Robert Stern. 1997. "Some Economic Effects of the Free Trade Agreement between Tunisia and the European Union," in A. Galal and B. Hoekman (eds.), *Regional Partners in Global Markets: Limits and Possibilities of the Euro-Med Agreements*. London: Centre for Economic Policy Research.

CAPMAS. 1997. *Annual Industrial Production Statistics (Public and Private)*. Cairo: Central Agency for Public Mobilization and Statistics.

Claessens, S., and T. Glaessner. 1998. "The Internationalization of Financial Services in Asia," *Policy Research Working Paper 1911*. Washington, DC: The World Bank.

Clements, K. and L. Sjaastad. 1984. "How Protection Taxes Exporters," *Thames Essay No 39*. London: Trade Policy Research Centre.

Codsi, G. and K. Pearson. 1988. "GEMPACK: General-purpose software for applied general equilibrium and other economic modellers," *Computer Science in Economics and Management* 1: 189-207.

Corden, W. M. and J. P. Neary. 1982. "Booming sector and de-industrialization in a small open economy," *Economic Journal* 92: 825-48.

De Melo, Jaime and Arvind Panagariya (eds.). 1993. *New Dimensions in Regional Integration*. Cambridge: Cambridge University Press

De Melo, Jaime and David G. Tarr. 1992. *General Equilibrium Analysis of U.S. Foreign Trade Policy*. Cambridge, MA: MIT Press.

De Melo, Jaime and Sherman Robinson. 1989. "Product Differentiation and the Treatment of Foreign Trade in Computable General Equilibrium Models of Small Economies," *Journal of International Economics* 27: 47-67.

Dean, J., P. Desai, and J. Riedel. 1994. "Trade Policy Reform in Developing Countries since 1985: A Review of the Evidence," *World Bank Discussion Paper 267*. Washington, DC: The World Bank.

DeRosa, D. A. 1992. "Protection and export performance in Sub-Saharan Africa," *Weltwirtschaftliches Archiv* 128 (1): 88-124.

———. 1995a. "Regional trading arrangements among developing countries: The ASEAN example," *Research Report 103*. Washington, DC: International Food Policy Research Institute.

———. 1995b. "International trade, regional integration and food security in the Middle East," in H. Kheir-El-Din (ed.), *Economic Cooperation in the Middle East: Prospects and Challenges*. Cairo: Dar Al-Mostaqbal Al-Arabi for Cairo University.

———. 1996a. "Agricultural trade and rural development in the Middle East and North Africa," Mimeo. Falls Church, VA: ADR International.

———. 1996b. "Regionalism and the bias against agriculture in less developed countries," in S. Arndt and C. Milner (eds.), *The World Economy: Global Trade*

Policy 1996 (Supplement to *The World Economy),* Cambridge, MA: Blackwell Publishers.

———. 1988. "Asian preferences and the gains from MFN tariff reductions," *The World Economy* 11: 377-396.

Devarajan, S., J. Lewis, and S. Robinson. 1993. "External shocks, purchasing power and the equilibrium real exchange rate," *World Bank Economic Review* 7 (1): 45-64.

Devereux, J. and M. Connolly. 1995. "Commercial policy, the terms of trade and the real exchange rate revisited," *Journal of Development Economics* 50: 81-99.

Devlin, J. and J. Page. 1999. "Steppingstones: Arab Integration, Competitiveness, and the Euro-Med Agreements," in Julia Devlin, Sebastien Dessus, and Raed Safadi (eds.), *The Dynamics of Open Regionalism in MENA*. Paris: OECD.

Drysdale, Peter, and Ross Garnaut. 1993. "The Pacific: an application of a general theory of economic integration," in C.F. Bergsten and M. Noland (eds.), *Pacific Dynamism and the International Economic System.* Washington, DC: Institute for International Economics.

Dunning, John. 1980. "Toward an Eclectic Theory of International Production: Some Empirical Tests," *Journal of International Business Studies* 11: 9-31.

Economic Research Forum for the Arab Countries (ERF). 1996. *Economic Trends in the MENA Region.* Cairo: ERF.

El-Erian, Mohamed et al. 1995. *Macroeconomy of the Middle East and North Africa.* Washington, DC: International Monetary Fund.

El-Imam, M. M. 1997. "Arab Common Market in light of the recent International and Regional Developments" (Arabic). *Journal of Arab Economic Union* 10 (14) May/June.

El-Naggar, Said (ed.). 1996. *The Uruguay Round and the Arab Countries.* Washington, DC: International Monetary Fund.

Erzan, R., H. Kuwahara, S. Marchese, and R. Vossenaar. 1989. "The profile of protection in developing countries," *UNCTAD Review* 1: 29-50.

Erzan, Refik and Alexander Yeats. 1992. "Free Trade Arrangements with the United States…What's in it for Latin America?" in Sylvia Saborio (ed.), *US-Latin American Trade Relations in the 1990s.* Washington, DC: Overseas Development Council.

European Commission. 1996. "Economic Evaluation of the Internal Market," *European Economy*, Reports and Studies No. 4.

FAO (Food and Agriculture Organization of the United Nations). 1994. *Food Aid in Figures*. Rome: FAO.

Fawzy, Samiha and A. Galal. 1998. "Assessment of the Business Environment in Egypt," mimeo. Cairo: Egyptian Center for Economic Studies.

Fernandez, Raquel and Jonathan Portes. 1998 "Returns to Regionalism: An Analysis of Non-traditional Gains from Regional Trade Agreements," *The World Bank Economic Review* 12 (2) May.

Finger, J. Michael. 1982. "Incorporating the Gains from Trade into Policy," *The World Economy* 5: 367-77.

———. 1998. "GATT Experience with Safeguards: Making Economic and Political Sense of the Possibilities That the GATT Allows to Restrict Imports," *Policy Research Discussion Paper 2000*. Washington, DC: The World Bank.

Finger, J. Michael and Philip Schuler. 1999. "Implementation of Uruguay Round Commitments: The Development Challenge," mimeo. Washington, DC: The World Bank.

Finger, J. Michael, U. Reincke, and M. Ingco. 1996. *The Uruguay Round: Statistics on: Tariff Concessions Given and Received.* Washington, DC: The World Bank.

Fischer, S. 1993. "Prospects for integration in the Middle East," in J. de Melo and A. Panagariya (eds.), *New Dimensions in Regional Integration*. Cambridge: Cambridge University Press.

Fischer, S., D. Rodrik, and E. Tuma. 1993. *The Economics of Middle East Peace*. Cambridge, MA: MIT Press.

Fishelson, G. (ed.). 1989. *Economic Cooperation in the Middle East*. Boulder, CO: Westview Press.

Francois, Joseph. 1997. "External Bindings and the Credibility of Reform," in A. Galal and B. Hoekman (eds.), *Regional Partners in Global Markets: Limits and Possibilities of the Euro-Med Agreements*. London: Centre for Economic Policy Research.

Galal, Ahmed. 1999. "Welfare Impact of Telecom Reform in Egypt: An Ex Ante Analysis," in Samiha Fawzy and Ahmed Galal (eds.), *Partners for Development: New Roles for Government and the Private Sector in the Middle East and North Africa*. Washington, DC: The World Bank.

Galal, Ahmed and Bernard Hoekman (eds.). 1997. *Regional Partners in Global Markets: Limits and Possibilities of the Euro-Med Agreements*. London: Centre for Economic Policy Research and Egyptian Center for Economic Studies.

Galal, Ahmed and Robert Z. Lawrence (eds.). 1998. *An Egypt-U.S. Free Trade Agreement.* Washington, DC: Brookings Institution Press.

Gamo, P. A., S. Fennell, and K. Sakr. 1997. "Adjusting to New Realities: MENA, the Uruguay Round, and the EU-Mediterranean Initiative," *IMF Working Paper* (Middle East Department), January.

GATT. 1966. *International Trade 1965.* Geneva: GATT.

———. 1979. "Agreement between the European Economic Community and Lebanon," *Basic Instruments and Selected Documents,* 25th Supplement (January).

———. 1994. "Trade Policy Review Mechanism Tunisia. Report by the Secretariat," C/RM/S/47 (May 24). Geneva: GATT.

Ghosh, Sukesh K. 1991. *Econometrics: Theory and Applications.* Englewood Cliffs, NJ: Prentice Hall.

Globerman, Steven and James W. Dean. 1990. "Recent Trends in Intra-Industry Trade and Their Implications for Future Trade Liberalization," *Welwirtschaftliches Archiv* 126 (1): 23-48.

Goldin, I. and M. Kherallah. 1996. "The Uruguay Round and international trade in agricultural products: implications for Arab countries," in S. El-Naggar (ed.), *The Uruguay Round and the Arab Countries*. Washington, DC: International Monetary Fund.

Goldstein, M. and M. Khan. 1985. "Income and price effects in foreign trade," in R. Jones and P. Kenen (eds.), *Handbook of International Economics, vol. II.* Amsterdam: Elsevier Science Publishers.

Gray, Peter. 1978. "Intra-Industry Trade: The effects of different levels of data aggregation," in Herbert Girsch (ed.), *On the Economics of Intra-Industry Trade: Symposium*. Tübingen: J. C. B. Mohr.

———. 1988. "Intra-Industry Trade: An Untidy Phenomenon," *Welwirtschaftliches Archiv* 124 (2): 211-227.

Grubel, Herbert and P. J. Lloyd. 1975. *Intra-Industry Trade*. London: Halsted Press.

Guasch, J. Luis and Pablo Spiller. 1999. "Managing the Regulatory Regime Process: Design, Concepts, Issues, and the Latin America and Caribbean Story." Washington, DC: The World Bank.

Gunter, B. 1995. "Survey on supply elasticities," Economic Development Institute, mimeo. Washington, DC: The World Bank.

Hamilton, Clive and Paul Kniest. 1990. "Trade Liberalization and Intra-Industry Trade: Evidence from the CER Agreement," *Discussion Paper No. 245.* The Australian National University.

Harberger, Arnold. 1990. "Reflections on Uniform Taxation," in R. Jones and A. Kreuger (eds.), *The Political Economy of International Trade*. Cambridge, MA: Blackwell.

Harrison, Glenn W. and H. D. Vinod. 1992. "The Sensitivity Analysis of Applied General Equilibrium Models: Completely Randomized Factorial Sampling Designs," *The Review of Economics and Statistics* 74 (May): 357-362.

Harrison, Glenn W., R. Jones, L. Kimbell Jr., and R. Wigle. 1992. "How Robust is Applied General Equilibrium Modeling?" *Journal of Policy Modeling* 15.

Harrison, Glenn W., Thomas F. Rutherford, and David G. Tarr. 1993. "Piecemeal Trade Reform in the Partially Liberalized Economy of Turkey," *World Bank Economic Review* 7 (May): 191-217.

———. 1996. "Increased Competition and Completion of the Market in the European Union: Static and Steady State Effects," *Journal of Economic Integration* 11 (3): 332-365.

———. 1997. "Economic Implications for Turkey of a Customs Union with the European Union," *European Economic Review* 41: 861-870.

Hathaway, D. E. and M. D. Ingco. 1995. "Agricultural liberalization and the Uruguay Round," in W. Martin and L. A. Winters (eds.), *The Uruguay Round and the Developing Economies*. Washington, DC: The World Bank.

Havrylyshyn, Oleh. 1997. "A Global Integration Strategy for Mediterranean Countries: Open Trade, and other Accompanying Measures," Middle East Department (August). Washington, DC: International Monetary Fund.

Havrylyshyn, Oleh and Engin Civan. 1983. "Intra-Industry Trade and the Stage of Development," in P. K .M. Tharakan (ed.), *Intra-Industry Trade*. Amsterdam: North Holland.

———. 1985. "Intra-Industry Trade among Developing Countries," *Journal of Development Economics.* Amsterdam: Elsevier Science Publishers.

Havrylyshyn, Oleh and P. Kunzel. 1997. "Intra-Industry Trade of Arab Countries: An Indicator of Potential Competitiveness," *IMF Working Paper*, April.

Hertel, T. (ed.). 1997. *Global Trade Analysis: Modeling and Application.* New York: Cambridge University Press.

Hertel, T., J. M. Horridge, and K. Pearson. 1992. "Mending the family tree: a reconciliation of the linearization and levels schools of applied general equilibrium modeling," *Economic Modeling* 9: 385-407.

Hirschman, A. O. 1958. *The Strategy of Economic Development.* New Haven, CT: Yale University Press.

Hoekman, Bernard. 1998a. "Beyond National Treatment: Integrating Domestic Policies," mimeo. Washington, DC: The World Bank.

———. 1998b. "Catching up with Eastern Europe? The European Union's Mediterranean Free Trade Initiative," in R. Safadi (ed.), *Opening Doors to the World: A New Trade Agenda for the Middle East.* Cairo: American University Press.

———. 1998c. "Using International Institutions to Improve Public Procurement," *World Bank Research Observer* 13 (2): 249-69.

Hoekman, Bernard and Simeon Djankov. 1996. "The European Union's Mediterranean Free Trade Initiative," *The World Economy* 19 (4): 387-406.

———. 1997a. "Effective Protection and Investment Incentives in Egypt and Jordan During the Transition to Free Trade With Europe," *World Development* 25 (2): 281-291.

———. 1997b. "Towards a Free Trade Agreement with the European Union: Issues and Policy Options for Egypt," in A. Galal and B. Hoekman (eds.), *Regional Partners in Global Markets: Limits and Possibilities of the Euro-Med Agreements.* London: Centre for Economic Policy Research and Egyptian Center for Economic Studies.

Hoekman, Bernard and Denise Konan. 1999. "Deep Integration, Non-Discrimination and Euro-Mediterranean Free Trade," *CEPR Discussion Paper 2095.* London: Centre for Economic Policy Research.

Hoekman, Bernard and Michel Kostecki. 1995. *The Political Economy of the World Trading System: From GATT to WTO.* Oxford: Oxford University Press.

Hoekman, Bernard and Michael Leidy. 1990. "Policy Responses to Shifting Comparative Advantage: Designing a System of Emergency Protection," *Kyklos,* 43: 25-51.

Hoekman, Bernard and Petros C. Mavroidis (eds.). 1997. *Law and Policy in Public Purchasing: The WTO Agreement on Government Procurement.* Ann Arbor, MI: University of Michigan Press.

Hoekman, Bernard, Denise Konan, and Keith Maskus. 1998. "An Egypt-US Free Trade Agreement: Economic Incentives and Effects," in Ahmed Galal and Robert Lawrence (eds.), *Building Bridges: An Egypt-U.S. Free Trade Agreement.* Washington, D.C.: Brookings Institution.

Ingco, M. 1996. "Agricultural liberalization in the Uruguay Round," *World Bank Working Paper No. 1500.* Washington, DC: The World Bank.

International Monetary Fund. 1994. *Government Finance Statistics Yearbook.* Washington, DC: International Monetary Fund.

———. 1997. "Globalization and Growth Prospects in Arab Countries," *IMF Working Paper No. WP/97/125.* Washington, DC: International Monetary Fund.

———. 1998. "Egypt: Beyond Stabilization, Toward a Dynamic Market Economy," *Occasional Paper 163.* Washington, DC: International Monetary Fund.

Jbili, Abdelali and Klaus Enders. 1996. "The Association Agreement between Tunisia and the European Union," *Finance and Development* 33 (3): 18-20.

John Mellor Associates, Inc. and Datex Inc. 1995. "Strategic priorities for sustainable agricultural growth in Egypt: Impact on growth, employment, trade, and privatization." Report prepared for the U.S. Agency for International Development. Washington, DC.

Johnson, D. G. 1995. "The limited but essential role of government in agriculture and rural life," in G. H. Peters and D. D. Hedley (eds.), *Agricultural Competitiveness: Market Forces and Policy Choice*. Hants, England: Dartmouth Publishing Company.

Johnston, B. and J. W. Mellor. 1961. "The role of agriculture in economic development," *American Economic Review* 51: 566-593.

Johnston, B. and P. Kilby. 1975. *Agriculture and Structural Transformation*. London: Oxford University Press.

Khaldi, N. 1984. "Evolving Food Gaps in the Middle East/North Africa: Prospects and Policy Implications," *Research Report 47*. Washington, DC: International Food Policy Research Institute.

Kheir-El-Din, Hanaa. 1998. "Enforcement of Product Standards as a Barrier to Trade," mimeo. Cairo University.

———. Forthcoming. "Enforcement of Products Standards as Barriers to Trade: The Case of Egypt," in Bernard Hoekman (ed.), *Trade Policy Developments in the Middle East and North Africa*. Washington, DC: World Bank Institute.

Kheir-El-Din, Hanaa and Ahmed El-Dersh. 1992. "Foreign Trade Policy in Egypt, 1986-1991," in Said El-Naggar (ed.), *Foreign and Intratrade Policies of the Arab Countries*. Washington, DC: International Monetary Fund.

Kheir-El-Din, Hanaa and Hoda El-Sayed. 1997. "Potential Impact of a FTA with the EU on Egypt's Textile Industry," in A. Galal and B. Hoekman (eds.), *Regional Partners in Global Markets: Limits and Possibilities of the Euro-Med Agreements*. London: Centre for Economic Policy Research.

Kirmani, N., N. Calika, R. Harmsen, M. Leidy, A. Subramanian, and P. Uimonen. 1994. *International Trade Policies: The Uruguay Round and Beyond. Volume II.* (Background papers. World Economic and Financial Surveys). Washington, DC: International Monetary Fund.

Konan, Denise Eby and Keith E. Maskus. 1997a. "A Computable General Equilibrium Analysis of Egyptian Trade Liberalization Scenarios," in A. Galal and B. Hoekman (eds.), *Regional Partners in Global Markets: Limits and Possibilities of the Euro-Med Agreements*. London: Centre for Economic Policy Research.

———. 1997b. "Joint Trade Liberalization and Tax Reform in a Small Open Economy: The Case of Egypt," mimeo. University of Colorado.

———. 1997c. "Is Small Beautiful? Trade Shares and Trade Creation with Differentiated Products," mimeo. University of Hawaii.

Kravis, I. and R. E. Lipsey. 1988. "National price levels and the prices of tradables and nontradables," *American Economic Review* 78 (2): 474-8.

Kravis, Irving. 1970. "Trade as a Handmaiden of Growth," *Economic Journal* 80 (December).

Krueger, A. O. 1974. "The political economy of the rent-seeking society," *American Economic Review* 80: 48-62.

———. (ed.). 1981. *Trade and Employment in Developing Countries.* Chicago, IL: University of Chicago Press.

Krueger, A. O., M. Schiff, and A. Valdés. 1988. "Agricultural incentives in developing countries: Measuring the effect of sectoral and economy-wide policies," *The World Bank Economic Review* 2 (3): 255-272.

———. (eds.). 1992. *The Political Economy of Agricultural Pricing Policy.* Baltimore, MD: The Johns Hopkins University Press.

Laird, Sam and Patrick Messerlin. 1989. "Institutional Reform for Trade Liberalization," *The World Economy* 12: 230-49.

Lakhoua, F. 1993. "The past and present of Arab economic integration." Paper presented at the Conference Establishing the Economic Research Forum. Cairo, June 4-6.

Langhammer, R. and U. Hiemenz. 1990. *Regional Integration among Developing Countries: Opportunities, Obstacles, and Options.* Boulder, CO: Westview Press.

Lary, Hal. 1968. *Imports of Manufactures from Less Developed Countries.* New York: National Bureau of Economic Research.

Lawrence, R. Z. 1996. *Regionalism, Multilateralism, and Deeper Integration.* Washington, DC: The Brookings Institution.

Lawrence, Robert et al. 1995. *Towards Free Trade in the Middle East: The Triad and Beyond.* Cambridge, MA: Harvard University.

League of Arab States. 1997. "Executive Programme of the Agreement on Facilitating and Developing Intra-Arab Trade for Establishing The Greater Arab Free Trade Area (GAFTA)." Secretariat of the Arab League, Directorate of Economic Affairs, Cairo, Egypt.

Lebanese Republic. 1995. *Report On Industrial Census: Final Results.* Ministry of Industry and Petroleum, Directorate of Industry (December).

Lee, Hyun-Hoon and Young-Youn Lee. 1993. "Intra-Industry Trade in Manufactures: The Case of Korea," *Weltwirtschaftliches Archiv* 129 (1): 159-169.

Leiberman, Ira. 1990. "Industrial Restructuring: Policy and Practice," *Policy and Research Series No. 9.* Washington, DC: The World Bank.

Limam, I. and A. Abdalla. 1998. "Inter-Arab Trade and the Potential Success of Arab Free Trade Area (FTA)." Paper presented at the International Conference on New Economic Developments and their Impact on Arab Economies, Arab Planning Institute (Kuwait). Tunis, June 3-5.

Lofgren, Hans. 1994. "Elasticity Survey," International Food Policy Research Institute, mimeo. Washington, DC.

MacBean, A. I. 1966. *Export Instability and Economic Development.* Cambridge, MA: Harvard University Press.

Mansfield, Edwin. 1994. "Intellectual Property Protection, Foreign Direct Investment, and Technology Transfer," *IFC Discussion Paper No. 19.* Washington, DC: The World Bank.

Markusen, James R. 1995. "The Boundaries of Multinational Enterprises and the Theory of International Trade," *Journal of Economic Perspectives* 9: 169-190.

Markusen, James R., Thomas F. Rutherford, and David G. Tarr. 1999. "Foreign Direct Investment in Services and the Domestic Market for Expertise," mimeo. Washington, DC: The World Bank.

Martin, Will. 1996. "Measuring welfare changes with distortions," in J. Francois and K. Reinert (eds.), *Applied Methods for Trade Policy Analysis: A Handbook.* Cambridge: Cambridge University Press.

Martin, Will and L. Alan Winters (eds.). 1995. "The Uruguay Round and the Developing Economies," *Discussion Paper 307.* Washington, DC: The World Bank.

———. (eds.). 1996. *The Uruguay Round and the Developing Economies.* Cambridge: University of Cambridge Press.

Maskus, Keith E. 1990. "Normative Concerns in the International Protection of Intellectual Property Rights," *The World Economy* 13: 387-409.

———. 1997. "Intellectual Property Rights in Lebanon," mimeo. Washington, DC: The World Bank.

———. 1998. "The International Regulation of Intellectual Property," *Weltwirtschaftliches Archiv* 134: 196-208.

Maskus, Keith E. and Denise Eby Konan. 1994. "Trade-Related Intellectual Property Rights: Issues and Exploratory Results," in Alan V. Deardorff and Robert M. Stern (eds.), *Analytical and Negotiating Issues in the Global Trading System.* Ann Arbor, MI: University of Michigan Press.

———. 1997. "Trade Liberalization in Egypt," *Review of Development Economics* 1: 275-93.

Maskus, Keith E. and M. Lahouel. 1999. "Competition Policy and Intellectual Property Rights in Developing Countries: Interests in Unilateral Initiatives and a WTO Agreement." Paper presented at the WTO/World Bank Conference on Developing Countries' in a Millennium Round. Geneva, September 20-21.

Massel, B. F. 1970. "Export Instability and Economic Structure," *American Economic Review* 60 (September).

Mattoo, A. 1999. "Developing Countries in the New Round of GATS Negotiations: From a Defensive to a Pro-Active Role." Paper presented at the WTO/World Bank Conference on Developing Countries' in a Millennium Round. Geneva, September 20-21.

Mellor, J. W. 1966. *The Economics of Agricultural Development.* Ithaca, NY: Cornell University Press.

——— (ed.). 1995. *Agriculture on the Road to Industrialization.* Baltimore, MD: Johns Hopkins University Press.

Mellor, J. W. and U. Lele. 1973. "Growth linkages of the new foodgrain technologies," *Indian Journal of Agricultural Economics* 28: 35-55.

Messerlin, Patrick A. 1998. "Technical Regulations and Standards in the EU," mimeo. Washington, DC: World Bank Institute.

Messerlin, Patrick A. and Jamel Zarrouk. 1999. "Trade Facilitation: Technical Regulations and Customs Procedures." Paper presented at the WTO/World Bank Conference on Developing Countries' in a Millennium Round. Geneva, September 20-21.

Michalopoulos, Constantine. 1999. "Developing Countries in the WTO," *World Economy* 22: 117-43.

Michalopoulos, Constantine and David G. Tarr. (eds.). 1994. "Trade in the New Independent States," *Studies of Economies in Transition 13.* Washington, DC: The World Bank.

Ministry of Industry and Oil. 1995. *Report on Industrial Census- Final Results*, Ministry of Industry and Oil, Beirut, Lebanon.

Mohieldin, Mahmoud. 1997. "The Egypt-EU Partnership Agreement and Liberalization of Services," in A. Galal and B. Hoekman (eds.), *Regional Partners in Global Markets: Limits and Possibilities of the Euro-Med Agreements*. London: Centre for Economic Policy Research.

Murphy, Kevin, Andrei Shleifer, and Robert Vishny. 1991. "The Allocation of Talent: Implications for Growth," *Quarterly Journal of Economics* (May).

Nabli, Mustapha and Annette De Kleine. Forthcoming. "Managing Global Integration in the Middle East and North Africa," in Bernard Hoekman (ed.), *Trade Policy Developments in the Middle East and North Africa*. Washington, DC: World Bank Institute.

Nathan Associates. 1996. "Research Study on the Quality Control System in Egypt," USAID/DEPRA Project Report, July.

———. 1997. "Egypt: Review of Selected Egyptian Organization for Standardization (EOS) Food and Manufactured Durable Goods Standards with Respect to International Norms," USAID/DEPRA Project Report, October.

———. 1998a. "Egypt: Review of Selected Egyptian Organization for Standardization (EOS) Food Standards with Respect to International Norms," March.

———. 1998b. "Enhancing Egypt's Exports." Final Report for USAID/DEPRA, June.

———. 1998c. "Pilot Study for Pre-Certification of Imported Products," March.

Ng, Francis and Alexander J. Yeats. 1999. "Production Sharing in Asia: Who Does What for Whom and Why?" *Policy Research Paper 2197*. Washington, DC: The World Bank.

Nordblom, T. L., A. V. Goodchild, and F. Shomo. 1995. "Livestock, feeds and mixed farming systems in West Asia and North Africa," in R.T. Wilson, S. Ehui, and S. Mack (eds.), *Livestock Development Strategies for Low Income Countries*. Nairobi: Food and Agriculture Organization and International Livestock Research Institute.

Nsouli, Saleh, Amer Bisat, and Oussama Kanaan. "The European Union's New Mediterranean Strategy," *Finance and Development* 33 (3): 14-18.

Olson, Mancur. 1965. *The Logic of Collective Action*. Cambridge, MA: Harvard University Press.

Page, J. and J. Underwood. 1997. "Growth, the Maghreb and the European Union," in A. Galal and B. Hoekman (eds.), *Regional Partners in Global Markets: Limits and Possibilities of the Euro-Med Agreements*. London: Centre for Economic Policy Research.

Panagariya, Arvind and Dani Rodrik. 1993. "Tariffs, Welfare and Endogenous Policy," *International Economic Review* (August).

Panagariya, Arvind, Shah Shekhar, and D. Mishra. 1996. "Demand elasticities in international trade: Are they really low?" mimeo. University of Maryland.

Puga, D. and A. J. Venables. 1998. "Trading Arrangements and Industrial Development," *The World Bank Economic Review* 12 (2) May.

Ranis, G. and F. Stewart. 1987. "Rural linkages in the Philippines and Taiwan," in F. Stewart (ed.), *Macro-policies for Appropriate Technology in Developing Countries*. Boulder, CO: Westview Press.

Ranis, G., F. Stewart, and E. Reyes. 1989. "Linkages in development: A Philippine case study," *Working Paper 89-02*. Manila: Philippine Institute for Development Studies.

Robinson, Sherman and C. Gehlhar. 1995. "Land, Water, and Agriculture in Egypt: the Economy-wide Impact of Policy Reform," mimeo. Washington, DC: International Food Policy Research Institute.

Robson, Peter. 1998. *The Economics of International Integration*. London: Routledge.

Rollo, J. and A. Winters. 1999. "Domestic Regulation and Trade: Subsidiarity and Governance Challenges for the WTO." Paper presented at the WTO/World Bank Conference on Developing Countries' in a Millennium Round. Geneva, September 20-21.

Roy, Jayanta. 1998. "Trade Facilitation: World Bank Experience." Paper presented at the WTO Trade Facilitation Symposium. Geneva, March 9-10, 1998.

Rutherford, Thomas F. 1989. "General Equilibrium Modeling With MPS/GE," Department of Economics, University of Western Ontario.

———. 1992. "Extensions of GAMS For Complementarity and Variational Problems Arising in Applied Economics," *Economics Working Paper 92-9*. Department of Economics, University of Colorado at Boulder.

Rutherford, Thomas F., Elisabet E. Rutström, and David G. Tarr. 1993. "Morocco's Free Trade Agreement with the European Community: A Quantitative Assessment," *Policy Research Working Paper 1173*. Washington, DC: The World Bank.

———. 1995. "The Free Trade Agreement Between Tunisia and the European Union," mimeo. Washington, DC: The World Bank.

———. 1997. "Morocco's Free Trade Agreement with the EU: A Quantitative Assessment," *Economic Modeling* 14 (2) April: 237-269.

Salter, W. E. G. 1959. "Internal and external balance: the role of price and expenditure effects," *Economic Record* 35 (71): 226-38.

Saudi Arabian Standards Organization (SASO). 1998. "Conformity Certification Program: ICCP." SASO Website: <http://www.saso.org/SERVICES/iccp.htm>.

Schiff, Maurice. 1997. "Small Is Beautiful: Preferential Trade Agreements and the Impact of Country Size, Market Share, and Smuggling," *Journal of Economic Integration* 12: 359-87.

Schiff, Maurice and L. A. Winters. 1998. "Dynamics and Politics in Regional Integration Arrangements: An Introduction," *The World Bank Economic Review* 12 (2) May.

Shafik, Nemat. 1995. "Learning from Doers: Lessons on Regional Integration for the Middle East," in Hanaa Kheir-El-Din (ed.), *Economic Cooperation in the Middle East: Prospects and Challenges*. Cairo: Dar Al Mostaqbal Al Arabi.

——— (ed.). 1998. *Prospects for Middle Eastern and North African Economies: From Boom to Bust and Back?* London: Macmillan Press.

Spiller, G. A. 1991. *The Mediterranean Diet in Health and Disease*. New York: Van Nostrand Reinhold.

Staples, Brian R. 1998. "Trade Facilitation," mimeo. The World Bank (download from http://www.worldbank.org/trade/).

Stone, Joe A. and Hyun-Hoon Lee. 1995. "Determinants of Intra-Industry Trade: A Longitudinal, Cross-Country Analysis," *Weltwirtschaftliches Archiv* 131 (1): 67-83.

Subramanian, Arvind. 1991. "The International Economics of Intellectual Property Right Protection: a Welfare-Theoretic Trade Policy Analysis," *World Development* 19: 945-956.

———. 1997. "The Egyptian Stabilization Experience: An Analytical Retrospective." *Working Paper No. 18.* Cairo: Egyptian Center for Economic Studies.

Togan, S. 1997. "Impact of the customs union with the EU on Turkey," in A. Galal and B. Hoekman (eds.), *Regional Partners in Global Markets: Limits and Possibilities of the Euro-Med Agreements.* London and Cairo: Centre for Economic Policy Research and Egyptian Center for Economic Studies.

Tullock, G. 1967. "The welfare costs of tariffs, monopolies, and theft," *Western Economic Journal* 5: 224-232.

———. 1980. "Efficient rent seeking," in J. M. Buchanan, R. D. Tollison, and G. Tullock (eds.), *Towards a Theory of the Rent-Seeking Society.* College Station, TX: Texas A&M Press.

Tumlir, Jan. 1985. *Protectionism: Trade Policy in Democratic Societies.* Washington, DC: American Enterprise Institute.

UIA (Union of International Associations). 1987. *Yearbook of International Organizations 1987/88.* Munchen: Saur.

UNCTAD (United Nations Conference on Trade and Development). 1987. *Handbook of trade control measures of developing countries 1987.* New York: United Nations.

———. 1994a. *Directory of Import Regimes.* New York: United Nations.

———. 1994b. *Liberalizing International Transactions in Services: A Handbook.* New York: United Nations.

———. 1995. *Trade analysis and information system, version 3.0* (computer CD-ROM). Geneva: United Nations.

———. 1996. *Handbook of International Trade and Development Statistics.* New York: United Nations.

———.1999. "Preparing for Future Multilateral Trade Negotiations," *UNCTAD/ITCD/TSB/6.* Geneva: United Nations.

UN Statistical Office. 1996. *UN Trade Data System* (computer database). United Nations, New York. (Data retrieved by International Trade Division, World Bank.)

Unter, Brian. 1998. "Maximizing Custom Benefits: A Global Model for Regulatory Reform," presented at the US-China Standards, Testing and Certification Workshop, Washington, DC, February 17-18.

USDA (United States Department of Agriculture). 1996. *World agriculture: trends and indicators* (USDA economics and statistics system data set, World Wide Web). Washington, DC.

Varian, Hal. 1984. *Microeconomic Analysis.* New York: Norton.

Viatsos, C. 1978. "Crisis in Regional Economic Cooperation Among Developing Countries: A Survey," *World Development* 6 (June).

Viner, Jacob. 1950. *The Customs Union Issue.* New York: Carnegie Endowment for International Peace.

WEF (World Economic Forum). 1994. *The Casablanca report: the results of the Middle East/North Africa Economic Summit, October 30-November 1, 1994, Casablanca, Morocco.* New York: Council on Foreign Relations and World Economic Forum.

———. 1995. *Record: 1995 Middle East/North Africa Economic Summit, Amman, Jordan, 29-31 October 1995*. Cologny/Geneva: World Economic Forum.

———. 1996. *The Middle East/North Africa Economic Summit, Cairo, Egypt, 12-14 November 1996 (Information Booklet for Participants)*. Cologny/Geneva: World Economic Forum.

Wilson, John. 1998. "Product Standards and International Trade," mimeo. Washington, DC: The World Bank.

Wilson, Rodney. 1998. "Banking and Finance in the Middle East 1999," *Financial Times*.

Winters, L. A. 1996a. "The European Union's Mediterranean Agreements: a comparative analysis and assessment," mimeo. Washington, DC: The World Bank.

———. 1996b. "Lebanon's Euro-Mediterranean Agreement: possible dynamic benefits." Paper presented to the Lebanese Center for Policy Studies' Conference on Lebanese-EU Relations. Beirut, July 1-2.

Wonnacott, R. 1996. "Trade and investment in a hub-and-spoke system versus a free trade area," *The World Economy* 19 (3): 237-52.

World Bank. 1992. *Global Economic Prospects of Developing Countries*. Washington, DC: The World Bank.

———. 1995a. *Claiming the future: choosing prosperity in the Middle East and North Africa*. Washington, DC: The World Bank.

———. 1995b. "Egypt: Into the Next Century: Volume I, Macroeconomic Framework," mimeo.

———. 1995c. *From Scarcity to Security: Averting a Water Crisis in the Middle East and North Africa*. Washington, DC: The World Bank.

———. 1995d. *World Development Indicators 1995*. Washington, DC: The World Bank.

———. 1996a. *From Plan to Market: World Development Report 1996*. New York: Oxford University Press.

———. 1996b. "Growing faster, Finding Jobs, Choices for Morocco," *Middle East and North Africa Economic Studies*. Washington, DC: The World Bank.

———. 1996c. *Social Indicators of Development 1996*. Washington, DC: The World Bank.

———. 1996d. "Tunisia's Global Integration and Sustainable Development," *Middle East and North Africa Economic Studies*. Washington, DC: The World Bank.

———. 1997a. "Arab Republic of Egypt: Country Economic Memorandum." Washington, DC: The World Bank.

———. 1997b. "Egypt: Issues in Sustaining Economic Growth," Main Report, Vol. II, Country Economic Memorandum, *Report No. 16207-EGT* (March 15).

———. 1998. *Egypt in the Global Economy: Strategic Choices for Savings, Investments, and Long-Term Growth*. Washington, DC: The World Bank.

———. 1999. *World Development Indicators 1999*. Washington, DC: The World Bank.

World Trade Organization. 1995a. *The Results of the Uruguay Round of Multilateral Trade Negotiations, The Legal Texts*. Geneva: World Trade Organization.

———. 1995b. *Trade Policy Review: Tunisia*. Geneva: World Trade Organization.

———. 1996a. "Accession of the Kingdom of Saudi Arabia," memorandum on the Foreign Trade Regime, *WT/ACC/SAU/4*. Geneva: World Trade Organization.

———. 1996b. *Trade Policy Review: Kingdom of Morocco*. Geneva: World Trade Organization.

———. 1996c. *Working Parties Memorandum on Saudi Arabia and Jordan.* Geneva: World Trade Organization.

———. 1998a. *Annual Report 1998*. Geneva: World Trade Organization.

———. 1998b. "Maritime Transport Services," *Document S/C/W/62.* Geneva: World Trade Organization.

———. 1998c. "Land Transportation Services," *Document S/C/W/60.* Geneva: World Trade Organization.

———. 1998d. "Sanitary and Phytosanitary Measures," *The WTO Agreements Series 4.* Geneva: World Trade Organization.

———. 1998e. "Telecommunication Services," *Document S/C/W/74.* Geneva: World Trade Organization.

———. 1998f. "WTO Trade Facilitation Symposium, 9-10 March 1998, Report by the Secretariat," *Document G/C/W/115* (May). Geneva: World Trade Organization.

———. 1999. "Trade Policy Review: Egypt." Trade Policy Review Body, *Document WT/TPR/S/55.* (May). Geneva: World Trade Organization.

Yeats, Alexander J. 1990. "Shifting Patterns of Comparative Advantage: Manufactured Exports of Developing Countries," *The Developing Economies* (Summer).

———. 1996. "Export Prospects of Middle Eastern Countries," *Policy Research Working Paper No. 1571.* Washington, DC: The World Bank.

———. 1998a. "Just How Big is Global Production Sharing?" *Policy Research Paper Number 1871.* Washington, DC: The World Bank.

———. 1998b. "What Can Be Expected from African Regional Trade Arrangements? Some Empirical Evidence," *Policy Research Working Paper 2004.* Washington, DC: The World Bank

———. 1999. "Does Mercosur's Trade Performance Raise Concerns about the Effects of Regional Trade Arrangements?" *Policy Research Working Paper 1729.* Washington, DC: The World Bank.

Zarrouk, Jamel. 1992. "Intra-Trade: Determinants and Prospects for Expansion," in Said El-Naggar (ed.), *Foreign and Intra-trade Policies of the Arab Countries.* Washington, DC: International Monetary Fund.

———. 1996. "Financial Services Liberalization in the Context of GATS: The Case of CAPAS Countries." Paper presented to the UNDP-UNCTAD Regional Seminar for the CAPAS Project. Benin, September.

———. 1996. "Policy implications of the Uruguay Round for Arab countries," in S. El-Naggar (ed.), *The Uruguay Round and the Arab Countries*. Washington, DC: International Monetary Fund.

———. 1999. "The Linkage of the Euro-Mediterranean Free Trade With Arab Free Trade Regional Agreements," in Julia Devlin, Sebastien Dessus, and Raed Safadi (eds.), *The Dynamics of Open Regionalism in MENA*. Paris: OECD.

———. Forthcoming. "Para-tariffs in Arab Countries," in Bernard Hoekman (ed.), *Trade Policy Developments in the Middle East and North Africa.* Washington, DC: World Bank Institute.

STUDIES IN INTERNATIONAL TRADE POLICY

Studies in International Trade Policy includes works dealing with the theory, empirical analysis, political, economic, legal relations, and evaluations of international trade policies and institutions.

General Editor: Robert M. Stern

John H. Jackson and Edwin Vermulst, Editors. *Antidumping Law and Practice: A Comparative Study*

John Whalley, Editor. *Developing Countries and the Global Trading System.* Volumes 1 and 2

John Whalley, Coordinator. *The Uruguay Round and Beyond: The Final Report from the Ford Foundation Project on Developing Countries and the Global Trading System*

John S. Odell and Thomas D. Willett, Editors. *International Trade Policies: Gains from Exchange between Economics and Political Science*

Ulrich Kohli. *Technology, Duality, and Foreign Trade: The GNP Function Approach to Modeling Imports and Exports*

Stephen V. Marks and Keith E. Maskus, Editors. *The Economics and Politics of World Sugar Policies*

J. Michael Finger, Editor. *Antidumping: How It Works and Who Gets Hurt*

Horst Herberg and Ngo Van Long, Editors. *Trade, Welfare, and Economic Policies: Essays in Honor of Murray C. Kemp*

David Schwartzman. *The Japanese Television Cartel: A Study Based on* Matsushita v. Zenith

Alan V. Deardorff and Robert M. Stern, Editors. *Analytical Perspectives and Negotiating Issues in the Global Trading System*

Edwin Vermulst, Paul Waer, and Jacques Bourgeois, Editors. *Rules of Origin in International Trade: A Comparative Study*

Alan V. Deardorff and Robert M. Stern, Editors. *The Stolper-Samuelson Theorem: A Golden Jubilee*

Kent Albert Jones. *Export Restraint and the New Protectionism: The Political Economy of Discriminatory Trade Restrictions*

Alan V. Deardorff, James A. Levinsohn, and Robert M. Stern, Editors. *New Directions in Trade Theory*

Robert Baldwin, Tain-Jy Chen, and Douglas Nelson. *Political Economy of U.S.–Taiwan Trade*

Bernard M. Hoekman and Petros C. Mavroidis, Editors. *Law and Policy in Public Purchasing: The WTO Agreement on Government Procurement*

Danny M. Leipziger, Editor. *Lessons from East Asia*

Tamin Bayoumi. *Financial Integration and Real Activity*

Harry P. Bowen, Abraham Hollander, and Jean-Marie Viaene. *Applied International Trade Analysis*